HELL OF A SIGHT TO SEE

HELL OF A SIGHT TO SEE

A TENNESSEE SAILOR'S JOURNEY THROUGH WORLD WAR II

Copyright © 2021 John E. Talbott
All rights reserved

Published by BrayBree Publishing Company LLC
FIRST EDITION

No part of this book may be reproduced, stored in or introduced into a retrieval system or transmitted in any form or by any means (electronic, mechanical, photocopying, recording, or otherwise) without the prior written permission of the publisher and copyright owner.

The scanning, uploading, and distribution of this book on the Internet or through any other means is not permitted without permission from the publisher and copyright owner.

ISBN-13: 978-1-940127-16-3

Printed in the United States of America

BrayBree Publishing Company LLC
P.O. Box 1204
Dickson, Tennessee 37056-1204

Visit our website at www.braybreepublishing.com

Dedication

This work is dedicated to the sacrifices and service of the men of the United States Armed Services during the Second World War (1941–1945) and especially to the men who served in the United States Navy. The author is appreciative of their dedication and sacrifice and retains the hope that the current generations of Americans may appreciate the lessons learned in the course of that worldwide conflagration.

Acknowledgments

It is a little difficult to sit down to write acknowledgments for a work like this. This was an intensely private project for me. It was not one which I chose to share with others as you would many writing projects. With most projects, you welcome the talents and insights of many. You seek the opinions and criticisms of others and their comments as to the manuscript you've given to them to review. However, in the case of this work, I chose to keep my manuscript largely to myself. As strange as it may sound, I did not want the suggestions or input of others. The reason was simple. I was extremely close to my grandfather. We spent years talking, visiting and documenting his youth. It was more important to me than it was to him, but he gladly entertained my questions and humored me as I inquired about every aspect of his youth.

I wanted to write this work as I saw him and felt his story ought to be told without suggestions or interference into my processes or thoughts. I have long treasured the stories of our World War II veterans. With the release of many memoirs of these veterans in the period of 2001 to 2010 and the death of my grandfather in 2007, I decided it was time to draw together the innumerable notes taken and interviews conducted while talking with my grandfather between the period of 1992 and 2006. This book is the result of those efforts.

Ultimately, I owe him, my grandfather, for his service to our community and country and the cause of freedom worldwide. I acknowledge his efforts and those of his colleagues and friends. They were the greatest of our generations. They saw many extraordinary things and came home to rather ordinary lives. I admire and respect them for the level of humility with which they performed their great service. Therefore, I respectfully acknowledge the service, humility, decency, life and memory of my grandfather, Luther Edward "Junior" Talbott and that of his generation.

CONTENTS

ACKNOWLEDGEMENTS vii
INTRODUCTION xi
1. EARLY LIFE IN LEAPWOOD AND KINFOLK 3
2. LIFE IN FINGER, SCHOOL DAYS, AND WANDERLUST 27
3. CHILDHOOD CHARACTERS AND ADVENTURES OF YOUTH 48
4. THE GREAT ADVENTURE IN TULIA, TEXAS 80
5. A WORLD IN TURMOIL 109
6. ADVENTURE AND PERIL IN THE NAVY 134
7. HIS SWEETHEART 160
8. FIGHTING THE GERMANS IN FRANCE 170
9. LIVELY DAYS BEFORE TRANSFER TO THE PACIFIC 208
10. BREAKING THE JAPANESE GRIP ON THE PACIFIC 227
11. OKINAWA AND HOME 247
12. COMING HOME AND MOVING ON 274
  EPILOGUE 282
  BIBLIOGRAPHY 295
  IMAGE CREDITS 303
  INDEX 307

Introduction

Seventy-five years ago, the young fighting men of the Allied armies and navies were preparing to embark upon what General Dwight D. Eisenhower deemed "the great crusade." They came from small towns, big cities; poor families, influence, power, and money. They were sons of the uneducated and the highly educated. Many were single, some were married, and others already had children at home. Some would perish within minutes of the first shot; others would live through the trials and return home to relive those days for decades. Some would put the nightmares behind them and embrace their actions; others would struggle until the end of their days.

On June 6, 1944, my grandfather, Luther Edward "Junior" Talbott, the subject of this work, was at his battle station ready to serve the great cause of liberating Europe from the grip of the German Armed Forces, the Nazi Party, and one of the world's foremost madmen, the German Führer Adolf Hitler. He was a young man, like so many others, from a humble background and a small American town. He was an otherwise average person among a generation of men and women living in extraordinary times. The Second World War was not their first struggle; they had been living through the greatest economic depression in history for the better part of their lives.

As Junior Talbott and his shipmates readied the big guns of the U.S.S. *Arkansas* to bombard the German positions on the coast of Normandy, they must have realized the gravity of the situation. D-Day would be one of the greatest assaults in the history of warfare. Despite their awareness, neither Junior nor his comrades knew the place they were about to take in history.

They served on a ship often overshadowed by larger, more distinguished battleships. Yet the U.S.S. *Arkansas* occupies a unique place in United States naval history. As the oldest battleship afloat during World War II, it was destined for the scrap heap before the Japanese attack on Pearl Harbor on December 7, 1941. That aggression and the horrendous losses inflicted on the U.S. Navy ensured the vessel's survival and continued use during the conflict. This grand old lady and her crew, including Junior Talbott, would render vital and brave service to their country in the effort to save the world from Fascist oppression. Part of this work is dedicated to telling that story.

In fact, this work serves several purposes. It tells the story of a young man who persevered and found both work and adventure in the Great Depression, came of age during that difficult period, and volunteered to fight a war neither he nor his fellow Americans asked for or wanted. It recounts the story of a spunky, broken-down battleship that showed her mettle and ability to be an effective and vital weapon in the worst and most deadly action. The young men manning the *Arkansas* not only escorted cargo and troop ships across icy submarine infested waters, but fought in two theaters of war and provided critical support and firepower at Omaha Beach on D-Day, the fall of Cherbourg, France, the invasion of Southern France, and the entire battles of Iwo Jima and Okinawa, all in less than twelve months.

This work has been at least twelve years in the making. It was borne out of a conversation between a 14-year-old and his 66-year-old grandfather in 1987. It became a desired goal almost twenty years later when that grandfather passed away. It is hard to explain exactly why I think

INTRODUCTION

Junior Talbott's story is so important to finally tell. It can honestly be said that many other men I've known had stories just as compelling. But then, they weren't my grandfather. There is a special relationship between a boy and his grandfather. The resentments between parent and child, father and son, simply aren't there. By the time his grandchild comes along, he has had time to mellow and gain wisdom. My grandfather had become a patient and gentle old man. Like most boys, I saw him—and still see him—in a light that borders on something damn near akin to idolatry. And I make no apologies for that fact. No kid could have been luckier than I was to call him my grandfather.

Still, there were reasons far greater than a blood relation or kinship that led me to write the history of Junior Talbott's first twenty-four years and the events he experienced. That relation alone could have been enough, but I had other motivations. In all truthfulness, as I grew up at the man's feet listening to story after story about his youth, I realized I had something interesting and special on my hands. He was a member of the generation now artfully termed "the greatest generation." I agree with that terminology whole-heartedly. This generation of Americans came of age in the greatest period of economic depression and turmoil our country ever experienced. They raised themselves out of that peril by conquering another peril: worldwide fascism.

Junior Talbott had much in common with his peers. He was born in a much simpler time and place. He was a boy from a rural background, a modest but proud heritage, but he yearned for more. His generation had to be resourceful and open-minded. They were among the first to migrate for opportunity. They couldn't afford to be complacent. Indeed, it was my grandfather's own story of resourcefulness that drew me closer to him.

He had to work and earn money his parents didn't have to enjoy what later generations received without sacrifice—a public education. Junior had to migrate hundreds of miles from home just to earn a mere eight dollars a week working full-time. He saw the Panhandle of Texas when pioneers still breathed and could tell him of olden days. He saw the world when that world was still considered rather large. He saw its old orders crumble and new forces rise. He was along for the ride and did his part to combat forces he couldn't understand at the young age of twenty-one. Still, like others from the greatest generation, he did what was asked of him without question and accepted that it had to be done.

He came home convinced that his leaders had asked no more of him than he was capable.

Junior Talbott didn't protest war, didn't seek a way out, and didn't bitch and complain when it was over that he had been mistreated, misled, or misused. He sought no special compensation for seeing some damn horrible sights. As he grew older, he didn't complain that the government had apparently forgotten him. He never complained at all. Instead, he kept new generations of young soldiers and sailors in his thoughts and heart when he heard stories of the horrors they had seen, smelled, or heard. He was proud to be an American and a citizen of a nation that had taken upon itself to lead the free world and free Europe and the Pacific from the shackles of evil Axis dictatorships. In his mind, his contributions paled compared to those of his comrades. He was humble about what he'd seen, experienced, and accomplished. He never bragged or felt he had done anything special.

As you read this account of one's man experience in hard times, peace, and war, I hope you will find it both informative and enlightening. It has gone through many transformations and stages of development. There were times when it sat for months without progress while I contemplated where I was going with it. There were times when I felt both frustration and hope. Still, there was never a time I gave up on finishing it.

Today, on this, the seventy-fifth anniversary of Junior Talbott's first battle and the first battle of the U.S.S. *Arkansas*, it finally feels that I have reached my goal. In doing so, I confess that it is a bittersweet experience. I loved my grandfather dearly. He has been dead for twelve years. Through this work and research, I felt like I've kept him, his adventures, and his voice alive in my head, heart, and soul. Now, as I complete the task and send it for publication, I wonder aloud at the effect of its completion on me. If I lose something, I can only hope that I have helped him come alive again in the minds and imaginations of my children, family, and others who choose to read the story presented on these pages.

The memory of my grandfather— the totality of the man as I saw him, still see him, and knew him—reminds me of Hamlet's response to Horatio's compliment of the late king in Shakespeare's *Hamlet*:

He was a man, take him for all in all, I shall not look upon his like again.

And I know that I won't. But I will remember.

John E. Talbott, J.D.
June 6, 2019

HELL OF A SIGHT TO SEE

1

Early Life in Leapwood and Kinfolk

The main street running through Leapwood, Tennessee, was dry and dusty, absent a heavy rain of course. The village and its most prominent citizens were ambitious to grow. These men had plans. They prepared for expansion and growth far beyond its boundaries that existed in July 1921. The main street was only a start. It would take much more investment and infrastructure to support the masses who would reside in the new town and the businesses that would spring up along its streets.[1] Young ambitious businessmen and entrepreneurs would stake their fortunes on the development of the small hamlet.

Things were bustling despite the lack of a bank, railroad line, or large industry. The town fathers included, among others, the Harris's, the Sewells, and the Whartons. They were folks with great plans and

---

1. The records of the McNairy County, Tennessee Register of Deeds reflect a plat for the Finley Addition to the town of Leapwood, Tennessee. This plat as shown on these pages demonstrate a vision for the village that was quite ambitious.

great dreams for the future. All was optimism and potential. Into such a community and such a world, a young child would be born who would see much more of the world than his neighbors. He would see it in the most tumultuous of times, in the heart of the American Century. Like the stories of millions of other Americans and future Allied soldiers and sailors of the Second World War, this young man would see things far beyond what even he thought possible.

There is little left of that small village in north McNairy County. The busy afternoons on dusty streets with folks milling around doing their business are long over. The indications of a community are still there. Much has changed in the last century. It was in Leapwood that Luther Edward Talbott was born on July 23, 1921. He was the only surviving son of Newton Perry "Newt" Talbott, a local merchant and farmer. Now an older father, Newt had raised two seemingly ungrateful and distant daughters. They had left their father for their own pursuits, both selfish and unselfish. Through his third marriage, Newt began a new family and a fresh start. It was not his first fresh start or his last.

"Junior" Talbott entered the world in a little plain wooden house located to the east of the present-day Enville-Leapwood Road (State Highway No. 224) somewhere beyond the stretch of the main road between the present-day Hardin Graveyard and Winding Ridge roads. It has long gone the way of the town itself. Nothing is left to mark its existence but the faded, recorded memories of a man dead now several years. The hearty young infant was born in a world of ancient and obsolete customs, in a time when rural West Tennesseans lived an existence not far removed from that of their pioneer ancestors.

In keeping with an old tradition whereby the grandmother had great latitude to name her own son's children, the wailing and healthy young male child was named by his grandmother, Angie Nora (Wright) Talbott. She named the newborn male child in honor of another of her sons, Luther Talbott. The name didn't sit right with the attending doctor who delivered him. Dr. L.C. "Cube" Smith, a friend of the family, wrote down the newborn child's name as John Henry Talbott. His mother, Beulah Varham (Matlock) Talbott, also disliked the name and nicknamed the child "Junior."[2]

Large-boned and sturdy, Varham Talbott was the daughter of Henry Thomas Matlock and Sarah Albertine (Moore) Matlock. Her parents actually named her "Varm" at birth. John Harris, a local banker and businessman in Finger, Tennessee, told her that Varm didn't spell anything and that she should change it to "Varham" as that would be more helpful on legal documents. It doesn't seem that it would be of any actual help or consequence, but she decided to change it. Varham and Dr. Smith were good friends. He often teased her by calling her by her first name, Beulah, and she returned his fire by calling him Cubit, which likely was his real name. A truce was reached when Dr. Smith agreed to call her Varham if she would refrain from calling him "Cubit."

Varham was a quiet, tall woman with rough-hewn features and a gentle, quiet nature. Much younger than Newt, she was his third wife. The theme and tradition of "poor but proud" seems to have run through her family history. Her family tree was full of good, honest, but struggling people. Her father was the son of Moses M. Matlock, a Confederate veteran and staunch Democratic farmer. He would prove to be the only Confederate in the family attic. Like her, many of these people were quiet in their demeanor.

On Junior's father's side, his ancestry was long and constituted a tradition equally comprised of hard work and struggle. His father was the eldest of five children belonging to William Alexander "Alec" Talbott and Angie Nora (Wright) Talbott. Newt's siblings were Ada (Talbott) Barton, Charlie Talbert, Willie Coleman Talbert, and Luther Talbott. One will note that two of Newt's brothers had different spellings of the last name. Will and Charlie were married on the same day, December

---

2. From this point in the account, Luther Edward Talbott will be referred to as "Junior." In the Finger community, he was known by most people as Junior. A few called him "Tater." The nickname "Tater" was the result of his wearing a toboggan in the winter which had a large fuzzy yellowish-gold ball on its top. The nickname originated from Raymond Hodges, who called him "Tater Top" after seeing Junior wear this particular toboggan. At the time, Hodges lived in Finger with his spinster aunt, Julia Hodges, across the road from the Finger School campus. The school's principal, Hugh Allen Basham, boarded with Miss Hodges as well. However, in Henderson, Tennessee, where Junior did much business and graduated high school in 1939, he was most often known as "L.E." or "Luther." However, his most common nickname was Junior and that is what he will be referred to for purposes of clarity and simplicity.

25, 1906, by the same justice of the peace, W.A. Loftin. Squire Loftin spelled the young men's names as Talbert rather than Talbott. The squire attached to their respective marriage certificates the legal name, Talbert. Afterwards, both men used Talbert as it appeared on their only legal document during those times prior to the Social Security Act.

Little is really known about Alec Talbott. According to Junior himself, his father never spoke of his grandfather. Interestingly, Alec's brother, Samuel Perkins "Perk" Talbott, never spoke of him on any occasion that could be recalled by Perk's step-daughter, Hattie Lee (Bray) Arnold Cone, whom Perk raised. No one seems to have discussed Alec and very little exists to give a good account of his life. It is believed that he was married prior to marrying Newt's mother. A marriage record for one W.A. Talbott exists in the marriage records of Henderson County, Tennessee, where Alec's home and domicile were located prior to the formation of Chester County. That record reflects the marriage of this W.A. Talbott to Martha Harrill on April 25, 1874. At that time, William Alexander Talbott was the only W.A. Talbott living in Henderson County. Although it has yet to be conclusively confirmed, it does appear that Alec Talbott may have been married twice. We have no knowledge of the fate of Martha Harrill, who may have died. Alec may have proven as difficult as some speculate and a divorce ensued. His marital history is as enshrouded in mystery as other aspects of his long ago life.

Still, some things about Alec's life are known. He was born to Theodore Perry Talbott and wife Elizabeth Ann (Walker) Talbott on August 7, 1846. He was the couple's second child and eldest son, born near Jack's Creek in present-day Chester County.[3] His father was known as a kind, gentle, quiet, and industrious man who enjoyed a close relationship with his children.[4] His mother was of true pioneer stock, the Walkers of Pittsylvania County, Virginia. She was a tough woman who came from hearty forbearers. Her own grandmother had ridden an ox from Virginia to Henderson County, Tennessee, to the Jacks Creek area

---

3. At the time of Alec's birth, the Jack's Creek area was a portion of Henderson County, Tennessee. Chester County was formed by legal proclamation and statute in 1879, but was not formally and officially established and governing itself until 1882. The county was originally slated to be known as Wisdom County after William Sargent Wisdom, a prominent businessman and banker of Purdy, Tennessee.

4. This information was passed from Theodore Perry Talbott's son, Perk Talbott, to his stepdaughter, Hattie Lee (Bray) Arnold Cone, who passed it on to the author (2002).

to visit her son, William Parrish Walker. After a lengthy visit, she returned on her ox back to Virginia.[5] At her best, Alec's mother, Elizabeth Ann, was a demanding and difficult woman.

Thus, Alec appears to have grown up in a household with a gentle father and a demanding, stern mother. His younger brother, Perk Talbott, once told the difference between the parents as no other example could. Perk was no more than ten years old and had gotten into his mother's tobacco. His father came in from the fields to find an angry wife demanding something be done about the boy's transgression. Exasperated, Theodore Perry asked Elizabeth for a suggestion of punishment. She tied young Perk's hands tightly behind his back and handed Theodore Perry a sturdy limb and commanded her husband to beat their son about his back. According to Perk Talbott later in life, his mother yelled and harangued her husband to continue the beating. He beat young Perk until the limb broke and then cut the boy loose. He took the boy to the fields with him, leaving a satisfied Elizabeth at home. Once in the fields far away from the house and the ears of his demanding wife, the father apologized to the son for having to inflict such a beating. Still, he instructed Perk to never steal his mother's tobacco again.

Such harsh discipline and apparent lack of motherly affection may have had a significant impact on Alec. Certainly, the impression has been left that he himself was not an affectionate person, not by description but from the lack thereof. It has been said that Alec was present with his brothers on the family farm cutting wood when their beloved father succumbed to a sudden and fatal heart attack. The boys saw their father's life ebb away from him—and them—on an otherwise ordinary afternoon while performing a routine farm chore. In what may have been an old Appalachian custom, the boys planted a cedar tree to mark the spot where their father's head landed and a pine tree to mark where Theodore Perry last stretched out his feet.[6] Theodore Perry's obituary ap-

---

5. Information regarding Ms. Walker's ox trip from Virginia to Tennessee and back was taken from an old unidentified nineteenth-century newspaper clipping found in the possession of the late Hattie Lee (Bray) Arnold Cone, the step-daughter of Perk Talbott, now in the possession of the author.

6. Photographs of these trees were found in the Samuel Perkins Talbott family papers and are included in this work.

peared in a Cumberland Presbyterian publication and bears witness to his character. It reads:

> T.P. Talbott died at his residence, near Jack's Creek, Henderson County, Tenn., on Jan. 24, 1878.
>
> He was born October 3, 1817, in Jefferson county, East Tennessee; professed religion in 1858, and joined the Cumberland Presbyterian Church in 1860, in which he lived a respected and beloved member until his death. He bore the name of "a good man" by all who knew him; was a kind husband and father, agreeable neighbor, peaceful citizen, and an honest man.
>
> Bro. Talbott died without a minute's warning; dropped dead while choping [sic] wood. But he was ready, his lamp trimmed and burning, and we believe he is now in the Cristian's [sic] home, where the wicked cease from troubling and the weary are at rest. I say to all, Be ye also ready.

Theodore Perry's obituary sets forth the kinds of character traits that would mark more than one generation of Talbotts.

In 1876, Alec married Angie Nora Wright (1849–1926), the daughter of Henry P. Wright and Sarah Jackson (Lloyd) Wright. The Wright family was native to Giles County, Tennessee. Other than what has already been discussed about him, little else is known. A photograph of Alex exists that gives at least a face on which to reflect. He had a stern appearance with a stocky build and a white beard that grew under his chin. Still, Newt did recount one story. He recalled that the first fish he ever caught had to be boiled because the family had no grease in which to cook the catch. This seems to indicate the dire circumstances of the family's existence. It has always seemed that Alec and Angie Nora were quite poor.

Like his father before him and his son afterwards, Alec's death was quite sudden. According to family members, he died while sitting at the table from an apparent heart attack. It is believed that he may have been much like his mother in temperament and personality. If so, that might explain much about everyone's silence regarding him. If Alec's personality was indeed anything akin to that of his mother, it may have been that he did not get along very well with his relatives, including his children. He died in August 1916 and was buried in Hopewell Cemetery in northern McNairy County. His and Angie Nora's graves remained unmarked until Junior and other family members purchased a cemetery stone to mark their graves. The fact that Alec and Angie Nora lay in Hopewell Cemetery so long without a headstone is another possible indication of their poverty.

After Alec's death, Angie Nora lived at various times with her sons, especially Newt and Luther. This was another old custom of the day, the widowed mother staying with various children. She often stayed with Newt and his family, but died while visiting her son Luther on August 12, 1926. Junior was only five when his grandmother passed away, but could remember her being a "fleshy little woman" who usually sat in her rocking chair next to the hearth.

Hopewell Cemetery is located in a hilly area and in 1926, the roads were in terrible condition. This was at a time when most were primarily dirt roads with little or no gravel. Mr. Tom Sims, a family friend, drove Newt, Varham, Junior, and his younger sister Vonnie Mae to the cemetery for the graveside service.[7] Tom's car was a Ford Model T, a type of automobile with no fuel pump. Instead, the car's engine relied upon gravity to feed the fuel to the line. Therefore, any time that he started up one of the steep hills, the car would go dead when gravity pulled the fuel away from the line. As a result, Tom had to start back down the hill, turn around, and then proceed up the hills in reverse gear. On the day of Angie Nora's funeral, there were large storm clouds hanging in the sky and the trees swayed wildly in the winds. The day was memorable for the young man who would retain his memories of it for the duration of his life.

Junior's memory brimmed with recollections of times when his grandmother, Angie Nora, spoke of her youth in eastern Middle Tennessee. She grew up in Giles County, near the town of Pulaski. This portion of Middle Tennessee lies within the Nashville Basin or the Central Basin. It was in this hilly area of thin soils and exposed limestone rock that Angie Nora grew into womanhood and came of age. One of the stories she often liked to tell concerned the family's method of gathering corn

---

7. Tom Sims lived at Leapwood, where Newt and his family lived at the time. He was a night guard at the cotton gin at Leapwood and was later shot and killed by a thief at the gin. Tom was found dead the next morning and robbery was presumed as the motive.

during the fall harvest. Due to the steepness of the ancient hills, Angie Nora's father, Henry P. Wright, would not take the wagon and team up or across their steep slopes. Instead, he would pull the wagon around the base of the hills as the others pulled the ears of corn and threw them down the hillside to be gathered into the wagon.[8]

As for Junior's ancestry on his father's side, there is an interesting thread that appears to run through the family's history. Until the Second World War, there appeared no direct involvement by any direct Talbott family ancestor in any war or other military action. There was one collateral ancestor, Colonel John Talbott of Jefferson County, Tennessee, who served in the pre-Civil War Tennessee State Militia. Otherwise, the direct line of Talbotts included men of age who could have served in the Revolutionary, Civil, Indian, and Spanish-American Wars, as well as the First World War, but did not fight in any of these conflicts. Generally speaking, the Talbott men were by nature quiet, peaceable, and non-confrontational.

It appears that the Talbott family eventually migrated to Tennessee from the area surrounding Chester County, Pennsylvania. Their religious background seems to have included generations of membership within the Society of Friends or the Quakers, a historically pacifist religious group. In short, their religious beliefs precluded service in the armed forces in any form. This may have impacted the decisions of generations of young Talbott men. By Junior's time, pacifism was not a popular stance following the Japanese attack on Pearl Harbor on December 7, 1941.

Junior Talbott spent his first six years in the little village of Leapwood. His father's farm was located on the present-day Beauty Hill Road in the vicinity of Dry Creek, just a little east of that otherwise dry branch.[9]

---

8. Junior knew little about the Wright family. It appears that Angie Nora's mother, Sarah Jackson (Lloyd) Wright, died while the family still resided in Giles County, Tennessee. By the time the family shows up in the 1870 Henderson County, Tennessee, Census, only Henry P. Wright and his children are counted. It appears that he migrated to this area with his children. According to family sources, he is buried in an unmarked grave next to his son Landon Wright at Cabo Cemetery in Chester County, Tennessee.

9. It was located about halfway between the present-day McIntyre Road and State Route 224 on the south side of Beauty Hill Road on the present day Doc Miller place. Miller's current home is almost on the site of the old Newt Talbott home.

The family's home was a two-room structure with a dog trot and possibly made of logs covered by weatherboarding.[10] The farm itself consisted of sixty-eight acres purchased by Newt and his first wife Nancy (Jackson) Talbott from a gentleman by named Haywood Hair on November 26, 1908. The couple paid $1.83 an acre.

Newt was married three times. His first marriage was to Nancy Jane Jackson on November 7, 1900, with local magistrate W.F. Maness officiating. Nancy was born in McNairy County in 1876. She and Newt had three children: Annie (Talbott) Peeples Henry, Nona "Nonie" (Talbott) Moore, and a son who died in infancy in 1905 (perhaps stillborn) who was buried in Hopewell Cemetery. Annie was a troublesome girl who gave her father great concern. She was sent to a boarding school at Purdy at one point and got into trouble there. According to Junior, she was a constant source of worry, concern, and trouble who gave little thought to the aftermath of her actions. She eventually relocated to Arkansas.

The second daughter, Nona, married John Moore. That union produced two sons, W.B. Moore and J.C. Moore, and one daughter, Marie (Moore) Thomas. They too lived in Arkansas. When Newt died in 1947, Nona had not returned to visit her father since 1925, more than twenty-two years of absence. She returned for the funeral and settling of the estate and was a solemn mourner, dressed in a black mourning dress complete with veil and black gloves. In fact, Junior's opinion of Annie and Nona was never very high or never appeared to be so. A man who seldom spoke ill of others, he never had anything good or constructive to say about his half-sisters. Their treatment of him upon the settling of their father's estate in late 1947 and early 1948 may have been a primary reason for his attitude toward them.

Yet things are not always as they seem. Interestingly, in 2013, a letter was discovered in the papers of Junior and Faye Talbott that gives a different view to the relationship between Junior and his much older half-sister, Nona Moore. The letter appears to be addressed to both Junior and Faye. One could assume the letter is to Junior and his sister, Vonnie Mae, but most likely not. First, it was written five days after the marriage

---

10. According to the late J.R. McIntyre, an adjoining landowner and a brother-in-law to Junior, this describes Newt's old home. Interview and tour with J.R. McIntyre on Sunday, June 3, 2007, in which J.R. McIntyre showed the author the site on which Newton P. Talbott and his family lived until 1927.

of Junior and Faye and addresses the subject of their recent marriage. Further, the letter makes no mention of anything that remotely relates to Vonnie Mae. Had the letter been addressed to Vonnie Mae, it is highly doubtful that it would have ever made its way into Junior's possession. The letter is dated October 8, 1944, and is addressed to "Bud" and "Sis" and uses the plural pronoun "you" when discussing Junior's marriage. The following is a transcript of this letter:

Cabot, Ark.
10-8-44

Dear Bud and Sis.

Was surprised of corse [*sic*] but you can't ever tell about a Navy boy ha ha and I'm sending to bouth [*sic*] of you my very best wishes of success and happiness. I don't know who I had rather congratchlate [*sic*] than you Bud. So may God richest blessing be with both of you. I would sure liked to have been home while you was in but I guess it was imposable [*sic*]. I know Dad and Mrs. Varham was taking the rag off the bush[11] with joy was they not? I know just how that felt only you hadn't been gone so long when you got home as W.B. was. And I didn't eaven [*sic*] now [*sic*] he was in the States when he come in. I had started to work just about ½ block from the house when I saw him and Boy O Boy I cryed [*sic*] with joy. I was never so happy in my life I know and he left wen [*sic*] J.C. come 2 weeks to a day. It was such a shame they couldn't got to see

---

11. The phrase "take the rag off the bush" was an old Southern idiom or phrase that was or has been used when scandalous relationships are revealed, but it's also applicable to anything surprising. It is closely akin to the phrases, "Don't that beat all?" and "Doesn't that take the cake?" According to authorities, its etymology is uncertain but some have speculated that its origin may have something to do with old-fashioned shooting contests in which somebody would drape a rag on a bush as a target and the winner was the person who shot it off the bush, A Way With Words: A public radio program about language examined through history, culture, and family, www.waywordradio.org/tear-the-rag-off-the-bush/. The phrase is also described as an old country expression which denotes something outrageous, going above and beyond the ordinary and surpasses everything, as defined in the Urban Dictionary, a popular online dictionary which also gives background for words, found at www.urbandictionary.com/define.php?term=Take%20the%20rag%20off%20the%20bush.

each other. But W.B. went and spent one night with J.C. I was so glad and I'm so glad W.B. is coming back to the states. Say J.C. is still at Front Royal, Va. I give you his address & Boy I would like to see him. I have saw W.B. since I saw him now and I thank [sic] he has a real girl to [sic] haha. But W.B. you can't ever tell about him. If you would like to right [sic] J.C. his address is John C. Moore, S.P. 2/c, W.R.D.T.C.K-9. Front Royal, Va. He would like to hear from you all. And say you do send me one of you all's picture. I thank [sic] the snap shot was grand. She is a real nice looking girl. So you all right me real often and tell me all the news about Finger as I never hear. I don't have time to right [sic] to no one. With lots of love to you both.

Sis. Nona

P.S. when you boys get home maby [sic] you all can get together and have a swell time. As I will enyway [sic] haha J.C. never was away eny [sic] at all, always with me but boy he is a swell looking boy 6ft 1 in tall and weighs 208 lbs. and don't look like he would weigh over 175. He is just firm. Guss [sic] you are tall to [sic], you never have told me. WB. Is 5 ft. 9 in and weighs 180 lb. and of corse [sic] we thank [sic] a good looking boy. I sure did like your picture, you looked so nice in your uniform, would make eny [sic] girls [sic] eyes fall for you. I had better shut up now before I say to [sic] much haha and have some one jelous [sic] haha.

Love
Nona

This letter seems telling in many ways. Despite the impression that Junior and Nona never had a relationship, this letter appears to indicate otherwise and there are some facts that probably should be taken into account. First, Nona was a full fourteen years older than Junior. She was married to John Calvin Moore (1884–1966) on May 21, 1922, before Junior was even a year old. Sometime in 1925, she and John moved to Arkansas. At that time, Junior would have been about the age of four. She did not return until 1947 and he never saw her again until that time. Regardless, it appears that she did write Junior on occasion and he wrote to her.[12]

At one time, a photograph of Nancy Jane (Jackson) Talbott was in the possession of Vonnie Mae (Talbott) Garner. This image showed an attractive and stylish woman. Nancy passed away on December 21, 1915, and was interred at Hopewell Cemetery. After her death, Newt remarried to Mary Gilbert Martin. This marriage occurred either in late 1916 or early 1917. Mary was the daughter of Dr. Thomas A. Gilbert and Ellen (Presley) Gilbert. Her first husband was James Nathaniel Martin. The couple had two children, Martha Ellen Martin and James Thomas Martin. Mr. Martin died on April 1, 1912. Newt and Mary had one child, William Perry Talbott, born in October 1917.

Happiness was not to belong to Newt and Mary. Their son died in April 1918 and the couple buried him in Hopewell Cemetery near Newt's first wife. That fall, they fell victim to the great influenza epidemic of 1918. Mary did not survive and passed away on October 21, 1918. Her family retrieved her body and buried her in the Cedar Grove Cemetery near her hometown of Scotts Hill in Henderson County, Tennessee.

Newt was so ill that he was not aware of Mary's death. That particular epidemic brought about the deaths of approximately 675,000 Americans between 1917 and 1920. The effects of the illness caused great deliriousness and deprived him of his ability to remain conscious. Mary was buried at Cedar Grove for more than two weeks before Newt realized that she

---

12. For example, the letter is dated only five days after Junior's marriage. Thus, the news must have traveled fast and Nona is responding quickly and with enthusiasm and humor, as if the relationship, although long-distance, is easy and familiar. There is also the fact that Nona refers to Junior with a nickname, that of "Bud." She mentions her sons, Junior's nephews, W.B. Moore (1923–1974) and John Calvin "J.C." Moore, Jr. (1925–1970). J.C. was born in Natural Steps, Arkansas, shortly after the Moores' arrival in that state. Both served during the war. Nona provided her sons' addresses to Junior and they were found in his papers after his death. She alludes to a snapshot (apparently of Junior and Faye) that Junior seems to have sent to her. She also mentions that he has never told her whether or not he is tall. This indicates that they have shared letters or communication of some sort, but this subject was never raised. Further, she mentions a photograph in her possession of Junior in his uniform, but it is unclear as to whether he provided it to her. Regardless, she seems proud of her much younger brother and is very complimentary to him. Such correspondence makes one wonder what kind of relationship these siblings could have had under different circumstances.

had died. Following her death, he remained in contact with her children and often provided support to them when it was needed. This unique gesture was most likely an example of Newt's respect and love for Mary.[13]

Junior was the product of Newt's third and final marriage. After considerable heartbreak and despair, Newt married Beulah Varham on October 16, 1920. She was born on August 30, 1889, the daughter of Henry Thomas Matlock and wife Sarah Albertine (Moore) Matlock (ca. 1863–1897). Henry was a local Democratic magistrate in the Twelfth Civil District of McNairy County. Sarah married Henry on August 18, 1881. She was the daughter of George W. Moore and Katherine (Pickett) Moore. Her siblings included William Nathan "Billy" Moore (1852–1937), the father of Curt Moore. According to some sources, Sarah died in February 1897, making her death likely the result of the birth of Cassie Matlock or some resulting complication. Her great-nephews included Odie and Millard Moore.

Henry was a friend of the Abernathy family of Selmer, Tennessee, strong Democrats, leaders in local and state Democratic politics, and the owners and publishers of the local newspaper, the *McNairy County Independent Appeal*. Matlock was an ardent Democrat and his son-in-law was a stubborn Republican. In fact, he was a Hoover man. Certainly the dinner conversations must have been interesting. Henry was interested in many things and was well-known in his community.

Varham's sister, Belle (Matlock) Martin, was a maid or house servant to Newt and Nancy Talbott. It may well have been through Belle that they became acquainted. Varham and Newt had two children, Luther Edward Talbott and Vonnie Mae Talbott. It is here that we pick up the story of Junior's early life once again. As stated earlier in this work, his first six years were spent in Leapwood. In his old age, Junior recalled many happy and interesting memories of his childhood.

One of his first memories pertained to a transition in his young life. During the very young days of a boy's life in the early twentieth century, he traditionally would wear a gown until such time that his parents put him into long pants. Junior was no different. On the memorable day in question, he reached across the dinner table for some item and his father jokingly proclaimed, "Varham, better get the boy some long pants...his

---

13. At the time of Junior's death in 2007, he still had in his possession a pocket watch that belonged to Dr. Thomas A. Gilbert, that his his father Newt Talbott had passed on to him.

peter's dragging the butter." Junior was old enough to hear and remember this amusing exchange. His ability to recall this humorous if earthy proclamation gives some hint to his advancing age at the time. The story provided him great laughter and mirth in his old age.

On nice days, Varham performed her wash duties at a spring somewhere off the Enville-Leapwood Road across from Newt's store and up behind the Leapwood Schoolhouse.[14] Ladies in the community met to do their washing at this rather large freshwater spring. Junior remembered there being a large cast iron wash kettle with a hot fire underneath that often remained stoked and ready. On one occasion, he was told to remain at the store with his father while Varham tended to the wash. But as young boys often do, he became restless and wandered off in search of his mother. Although Junior did find her, his father was quite angry that he had wandered off without any warning. When he found Junior, Newt stripped a peach tree limb and walked him back to the store, all the while swiping the backs of his bare legs with the willowy limb. Junior was wearing short pants and the punishment was memorable.[15] Varham often performed her wash duties at the spring with the wives of Ed Harris and Julius Harris and others. Almost every local family kept an iron wash kettle at the spring. A black lady by the name of Margaret Jones often came and did Varham's washing for her, especially on Mondays. She usually brought her son with her and he and Junior played together while the washing progressed. At that time, even in the South, it was not unusual for children of both races to play together and enjoy youthful adventures. The societal distinctions would come later, but Junior was never very observant of them.

Junior first attended school while living in Leapwood.[16] He always maintained that he was technically too young to enroll, but the principal, Miss Florence English, allowed him to attend.[17] According to Junior,

---

14. The Leapwood School did not occupy its later site where the former school building currently sits.

15. When failing to punish his own grandchildren for some infraction of the rules many years later, Junior never failed to recall this punishment as a way of telling his grandchildren they were getting a good deal!

16. Junior recalled his first school days in an interview dated March 22, 2004, in which he detailed his first experiences in school and the teachers he grew to know there.

17. Miss English was later the principal of the Finger School.

he attended classes, sat quietly, and listened to the teacher as she taught. He always thought he was an unofficial student there. However, later research revealed that he was enrolled in the class of Ms. Irene Moore from August 10, 1925, to March 26, 1926. Interestingly, Junior was barely four years old when he started to school at Leapwood.[18] His birthdates, upon enrollment, was altered on the school records to show his date of birth as August 10, 1920. His enrollment records show him being five years old in August 1925. Indeed, he was barely four years old when he was enrolled in the first grade.

Junior recalled only two teachers at the Leapwood School, Miss Florence English and Miss Cora Hair. Apparently, he did not remember Ms. Moore, but given the fact that he was so young, it is entirely possible that he simply didn't remember this teacher so many years later. Miss English informed Varham that she did not mind Junior's attendance at the school because he was a quiet and attentive child. The school was within sight of Newt's store and Junior stayed only until lunch and went back to the store when dismissed. Miss English watched him as he walked back to his father's store each day.[19]

During his childhood days in the small village of Leapwood, Junior played with another young boy named Raymond Sewell, who was the son of Eb Sewell.[20] Mr. Sewell owned the brick store building next to Newt's store.[21] Raymond and Junior played together between the two buildings. Junior would grow into old age, but Raymond was not so fortunate. He died when he was only 48 years old.

The general store owned by Junior's parents in Leapwood was much like the one they later operated in Finger. In addition to running the

---

18. McNairy County School Records: Leapwood School, 1925-1926. These records did indeed show Junior's birthdate as August 10, 1920, and identify him as "Junior Talbott," the son of N.P. Talbott, a merchant who lives 1/8 mile from the school.

19. Due to his young age, it may have been that Junior remained at school all day but didn't recall it so many years later. It may also have been that due to his young age that his teachers may have excused him early each day.

20. We do not know much about Raymond Dee Sewell. He was born on May 16, 1919, and died in Jackson, Tennessee on July 23, 1967. He was buried in Mars Hill Cemetery.

21. W.E. "Eb" Sewell (January 5, 1889–April 29, 1959) also served as McNairy County Clerk for a period of years.

store, Newt also worked on the family farm.[22] He admitted that while he could grow great corn, he was not much of a cotton farmer. The quiet but personable merchant divided his time between his store and his farm. One of the salesmen who often called upon Newt was a tobacco salesman for Garrett Tobacco Company named Mr. Barksdale. Barksdale made his rounds by carriage or on horseback for many years. Years after Newt's death, Barksdale told Junior that he often had to go to the fields to take Newt's tobacco order. He sat on a plow stock as Newt recited his tobacco order. Incidentally, Newt had to make all such orders because his Leapwood business partner would not make decisions.[23]

Newt always told his son that he and his "Uncle Wright" established the store at Leapwood. Yet Junior's memory could never bring to light the actual given name of the "uncle."[24] The Talbotts' general merchandise store, both in Leapwood and later in Finger, provided a wide variety of necessities and goods such as axes, saws, harnesses, staples, nails, hoes, rakes, pick sacks, soda and baking powders, fatback, dry salt middling, lard, sugar, coffee, flour, canned tomatoes, salmon, peaches, potted meats, tobacco products including snuff, chewing tobacco and cigarette tobacco, straw hats, shoes, work clothes, bolts of cloth with which to make dresses and threads for sewing machines, embroidery, and quilting.[25]

Junior often recalled a story about the days of the Leapwood Store that both amused and frustrated him. It dealt with the theft of a large amount of sugar. In the era of Prohibition, many people resorted to

---

22. The wooden store building was torn down in the mid 1990s. The lot is now overgrown with brush and small trees. The coordinates for the lot are 35º 18' 17.66" N, 88º 27' 22.99" W.

23. As will be seen in the succeeding paragraph, Newt's business partner was likely G.G. Wright.

24. A 1923 deed shows that Newt Talbott bought one-half of the interest in the store building and lot from a G.G. Wright for $112.50. Whether or not this is the "Uncle Wright" of whom Newt spoke cannot be established. It can be surmised that G.G. Wright was his partner. Mr. Wright is buried in the Mars Hill Cemetery in Leapwood, Tennessee.

25. Whenever Newt took his annual inventory, he had to figure in the selling price and what the goods cost him. Like all merchants, Newt had a cost mark written on the products and his mark was different from that of other merchants. Newt's cost mark for inventory was as follows:
    B E   W A T C H F U L
    1 2   3 4 5 6 7 8 9 10

The numbers in the price of each item were represented by some of the ten letters. For example, if an item cost Newt the sum of $2.45, the letters EAT were to be found under the selling price.

stealing sugar to make bootleg whiskey.[26] Newt kept the sugar in a large wooden barrel near the center of the store building. One day, a customer or loafer apparently stepped off and measured the exact location of the center of the sugar barrel. During the night, this fellow or his confederate slid under the building through a crawl space and drilled through the floor and into the bottom of the barrel. The sugar was drained through the hole and into a bucket or a sack. The sifting of the sugar left a cone shaped void in the barrel. The next day, Newt fetched sugar for a customer and discovered the theft. Junior always believed his father knew the identity of the bandit but feared he might falsely accuse an innocent person. Such was the character of Newt Talbott.

In October 1923, Newt moved off the farm to be closer to the store. He purchased from R.J. Landreth another house and nine acres for $175.00. This property bordered G.G. Wright, Manley Harris, and Matt Wharton with the house itself located across from Harris.[27] Mr. Harris was a "jake-leg" or "jack-leg" veterinarian who castrated colts and performed other animal husbandry chores.[28] This particular home had about two or three rooms and was located somewhere behind the Cora Hair home. The old Leapwood School building also stood near the Hair home.[29] The old road ran behind Miss Hair's home and the Talbott home was up the road towards the Mars Hill Cemetery. The Talbotts lived on the left side of the road and the Harris home was directly across the road.

The town of Leapwood where Junior was born and spent his first years was much different in 1921 than it is today. It was a busy little village at that time with a viable commercial district of sorts. Aside from

26. Sugar was still purchased in great quantities even in later years for the production of bootleg white whiskey. Junior often recalled a story that occurred in the 1950s while making his own peddling route while he was as a merchant. He was delivering a one hundred pound bag of sugar in the Byrd Locke Community in McNairy County. The gentleman who ordered it instructed Junior to take the sugar deep into the woods, apparently to the site of his whiskey still. Junior told the fellow that he would not get that involved. Instead, he would drop the sugar off at the road and assume the man's wife was making a large quantity of cookies and pies.

27. L.E. "Junior" Talbott interview, March 22, 2004. Manley L. Harris (May 25, 1876–November 22, 1960) was a well-respected individual in the Leapwood community.

28. Harris had a brother known by the nickname of "Caesar" Harris.

29. The Cora Hair home still stands in 2019. The Leapwood School referenced here does not refer to the later school building that also remains. Incidentally, this Cora Hair home was probably not standing at that time. Instead, it serves as a landmark to identify the area about which is being written.

Ebb Sewell and Newt Talbott, there was at least one other merchant, the cotton gin and mill, a post office, a doctor, and the local school. The town planners and the village fathers were ambitious. There exists a plat entitled "Findley's East Side Addition to Leapwood, Tenn."[30] This demonstrates the almost unrestricted ambition of, at the least, Mr. G.L. Findley in regards to the future of the community. Even small towns like Leapwood had visionaries with boundless ambition and hope.

One of the moving spirits of Leapwood was J. Matt Wharton (1881–1944), an astute businessman who built one of the first truly modern homes in north McNairy County. It was located on his farm on the Finger-Leapwood Road. The brick house had a design vaguely akin to modern ones during the era of modern and innovative architects like Frank Lloyd Wright. Junior remembered being in the home as a child and recalled it was like no other he had ever seen. He recollected the large picture window and the view from the parlor. The kitchen had interesting and unique features, including cabinets with hidden compartments within them.

Wharton was a local notary public and his signature could be found on many of the legal documents of the day in Leapwood. Always very active in the stock markets as well as other financial and banking affairs, the Great Crash of 1929 ruined him. He was forced to sell his nice home in Leapwood and relocate to nearby Finger, where he built another residence. Though far less impressive, it still had many interesting innovations that Wharton enjoyed in his previous home.[31]

There were many families with whom Junior's parents were acquainted. These included the Alexander, Barham, Barnes, Carothers, Davis, Droke, Findley, Hair, Hardin, Harris, Hysmith, Jackson, Kerby, Kirk, Landreth, Lott, Martin, Massengill, Pyron, Stevens, Tacker, Vires, Wharton, and Wilkerson families. Other leaders of the community whom Junior well remembered included the Eason family and the Sewell family.

The Eason family included many physicians. This family was especially close to Newt Talbott and was often guests in each other's homes.[32]

---

30. This plat is found of record in Deed Book 16, page 620, in the McNairy County, Tennessee, Register of Deeds' Office.

31. This home was later occupied by Pearl Gilbert.

32. In the fall of 2002, one of the late Dr. Eason's sisters shared with the author that she had often spent evenings with the Talbotts in their small Leapwood home.

One family member, James A. Eason, was born just a month shy of Junior on June 28, 1921. The two spent their first few years together growing into young boys in Leapwood. After World War II broke out, James joined the 375th Fighter Squadron, 361st Fighter Group, 8th Army Air Force. He was killed over England on November 1, 1944, and brought home and buried in the Mars Hill Cemetery. In a world war, tragedy and loss were inevitable and reached all corners of the earth, even north McNairy County.

The Sewell family was the preeminent family of Leapwood during Junior's childhood years spent there from 1921 to 1927. W. Ebb Sewell ran the store next to Newt's. Married twice, his first wife died in the first few years of the twentieth century. He remarried and his second wife, Mary, also died early in life. Mary Sewell (March 5, 1898–March 31, 1928) was a very attractive young lady. Following her death, she was buried in the Mars Hill Cemetery. Sewell was an astute businessman, politician, and a good neighbor to the Talbotts.

Junior's memories of the days in Leapwood were varied. He recalled his mother keeping her butter and milk in a bucket that she lowered into the well to keep them cold and prevent spoilage.[33] Unfortunately, neither of Junior's parents dwelled on their own childhoods, their parents, or discussed these types of things in any detail. No known photograph of Sarah Albertine (Moore) Matlock exists and only one is known to survive of Henry Thomas Matlock. According to Junior, his mother did speak of the Cosbys, whom she said were her cousins. Of the various older Moores in the area, Junior always believed that "Uncle Billy" Moore was a brother to Sarah Matlock and that John Robert Moore and William Moore were nephews. He also believed that Mr. Curt Moore was perhaps a nephew to Sarah as well.[34]

---

33. L.E. "Junior" Talbott interview, March 22, 2004.

34. Later research verified Junior's memories on the subject as well as those of a distant cousin, Mandy (Jamerson) Amerson. Indeed, Sarah (Albertine) Moore Matlock (born ca. 1863 and died ca. 1897) was the daughter of George W. Moore and Katherine "Kitty" (Pickett) Moore. Her brothers included William Nathan "Billy" Moore, John W. Moore, Jesse Alexander Moore, George W. Moore, and James B. Moore. She was an aunt or great-aunt to such local individuals as Essie Mae (Webster) Vires Talbott, Washington Curtis "Curt" Moore, Millard Moore, Odie Moore, Vadie (Moore) Droke, and John Calvin Moore, the husband of Junior's half-sister, Nona Mae (Talbott) Moore.

Junior was not quite sure where Henry Thomas Matlock lived. He always believed that it was in the vicinity of the Mount Zion Cemetery near Enville. In fact, he owned an 81-acre farm in the Twelfth Civil District of McNairy County, which he sold to Emma Browder for $200.00 in 1912. After selling it, he lived at various times with his daughters, Miranda (Matlock) Tidwell and Cassie (Matlock) Herring. Often, Henry spent a week or so at intervals with Varham and her family leaving vivid memories in the mind of his young grandson.

Junior often recounted his admiration for his maternal grandfather. Henry Matlock objected to dove hunting and often instructed his grandson that it was extremely bad luck to shoot or otherwise harm a dove. The young boy's mother also told him on many occasions that it was not good to kill them because they were "the Lord's birds." He violated this rule only once in his lifetime. One Sunday morning in 1935, while hunting in the bottoms of Finger, he shot a dove out of an elm tree. He was standing on the old levee near the old creek run and the old iron bridge spanning Huggins Creek. After he returned from his hunting and wandering that morning, he and the rest of the family learned that his beloved grandfather Matlock had died that same day at about noon. To the best of his knowledge, Junior had shot the dove at about the same hour. He always stated that this incident confirmed his now late grandfather's advice. He never shot another dove again. The instrument of death was a homemade slingshot.[35]

Junior's grandfather had been sick and Varham had gone to Leapwood to sit with him. He died at the home of Cassie Herring, a little box house located behind the Horace and Miranda Tidwell home.[36] The night his grandfather "lay a corpse" or lay in state, eight or ten people sat up with the body. According to Junior, everyone present for the wake had to fight the cats all night long. The wake was held in Cassie's little house and as it was summer and hot, the doors and windows were all kept open. The neighborhood cats crawled in and circled the room. Cats were believed to light on corpses and defile them by attempting to feed on them. So, as with all others during those days, the Matlock family and friends spent

---

35. Junior recalled the events of his grandfather's death with great emotion in an interview on March 22, 2004. He often grew visibly emotional when discussing his grandfather and his memories of the man.

36. This location was just a little south of the latter day Leapwood School.

the evening fighting off the cats and shooing them away. Junior would later recall that the cats squalled and "carried on" all night long.[37]

Frank Herring, Cassie's husband, once carried Varham, Junior, and Cassie to Adamsville in his wagon for a shopping excursion.[38] At the time, a feud was raging between the Abernathy and Plunk families. Frank got wind of the trouble brewing that day and told Cassie and Varham to get their packages together and get in the wagon as quickly as possible. Trouble was about to start. When Frank got to Dollar Hill, the party could hear the gunfire blazing. Such feuds and conflicts were common even in that late day and were taken very seriously. They were the ultimate test of a family's honor or lack thereof.[39]

When Junior was still rather young, the family, including all or most Varham's sisters and their spouses, made trips to nearby Winding Ridge to gather scaly-bark hickory nuts. Winding Ridge was, and is, just as the name indicates. The ancient ridge winds through deep hollows with a snake-like winding and curving path. The hollows are deep and shadowed by great hardwoods. In the 1920s, Winding Ridge was especially populated by large hardwood trees, many of which were grand scaly-bark hickory trees. These old trees were large and the limbs were full with hickory nuts. The family would gather them by the "sack-full" and use them to make cakes and pies. Junior, who was rather small at the time, recalled dragging a ten-1 pound sugar sack as he gathered. It seemed in his mind that the sack grew as heavy as he was. He gleefully recalled these hunting and gathering trips as part of a happy and fulfilling childhood, quite content with the family's circumstances.[40]

Junior's grandfather encouraged his hunting and interests. He once instructed Junior to go next door to Ebb Sewell's store to buy some No. 4 shot.[41] After purchasing the shot, Junior and his grandfather Matlock

---

37. Miranda (Matlock) Tidwell's home, located next door, would later become the Jack Loving home. At the time, it was a weatherboard house painted yellow, not the brick edifice that it became and is today (2019).

38. Benjamin F. Herring (1894-1970) and wife Cassie Matlock Herring (1897-1988) had no children of their own and Cassie often doted on her sister Varham's children. The author well remembers Cassie Herring himself.

39. L.E. "Junior" Talbott interview, March 22, 2004.

40. Ibid.

41. L.E. "Junior" Talbott interview, October 23, 2002. At that particular time, the Sewell store was also being ran with the assistance of Sewell's son-in-law, Rudolf Barber. According to

went out to the Eason farm. That farm abounded with hickory nut trees and both gray squirrels and fox squirrels. Junior and his grandfather killed eight to ten squirrels on this particular trip. Afterwards, Frank and Horace skinned the creatures and a stew was made with the meat. The squirrel meat, some chicken, tomatoes, peas, beans, corn, and anything else suitable were mixed together to make mulligan stew.[42] The meal proved memorable because Junior broke a tooth on a piece of the No. 4 shot that was still imbedded in a piece of squirrel meat. From that point, he avoided squirrel meat whenever possible.

Junior's aunt Belle Martin appears to have been prominent in his very early life. Belle and her husband John had only one child, a daughter, Mary, who was born and died on the same day, June 6, 1916.[43] A photo exists of Belle and Junior standing at Mary's grave at Mars Hill Cemetery while Junior was still just barely more than a toddler.

There are not many facts or stories which have survived regarding John and Belle. Junior did, however, hold dearly to a few reminiscences about his aunt and uncle. Belle was a very large woman but also quite big hearted. After the family moved to Finger, Junior visited John and Belle on occasion. On one visit, he was helping his Uncle John, who ran a grist mill.[44] Junior came across some soured corn and mentioned to his uncle that maybe they should dispose of it. John became gravely serious and told Junior in a hushed tone, "Shh! Be quiet, son. Don't you say nothing about that corn." He made it evident to Junior that he wanted the existence of the spoiled corn to remain a secret. After all, the sour corn was worth more than the "good" corn. It would make good whiskey, which

Junior in an interview in 1992, the No. 4 shot or shell contained approximately 3¾ grams of gun powder. The gun used on this squirrel hunting escapade was a 12-gauge double barrel shotgun with a twenty inch (20") long barrel. The barrels were shorter than regulation length because one barrel had blown up and the entire barrel apparatus had to be sawn short to accommodate.

42. Mulligan stew is an improvised or "thrown together" dish which was reputed to have been prepared by American hobos in camps along the railroad lines during the first part of the twentieth century. Mulligan stew is an Irish stew that consists of meat, potatoes and other vegetables as well as any other items that can be gathered up for inclusion into the mix.

43. John T. Martin (January 7, 1879–April 10, 1961) was married previously to M.E. Martin (1884–1912). The author has always been under the impression that John did have children by his previous wife. Sarah Belle (Matlock) Martin was born on January 8, 1885, and died on March 14, 1953.

44. John Martin's grist mill was located across the road from Newt Talbott's store. It was powered by kerosene.

was its intended purpose. Sometime late in her life, Belle fell into the fireplace and sustained terrible injuries that led to her death.

Junior's uncle, Horace Tidwell, raised pigeons and hogs. He drew a pension for his service during the Great War and so he often piddled around with various hobbies. Horace had one of the first Duroc boars in the area. It was roughly four feet tall and everyone around brought their sows to be serviced by this Duroc boar.[45] Horace and Miranda were by no means ambitious people, but they maintained themselves during his lifetime. It was a different story after Horace's death. Miranda was often dependent upon her then grown nephew Junior and his wife for support.

The Talbott family remained in Leapwood until January 1927. No railroad ran through Leapwood or anywhere nearby. The closest line came through nearby Finger. Newt moved the family and the store's contents there in 1927 because of the town's location on the Mobile and Ohio Railroad. The reason for the move was simple. At this time, the road between Finger and Leapwood was basically a dirt road that turned to mud during wet weather. It was often impassable and virtually impossible for heavy loads of groceries, hardware, and stock to be carried over. Any major order of stock from a wholesaler or other supplier had to be delivered by train to the Finger Depot, then transported over the Finger-Leapwood Road to the store twelve miles away. After more than twelve years of business in Leapwood, Newt was weary of struggling to get stock between the two towns. Finger was growing and another store could certainly be sustained. Therefore, Newt made the decision to relocate his family and store to Finger—lock, stock, and barrel—a move that put him just yards from the depot.

When Newt moved his family, he brought two completely loaded wagons. His brothers-in-law, John Martin and Frank Herring, helped. Junior recounted that his father and uncles stopped the wagons on the side of Huggins Creek.[46] The men unhitched two mules from one of the wagons, hitched them to the team pulling the other wagon, and took the first full load across the bridge. After crossing the bridge, the four mules were unhitched from the first wagon, taken back across the bridge, and hitched to the second wagon to complete the crossing. Although it was

---

45. Junior discussed Horace Tidwell's farming practices with great interest in an interview on October 23, 2002.

46. Luther E. "Junior" Talbott interview, 1994.

January and very wet, the journey was successfully made. The family's ties to Leapwood remained, but now they would have new ones to the community of Finger that would last for generations.

2

Life in Finger, School Days, and Wanderlust

The winter was cold and wet when the move to Finger was made. Despite Newt Talbott's age, then forty-nine years old, his family was young and in a new town. It was 1927 and the country was still prospering. The Jazz Age was in full swing. Prohibition was ignored in big cities and small towns alike. The Roaring Twenties roared on without heed to the trouble looming in the distance like storm clouds brewing. The cities and urban areas were running wide open, in every sense of the meaning. Out in the country, ways were still simple and towns like Finger were innumerable. Being there was a larger, more expanded version of living for Newt, his wife Varham, and their children. It was bigger than Leapwood and had many advantages over the smaller village the family had left behind. It would provide the Talbott children with opportunities and their father a chance to begin anew.

Once in Finger, the family needed a roof over their heads. Newt rented a place to get them through the winter, a small wooden frame home in a grove of hardwoods just below the old McIntyre home. It was much smaller than the more substantial McIntyre residence up the hill that housed two batches of Jim McIntyre's children as well as many of his extended family. Now old Jim McIntyre was dead some six winters and his widow wanted to rent out her smaller house. Fannie (Carroll) McIntyre still had children at home, including her daughters, Alice and Wilma. The house was small but close to Newt's new store, only a short walk to town for the middle-age merchant. During their stay, six-year-old Junior fell from the front porch, a minor injury he would never forget.[1]

Finger, Tennessee, in 1927 was a busy place. The downtown area was bustling. There were no less than twenty-four commercial buildings in the business district. These generally included nine general merchandise and dry goods stores, one hotel, two livery stables, two physicians' offices, a cotton gin, a bank, the Mobile and Ohio Railroad depot, and three warehouses, as well as small sheds and shacks used for various commercial purposes. Junior experienced a number of impressions upon arriving in Finger. One memory was a *sound*. Leapwood was much smaller without the appearance or function of a larger town. When Junior arrived in Finger, it seemed like entering a great, large place. He recalled vividly hearing the church bells of the Methodist Church ring on the occasion of a funeral or a wedding. He was also taken with the very thing that brought his father to Finger—the railroad. The railroad would fascinate Junior as a young man and throughout his long life.

As he crossed the tracks of the Mobile and Ohio Railroad into town, he saw what appeared to a young boy as a "big town." On the south side of Main Street in successive order could be found the Mobile and Ohio Railroad Depot; the office of Dr. William Mark Barnes, MD; Bishop & O'Neal General Merchandise; Bishop Funeral Home and Finger Burial Association; the Farmer's Progressive Store (soon to be N.P. Talbott General Merchandise); H.L. Hodges' Produce and Commission House (shortly thereafter to become Gardner Motors); Ed Stephens' Barbershop; a dry goods store that by 1930 would belong to Albert Weaver; a café; Logan McCaskill's barber shop; and Ernest Clayton's Dry Goods Store.

On the north side of the street heading west from the railroad tracks could be found the wooden framed warehouse and brick storehouse of John

---

1. Incidentally, this house remained until it was razed in 2015. Junior lived across the road from that first residence in Finger from 1948 until his death in 2007. He saw that old home every day.

R. Harris General Merchandise; the office of Dr. Nathaniel A. Tucker, MD; Home Banking Company; the warehouse and brick storehouse of W.P. Massey General Merchandise (which also housed the Finger Post Office); Rube Young General Merchandise; Dolf C. "Pa" Holder's General Merchandise Store; and the Jess O. Mitchell General Merchandise Store. Up the hill from these last three stores was the Finger Hotel and Livery Stable. Behind the Bishop & O'Neal General Merchandise Store, across an unnamed alley, was a livery stable and blacksmith shop.[2]

The old gin site was one of those early places in Finger that interested young Junior Talbott. The old gin had been constructed originally by Isom P. Womble. He later sold it to Finis E. Miller, a Civil War veteran of the Union Army and a survivor of the notorious Confederate prison camp of Andersonville, Georgia. Eventually, it was purchased by Albert Pickett to be a steam-powered mill. It ginned cotton during the fall and was a stave mill and sawmill the rest of the year.[3] Two of the workers at this gin were Junior's much older friends, Hartle Hayre and Eddy C. Peeples.

When Junior and his family arrived in Finger, the main street running through town was dusty in hot, dry weather and wet and muddy in cold, wet weather. The road would later be relocated. As a young man about 1929, he watched the construction crew build the new road using a team of mules and a breaking plow. The road hands ran the breaking plow through the ground, then scooped the loose dirt and piled it on layer after layer. The bridge across the Huggins Creek Canal, a site for many of Junior's fishing, trapping, and swimming adventures, was built of wood and the lumber soaked in creosote. When heavy rains occurred, parts of the levee would be submerged and waterlogged. Loads of gravel had to

---

2. In the early 1990s, Junior sat at his dining room table and with a No. 2 pencil sketched a map of Finger as he recalled it upon his arrival in 1927 and up to 1930. The reader will note the inclusion of the Finger Gin Company as located north of Main Street and just south of the John R. Harris residence (later the Coy Russom home). In 1927, this gin had not yet been constructed but was by 1930. In 1927, the Finger Gin was located south of Main Street along the Mobile and Ohio Railroad off Mill Street (now Talbott Street).

3. White oak logs were sawed at this mill and turned into staves that were shipped down the Mobile and Ohio Railroad for use in making white oak barrels.

be hauled in and spread over the top of the levee.[4] In the spring of 1930, the Finger and Enville Road was improved and graveled.[5]

Newt Talbott already had a plan for his mercantile business when he contemplated the move from Leapwood to Finger. He purchased shares and interests in the Farmers Progressive Store building. Its investors, who included H.H. Kirkpatrick, R.N. Barham, E.H. Plunk, and W.L. Plunk, were willing to sell. Newt bought each of their shares at a staggering sum of $872.50 each.[6] This transaction alone cost him the sum of $3,490.00.

That first winter spent in his father's store stayed in Junior's memories. At the center of the brick building was a potbellied wood stove. He recalled that his first memories of Finger and its people began there around that potbellied stove where country folk and town folk gathered on cold winter days to talk of news and gossip, trouble and celebration, happiness and pain. Here he learned that a store was also place of gathering where knowledge could be picked up and learned from others. It could be a center for politics and a forum for local folklore. Much could be learned from his elders as they gathered here for company and to give themselves a break from the tedium of their everyday lives.

During those days, the local general store had a very special purpose. Transportation was limited in rural areas like Finger and families sustained themselves on their farms. The average farmer in and around north McNairy County grew most of his family's food. Late winter and early spring gardens produced cabbage, Irish (pronounced locally as "Arsh") potatoes, radishes, turnips, and onions, which could be eaten throughout the year. Late spring and summer gardens produced fresh vegetables and fruits such as corn, tomatoes, lettuce, cucumbers for pickling, squash, beans, peas, watermelons, and cantaloupes. Fall gardens and patches

4. In 1993, the author and Junior discussed the construction of the Finger-Leapwood Road and detailed notes were recorded regarding Junior's memories of the process by which the road was constructed. Incidentally, the levee was raised and reconstructed so that it would not flood so easily.

5. The progress on the nearby Finger and Enville Highway was reported in the in the "Bushel Creek News" section of the March 27, 1930, April 10, 1930, and April 24, 1930, editions of the *Chester County Independent* newspaper. Further, the Huggins Creek bridge was improved with the construction of concrete abutments.

6. The deed for this transaction may be found in Deed Book 21, page 7, in the Register's Office of McNairy County, Tennessee.

enabled them to put up sweet potatoes and peanuts. Families canned pickles, beans, peas, potatoes, corn, and okra for consumption during the winter months. Most homes had a hand-dug cellar for cool storage.

These families also raised and slaughtered beef and pork for curing and consumption. A hog killing was a big event. The hogs were scalded and all parts were used. The men and sometimes the women gathered around large scalding vats and stoked a hot fire. The hog was placed in the scalding water just long enough to condition the hair so that it could be scraped from the carcass, leaving a smooth hide. Nothing was wasted. The heads were scraped of all their meat and used for souse meat and the intestines for either chitterlings or as sausage casings. Junior gleefully recalled that everything on the hog was used but the "squeal." Some farm women like Junior's future mother-in-law, Ollie Pearl (McCann) McIntyre, fried sausage and canned it, turning the capped jar upside down so the hot grease would cool around the lid and seal it. Hams, sides of bacon, hog jowl, stands of lard, and cracklings were put up for later use.

Having raised most of their food, local men traveled to town and went to the general stores for their wives and families. Women sent their husbands to pick up items such as baking powders, sugar, coffee, tea, extracts, and spices, as well as buttons, lace, thread, zippers, household goods, and items they could not make or produced at home. Farmers would come to town when their work allowed them the luxury to visit with the shopkeepers like Newt. They talked about what they were hearing from the county seat at Selmer, Tennessee, news from this ridge or that hollow, the deaths and births in the larger community, predictions about the weather, or the insects that might cause harm to the next season's crops. Often these farmers read their only newspapers and heard their only news about the greater world at the local store. Junior grew to know many families and men through his father's store.

It may seem odd that the world he knew was largely made up of men. In those days, small towns could be rough and women generally didn't visit. Their lives at home demanded much of them and work was never truly done. Because it was common in small towns to see a fight, a knifing, or other kind of brawl, polite womenfolk stayed away from the hurly-burly of the small towns. The husband, often themselves the participants in these affairs, were the family emissaries to the nearby small town or hamlet. Of course, Junior did learn of the kindnesses of the little old gentle ladies of his small town. He often did some odd job or made a delivery for them and developed friendships with many that lasted for years.

Newt Talbott's family lived in the McIntyre rent house for about a year until he purchased a house of his own. He bought the Bruce Barnes house and lot, located just around the corner of Main Street and Mill Street, for $1,250.00. Great sums of money were spent establishing himself and his family in Finger just two years prior to the great economic crash of 1929. He could have bought the Ily Brown house and three or four acres for the same amount, but the Barnes house was closer to the store. There on Mill Street, the family lived across the way from the Methodist Church, where Varham would be a member for the next four decades. The next few years would see much development in Junior's character and personality. Over the next decade and a half, he would soak up much life and learning.

Junior Talbott attended the Finger School as early as August 23, 1927, when he was six years old. Despite his time spent at the Leapwood School, he was enrolled in the first grade. Too young to walk himself to school, he went with his older half sisters Alice and Wilma. They acted as his protectors each morning along the old road going into town. That winter, school was held in two separate locations after a fire had destroyed the Finger School in July. High school students attended classes on the second floor of the Home Banking Company building. The elementary students, like little Junior, went to classes at the Finger Methodist Episcopal Church South on Mill Street.

The old school was a large two-story wooden white frame structure. Classes were held on both floors. The top floor was also used by the local Odd Fellows and Masonic lodges. Several classes of the community's bright youth had passed through the doors of the building.

As Finger grew, the town fathers wanted a new schoolhouse. Inquiries had been made for the construction of a larger and more modern structure. County officials considered the old one sufficient and refused to fund a new building project. One afternoon, a secret meeting was called at the home of Freelin Dickey.[7] Dickey's nephew, a young man named Clifford Young, was asked to attend. When he arrived, a group of the village's leaders was already present and in deep discussion. The mood in the room was somber and quiet. The men made him a proposition. Clifford listened attentively and responded, "I'll have nothing to do with this. I'm sorry; you'll have to get someone else."[8] Young had been asked to commit the act of arson itself for the sake of procuring a newer and better facility.[9] The old building was an impediment to progress and the town fathers felt something needed to be done. Clifford refused to participate. In any event, the old school building burned down. Young Junior saw the sparks from the blaze lift into the air. It was a spectacle that caused great excitement in the town. After the fire, Finger got its new school.

Junior's first teacher at Finger was Miss Ethel Plunk, a spinster and the daughter of C.C. Plunk. She had been engaged earlier to Professor Harvey Hodges, but the engagement ended with Hodges' death in 1922. Junior's other teachers in these early years included Mrs. J.B. Teague for second grade (August 27, 1928–April 26, 1929) and Miss Florence English for both third grade (August 12, 1929–April 30, 1930) and fourth grade (July 21, 1930–March 27, 1931). Although Miss English was another strict old maid school teacher, Junior's memories of her weren't particularly bad.[10]

No records were found for Junior's fifth grade year, though his studies progressed during the 1930s. For the sixth grade from August 19, 1932, until April 21, 1933, he had Miss Aline Tucker as his teacher. She was

---

7. According to Junior's old friend, the late Clifford Young, the son of James and Sally Young, this meeting was held in the home of Freelin Dickey, a leading promoter of Finger and known locally as the Barbecue King of Finger. Dickey, like the author, was a grandson of some degree to one of the area's leading founders, Robert Thompson McIntyre. Incidentally, Clifford Young was a nephew to Dickey.

8. The author interviewed Clifford Young in 1994 on the grounds of the old Finger School. It was then that Young shared the information regarding the school fire with the author. He directly implicated his own uncle and stated that he did not wish to get himself into any trouble and felt the whole affair was risky.

9. A July 1927 edition of the *McNairy County Independent Appeal* newspaper commented on the fire: "The Finger school building was burned last Thursday night, the origin of the fire unknown. It was valued at about $4,000 and there was very little insurance. Besides the loss of the building, there was also that of a piano, library, and laboratory equipment. The enterprising people there will soon erect another school building."

10. McNairy County School Records: Finger School, 1927–1936.

the daughter of Dr. N.A. Tucker and never married. Junior was fond of her. J. Clifford Hodges taught him in the seventh grade (July 24, 1933–April 20, 1934). He often spoke of Mr. Hodges and found him to be an interesting and easy-going fellow. Junior's teacher in the eighth grade from July 23, 1934, to April 26, 1935, was Miss Edna Barham. A spinster and daughter of Squire Charlie Barham, she was a teacher whom he held in high regard. His last teacher at Finger was Hugh Allen Basham from 1935 until 1936.[11] Junior was never fond of Mr. Basham.

During his youth, Junior loved to read and contemplate the world outside of the small village of Finger. He read of different nations in geography and history classes and loved history, literature, and adventure stories. This reading habit stayed with him throughout his long life. For Junior, much of his formal education came to life on the road and in the world. He was a firm believer in the concept of an education acquired through travel, experience, and independent reading. He was fond of saying that history takes on new meaning when you actually stand in the middle of it. World history and geography were interesting subjects once he crossed the International Date Line or stood on a street in an English or North African coastal village. Of course, such moments would all come later in his life.

Junior attended the Finger School until about 1938, when he spent his final year of high school at Chester County High School in Henderson, Tennessee, in the old Georgia Robertson Christian College building.[12] While going to school, he worked to earn money. The Great Depression began in 1929 when Junior was eight years old and did not effectively end until the outbreak of World War II in 1941 when he was twenty. His entire youth was spent in the depths of America's greatest economic depression. During this period, few people had the opportunity to finish school. Free textbooks for school children were a luxury available only in a few isolated states. Junior hunted, fished, and trapped to earn the bulk of his funds to continue his education.

11. Interestingly, all of Junior's school enrollment records listed him as "Junior Talbott." None of his records listed him as L.E. Talbott, Luther E. Talbott, or Luther Edward Talbott.

12. This wonderful old building would remain until 2005 when it was dismantled to make way for a new and less impressive building known as the Bulliner-Clayton Fine Arts Building. Interestingly, the author received many of his own college classes in this very building between 1991 and 1995, while it was known as the Milan-Sitka Building, the headquarters of the School of Business for Freed-Hardeman University.

Junior swept the classrooms at school and built fires to warm them during the winter. He arrived early in the morning before the students and teachers and lit fires in the stoves: one in the basement furnace and four others throughout the rest of the building. After each fire was lit, he went back to each stove and placed a scuttle of coal in each one. He was paid five cents per fire and five cents per sweeping. During cold weather, he earned up to $2.50 per week performing these chores; in warm weather, he earned up to $1.25 per week.

Something happened on one occasion and the fire went out in the study hall. Mr. Hugh Allen Basham, a coach and teacher as well as principal of the school, tracked Junior down and gave him a verbal flogging over the extinguished fire. Mr. Basham told him sternly that if he wanted to continue building fires and sweeping rooms at the school, he would have to cease hunting, trapping, and fishing. He thought Junior's attention was being diverted from his school chores. In fact, these very activities were helping to pay for his school necessities. After listening to Mr. Basham's ranting, Junior told him to forget it. He made too much money from hunting and trapping. Mr. Basham would have to find someone else. These were the days before janitors were hired to clean and maintain rural schools. Teachers were responsible for such janitorial duties and often paid a student to do them. By the end of the day, the other teachers told him they wanted him to stay on and continue building their fires and sweeping their rooms.

Junior continued with his chores, but he refused to sweep or build any fires in the study hall where Mr. Basham was stationed. A week later, after failing to find a dependable person to assist him, Mr. Basham approached Junior and asked him to resume building his fires and sweeping the floor in the study hall. Junior told him he was not interested in the job. "You've already told me I'd have to quit hunting and fishing and trapping and I can't because I make more money at that than anything, so I won't do it," he said.[13] Basham conceded and offered him the sum of twenty-five cents per day. Junior accepted at the higher rate.

---

13. Junior remained indignant over Mr. Basham's treatment of him and never developed a positive or friendly attitude towards him. He often said that Mr. Basham was friendlier to the town's wealthier citizens and their children and thought himself above many of the poorer folks in town or in the countryside. Of course, this view may simply have been the result of this early exchange between the two.

There are not too many stories about Junior's days at school. Despite his great desire for education, he told few anecdotes about this period of his life. An interesting one was recalled by his childhood friend, Hayes Hayre. One early morning in the early 1930s, while standing in the front yard at school, Hayes and Junior looked into the sky to see the first airplane they had ever seen flying over. Both boys had heard of planes and read about them, of course, but that was the extent of their knowledge of aviation. Junior told Hayes that he believed that by the year 2000, air travel would be as common as walking, riding horses, or driving in automobiles. Hayes laughed the matter off and told him neither of them would ever live to see the year 2000. When World War II broke out and both boys volunteered for service, Hayes served in the newer Army Air Corps and Junior served in the U.S. Navy, the older branch of service.[14]

Junior often recalled an incident when he fell on the long brick walk leading up to the front door of the Finger School.[15] He cut his scalp and required stitches. Dr. W.M. Barnes, one of Finger's local medical doctors, performed the minor procedure. Unfortunately, keeping with his nature, Dr. Barnes performed the procedure without the benefit of a local anesthetic. Junior recalled the experience as being very painful and the pain never ended.[16] One of his classmates, Mary Frances Brown, often referred to him playfully as her old "boyfriend." Junior cheerfully recalled that the two of them, along with others, would cut class and run off to

14. Hayes Hayre related this story to the author on a cold winter morning, New Years' Day 2000, while ill and slowly declining from a lung disease that would claim his life that July. Junior survived him by almost seven years. The author was instructed by Hayre to ask Junior if he recalled this incident. The author did later that morning. The resulting conversation went as follows:
> John E. Talbott: "Hayes Hayre told me to ask you if you remembered a conversation the two of you had back in the thirties in the school yard about the year 2000."
> Luther Talbott: (After a short laugh) "Yeah, I sure do. We saw an airplane fly over the school and I told Hayes that everyone would be riding around in airplanes one day just like they walked back then. He laughed at me and told me that it wouldn't matter because neither of us would make it to the year 2000 anyhow. But we did make it, even if by just a little bit."

Both men found humor in recalling the story. The author was amazed at their ability to recall the story independently of each other all those years later.

15. This walkway still existed into the twenty-first century until it was obliterated in the summer of 2014, when the area was prepared for the construction of the new Finger Fire Department.

16. From that point in the 1930s until his death in 2007, Junior felt a tinge of pain every time he combed over the area of the cut.

smoke cigarettes. Mary Francis always told happy stories about growing up with him and was very fond of him.[17]

During his first winter spent in Finger, Junior experienced and witnessed a number of events that remained with him throughout his lifetime. One was the tragic death of a childhood acquaintance, Troy Clayton. He was born in 1917, the son of John P. and Ada D. Clayton. He was four years older than Junior.

Like many other young boys in and around Finger, Troy loved to hunt the swamps and woods in and around town. He and his friends Jack Dickey, the son of Freelin Dickey, and Raymond Patterson, son of Lucian Patterson, decided to try a little rabbit hunting. Early on the morning of December 17, 1927, they walked down the tracks of the Mobile and Ohio Railroad to try their luck at swamp rabbits. Troy spotted a rabbit and jumped up to point out the rabbit at the same time that Jack was sighting it with his shotgun. Unfortunately, Troy jumped in the path of Jack's fire and was fatally wounded. Jack ran up the tracks toward town to get help for his mortally injured friend. Many years later, when he was an old man, Junior recalled with vividness seeing the town's men running frantically down the railroad tracks to the boy. The memory was vague, and yet it wasn't. As he recalled, the town was quickly excited and saddened by what had just happened. The sight of these scared and heartsick grown men never left him.

Not long before his death, in his late nineties, Clifford Young recalled the incident. He was one of the men who ran down the tracks to find the boy. Young shook his head and grimaced as he remembered the sad

---

17. Junior got along with most everyone and didn't easily make adversaries. However, he did have problems with one fellow during his youth. There was a bully who enjoyed picking on kids younger and smaller than himself. One day, the bully began picking on Junior and continued to do so while Junior remained patient. Finally, one afternoon while Junior was walking down Mill Street (now Talbott Street) in front of his own home, the young aggressor approached him and attempted to bully him again. This time, Junior had taken enough. He pounced on the young bully without warning and proceeded to give him a pounding. The boy begged Junior to stop and went running off crying. According to both Junior and his wife Faye, he never again bullied anyone around the Finger School. The young bully, whose name is now lost to us, was later killed by another individual while still relatively young.

event.[18] Robert Beene, a friend of Junior's, was one of the first to arrive on the scene. Some seventy-seven years later, he shared his memories:

> I was one of the first ones out there when he [Troy] was killed a short distance in front of the depot in the bottom. There were three boys in the rabbit hunt—Troy Clayton, Jack Dickey, and Raymond Patterson, Lucian's boy. They had only one gun, Troy's gun, a 20 gauge. It was said his [Troy's] Dad bought it [for] Christmas. The top of his head was blown off, his brains was [sic] on the ground when his dad got there. He [his father] picked up his brains with both his hands and put them back in his head. That was an awful sight to see. The section hands was [sic] working close to the depot. They came out and carried him on a tarp to Guy Bishop's. He was the undertaker at that time…I doubt if anyone is living now that was out there but me.[19]

Troy Clayton died almost instantly at the tender age of ten years old. Junior never forgot such a traumatic event. It was his first experience with the death of someone young.[20] There would be other tragedies that he witnessed, but this first one never left him. As the years passed, he became close to the boy's father, John Clayton. The aging gentleman spent much time at Junior's store and became very close to his family.

As a young man, Junior spent much of his time hunting, fishing, and trapping. The hunting and trapping helped him to earn the bulk of his funds for schooling. Fishing was a wonderful pastime for a young man growing up in a small rural town in otherwise lean times. Often he went down into the bottoms near the Mobile and Ohio Railroad. He even spent nights in the woods, out on a sandbar in the creek, or on the creek bank, lying under the night sky and stars. This was a lifestyle akin to

18. Clifford Young interview with the author, 1994. Young was very forthright and told the author of many events that had been seldom discussed over the years since their occurrence.

19. Robert Beene letter to the author, May 15, 2004. According to Beene, the boys had only one gun amongst themselves. Other contradictory sources claim that both Troy and Jack each had a gun.

20. Mr. John Clayton remained a lifelong friend of Junior's and frequently visited and traded at the store. John Clayton (September 23, 1887–April 8, 1975) and Ada D. Clayton (October 31, 1889–August 30, 1957) are buried along with their son at the Finger Cemetery.

much older times and eras. One evening, Junior went down to Huggins Creek to check a trot line he had set in the creek. It was early spring and the night seemed warm to him. He checked his lines and then made his bed on the exposed sandbar for the night. When he awoke the next morning, he was covered with a light dusting of snow. The temperature had fallen during the night and snow had begun to fall.

Junior fished all of the creeks in and around Finger. They shared many of the same attributes. The waters were often murky and a bit muddy with the outspread limbs of nearby sweet gums and poplars reaching over the waters to provide shade and protection. The creeks flowed slowly and languidly short of a hard rain. They were quiet places with plenty of young and old men who fished and watched the waters flow. Still, honey holes abounded in these otherwise shallow creeks. They made for afternoons of fun and relaxation as Junior stood on the clay banks of north McNairy County's creeks.

Junior fished and trapped around Huggins Creek, Hogwallow Creek, Billies' Creek, Bushel Creek, and Tar Creek. Hogwallow Creek was and is a stagnant branch that runs through and around Floyd's Crossing. He spent many days roaming the swampy bottoms around Hogwallow Creek looking for swamp rabbits and other fur bearing creatures. It was in these creek bottoms that Junior first saw the majestic chestnut trees.[21] These trees were on the wane and close to disappearing from the earth at that time. Chestnut trees had been used for years to construct split rail fences, furniture, and other items necessary for use by early settlers. Around the turn of the century, a blight infected these wonderful old trees until they disappeared by the mid-twentieth century.

Bushel Creek originated largely in the vicinity of and on the farm of John Robert McIntyre, Junior's future father-in-law. Bushel Creek wound its way through the McIntyre farm and onto the Adrian McIntyre farm and down into the bottoms around Finger. Eventually, it emptied into Huggins Creek. Bushel Creek ran past the first site of the Finger

---

21. American chestnut trees, more properly known as Castanea dentate, were wiped out in the Southern United States due to a blight known as Endothia parasitica that destroyed these nut bearing trees. This blight was first noted in 1904 and had destroyed almost every specimen of the native chestnut tree by the middle of the twentieth century. Eliot Wigginton, ed. *Foxfire 6: Shoemaking, Gourd Banjos and Songbows, One Hundred Toys and Games, Wooden Locks, A Water-Powered Sawmills and Other Affairs of Just Plain Living.* Garden City NY: Anchor Press/Doubleday, 1980.

Barbecue. It was in these very creek bottoms and on these creek banks that Junior hunted, fished, trapped, and lived a Huckleberry Finn/Tom Sawyer kind of life.

Junior and his father often set live traps for opossum, commonly known as the "possum." Newt enjoyed a good meal of possum. He would place it in a cage out behind the house for about a month and feed it table scraps to get the wild gamey taste out of it. This type of fare differed greatly from the natural fare of the possum. Normally, they eat insects, other small animals, birds' eggs, mushrooms, grains, fruits, and carrion.[22] Newt then roasted the possum on a tray surrounded by sweet potatoes, which in turn soaked up the grease as it cooked out of it.

Both Junior and his Dad enjoyed a meal of baked possum and treated it like a delicacy. Still, there comes a time when a man gets enough of something, especially possum! Junior was tramping through the woods early one morning around Finger and came upon an unusual sight. He was hiking along the area of the swamp near the old road into town just east of the railroad tracks and came upon a dead mule lying in the woods. Its stomach looked distended. Junior noticed it seemed to be crawling and almost moving in and out as if it were breathing. After a moment, he gave the mule a swift kick. Five or six possums came waddling out of the rectum of the mule. This sight killed his appetite for possum the rest of his life.[23]

Junior also hunted and trapped opossum for their skins and furs. He trapped rabbits, mink, raccoon, and other small animals. His nights and early mornings were often spent in pursuit of game in the swamps around town. His parents were very tolerant of his activities. In fact, they were quite indulgent of him. For a young man growing up in such

---

22. Susan J. Wernert, ed. *North American Wildlife*. Pleasantville NY: Reader's Digest Association, Inc., 1982, 44.

23. This incident provided a great deal of laughs and chuckles afterwards. For years, Junior told his children and grandchildren that possum was great and very tasty. He also maintained that he would "just as soon eat a possum as a steak" and might just eat one if he had a chance. His family always laughed about this because it seemed he never once substituted a steak for a possum. In fact, the author is sure that Junior never forgot the sight of those possums crawling out of the rear end of that dead mule. He is certain this is why he never ate another possum. Junior often caught an opossum in his live traps while trying to capture rabbits. The author often accompanied him while he carried these opossum off the premises and disposed of them. However, Junior never roasted, baked, fried, or cooked a single one of them in any manner.

a rural community, his parents gave him wide latitude and allowed him to roam. This freedom gave him quite an adventurous youth.

Although Junior enjoyed hunting and trapping and made money doing it, he also labored for others doing various types of chores and work as well. While a student at the Finger School, he and all other students were given a six-week break in the fall for picking cotton and harvesting other crops. One of Junior's more memorable stories regarded pulling corn for the Woodward family, who lived across Highway 45 in the Old Friendship community. He was working with an old fellow named Mr. Will Hurt. The old man had broken his back many years before in an accident and was literally bent over at the waist. Mr. Hurt walked in a stooped position permanently and his fingers literally brushed the ground as he walked. Years later, with a chuckle, Junior recalled standing in the cornfield one autumn morning and seeing Mr. Hurt look at everyone and say, "I guess ya'll want me to get the down rows."[24]

There was a black family by the name of Burton who lived down the road past the W.L. Plunk place (later the Arl Davis place) near the McNairy-Chester County line. Junior knew this family and sometimes worked with them to earn extra money. He picked cotton and sometimes helped in the hay fields. Junior always had a good relationship with the local black people in and around Finger. He also knew the Draper family, including a young Draper girl who turned up white moss growing on ditch banks and roadsides to eat the dirt under the moss.[25] He also talked about a girl by the name of Cora Draper who did washing for the local white folks. Junior and Hayes Hayre both recalled an ancient black man known as "Uncle Enoch." He was a former slave named Enoch Overman, who had a wild, unruly head of coarse white hair and a wiry white beard. He often sat in the alley that ran behind Newt's store near the livery stables. Both men often wondered what this ancient and weathered Negro had seen in his life.[26]

24. For those who have never picked corn by hand in the old fashioned way, the down rows were those that were still unpicked but trampled down by the horses or mules pulling the wagon. A person on each side of the wagon would get at least two rows at one time. The person walking behind the wagon would pull the corn from those rows put on the ground by the horses or mules and the wagon moving along. Naturally, because of his injury and the resulting shape of his body, Mr. Hurt did not have to overexert himself to pick the ears of corn from the down rows.

25. Junior and Faye Talbott interview with the author, October 23, 2002.

26. Ibid.

Junior often recalled a black man by the name of Robert Bass. He had once owned a farm off the old Purdy-Lexington Road. A prosperous black man, he had the respect of the local white population because of his intelligence and industrious nature. According to Junior, Bass built the house located on the Finger-Leapwood Road known today as the Pete Lemons home. Willie Martin bought the home from Bass and moved his family there. Bass did business with the local merchants and was well-received by them.[27]

Junior's mother didn't push him and both of his parents encouraged his youthful independence. One evening, his future bride, Faye McIntyre, got a glimpse of his harder-to-please side. She was about nine years old and spending the night with Junior's sister, Vonnie Mae. She and Vonnie Mae sat down to eat supper and Varham sat Junior's plate in front of him. She had cooked English peas. As soon as Junior saw his plate, he began to complain. "English peas! I can't stand English peas. I'm not eating this. I'll go to the store and see if I can find something else." With that, he got up and made his way to the store. After witnessing Junior's "hard to please" side, Faye looked at Vonnie Mae and said, "I'd sure hate to have to cook for him." She was certain she would not have gotten away with such antics at John Robert McIntyre's dinner table![28]

In 1937, Junior's younger sister, Vonnie Mae, married Earl McIntyre, the son of Hubert and Maggie McIntyre. She was only thirteen years of age when she married Earl. Junior always felt disappointed that his parents allowed his little sister to marry at such a young age. Her childhood friend, Faye McIntyre, was Earl's first cousin. According to Junior, Earl and Vonnie Mae had a tumultuous relationship. Of course, she was

---

27. Ibid.

28. By contrast, Junior's future father-in-law, John Robert McIntyre, was not so indulgent of his children in that regard. Faye often recalled the atmosphere around her parents' dinner table. While her mother was fun-loving and light hearted, her father was more stern and stoic. He demanded respect and a quiet atmosphere at the dinner table. There was to be no laughing or horsing around at his table. There was also no refusal to eat what was served. He expected his children to act with respect and quiet reserve at the table where dinner took on a more formal tone than in the Talbott household.

so young and had not yet matured emotionally to be married to an older fellow.[29]

Regardless of the difficulties of the relationship, during the fall harvesting break of 1938, Junior and Earl decided to travel to the vicinity of Hayti, Missouri, to pick cotton. There would be at least a couple of trips. On the first trip, Junior, Earl, and another individual traveled by Greyhound bus. The party caught the bus at Henderson, Tennessee, changed buses at Jackson, and proceeded to Dyersburg. There they boarded Shorty's Bus Line and journeyed to the Mississippi River. Upon reaching the river, they boarded a ferry, crossed the river, and continued on foot. The first trip lasted for one week. They stayed in a small shack about three or four miles south of Hayti.

Because the cotton was not yet ready for harvest, they were forced to head back home. On the trip back, they hitchhiked and walked to Cottonwood Point, Missouri, and took the ferry back across the Mississippi River. On the east side of the river, the party learned the last bus had already left and another would not return until six o'clock the next morning. They walked the rest of the night until they reached Dyersburg. There they ate breakfast at the bus stop. From there, the party caught the bus to Jackson and then changed buses to proceed south to Highway 45 just outside of Finger. Interestingly, at that particular time, the highway from Dyersburg to the Mississippi River was graveled on one side of the road and paved on the other side. The graveled side was approximately four to five inches lower than the paved half.

The next week, the party set out again for the same destination. This time, they stayed for four weeks and worked in the cotton fields for one farmer. This farmer had a large number of black sharecroppers working and living on his property. They called him "Boss." Every Saturday night, he took his family and white laborers to Hayti to watch a movie at the local theater. While the farmer was away, the black sharecroppers would steal stove wood from him. One night, the Boss stayed home while his wife, children, and farm hands went to town to see the movie. He caught the thieving sharecroppers "red-handed" and told them that he would take them to buy one half a cord of firewood. He would keep one quarter of a cord for himself as repayment and they could keep the other

---

29. The couple never had children. Both later married a second time and had children and longer marriages.

one-quarter of a cord for themselves. Junior admired the humaneness of the farmer's punishment in a day when men of some means could be quite harsh with those less fortunate who were powerless otherwise.

The farmer for whom they picked cotton also grew watermelons. He allowed his hands to pick any melon they desired for a price of 25 cents each. One afternoon, the farmer suggested they head towards Caruthersville, Missouri, to see a cotton farm that supposedly produced two bales of cotton per acre. The cotton rows on this particular farm were crossways, diagonal, and checked in a square. This cotton was described by Junior as "pretty cotton" being spaced apart 38 inches per stalk. The Boss couldn't believe that this farm yielded that much cotton.

One of the individuals whom Junior and Earl worked with was a man by the name of Perry Clark. He was from Arkansas and he and his wife both traveled to Hayti to work. Perry could pick large amounts of cotton. Junior really wanted to outdistance him and beat his numbers, but knew it would be almost impossible. One morning, he made up his mind to pick at least one half of what Perry picked that day. Perry had picked some 300 pounds by lunch and by the end of the day had totaled over 600 pounds. Junior picked some 260 pounds, and then picked another 103 pounds that evening, totaling 363 pounds for the day. His goal was met. Junior remembered earning about 75 cents per one hundred pounds of picked cotton. He recalled the long, flat, even fields in Southeast Missouri. One field might have as much acreage as an entire farm back home. Junior recalled he could see "forever."[30] The little town of Hayti, like so many of the day, was sustained largely by farmers and their families who shopped there and supported the businesses. It was small with a downtown that surrounded a court square.[31]

Junior, Earl, and Vonnie Mae stayed in a little two-room box shack. They did their own cooking. Junior and another boy slept on a pallet on the floor and Earl and Vonnie Mae slept in the only bed in the little shack. There were sand fleas in the shack that infested everything. They bought Bee-Brand Insect Powders to sprinkle on the floor to kill the fleas and get

---

30. Later in life, the Great Plains would especially captivate Junior for their openness and spaciousness.

31. The author visited Hayti, Missouri, in the fall of 2013. It was a town that had seen better days and was struggling to survive. To some degree, it was still somewhat busy though it had changed little in physical appearance from the late 1930s.

relief from them. When the picking was finished for the day, Junior and the others would stop at a local grocery store and buy a 15-cent quart of ice cream. They would slice the quart into pints and share it.

For Junior, the purpose of this trip was to raise money to better equip himself for his hunting and trapping pursuits. They made him a fairly substantial amount of money for that day and time. He made enough money to buy himself a pair of high-top leather boots, being sixteen inches in height; a case of shotgun shells containing twenty boxes; a new single-barrel Stevens 20 gauge shotgun;[32] twelve steel traps; a pair of hunting pants; a brownish-khaki hunting coat made of heavy twill; that year's hunting, trapping and fishing licenses; a cap and headlight for hunting; and a five-pound can of carbide for the headlight. He also purchased a suit of school clothes. Interestingly, the new shotgun cost him $6.45 from Sears, Roebuck & Company, and the shotgun shells were about twenty-five cents per box. These items allowed him to more seriously pursue his work.

Junior never forgot his experiences picking cotton in Missouri.[33] It was the first chance he ever had to travel outside of his own region. Like most Talbotts historically, he had the desire to travel and the gift of wanderlust. He wanted to see the world and experience adventures that only travel could bring. He took great pride in his hard work and the fact that it took this kind of hard work to further pursue his education. He did just that.

Junior trapped swamp rabbits and hill rabbits for shipment to New Orleans. He broke the rabbits' necks after catching them and put them on the southbound train. These rabbits were bought for their meat and the Louisianans did not want them placed in a refrigerated car. The buyers considered them right for consumption when the fur and skin slid off the backbone. Perhaps they were more ripe than right. Although rabbits were sometimes trapped for their meat, others were primarily trapped for skins and furs. Raccoons, beaver, mink, and other game were trapped and killed for their hides. As a young man in the 1930s, Junior learned the fur trade could still be lucrative.

32. Junior loved the old shotgun and it was still the only shotgun in his collection at his death in 2007.

33. Hayti, Missouri, was and is today a very small town with very flat terrain. It is a poor area that has little or no industry other agriculture. Cotton is the major crop in the area.

One interesting hunting trip involved Junior and his friend, Warren Williams. This story was recorded just as he related it to the author in the mid 1990s.

> Once me and Warren Williams, Ward Williams, and I think Orby Brown, he ran with us, went hunting and Warren and Ward lived down on the Chandler place below Mount Carmel [Cemetery]. Well, we took a shortcut up the hill and was going to go through the graveyard and on what's now Ronald's hog pen and Bill Cone's farm. Well, we were going through the graveyard and all of a sudden, I just went down. I stepped on a grave and it sank in and I went down to my waist. I'll tell you, I was about to flitter in my breeches. Anyway, Warren, Ward, and Orby helped pull me out of the hole but that gave me a good scare.

Hatton Williams, the father of Warren and Ward Williams, lived on the old farm located just below the Mount Carmel Cemetery, now commonly known as the Chandler place. Hatton would sing and whistle and his song could be heard for a mile. When the wind was right, Hatton could be heard singing while cutting wood on his farm. He would cut wood and haul it up to the house, but would not split the wood until he got ready to burn it. On quiet days when there was no wind, people might stop what they were doing after hearing a faint distant sound and then realize they were still hearing Hatton sing.[34] His voice certainly carried.

Given the serious nature of Junior's hunting and trapping activities, it is no wonder that he might occasionally stretch the limits of the hunting seasons. Given the times, they were not so strictly enforced unless someone complained to the authorities. Many relied on what they hunted to supplement their income, diet, or both.

Haven Garner, a local school teacher and friend, thought Junior was doing *too* well. Convinced that he was poaching, he reported him to the game warden. Haven told him the approximate time and location of Junior's probable activities. Sure enough, Junior was just where the game warden expected. But the young man would not to be outfoxed. He was

---

34. Hatton Williams (March 10, 1885–March 16, 1972) and his wife Euda Williams (November 23, 1887–September 26, 1972) were well-respected by both Junior and Faye Talbott.

on the farm that belonged for generations to the Ward family (later the Jere Redmon farm). The night was dark and the woods were thick. The game warden got within just two or three feet of him but didn't catch him. Junior was lying on the ground in a depressed area behind a large log, obscured from sight. The game warden stood with his back to him and shone his lamp around, but never caught sight of him. Junior took no real offense to being reported by Haven. In fact, he laughed about it and seemed to think of it almost as a game.

Indeed, Junior's youth could be considered idyllic for adventurous and high-spirited young men today. Despite the leanness and conditions of his time, he soaked up the world around him. He observed and studied it and considered life a school. Characters and individuals of all kinds, sour and savvy, lively and leaden, mirthful and mournful, could teach a young man much. This lesson was not lost on young Junior Talbott.

3

Childhood Characters and Adventures of Youth

It's difficult to define someone who is a *character*. You simply know one when you see one. *Webster's Dictionary* defines a character as a person with reference to behavior or personality; an odd or eccentric person.[1] Life in the 1920s and 1930s was full of characters. Every small town in America had their share of odd, eccentric individuals who left their marks on young men like Junior Talbott. He thoroughly enjoyed getting to know them throughout his long life.

Many stories that Junior shared from his youth involved his sense of mischievousness and the interesting characters that he encountered. They were earthy folks with amazing insights into life who had lived fascinating lives. These people had oddities and ways from bygone days that may never be seen again. His memory never failed to recall them and their varied ways. Their influence on him lasted a lifetime.

---

1. *Webster's Unabridged Dictionary of the English Language.* New York: Portland House, 1989, 247.

Arthur Petty was a local farmer who befriended Junior when he was a young man. He lived in a house behind the Finger School campus, his property fronting the street that connects Brown Street with Massey Street.² Mr. Petty planted watermelons on what is now part of Murray Cook's property. Junior and his friends often raided his watermelon patch. On one occasion, he and a young man by the name of Brown (a cousin of Lorraine Meadows) got Mr. Petty's seed melon. It was a big beautiful melon, so big that neither boy could carry it. They had to roll it to their destination. After the boys finished eating what they could, they took the seeds from the melon and spread them out on paper somewhere about where Murray Cook's house is now located. Not long afterwards, Junior ran into Mr. Petty. The old farmer asked him, "Did you get my seed melon?" Junior replied, "Yes, sir. Did you get your seeds?" Mr. Petty answered with a smile. He had indeed gotten his seeds and there were no hard feelings.³

On another raid, Junior, the same Brown fellow, and a couple of other boys made off with about five good large melons. They hid the absconded melons in a sage grass field down the hill behind the Finger School where they could be retrieved on the weekend. Junior always said that no malice was ever intended. It was almost a game of sorts and that his friend, Mr. Petty, basically winked at these antics.⁴ After church services on Sunday afternoon, Junior walked past the home of local merchant Guy Bishop and saw him and the local Methodist minister sitting on Guy's porch eating watermelon.⁵ Junior wondered where they came from

---

2. The Petty home stood in the area where Larry Franklin later located a trailer.

3. Charles Haze Petty, the son of the late Arthur and Pearl Petty, gleefully recalled these same stories at the author's office on October 28, 2014.

4. The story of the seed melon certainly seems to verify this view.

5. The Alsworth Guy Bishop home was located on the lot just west of the Finger School campus. This home stands even today (2019) and was, until about 2006, the seat of this family since its construction around 1910. When telling and retelling this story, Junior often chuckled, grinned, and commented that it was no surprise that Guy Bishop would take watermelons from young boys. He had little respect for Bishop and often mused on the fact that the minister was probably feasting on a watermelon that was twice pilfered. Junior had little use for organized religion and was suspicious of preachers in general. The thought of a preacher eating of a fruit that had been the object of two raids seemed somehow appropriate in his sharp analytical mind. Junior did hold some respect for Mr. Bishop. During the Great Depression, he suffered significant losses and was left basically penniless. But rather than file for bankruptcy protection or otherwise cheat his creditors as many in his position had chosen to do, he worked through his debt until he had paid every

and thought it prudent to check on his pilfered melons. After all, he and his school chums had made the honest effort to raid the Petty patch. As he suspected, the melons were nowhere to be found. He always believed that Guy had commandeered them for his own consumption.

Mr. Petty used to say that he knew when Junior and his gang had raided his melon patch. They would eat from a melon without causing great waste and then turn it over so the crows would not feast on it. This was important because once a flock of crows began feasting on one melon, the flock would become greedy and continue eating until they had consumed or damaged most of the melons in the entire patch. Mr. Petty appreciated the fact that Junior sought to protect the rest of his crop and was not given to waste. In fact, one of Junior's most known traits was his penchant for using something until it could not be used further.

When he was older, Junior found great joy in telling of his youthful exploits. He often amused himself by telling stories that seemed to come right out of a Mark Twain novel or a memoir from an earlier time. It is hard for those reared in the latter twentieth century to understand that children of Junior's generation were raised basically in the same tradition and manner as children had been in America since the late 1700s. Little had changed for rural Americans in the South up to the 1920s and 1930s.

One story that often brought a laugh involved Mrs. Pearl Petty, the wife of Junior's watermelon growing friend, Mr. Arthur Petty. Pearl often took some of the kids in town down to the Huggins Creek Canal so they could swim and play in the creek. There was a large sandbar in the midst of the canal from which boys would dive into a fairly deep hole. On one occasion, Junior dove from the sandbar. While coming back up from under the water, a large bullfrog got into his bathing suit. It was an old style bathing suit popular at that time with shoulder straps and material covering the boy's chest. The bullfrog, which was rather large and measured about a foot long from its head to the tips of its webbed feet, got down into the lower regions of the one-piece suit and fooled Junior. He actually thought the bullfrog was a snake. Frightened, he quickly came

---

creditor in full. Junior respected this mentality as he himself felt strongly that people should pay their just debts. He often related a story about a man who went to see a lawyer in Henderson. The man asked the lawyer, "What does it take to file bankruptcy?" The lawyer replied, "Fifty dollars and a son of a bitch." Junior seemed to like the lawyer. Mr. Talmo Johnson recounted this same story and attributed the advice to the late attorney, Judge J.I. Galbraith, of Henderson, Tennessee.

up from the water and began to strip himself down to the waist. At that point, the bullfrog jumped out. According to his recollection some seventy years later, Mrs. Petty looked at him and said, "You were going to take that bathing suit off!" Junior was not bashful at that time. He answered, "Yeah, I was going to if that frog didn't come out."[6]

Often Junior's humorous anecdotes were about older women who were very central in his young life. Doll Dickey was a spinster who lived with her sister Ophelia Dickey and Ophelia's granddaughter Elizabeth Stovall (later Droke). Doll gave the appearance of a stern woman who was sturdy and stocky of build. Actually, she was a gentle and quiet woman with very traditional manners. She always wore dresses and when more formally dressed, she wore a petticoat. Junior never failed to laugh when recalling that he and some other young men were throwing firecrackers and one landed on the ground under Doll's skirts and petticoat. This heavy-set woman began to dance around and jump trying to avert the firecracker's explosion. He always laughed heartily at the memory of this normally leisurely paced woman dancing and pulling up her skirts to find the offending firework!

Another woman that Junior remembered was Annie (Davis) Holder, commonly known to Finger's old-time residents as "Ma" Holder. She and her husband, Dolf C. "Pa" Holder, ran a small general merchandise store in Finger. Ma Holder was a gentle, kind, and humble woman. She was known through the village for her kindness and generosity to the town's children. Junior himself recalled her kindnesses. As a merchant, he also recalled a quote from Ma Holder. She once told someone that it didn't cost her anything to eat because she and Pa just ate out of the stock in their store. She seemed to forget that the stock did cost Pa something. Junior never knew of Pa and Ma Holder having any children. He always thought that to be the reason for their many kindnesses to him and other children.

At the end of Mill Street (now Talbott Street) lived two spinster sisters named Callie and Mattie Miller. These ladies were the daughters of Finis E. Miller, local merchant in Finger and survivor of the Andersonville Prison during the Civil War. These ladies lived in a large,

---

6. According to Junior, for an average-sized boy standing in the Huggins Creek Canal in the 1930s, the water would easily reach a boy's chest. Haze Petty was present on the creek bank and witnessed this incident. Haze Petty Interview, about October 28, 2014.

beautiful, two-story home built by their father on the east side of Mill Street near the corner of Mill and Apple Streets. It was well-furnished and much nicer than most in town. Mattie was older than Callie and of a more reserved nature. Although very kind, Mattie was apparently less sociable that Callie though a very likeable and sociable lady who had a fun-spirited way about her.

The personality of the two ladies appears in contrast to the nature of their sister, Ella (Miller) McIntyre. Ella was the wife of Adrian McIntyre and apparently a very sour woman who thought herself above many others. Her and Adrian and their daughter Cecil moved to St. Louis, where Adrian worked on a street car. She returned home later more haughty than she had been before. Her husband's family disliked her so much that they called her "Puss Ella" because she was such a sourpuss. While chasing a chicken from her flowers, Ella fell on a "stob" (the sharp cut end of a plant stalk) that impaled her in the stomach. She died shortly afterward.[7]

Interestingly, Callie and Mattie were quite different from their sister. They had great affection for the town's children and were quite hospitable to them. These ladies ran the switchboard for the Finger Telephone Company out of their home. Like many children, Junior made the trip down Mill Street toward the area where the old cotton gin was located and passed by the old Miller home. At some point, the sisters acquired a parrot that liked to talk and often tricked youngsters. It had the habit of calling out to children by their names. The parrot lived with the sisters from the late 1930s through the 1950s.

Over the years, Junior discussed several of his friends. One seldom mentioned was Joseph P. "Josie" Adams. He was born on September 17, 1918, to Estilee Adams, who was 44 years old when he was born. His

7. Ella (Miller) McIntyre was so disliked by her brother-in-law, John Robert McIntyre (Faye McIntyre's father), that he cut her face out of photographs sent back home by Adrian McIntyre. When looking through the McIntyre family photographs, one would find a jagged remnant of a photograph showing Adrian and Cecil, but not Ella. Given John Robert McIntyre's gentle and kind nature, it is very telling that he would dislike Ella so much. Indeed, she must have been as insulting and haughty as was remembered so many years later. On the day of her funeral in June 1935, John Robert McIntyre and his family were down in the bottom on their farm working in the fields when Ollie Pearl asked John, "Are we not going to go to Ella's funeral?" Apparently, John's answer was swift and terse, "No, she didn't want us around when she was alive, we're not going to disrespect her now that she's dead." So the family did not attend the funeral. His daughter Faye never forgot this exchange.

father, Arch Willis Adams, was 64 years of age at the time of Josie's death. Josie grew up outside of town toward Talleytown. He lived with his mother and Junior never knew what became of his father. Josie was a jovial young man who had an easy bearing and ready smile. Being younger than Josie, Junior had great affection for him.

Some of Junior's stories and anecdotes regarded the roughness and coarseness of small-town life before and during the Great Depression. In those days, few women ventured into town and seldom if ever without the company of their husbands or older sons. As a young boy and adolescent, Junior witnessed many sights and many fights. He often recalled the story of Leonard Sheffield.[8] Mr. Sheffield was a rough man who drank to excess.[9] He owed Newt a debt on an account at the store. On this particular day, Newt asked Mr. Sheffield for the money to satisfy his delinquent account. Sheffield got rowdy and it appeared that he might actually start some real trouble. Junior went to the cash drawer and retrieved his father's .38 caliber revolver.[10] He stuck it underneath his shirt and continued to hang about in the event of trouble. Within seconds, Mr. Dewey Gilbert walked over to Junior and asked, "Where's Newt's gun?" Junior told him he had the gun and would use it if such an action was required. Out of his concern for his friend Newt, Gilbert stayed with Junior in case he was needed. Fortunately, Sheffield did nothing other than talk and bluff. It was assumed that he had sense enough not to start any fracas in the store.

Another occasion that Junior remembered was a fight between two fellows named Fate Ingle and Alfred Cook. Fate was getting cut up pretty badly and it appeared that Alfred was going to knife him to death. Because of this possibility, a bystander, Gordon Kirk, picked up a wooden slab and hit Alfred upside the head. Alfred ran around to the side of the Talbott store building and collapsed. Another bystander told Gordon that Alfred had fallen dead from the strike to his head. This false report gave a Gordon quite a scare. He immediately thought of ways to flee the ter-

---

8. It is possible that Mr. Sheffield's last name was Sherfield. Often the name Sheffield was pronounced "Sherfield" in error and in the local dialect. It is most likely that the name was indeed Sheffield.

9. Junior actually referred to the man as a "rough old drunk."

10. This revolver remains in the family to this day.

ritory. It gave Junior quite a laugh for the next two or three generations. It was a story that he never tired of telling.

Junior often ruminated on the possibilities of things that could have been worse had it not been for some cooler head prevailing. He often told a story regarding Allen Patterson, a local drunkard. Some old fellow and Allen got into a verbal scuffle over something long forgotten sixty years later in the retelling. Allen had no desire to fight the fellow, but the other man was a bully and always itching for a fight. Allen walked away from the argument and made his way into Newt's store. A short time later, the bully walked into the store and started up again. This time Allen wasn't going to hear anything of it. He picked up a gallon of coal oil and swung it at him. Whether it missed the fellow or slightly grazed him, Junior never knew. Regardless, Newt heard the commotion and proceeded to get onto both men. He told them that he would have no trouble or commotion in his store. Allen left out the front door and the bully proceeded out of the back door. Allen went to his home to get his gun. Someone advised the bully that he needed to leave because Allen would kill him. The aggressive bully didn't stick around to see if it was a bluff.

One of the Davis brothers, Martin Davis, was drunk one night and began running up the main street firing off his gun. When he had sobered up, Davis realized he was in trouble. He packed his things on his back and headed out of town. He ran into Junior, who asked him where he was going. Davis responded, "Headin' for Arkansas! Parts unknown!" Until his death in 2007, Junior never tired of telling this story, often acting out Davis' response in the retelling.

There was a local bootlegger named Lipford. He was caught by the authorities and brought before the local judge, who fined him fifty dollars. Mr. Lipford grinned and told the Judge, "Aww, hell, Judge, I got that in my pocket." The judge then looked at Lipford and responded sternly, "Alright, thirty days then! You got *that* in your pocket?" Junior was sure the fellow's main transgression was not bootlegging, but failing to pay the sheriff a healthy bribe.

The roughness of the times was illustrated in another story from Junior's childhood. John Harris, a local merchant and banker, once hired some black laborers to work for him. He housed them in a small shack of a house located on the backside of Finger near the tracks of the

Mobile and Ohio Railroad. One of the men was particularly haughty and prideful. He carried a knife known as an "Arkansas toothpick" with him. This was a pocket knife with a particularly long narrow blade that he liked to brandish. Junior recollected that this man finally "got too big for his breeches" and a few of the men around town decided to go after him. The man got word and fled to John Harris' house for refuge. He left town the next morning and did not return. His departure was so hasty that he left behind his few scant possessions.

Afterwards, John Harris made a great deal of noise and protest over the treatment of his hired help and criticized the actions of his fellow town folk. Finally, after so much ruckus, John's cousin, Thee Harris, went to John and told him it was in his best interest to drop the subject quickly and quietly. If he didn't, the same men would run *John* out of town. It always impressed Junior that these men were not intimidated by John Harris' wealth and influence.

During Junior's childhood, it was common to hear reports of the robbery and murder of common farmers along the tracks of the Mobile and Ohio Railroad between Finger and Henderson as well as between Finger and Selmer.[11] He remembered the husband of Icey Amerson being one of those murdered robbery victims. The newspapers of the day are filled with stories of men found dead along the tracks having been robbed of their crop proceeds and other earnings. A certain gang consisting of warring factions of the same family in Henderson was often believed to be responsible for most of the killings.

The Mobile and Ohio Railroad played an important part in Junior's youth as it did many other young people during that time. The railroad always seemed to Junior a road to the strange, the mysterious, and the different, to lands about which he could only dream. It was a time of hoboes and traveling men. The Great Depression crippled the nation and many men moved from region to region looking for work and wages that did not exist. Many communities erected signs that read, "Unemployed men, keep moving. We don't have jobs enough for our own."

Stories of the hobo and the wayfaring man intrigued Junior. Deep in his nature was an urge to travel and explore, to see and to learn and to

---

11. Junior once recounted that when his father went to Henderson in the fall to sell his cotton, he and any others accompanying him had to cross the railroad tracks and the bottom down around Talleytown. They almost always had to carry their guns in case someone tried to rob them.

experience things that a young man could not experience in north McNairy County, Tennessee. Junior Talbott was at heart a wandering man. Later in life, his favorite memoir was that of Louis L'Amour, *Education of a Wandering Man*. It reminded him of his own youth and his own innate love of travel, reading, and informal education.[12]

One of the traveling men of whom Junior liked to tell tales was Jenkins Miller. Known as "Red" to his friends, Miller was a renowned hobo. He had traveled the country and even made his way into Canada. Many people contended that Red was "touched in the head." There's no question he was peculiar and possessed many quirks. He was often the subject of many taunts and tricks by others. Perhaps the unceasing taunting caused some of his problems. He was known to curse a man for the taunting and then pray that a rock would fall on the tormentor's head.

Red was said to be related in some manner to the spinster sisters, Callie and Mattie Miller, who lived on Mill Street (now Talbott Street) behind Newt's store. On one occasion, the sisters had relatives visiting and Red wanted to see them while they were in Finger. By the time he arrived, they had already departed by rail to their home many miles away in another state. It was told that when these relatives arrived back home, Red was waiting on their front porch. He had gotten to their home before they had themselves. He taught Junior many things about riding the rails and the life of the hobo. When Red had to go live at the county poorhouse in Selmer, Junior and others in the community went down to the depot to see him off. The entire community was saddened by his departure. At his death, Junior and others contributed to the purchase of a granite headstone to mark his grave in the old Mount Carmel Cemetery.

Interestingly, hoboes like Red Miller marked friendly homes where the residents were helpful and sympathetic to them and their fellow wayfarers. Once a hobo realized the kind nature of an individual or family, he would mark the home for the benefit of other hoboes. Usually, the identifying mark was found on a seal or floor joist under the porch of the home or in another inconspicuous place where only a hobo knew to look. According to Red, the Newt and Varham Talbott home was marked, a testament to their kindness and generosity. Red taught Junior about the system for marking friendly homes.

---

12. Junior recommended this book to the author as a guide to the times in which he had lived.

The hobo captured an interesting place in Junior's mind and imagination. Their love of travel and boundless wanderlust attracted the young man's attention and interest. He recalled with great fascination the small hobo encampments that occasionally could be found along the old Mobile and Ohio Railroad. He saw hoboes camp out at the Double Trestle as well as the small trestle located along the line behind the John Harris home. In these very temporary camps, the old tramps of the locomotives could be found around a fire talking, singing, or sharing stories with one another. There were times when these tired old traveling souls sat around in the waiting room of the Finger Depot or in the nearby seed warehouses. Their ways and their own peculiar culture fascinated Junior.[13]

Another interesting character who impacted Junior's interest in travel and the itinerant lifestyle was Tom Staton. He was a brother to Vroner Staton and said to be a half-blood Native American. Tom was often stricken with "rambling fever" and would take off and stay gone for months at a time. On one occasion, he was staying with his sister, who was married to a Bullman. One morning, Tom told her that he was going out to pick up some tobacco. About six to eight months later, Mrs. Bullman received a letter from Tom. He was in Paul's Valley, Oklahoma, working in the broom corn harvest. Paul's Valley was the self-proclaimed broom corn capital of the world. Junior always thought that Tom did settle long enough to get married. However, he did not stay settled long for he and his wife separated either shortly before or after their only child was born. After his death in 1962, at the advanced age of eighty-two years, Tom was buried in the Finger Cemetery.

The railroad was an important landmark in a small town and the Mobile and Ohio Railroad was an important focus of young Junior Talbott's attention in Finger. The depot itself represented the coming and going of people and things. It was there that these people and things were introduced to young impressionable boys like Junior. He regularly kept up with trains schedules and arrival times. One never knew what would arrive at the Finger Depot on any given day. The depot was a wooden structure where Western Union telegrams could be sent and received. Trains from all over the country eventually make their way through Finger carrying all varieties of cargo.

---

13. Interview with L.E. "Junior" Talbott, no date.

During Junior's childhood and early adolescence, a train known as the "Doodlebug" ran southbound in the morning and northbound in the evening. It carried both packages and passengers.[14] The formal names of the two main engines that pulled trains through Finger were the "City of Miami" and the "Spirit of St. Louis." The train times in those days were 8:00 A.M., 10:00 A.M., 4:00 P.M., and 6:00 P.M. The 10:00 a.m. Doodlebug was bound for Corinth, Mississippi, and the 4:00 P.M. train was bound for Jackson, Tennessee. Many of the town folk would come out to the depot in the evening at 6:00 to "meet" the train. This was a common practice at that time and town folk would meet friends and strangers alike to learn of news and events and the fate and whereabouts of others. When folks began to gather down at the Finger Depot, someone would usually call out, "the train's in the block!" thus signifying its arrival.

As a child, Junior often watched the elderly Tom McCaskill push his wheelbarrow to the depot and pick up the mail after the train had delivered it. Mr. McCaskill then pushed the mail back to the post office in the corner of the W.P. Massey General Merchandise Store. Junior watched depot agents such as E.O. Parrish, Van Young, and Harrison Naylor assist passengers, send telegrams, and load and unload cargo and freight. It was at the Finger Depot that Junior saw for the first time large stalks of bananas, large sacks of coffee beans, and other exotic items as well as boxcars full of coal, grain, and other items of bulk being carried down the tracks.

The Finger Depot had a room that ran from end to end. The agent worked in this room and could see out the bay window toward the direction of Henderson. The telegraph operation was set up and the agent operated the signals and flags from there. On one side of the depot were two passenger waiting rooms, one for whites and one for the "colored." On the other side of the agent's office was the freight room. The depot had a covered porch or loading dock on its two main sides. At the end of the depot facing toward McNairy Station was a door. If the agent had a letter or mail for the train to pick up and the train wasn't going to stop, the agent would attach the mail to a clothespin-like device and hang it out toward the tracks. There was a spot for the engineer or conductor to run his hand and arm through and snatch the mail and never have to stop the train. These facts remained vivid in Junior's mind throughout his life.

14. Others at the time called this train the "Dinkie."

It is important to remember that Newt Talbott was forty-three years old when his only surviving son was born. There's no doubt the aging father doted on the young boy. For his part, Junior was devoted to his father and recounted many stories about him. According to many who remember him, the elder Mr. Talbott was a quiet and very peaceable man. His nature was much like that of his brothers and their grandfather, Theodore Perry Talbott. They were quiet but strong men with dominant wives. They avoided trouble when possible but were not fearful people. They stood their ground when it was needed. The Talbotts are of old stock and, by their nature, of strong fortitude. A good example of the nature of their forbearers is Junior's great-great-great grandmother Walker, the mother of William Parrish Walker.[15]

For his part, Newt was a very honest man. He treated others with respect and decency and expected the same in return. It seems from the stories that he was not easily impressed by authority or authority figures, especially dishonest ones. Still, he gave people the benefit of the doubt. Until proven otherwise, Newt believed people were basically honest and he would view them as such until proven to the contrary.

On one particular occasion, Alec Lowrance, the son-in-law of Dr. N.A. Tucker, a salesman living in Henderson, conspired with merchants John R. Harris, Guy Bishop, and J.O. Mitchell in what appeared to be a price fixing scheme. According to Junior, these men allegedly agreed to fix their prices on certain goods and sought Newt's agreement to do the same. This was during the Depression and just prior to the outbreak of World War II, when goods were often scarce. In fact, these merchants lowered their actual prices even lower than what they had disclosed to Newt. According to Junior, he caught on to this scheme and reported it to his father. Junior attempted to talk his father out of taking the action he had promised to Lowrance, but Newt refused his son's advice. He told Junior that he had agreed to the proposition and that regardless of these men's actions, he would keep his word. Others' failure to behave properly did not affect his ability to do the right thing. Times were hard and he was trying to do something bigger: make groceries affordable to those he served.

---

15. William Parrish Walker's daughter, Elizabeth Ann Walker, married Theodore Perry Talbott, which was Junior's great-grandfather. See Chapter 1, 6–7, for a story about her fortitude.

In the same vein, while Newt was not self-righteous about his belief in honesty, he made no qualms about expecting other people to honor their word once it was given. At the same time, being a quiet man, he was not given to be loud or boisterous. He plied his morals and ethics in the same quiet manner in which he behaved otherwise.[16] One story that demonstrated to Junior the level of his father's integrity involved an official in McNairy County government. During the 1940s, the brother of Logan McCaskill, Dennie McCaskill (1892–1975), was serving as Trustee of McNairy County. He was responsible for the issuance of county warrants to county employees and the collection of county property taxes, among other duties.[17] It became apparent during McCaskill's tenure in the Trustee's Office that warrants were not being honored. According to McCaskill himself, who, as Trustee, was effectively the county's banker and investment manager, the county did not have the money to back up the warrants. In reality, it appeared that he was not being truthful with the warrant holders. He was buying the warrants from their rightful holders, as a "favor" to these people, at a rate of fifty cents on the dollar. Afterwards, he would cash them for full value from the county coffers.

This scheme was being perpetrated county-wide. While it was not confined only to the Trustee, it has often been surmised that he was a principal in the organization of the scheme. According to those who were around at the time, the Trustee was one of a handful of people who were buying these warrants. As the scheme went, the rightful holders of the warrants were told by the Trustee and these certain few others that their warrants were essentially worthless because the county was broke and did not have the funds to honor the warrants. However, these gentlemen were certainly in the position to know that the county did have the funds but gave the appearance that it did not and that they were buying

---

16. According to Junior and his wife Faye Talbott, both Newt and Varham Talbott were quiet, unassuming people. They were of a more serious nature and kept their own counsel.

17. County employees were paid with checks known as warrants. These warrants looked like checks and functioned the same. They basically warrant that the public funds paid to the employee were good and would be honored upon presentment. Such warrants are still issued by county governments in Tennessee today. Employees who received such warrants in the 1940s were school teachers and bus drivers. During that time, there were few county employees as county government was quite limited. A warrant would be issued to an employee, cashed, and the funds paid out of the county's budgeted funds as previously approved by the county's Quarterly Court (in modern terms known as the County Commission).

them back from these poor souls out of kindness and because they felt badly that their county government would issue such "worthless" warrants. Again, they were paying approximately 50% of the value of the warrant's face value.

Newt caught on to the scheme and found it a terrible thing. Some of his customers were among those individuals who received the warrants. The fact that poor people earning honest wages lost a portion of them during already difficult days angered Newt, knowing that certain members of the local courthouse ring were getting wealthier off the backs of these honest, powerless people. Newt decided to act against it. One day, an individual came into Newt's store and told him that he could not pay his entire bill because all he had was his county warrant that apparently wasn't worth much. Newt decided to call the Trustee out on the issue despite his friendship with the Trustee's brother, Logan McCaskill. Newt took the warrant as payment and took other such warrants as payment despite the holder's advice that the warrants were not very valuable.

Newt gave his customers full face value on every occasion. Despite the hard times and the fact that he himself had very little money, he made sure that his customers were treated fair and decently. Newt collected a number of these warrants until he had enough to cover his real property taxes and then travelled to the courthouse at Selmer to pay his annual taxes. He walked into the Trustee's office with a wallet full of warrants with which to satisfy his county taxes. Mr. McCaskill jumped up from his chair and greeted Newt, whom he knew well and for many years. After their greetings, Newt pulled the warrants from his wallet and threw them on the counter toward the Trustee. Newt told him that he had just enough warrants to cover his taxes and still have a little money due him. The Trustee turned pale and stuttered, protesting that he could not accept the warrants. Junior never forgot his father's response. According to Junior, he calmly said, "Dennie, you issued those warrants and you're going to honor them for every cent they're made out for." Newt stared him down. The Trustee honored them and the worthless warrant scheme folded quickly thereafter. Junior was always very proud of his father's courage against the machinery of county courthouse politics.[18]

Newt was an independently minded and ruggedly individualistic person. Although quiet and reserved in his demeanor, taking a stand was

18. Whether Junior was actually present is not known, but he recounted the story nonetheless.

not difficult for him. In the 1930s when President Franklin D. Roosevelt was implementing his New Deal legislation, the centerpiece of his legislative program and hence the New Deal itself was the National Recovery Administration (NRA). The NRA was proposed to serve to assist in increasing workers' wages and spread work among workers by shortening their hours. More specifically, the NRA ostensibly functioned to eliminate ruthless competition and create codes of fair practices and set prices. The NRA was represented by the now famous Blue Eagle, which could be found in thousands of store windows across the United States.

But the Blue Eagle was not displayed in Newt's store window. Despite the fact that merchants were expected to participate, he absolutely refused to join the NRA. Newt took the position that it was basically unconstitutional and no merchant should be forced to join or participate in the Administration's work or goals. He was a staunch Hoover Republican.[19] He and other merchants like him were proven right when the U.S. Supreme Court struck down the NRA as unconstitutional. Despite political fortunes and changes, Newt had remained a Hoover Republican. President Herbert Hoover believed the free market should be left just that, an independent force unhindered by government interference.

Although not a drinker by habit, Newt usually took a teaspoon of whiskey in the morning and one in the evening. One of his customers, Alec Vandiver, came to the store one day, sat down, talked to Newt for a few minutes, and then promptly left. He returned a few days later and told Junior that he and Newt had worked out a trade and that he needed a one-hundred pound bag of sugar. Not too long afterwards, Alec brought something to the store, took it to the back of the building, and left. Quite curious, Junior went back to investigate. There he found two gallons of homemade whiskey. Now Junior knew the particulars of the trade.

In addition to running the store, Newt worked in the cotton ginning business and farmed. He also engaged in some of the older trades and crafts from a simpler time. Newt, like his brother Will Talbert, splinted and caned chair seats, i.e. weaved the white oak strips in the bottoms of ladder back chairs, as well as crafted white oak baskets. These were old skills still being practiced and such chairs and baskets were still being

---

19. Herbert Hoover, who served as U.S. president from 1929 to 1933.

used for real and practical purposes.[20] A fellow by the name of "Popcorn" Jimmy Davis sold Newt the white oak saplings to cut into strips.[21]

The store owned and operated by Newt in Finger where Junior was literally raised was not different from that which he ran in Leapwood. The general store of that day served a number of functions. Certainly, it was a place of commerce, but it had a deeper function. It served as a sort of community center where news and information could pass and be verified. The merchant's customers became an extension of his family in many ways. The ties between merchant and customer were often lifelong and, in some cases, multi-generational. Multiple generations of a family did business with multiple generations of the Talbott family. This all began with Newt. However, though "raised" in the store, Junior was not one to stay in the store. He enjoyed hunting, trapping, fishing, and exploring the little world around him much more. He would later enjoy exploring the greater world around him.

Like many young men, Junior did various odd jobs to earn a little money during those days of hardship and privation. Aside from hunting and trapping in the woods, building fires and sweeping classrooms at school, and occasionally working in the fields for others, he also maintained Dr. Tucker's yard for him. He was the type of kid who did not like to be told he wasn't big enough or strong enough for any job. He did not take well to being underestimated. Baxter Gardner, a local businessman and car dealer, owned a farm and was building a levee on his property. He needed someone to work alongside his other laborers doing such menial chores as picking up roots and hauling brush. Junior asked Baxter about the job and was told that he was not big or strong enough to suit his needs. This angered Junior and he discussed it with his father. After other men didn't work out for Baxter, he decided to hire Junior. Being more than a tad prideful, Junior turned down the job and told Baxter that he wouldn't work for him under any circumstances. Knowing now that once he was hired Junior would stay at the job until it was completed, Baxter persisted. Finally, he agreed to take the job, but only for a higher wage than originally offered. Baxter agreed to Junior's demands and paid his wage.

20. L.E. "Junior" Talbott interview, 1992. Junior related this information while discussing his father's many talents and the level of his practical knowledge.

21. Ibid.

Junior's childhood exploits and adventures were of the style often enjoyed in the nineteenth century—the Huckleberry Finn/Tom Sawyer experience. There is a quote from Mark Twain's speech to The Metropolitan Club on his 67th birthday in 1902 which sums up the type of life Junior Talbott enjoyed in his own youth:

> Well, it was a beautiful life, a lovely life. There was no crime. Merely little things like pillaging orchards and watermelon patches and breaking the Sabbath—we didn't break the Sabbath often enough to signify—once a week perhaps.

In keeping with Twain's own view of his eventful childhood, Junior often recalled experiences that were very humorous and of a nature that seem foreign in today's sterile, politically correct atmosphere. He told of a couple of adventures involving his attendance at church services at a local black congregation. Junior had personally befriended and respected many older black folks in his youth.[22] One hot, swelteringly humid night, Junior attended the services of Tillman's Chapel CME Church. During the heat of an excited revival sermon, some devious young friend of Junior's had crawled under the old church building with a small hornet's nest trapped in a large jar. The young man picked a heightened moment in the hand-raising, clapping, and praying to remove the lid and hold it to a hole in the floor. In a short few minutes, the hot angry hornets were flying through the hole. Junior often chuckled at the mental vision of his black friends running from the church building, swatting hornets and jumping when stung. He always shook his head at this memory with a mischievous grin while acknowledging that such antics weren't right and certainly weren't proper.

Another story that brought laughter and mirth to Junior involved an old aged black preacher. It was a Sunday sermon and Junior was again attending the services at Tillman's Chapel CME Church. In fact, he probably attended and enjoyed local black church services in his youth far more than he attended white church functions as an adult. He sat quietly in a back pew with his friends as the ancient preacher admonished

---

22. Another incident is recounted in Chapter 6. Although it may appear to be inconsistent with Junior's character, the difference is between free association and forced integration. In those days, the two were treated differently.

his parishioners in a high-pitched and crackly voice. He was a wiry little man, ancient in appearance and had weathered many seasons. The gist of his sermon was that you can't behave one way outside church and another way while in worship. As the preacher reached the climax of his sermon, he called out, "You niggas ain't gonna get to heaven with chicken feathers in your picksacks!" The old brother's point was that you can't steal chickens by night and pray yourself into heaven by day. This message both resonated with and amused Junior to no end.

Aside from fishing and hunting, there were other occasional diversions from everyday life that Junior recalled from his childhood. He remembered a circus that came to town and camped in the grove in front of the home most recently known as the J.L. Joyner home. Seeing an elephant, a gorilla, and the types of circus tramps and artists that fill such camps in Finger was a truly unique sight, one that Junior never forgot. He also recalled traveling movie "houses" coming to town and showing old silent movies. These affairs involved a canvas screen being tacked up against a barn wall and the film projected onto it. Admission cost a nickel. He recalled that the future Mrs. Herman (Bessie) Plunk and her brother ran these shows. Some of them were held off Mill Street (now Talbott Street) near the old cotton gin/sawmill site.

Junior had friendships with many older people in the village of Finger and the surrounding areas. He enjoyed older people and their wisdom. He liked to retell stories he learned from people who had lived prior to, during, and following the Civil War and the latter part of the nineteenth century. He carried these stories with him to the end of his life. He enjoyed the good fortune to retain his mental faculties and sharp memory for events of long ago until the very day of his death.

One of the older people for whom Junior felt great love and respect was his uncle, Willie Coleman Talbert, known as Uncle Will.[23] This uncle was a quiet and simple man who enjoyed simple pleasures and an old way of life. He often walked about barefooted, wore overalls at all

---

23. Two of Junior's uncles, Will and Charlie, spelled their names "Talbert" rather than Talbott, the correct spelling. The reason is a clerical error by the justice of the peace. The two brothers were married on the same day and simply misspelled it. At that time, the only official document most people had was their marriage certificate or license. Charlie and Will were married during the first decade of the twentieth century before the passage of the Social Security Act and prior to the use of birth certificates in Tennessee. Therefore, the only legal documents with their names were their respective marriage certificates.

times, and had an old-style long beard. He and his wife, Arcana Edgar (Russell) Talbert, had only one child, who died as an infant and was said to be buried in the O'Neal Cemetery in Enville, Tennessee. A photograph of the child exists, but that is the only record otherwise of its existence aside from fragmentary oral history. The child's name was never recorded to anyone's knowledge. Junior's Uncle Will and Aunt Edgar lived in the Sweetlips area near Hopewell Baptist Church and cemetery.

Junior often helped his Uncle Will on his farm. He stayed for days on end with his uncle and aunt. When he walked back home to Finger through the old hills of north McNairy county, he would scratch the ground at the bottom of the grader ditches along the edges of the road and draw water to drink. He claimed that it was better than well water. Oftentimes in the spring, Junior helped Uncle Will as he planted his corn. His Aunt Edgar raised calves and carried out her own farming pursuits and enterprises. Uncle Will made white oak baskets and repaired and splinted cane bottomed chairs. They were an interesting couple and she was certainly not a housekeeper. Their old home has been beautifully expanded and restored in the present day.

Another of Junior's older friends was an old bachelor, Marcus Dee Malone.[24] Dee, as he was known to his friends, was the son of an old Confederate veteran and Tennessee state representative, William Barney Malone. He was a short, heavyset, bald man. During the time that Junior knew him, Mr. Malone was living in what was later known as the Eula Kirkpatrick home, a white frame house that once stood immediately next to the Finger Church of Christ. Dee moved to Nashville when he was young and worked for a fertilizer company. In 1918, he was a conductor for the Nashville Railway and Light Company.[25] Dee returned to Finger many years later when he retired. His interests included fly fishing and he usually took Junior with him. He carried a little tin box full of flies that he had tied himself. Dee taught Junior the rudimentary skills of fly fishing. They spent time together on the banks of Huggins Creek

---

24. Malone's name is listed as Markus Dee Malone on his death certificate. Registration Number 27379, State of Tennessee, State Department of Health, Division of Vital Statistics. Certainly, Malone seemed like an old man to Junior, but he was only 59 years of age at the time of his death.

25. This information was provided on Malone's World War I registration card.

discussing fishing and life. It was an important relationship during his formative years.²⁶

Junior's lessons from Dee began one day while Junior was fishing in the bottoms around Finger. The boy had cast his line around an underwater stump thinking he could hook a decent catch in this particular spot. He was using a No. 2 hook, a big hook typically used for catfish. On this day, Junior was fishing for whitefish or bluegill, but they were only getting his bait. The older man saw the problem and told him that he was using too large a hook. Dee gave him a smaller one and almost immediately Junior began catching fish.²⁷

The two companions also enjoyed playing pool at Chili Davis' pool hall. It was located on the corner of what is now Main Street and Massey Street. They were playing late on the night of March 16, 1938, and had played several games, approximately three or four matches. Junior beat poor Dee each and every time. Finally, out of frustration and exasperation, the older man threw his cue stick on the table and declared that it would be the last game of pool that he would ever play with him. Dee and Junior parted ways that evening; Dee went home and died in his sleep.²⁸ True to his word and very unintentionally prophetic, he never played another game. Junior made up his mind never to play another round of billiards out of respect for his old friend Dee. He kept that promise for almost 70 years.

Another older friend of Junior's was Logan McCaskill. He was the husband of Alice McIntyre, who had walked Junior to school as a child along with her sister, Wilma (McIntyre) Sharp. Logan was a large man with large appetites. He enjoyed business and commerce and was engaged in a number of pursuits. He was a barber, a merchant, a restaurateur, an innkeeper and resort owner, and an insurance agent. He ran the resort on Highway 45 in the area known as Logan's Lake. It consisted of a large three-story lodge house, several guest houses, a store, a large lake, and

---

26. Another of Junior's older fishing buddies was Mrs. Lillian Brown, the wife of Harrison Brown. Her daughters, Lorraine (Brown) McKenzie and Christine (Brown) Harris, were of Junior's generation.

27. Junior carried these memories with him the rest of his life and always spoke very affectionately of Dee Malone.

28. Malone died of *myocarditis angina*, in short, a heart attack, per his death certificate. At the time of death, he was identified as a merchant, McNairy County Death Book B, page 36.

a swimming pool. Junior often recalled an occasion when he and Logan drove over to the Tennessee River to fish. They caught so many fish that they filled the back of Logan's car. He served the fish at his lodge and his restaurant. The two brought back more fish than would be allowable otherwise, but Logan was creative in finding places to stash the fish inside his vehicle. Junior recalled this fish caper with a certain amount of glee. Incidentally, he also helped Logan stock his lake, commonly known as "Logan's Lake," with fish caught at the river and transported back in wooden barrels.

There was an interesting story involving Logan remembered by both Junior and his childhood friend, Hayes Hayre. On August 23, 1929, sometime after Newt had purchased the Bruce Barnes home and moved the family into it, Home Banking Company was robbed at about 2:30 in the morning. The initial story was told by the local newspaper:

> At about 2:30 last Friday morning four bank robbers made an unsuccessful attempt to break into the Home Banking Company at Finger. They had driven to a point by the side of the building and parked their car. Entrance was made through the rear west window, and when discovered they had burned through the outer steel door of the vault and had gone unto that preparatory to burning a hole in the money vault. They had all the equipment required, a complete asceteline [*sic*] outfit.
>
> Mrs. Aubrey Massey was attracted by a noise and she aroused her husband. He hastily notified Logan McCaskill, deputy sheriff Frye and J.R. Harris. These citizens armed themselves and proceeded towards the parked automobile. The robbers on being discovered left the whole outfit and ran to the car, and drove from the alley into the street, going down a steep embankment. Turning west they were met by these citizens. The robbers opened fire which was returned. In the exchange of shots it is believed that one or more of the robbers were wounded. Mr. Frye was using a shot gun and was firing at reasonably close range. The others were using revolvers.

From the tracks of the fleeing car it is thought they came down number 5 as far as the filling station on the west side of Selmer and turned into number 15.

But for the prompt and fearless action of the citizens at Finger, another bank robbery would have been committed.

From the names and tags on some of the outfit, a lot of the stuff came from Jackson. J.R. Harris took the whole of the outfit to Jackson where with the aid of the Jackson police and other officers it was sought to get other clues. The officers in many other places have been notified and all efforts will be made to apprehend the robbers.[29]

Junior recalled vividly being awakened in his back bedroom by the sound of gunshots in the streets. His father told him to "stay put." He would not allow anyone to go outside.

Both Junior and Hayes Hayre remembered another event specifically regarding Logan McCaskill. They were never sure if it occurred during the course of the Home Banking Company robbery or on another night. Regardless, Logan, a rather large individual, was quietly and carefully investigating with his revolver drawn. He passed a mirror and caught the glimpse of an individual (who turned out to be himself and not some notorious criminal) and turned toward the mirror image and fired his revolver at it. Both Hayes and Junior laughed at the prospect of Logan McCaskill shooting his own reflection!

While on the subject of the bank robbery, Junior's old friend, Clifford Young, added to the story in the author's interview with him in 1994. The following are the notes from that portion of the conversation between the author and the ninety-year old Young:

> The men who robbed or tried to rob Home Banking Company in 1929 were construction workers, working on the overhead bridge at Jackson, Tennessee. They had a black man watch the front while they went around the back of the building and entered there. After Orby [Aubrey] Massey became aware of the break-in, he alerted Logan McCaskill, who lived across the street from Massey. Conard [locally pronounced as Con-erd]

29. *McNairy County Independent Appeal*, Friday, August 30, 1929.

Frye was a deputy at that time and carried a shotgun. He shot at the men at a fairly close range. The bank robbers themselves were scared when they heard Dr. N.A. Tucker drive his car through Main Street in front of the bank. When the robbers heard the doctor's car, they thought they were caught and decided to leave. As the robbers roared down the road toward the new Highway 45, their battery cable came loose and their car went dead close to one of the old wooden bridges there in the hollows between town and the highway. They came across a young man who was walking back toward town carrying an inner tube as he had had a flat. It was surprising to many that they did not kill the boy. Anyway, they managed to get their car going again. They made it to Bolivar, Tennessee, where they were treated for their wounds. They were captured, but later they escaped from jail and were never heard from again.[30]

Mr. William Ivy Barton (more commonly known as Ivy Barton) was another interesting character from Junior's youth. He was born on February 21, 1870, and was more than sixty years of age by the time Junior became acquainted with him. He vividly recalled Ivy and his strange mode of transportation. The old eccentric had built a small cart made from the frame of an ancient cultivator and old lumber and hitched it to his small team of mules. One day, Junior and Hayes Hayre were fishing on the creek bank of Huggins Creek when Ivy came rattling across the old wooden bridge. As the mules pulled the makeshift cart across, it wobbled and made awful noises. Ivy looked down toward the creek and saw Junior and Hayes fishing. They had eight to ten little fish and Ivy wanted to make a trade. He asked the boys what they wanted for the little fish. The two replied they didn't know what they were worth. So Ivy gave them some peanuts for the fish since he didn't have any money with him. Having made the trade, Ivy Barton, his mules, and the little fish made their way back to Mount Peter, where he lived.[31]

Both Junior and Hayes recounted another amusing story about Ivy Barton. He made a trip to Bethel Springs one day and then decided to

30. Clifford Young interview at the Finger Barbecue, August 6, 1994. He was ninety years old at the time.

31. L.E. "Junior" Talbott interview, no date. Hayes Hayre interview, 1993.

proceed to Selmer. When Ivy reached the city limits of Selmer, he read the 30 mile per hour speed limit sign. Looking over it for a moment, he then fiercely whipped his mules and called out that he didn't know if he could get those mules to go thirty miles per hour or not, but he would sure give it a try![32]

Another playful story passed on by Junior and Hayes Hayre involved Mr. Alfred Plunk (perhaps Alford Plunk). Mr. Plunk would sit on the old wooden bridge that spanned Huggins Creek and fish with a cane pole. Mr. Plunk would fall asleep and the local boys would go under the bridge, tug at Mr. Plunk's line and pull it for a little spell, making him think he had hooked a big fish.[33] Such pranks were common among young boys in those days. Young men were creative and pranks were the most common form of entertainment.

When he was young, Junior became acquainted with the various merchants, businessmen, and craftsmen of Finger. He thought one of the greediest men in town was Mr. John R. Harris, who owned the John R. Harris General Merchandise Store and the Finger Gin. He was also a major stockholder in the Home Banking Company. Mr. Harris was known for loaning money to farmers and individuals in trouble. Junior and others recalled that he would loan a relatively small amount of money against a farm worth far more than the loan, knowing they would have trouble repaying it. Mr. Harris eventually repossessed and took personal ownership of more than sixty farms around north McNairy County and south Chester County. He was first married to Ora Lee Brown. They had three daughters: Doris (who died as an infant), Anna Lee, and Gretchen. He left his wife for the cashier at Home Banking Company, Miss Zaida McCaskill. According to Lee A. Weaver, he came in from lunch one afternoon and caught Mr. Harris and Miss McCaskill in an inappropriate way on Mr. Harris' desk in the office. Weaver quietly placed his hat back on his head and walked out of the bank. He resigned and later built and operated the Union Savings Bank.[34] Harris built a substantial brick home for Miss McCaskill on Droke Road, behind the Massey Store.

32. Hayes Hayre interview, 1993. This story was later reaffirmed by Junior in a discussion with the author.

33. Ibid.

34. The information regarding the disagreement between John Harris and Lee A. Weaver was recounted by the late Hayes Hayre in the 1990s.

Harris' cousin, Thee Harris, was a much nicer fellow. According to Junior, Thee was also an able businessman but a nicer fellow than John. He and his wife, Lela, lived in the home just across the railroad tracks from the depot, a house down in the hole below the present road. Thee ran the Harris General Store after John sold out to him. Thee and Lela had two children: Mary Harris Gardner and Prince Harris. Mary married Baxter Gardner and lived to an advanced age. Prince was a rambunctious young fellow. Junior remembered that Prince once tore a dollar bill in half in anger and Thee, a very tight fellow, decided he ought to go to reform school.[35]

Junior had a high opinion of Dr. Nathaniel A. "Al" Tucker and his wife Beulah (Harris) Tucker. Beulah was a sister to John R. Harris. Al Tucker was Finger's most prominent doctor during Junior's youth. He smoked cigars and made his rounds with patience. His office was located between the Home Banking Company building and the Harris General Store building. He was well-respected in the medical circles and of a very kind disposition. Miss Cora B. Clayton worked in his office. He also had a drug store there and often bought old glass medicine bottles from folks for one penny apiece. Junior and Faye and others provided valuable information regarding Dr. Tucker for the work, *Let's Call It Finger!: A History of North McNairy County and Finger, Tennessee and Its Surrounding Communities*:

> Dr. Tucker was known for being a straight talker. He didn't mince his words and he got straight to the point. Yet he was a compassionate doctor who understood the problems and heartaches that people faced. One story which has passed in the author's family regards Dr. Tucker's professional and personal fidelity. In 1947, Faye (McIntyre) Talbott gave birth to a little boy who unfortunately would not live for long. The birth was a difficult one, but Dr. Tucker remained. In fact, the good doctor tarried long after the event, sitting out in the front yard with Luther Talbott, John Robert McIntyre, and Dave Alexander until two o'clock.

---

35. Thee Harris (1879–1948) and Lela Harris (1880–1958) are buried in the Finger Cemetery near Junior and Faye Talbott.

CHILDHOOD CHARACTERS & ADVENTURES OF YOUTH

As for his professional reputation, he was widely known as a diligent and dedicated doctor. The late Dr. Webb, founder of Webb-Williamson Hospital of Jackson, Tennessee, stated that Dr. Tucker was one of the best diagnostic doctors in the area. In other words, Doctor Tucker had great ability to diagnose medical conditions and problems.

As to his straightforwardness, the following story serves as an example. During his term of service in the United States Navy, Luther Talbott had been exposed to malaria and occasionally had needed a strong dose of a certain type of medicine to treat his recurring malarial symptoms. He walked into Dr. Tucker's office and requested the medicine. Dr. Tucker responded somewhat suspiciously, "What do you need with that?' Talbott explained that he had taken them regularly while in the Navy and needed some now. The old doctor told him to wait a moment and shortly he returned to his work desk with a small white envelope. He proceeded to pour white tablets from a two gallon glass bottle. When he finished, he handed the envelope containing about twenty-five tablets to his young patient. Talbott asked what he owed Dr. Tucker and the old doctor gruffly replied, "Oh, about 25 cents."

Before Dr. Tucker retired from his practice, he was beginning to have problems with his memory. Perhaps a patient would pay his bill and Dr. Tucker would forget to make the proper notation resulting in the expectation that such debt would be paid again. Most of his life, Doctor Tucker was a cigar smoker. One Sunday morning he came walking up through town and stopped in at N.P. Talbott's house and asked if Luther could help him out. The young Talbott responded that he could and the old doctor said, 'I was heading out east to see a patient and I ran off the levee out there just past the bridge about 100 feet before you get to Centerhill Road' and on the left. Because there was concern that the car, a business coupe, might turn over, Luther rounded up some plow lines to tie to the vehicle. With the help of a group of young men, the two managed to get the car out. Dr. Tucker denied it, but what is believed to have happened is that while he was driving across the levee, he lit up an unwrapped cigar and the cellophane wrapping flashed up in smoke, causing him to become distracted.[36]

Dr. Tucker finally moved to Henderson after his mind began to deteriorate. He lived there until September 3, 1951, when he died and was buried in the Finger Cemetery.

Junior also knew one of Finger's other doctors of note, Dr. W.M. "Mark" Barnes. Dr. Barnes and Dr. Tucker could not have been any more different. Dr. Barnes was not terribly respected for his medical ability. He was more interested in making money than in practicing medicine. Dr. Barnes had a shooting range located on land that would later belong to Richard and Arlie Smith, but was then the Lee Weaver farm. He shot clay pigeons and entertained his fellow gentlemen on many afternoons.

Gentlemen were not the only company the old doctor liked to entertain. According to the late Arlie (Harris) Smith, a native of McNairy Station and longtime resident of Finger, Dr. Barnes had a mistress who lived in McNairy Station. Arlie recalled that she and a friend, while still younger girls, once stood outside the parlor window of the woman's house and watched the lady and Dr. Barnes dance across the parlor to the sound of the woman's phonograph. According to Smith, the doctor regularly visited the woman, whom she never identified by name.

Junior recalled the doctor's office located on the side of the Bishop & O'Neal General Merchandise Store where Dr. Barnes plied his vocation. He also kept a little drug store with a soda fountain and a couple of small ice cream parlor tables and chairs. Callie Miller sometimes worked for Dr. Barnes. Inside this little office, Dr. Barnes kept strange artifacts of his practice, including the foot of Hard Leath in a jar of formaldehyde. Junior recalled that old Dr. Barnes was actively engaged in pursuits other than practicing medicine.[37] In fact, it was common practice for him to pick up people's livestock when they failed to pay their family's medical

---

36. John E. Talbott, *Let's Call It Finger! A History of North McNairy County and Finger, Tennessee and Its Surrounding Communities*. Henderson, TN: Self-published, 2003, 219–221. Junior was referred to as Luther in this book.

37. Chapter 2, page 36, contains an account regarding an incident resulting in an injury at the Finger School which required Dr. Barnes' attention.

bills. He was often seen towing a livestock trailer that he used to retrieve a cow, horse, mule, or hog. The late Marvin Hand once recounted, "It took Dr. Tucker to make a cowboy out of Dr. Barnes."

He and his wife, Estelee (Bishop) Barnes, had no children, but they raised Roy and Inetha Bishop, the children of her brother Dorsey "Dossie" Bishop and his wife Lela (Woodward) Bishop. Dorsey and Lela were killed along with Scott McCaskill when a train collided with their touring car in 1922. Both Roy and Inetha were in the car as well, but they survived despite Inetha's horrible injuries.

Another old-time character whom Junior often discussed was Mr. Tom Stewart. If someone needed to sell some old butter or had a dried up old milk cow and a litter of pigs that they needed off the feed bill, they could stop by and deal with Mr. Tom M. Stewart, "Produce Buyer and Trader of Cattle and Hogs."[38] Tom was well-known to many of the little ladies who were looking for a market for their old butter. For those who aren't old enough to remember the distinction between old and new butter, the following will serve as an explanation. In the early years and decades of the twentieth century, everyone around Finger and most rural areas had an old milk cow. The people would churn their own fresh butter. No one locally bought fresh butter; they didn't have to. Someone might have to buy new butter if their milk cow went dry, but even then, their neighbor usually would help them out. A family might churn a pound or so of fresh butter and use that butter. If they didn't use it fast enough and it started to get an old taste to it, they would take it to town and sell it for usually about 10 cents a pound. This butter was referred to as "old butter."

Tom Stewart had his fair share of mishaps with the butter business. Once, a lady came into his shop and told him that she had some old butter to sell. He took the package from her and sat it underneath his counter. She then said, "To be honest with you, Mr. Tom, I got a mouse in my churn. But what folks don't know won't hurt them." After pretending to change out her butter for new butter, Tom handed the woman back her own old butter and stated, "You know, you're right, what folks don't know won't hurt them." Another humorous story involved the son of the local depot agent, Van Young. The young man wanted money to

---

38. Stewart was identified as such by an advertisement for his service from the 1920s and 1930s.

purchase candy and devised a plan. He put some horse manure in a paper bag and walked in Tom's shop. He placed it on the counter and told Tom he wanted to sell some old butter. Tom immediately placed it on the scale, figured the price, and paid the young man. After a few moments, he opened up the bag and discovered the manure. Needless to say, the elder Mr. Young was no more amused than Tom Stewart.

Junior often talked about certain friends who were older than him but whose interests and activities fascinated him. Frank Walker and Carroll Walker were two examples. Both played baseball and even traveled with teams to other towns. Probably the simple fact of the Walker boys being able to travel freely from town to town simply playing baseball along the way captured Junior's imagination and fueled his insatiable desire for travel.

Junior would have seen a number of other fine business establishments that could be reached from the sidewalks and little streets of Finger. Kids like him or gentlemen coming to town for a little treatment could walk into Stephens' Barber Shop for "first-class work and shower baths." Ed Stephens could go to work giving men and boys a first-rate haircut and shave for a nickel or for a dime at the most. After receiving the amount of pampering respectable men could afford, they could go on their way to check about their insurance at the office of Logan McCaskill's insurance agency. Perhaps they would stop by either of the banks to check on their loans, accounts, and the contents of their safety deposit box. Finally, with a hunger pang in the stomach, one could stop by Henry's Place, the local café, and see the owner, C.H. Kirkpatrick, and have a bite to eat. If they had brought along a shopping list lovingly provided by the wife, they had their choice of the following: W.O. Mitchell and Son General Merchandise, J.R. Harris General Merchandise, N.P. Talbott Staple Groceries and Produce, W.P. Massey, Dealer in General Merchandise and Brown-Built Shoes, Bishop and O'Neal, and Weaver's Grocery and Café.[39]

Despite the size and scope of Junior's world, Junior's parents were very important to him. He always expressed that his mother was quiet and withdrawn in many ways. She never showed him much affection and was very stoical. Her mother died when she was young and perhaps this affected her. Her father, Mr. Matlock, never remarried and raised four

39. All of these businesses in Finger were advertised in the late 1920s and early 1930s.

daughters on his own. His father Newt was warmer and more affectionate. He did show affection and was often concerned about his only son as the years wore on and Junior traveled into the wider and more dangerous world. Regardless, he loved and respected both his parents and refused to speak anything but good of them.

Junior, as has been stated, enjoyed his times and the traditions of those times. Halloween and Christmas were particularly special to him both as a young man and when he was older. As a young man, he particularly enjoyed Halloween. He loved the fall of the year and the added glee and mischief of the holiday only added to its charm. Often he recounted a certain amount of delight about the events surrounding Halloween night in and around town. He talked about some of the stunts that youngsters pulled while tricking others. One of the tricks he remembered most was how a group of young people removed the wheels and fenders from an automobile, set the partially disassembled vehicle on a porch in town, and then reassembled the vehicle behind the posts so that the owner could not remove it. He also recounted hearing stories of young men taking apart a car and placing it on a rooftop, where it was then reassembled. As Junior himself had a mischievous streak, he enjoyed retelling these stories.

Christmas involved the stocking and selling of wonderful treats at his father's store. These included peppermint sticks, hard candy, and other types of confectionary, as well as fruits like apples and oranges and various types of nuts such as pecans, walnuts, and chestnuts. He remembered the generous spirit of those around him during the Christmas season. He loved the foods and smells of the season. Junior enjoyed the festivities and the generous feelings that abounded during the holiday. Even in hard times, joy and generosity could be found and celebrated. This love for Christmas would abide with him the rest of his life.

Regarding the hard times of the Great Depression during which he came of age, Junior made only a few references. First, he said that hunger was no issue out in the rural areas of America such as his native South. Unlike the cities, where inhabitants found it necessary to eat zoo animals and stand in soup and bread lines, the people of his region knew how to garden and how to subsist. Second, he first knew things were not so good when he asked his father for a new bicycle and was told that it was not possible. Third, his most vivid memory of the hard times of the

1930s was learning of his father's ill fortune while trying to do good for his brother-in-law. Newt co-signed a loan at Home Banking Company in Finger so the brother-in-law could afford for his daughter to undergo surgery to repair her club foot. Following the surgery, he failed to repay the loan and it was left for Newt to satisfy the debt. Unfortunately, it was in the midst of the Great Depression and Newt could not afford the payments. He was forced to sell his farm in Leapwood to repay the loan. This piece of misfortune was never forgotten.

Junior continued his education at Chester County High School beginning in the fall of 1937. He had attended school at Finger High School through his completion of the tenth grade.[40] At the time that he enrolled in Chester County High, it was considered one of the finest and most innovative secondary schools in the South. The school was then under the management of Professor W.E. Montgomery (1886-1940), a very stern principal. Montgomery was an innovative educator who installed the first theatre in a high school in the southeastern United States. The high school was located in the old Georgia Robertson Christian College building, where members of the McIntyre family attended during that time and where the author attended many of his undergraduate university classes in the early 1990s.[41]

During those high school days, Junior had many stern and competent instructors, including Tom "Prof" Williams, Annie Davidson, Professor Montgomery, and James "Chick" Williams. At some point, he worked for a short period of time with James Williams, his history teacher, at a hatchery and chicken barn in Henderson on Hill Avenue. Williams picked up the nickname "Chick" during this time and Junior made the mistake of calling him by that name one day in class. Williams informed him that he was to never refer to him by that name again while at school. He also recounted the story of Professor Montgomery's astuteness. One day, he was walking too fast down the stairs and as he hit the floor at the bottom of the staircase, Montgomery called out his name and warned

---

40. Another incident of school life at Finger which Junior recounted involved his punishment for not finishing his school work. He was quite young and attending the Finger School. He didn't complete his work and his teacher made him stay after school until he finished. As it turned out, his teacher had to walk Junior home from school in the dark.

41. This old rambling brick building served the educational needs of the community as a college, high school, elementary school, and finally as a college/university facility. It was dismantled brick by brick in 2005.

him against the transgression of walking too fast. What made this most impressive to Junior was that Montgomery was sitting in his office and had his back to the staircase.

Junior rode to school each day with his friend, James L. Massey, in Massey's old car. James was always quite a whimsical character and remained so until his death in March 2011 at the age of 91. The two had known each other since they were about seven or eight years old and remained friends until Junior's death in January 2007. Although Junior was included in the class of 1939 and his photograph appears in the class composite, he did not actually graduate. He lacked one-half of a credit in order to graduate officially. Yet his education surpassed that of many others in his day. In the future, he would receive more schooling many miles away while serving his country in America's greatest foreign war. But first he would broaden his education as a migrant worker in the Panhandle of Texas.

4

The Great Adventure in Tulia, Texas

It was an interesting time to grow up. Life in a village like Finger was small but vividly alive with color. Adventure and experience gave Junior Talbott many lessons in life by 1941. He had grown up around a varied and eclectic arrangement of characters and people who taught him many lessons, helping him develop his own character. He had known old maids, eccentric bachelors, self-righteous but very fallible preachers, harsh schoolmarms, shady businessmen, hobos and vagabonds, rambunctious drunkards, prim teetotalers, and so many others.

Still, his world was small, not beyond the borders of his home area except the two trips to Missouri. Outside the walls of Chester County High School and the Finger School, an education still awaited him. It was the education of a man rather than a boy; a wandering man, one infected with the age-old penchant of wanderlust. The desire to see new lands had long been a Talbott family trait. It led Junior's forbearers from the British Isles to Pennsylvania, Virginia, and East Tennessee, before settling in West Tennessee. Now the desire to embark on his own trek overcame him.

In 1939, the nation was in its tenth year of economic depression. Work was hard to find and wages were low. There was little or no industry or manufacturing in the rural South outside of the large cities where major railroad hubs concentrated in and around centers of trade and commerce. Junior's opportunities in and around north McNairy County and south Chester County were exceedingly limited. Following his exit from school, he needed to find work and felt the need to seek out new opportunities and adventures. Given his adventurous spirit and desire to see the world, it was no major imposition to travel hundreds of miles, if necessary, to seek employment.

From 1939 to 1941, Junior assisted his father in the general merchandise business, worked odd jobs, and was a laborer at the Finger Gin Company.[1] Newt Talbott owned stock in the gin. There Junior worked with older fellows Lawrence "Red" Robison, John Rouse, and Robert Harris. Robison weighed cotton, Rouse was the engine man, and Harris and Junior tied the bales out. At some point, Junior worked two stints at the gin. He was always fascinated with the work and mechanics of the cotton gin. He became friends with his three older co-workers. Harris was the son of Bliss Harris, whom he held in high esteem.

Like many young men of the time, Junior decided it was time to hit the road and look for better paying work. After some consideration, he chose as his destination the small Texas panhandle town of Tulia. It's important to understand how he found his way there. It wasn't by accident. For many years, there had been a sporadic exodus of hard-working people from north McNairy County to Tulia, located in Swisher County, Texas. It was located in the vicinity of larger and better known Texas towns such as Silverton, Pampa, Amarillo, and Miami (pronounced by Junior as *Miama*).

Swisher County's agricultural products included cattle and wheat. At that time, it was the epitome of rural agrarian Texas. Beginning at the turn of the century, many people moved there from north McNairy County. Among those who made the journey for various motives were Blaine Barnes, Eulis and Earl Kirby, John Wesley Kerby, Hobert Patterson,

1. To the best of the author's understanding, Junior Talbott worked at the Finger Gin Company both before he went to Texas and after he returned, prior to going to the Navy.

Orville Plunk, Orby Plunk, and Emanuel Chandler. Of course, there were many others as well, but these men were all associates of Junior or family of his neighbors back in Finger.

A relatively thorough and extensive discussion of the McNairy County-Swisher County connection can be found in the author's previous work on the history of Junior's native area.[2] This partial narrative picks up the story:

> One of the common patterns to be noticed in history is the correlation between Tennesseans eventually making their way westward to Texas. So many early settlers of western Tennessee found their journey far from finished once they reached McNairy, Henderson, or Hardeman county. After a few years in this area, many often trudged on to Texas where they completed their long and arduous journey. Yet as the years passed, there were individuals who traveled only temporarily to the various sections of Texas to find work and then return.
>
> Interestingly, one of most common destinations was the town of Tulia in Swisher county, Texas. For those who haven't brushed up on their Texas geography lately, Swisher county is located in the Panhandle region of Texas. It is located relatively near to the towns of Amarillo, Miami, Silverton, and Pampa. It was known for its wheat farming and cattle ranching. It was also the stomping grounds for a large number of McNairy countians who migrated there in the period between the late 1890s and the early decades of the twentieth century.[3]

Many adventurous, hardy, and hungry individuals sought out a living and an opportunity in this land where the burdens and borders of the old one didn't exist. Each had their own reasons, but survival was the primary one of the time. Other than the Kerby brothers (Eulis and Earl) or Blaine Barnes, none sought to remain permanently or to become the barons of large ranch holdings. Rather, most sought to make a daily wage

---

2. John E. Talbott, J.D. *Let's Call It Finger: A History of North McNairy County & Finger, Tennessee & Its Surrounding Communities.* Dickson TN: BrayBree Publishing Company, 2015, 328–332.

3. Ibid, 328–329.

to support themselves and live decently before returning home to pick up their lives back in north McNairy County or south Chester County.

Junior's acquaintances in Texas were an interesting lot. Many had quirks and oddities that set them apart in his memory for decades to follow. Their eccentricities made them all the more memorable. Emanuel "Manley" Chandler had long ago found the small town where ranch work seemed always available. He was known in the town as an extremely hard worker who could endure a hard day's work regardless of his social activities the night before. Junior recalled that "he could drink all night and never miss a beat…go to work the next day and work all damn day!"[4] According to Junior, Manley was an eager, industrious man who gladly tackled any job, no matter how big or small.

Junior wasn't personally acquainted with the Kerby brothers, but Earl and Eulis (Ulyss) were among the earliest migrants to Tulia. Their uncle, John Wesley Kerby (1851–1922), lived there and it's likely the boys and their mother migrated to be near him. The Kerby boys were actually Naylors. However, their mother, Rosaline (Kerby) Naylor, left their father, Frank Naylor, when the boys were small and headed to Texas. She settled in Tulia and later died on June 2, 1924, having never returned to Tennessee. Both Earl and Eulis became successful farmers and owners of large tracts of land. The author's previous work picks up the story:

> One of the brothers married, but the other did not. Photographs taken in the early 1930s show a fleet of dozen or more combines to be utilized in the harvest of wheat. Both were good gentlemen whose first love was farming. Earl had bought a new Chevrolet business coupe and while driving across the farm he came across a newborn calf in need of assistance. He picked up the calf and put it in the backseat and proceeded on his way. The Kerby brothers' father made an attempt late in his own life to become reacquainted with his sons, who were taken away from him so early in their lives. He offered both brothers a new rifle as gifts upon their meeting. However,

---

4. L.E. "Junior" Talbott interview, 2001.

both brothers refused a meeting and showed no interest in getting to know their elderly father.⁵

Junior counted among his acquaintances members of the Plunk and Wamble families. The brothers Orby and Orville Plunk both wound up in the small Texas town working first in the wheat harvest. Afterwards, they found other work and new enterprises. The Wambles had a number of their family settle permanently in Swisher County. A brother of Marcus A. "Mark" Wamble lived out his life as a farmer in Tulia. Junior often recalled one particularly amusing story regarding the old adage that everything is bigger in Texas, but this one in reverse. One year, before harvesting a wheat crop in a field just off Highway 45 near the junction of Old Friendship Road, Mark Wamble walked out in the middle of his field and got on his knees to have his picture taken. According to Junior, he then sent the picture to his brother in Tulia with a caption that reported that his (Mark's) crop seemed to be doing well that year and was still growing.⁶

In June 1941, Junior decided to make his own journey to Tulia.⁷ He talked to a number of people including Emanuel "Manley" Chandler and learned that decent wages could be found there. Junior and his friend Horry Young (1906–1986) set out for Texas to find work knowing that other friends and acquaintances had already pioneered the same course. The two left Finger and caught a bus in Henderson, Tennessee, which they rode to Memphis. There they switched buses and travelled to Amarillo, Texas, having stopped only to eat breakfast in Fort Smith, Arkansas.

The young men arrived in Tulia one evening at approximately 11:00 P.M. in time to get a room in the local boarding house operated by Ms. Faye Townsend (1892–1969). She was a native of Kansas who, with her

---

5. These stories regarding the Kerby brothers were passed on the author by the late Hayes Hayre. He visited the Kerby brothers and family in Texas in the 1930s with his grandfather, Lee Andrew Weaver, whose wife was Dovie (Kerby) Weaver.

6. Junior Talbott recounted this story often and always with a laugh. Old Mr. Wamble's play on the Texas ego always tickled Junior's sense of humor.

7. Judge Dinwiddie paid Junior wages of $1.25 per day plus board, which was a little over $17.00 every two weeks. The Judge later raised his pay to about $2.25 per day. Junior's laundry bill was about fifty cents per week.

late husband James Anthony Townsend, ran the same boarding house on North Maxwell Street. Mr. Townsend had died in 1932. By this time, she was the lady friend of Blaine Barnes, a McNairy County native.[8] Blaine was the owner and operator of a livery stable between Silverton and Tulia. In his later years, he would move to town and reside at 402 North Maxwell Street. Blaine was a civic-minded individual and in his lifetime he served as a town commissioner, night watchman, and deputy. He was a deputy under Sheriffs Mosely, Tom Walters, and the legendary Texas sheriff of pulp magazine fame, Hugh White. Barnes was also a member of the local rationing board during World War II. He was an avid equestrian and a member of the American Quarter Horse Association as well as the National Quarter Horse Association. He and his wife, Ida Clayton Barnes, had thirteen children. It was following Ida's death that Blaine courted Ms. Townsend, Junior's first hostess while in this faraway little town.[9]

The next morning, Junior and Horry came downstairs for breakfast. Upon entering the room, they found one of Tulia's leading citizens and town fathers waiting for them at the lunch counter. Judge William Charlie Dinwiddie (1872–1947) was ready to offer them jobs. He began the conversation by telling the young men that he had heard of a couple of Tennessee boys in town looking for work and he wanted to get them before anyone else had a chance. Of course, this was a welcome development. Junior recalled the moment for a lifetime:

> We got in late. We were worn out and needed sleep but got up early anyway. When we came down, we went right to the dining room to get breakfast. Well, there sitting at the counter was this old man and he asked if we were looking for work. We told we were and he said that he'd heard we were from Tennessee. We told him we were and he said he wanted to hire us before someone else got to us. And he hired us on the spot. That was the first time I met the Judge.[10]

---

8. Faye Townsend and Blaine Barnes married sometime after 1940.

9. Sargent Blaine Barnes died on March 13, 1971, at the age of 89. He was the son of James A. Barnes and wife Martha Elizabeth (Plunk) Barnes of McNairy County.

10. L.E. "Junior" Talbott interview, 2001.

Judge Dinwiddie was himself a native of East Tennessee and relished the opportunity to get acquainted with other native Tennesseans. The Judge always maintained that Tennessee boys were the hardest working and most industrious of the laborers he saw. He asked Junior and Horry if they knew a man by the name of "Chan." They in turn asked if he was referring to Emanuel "Manley" Chandler of Finger, Tennessee. He was indeed and that he knew Chandler to be an honest and extremely hard working fellow who could drink white whiskey all night and still get up and work hard all day long without a hitch. His evening activities had no appreciable or negative effect on his daytime work. The Judge spent a good deal of time that morning getting to know Junior and Horry. After a little breakfast and a little more conversation, the young men made their way out to the Dinwiddie ranch with the Judge. They had found the employment for which they had journeyed so far.

Horry Young would not remain long in Tulia. After only a couple of days of work, he sustained a scrape or cut on his chin while performing some chore. It was certainly not a serious injury, but he insisted that he needed professional medical treatment to prevent it from getting worse. The Judge told Horry that it was nothing serious and that he was carrying on so for nothing. Horry persisted and was convinced that he needed to see a doctor. Judge Dinwiddie relented and he and Junior drove him to town. After receiving medical attention, Horry told them that he really felt he ought to stay a couple of more days as a precaution, then he would head back to the ranch. After a few days, Judge Dinwiddie and Junior returned to fetch Horry only to be informed that he had left for Finger, Tennessee, and was already home. Horry never ventured back to Tulia again to anyone's knowledge. Having been married twice previously with children, it's very possible that he missed his family and home.[11] Such a desire to return was understandable for a fellow in his position.

It is important for any understanding of Junior's time in Texas to know his relationship with the man who hired him. Judge William Charlie Dinwiddie was a man that he loved like another father and he had great respect and warm affection for him. Junior never saw the Judge as just

---

11. Horry Young married first to Ethel McIntyre and they had daughters, Marie and Lucy. After their divorce, he married Lessie Griffin and they had a son, Charles Young. Following his divorce from Lessie, he married his third wife, Nettie, in 1944, and they had a daughter, Becky. Nettie survived Horry and was still living in 2019.

another employer but rather as a friend and mentor whom he remembered the rest of his life. He talked about "The Judge" or "the Old Man" for the next sixty-five years. He never once spoke an ill word about him and found no fault in him in any manner. The old man must have had a profound impact on Junior for he talked about the old gentleman to his children and grandchildren for decades.

William Charlie Dinwiddie was born on July 29, 1872, in Jefferson County, Tennessee, to an old and distinguished family.[12] He was the son of John R. Dinwiddie and wife Elizabeth A. (Hankins) Dinwiddie.[13] Nothing is known of his childhood or adolescence. His father was a veteran of the U.S. Ninth Cavalry during the War Between the States.[14] Interestingly, Judge Dinwiddie rarely spoke to Junior about his youth. However, in 1941, he revealed that he had not returned to Tennessee in almost fifty years though he always hoped to return one day before he died. It does not appear that Judge Dinwiddie ever got that opportunity. Junior, still young and impressionable, often speculated that perhaps the Judge had gotten into some form of trouble when he was young and came west in order to escape it. However, such was only youthful speculation and there was no proof for such a theory. In fact, as of 1910, Judge Dinwiddie's mother, Eliza Dinwiddie, was living with the family in Swisher County, Texas.[15]

Dinwiddie came to Swisher County in November 1897. He later was a member of the Swisher County Old Settlers' Association, a group organized on July 17, 1933, for those residents who had lived in the county for at least 25 years or more. After a few years, people ceased registering for the Association and its membership was largely confined to early members and those shortly thereafter. Dinwiddie's three brothers, Sam B. Dinwiddie, J.R. "Jim" Dinwiddie, and John Wooten Dinwiddie, came

12. Jefferson County, Tennessee, was a place that Junior and the Judge shared in common, though Junior did not know it at the time. It was not only the seat of the Dinwiddie family but the Talbott family as well. It was from Jefferson County that Junior's great-grandfather, Theodore Perry Talbott, migrated to Henderson County (later Chester County), Tennessee.

13. This information was sent to the author from Zoe E. Smith via e-mail on August 28, 2001, with the information being taken from a history of Swisher County, Texas, entitled *Windmilling: Swisher County, Tennessee, 1876–1977*. Tulia TX: Swisher County Historical Commission, 1978.

14. *Tennesseans in The Civil War: A Military History of Confederate and Union Units with Available Rosters of Personnel*, Part 1. Nashville TN: The Civil War Centennial Commission, 1964.

15. 1910 U.S. Census, Swisher County, Texas.

to Swisher County about four or five years later, perhaps after the turn of the century.

Judge Dinwiddie was approximately twenty-five years old when he migrated to Texas. Apparently, he quickly became very active in the civic and business affairs of his new county. He was one of the organizers of the First National Bank of Tulia in 1902, serving as its first president until 1904.[16] That year, he was elected county judge of Swisher County, and held this position until 1906. During his tenure, Judge Dinwiddie helped the county make great gains and played a crucial role in the building of the Santa Fe Railroad through it. He was also the organizer of the Farmers Grain Company of Tulia in 1919, which still existed when the 1926 Tulia Telephone Directory was published.[17]

Of course, it was Judge Dinwiddie's agricultural and livestock operation in Swisher County that Junior was most concerned with in 1941 and 1942. The Judge spent almost fifty years farming and ranching, raising both wheat and registered cattle. He owned fourteen sections of land, which amounts to 8,960 acres, as one section consists of 640 acres. As of 1941, he had approximately 500 registered white faced Hereford cattle and maintained fifteen registered bulls to service his cows. He always kept approximately 200 young bulls on hand and sold these young bulls as well as many young heifers.

Each year, Judge Dinwiddie planted approximately 2,000 acres of sorghum, 640 acres of barley, 2,000 acres of wheat, and leased the so-called "Nanny Pastures" for grazing. These grazing grounds were located adjacent to his ranch. The Judge had two Caterpillar tractors in use in 1941 as well as a third of the same model to be used for parts.[18] At that time, the Judge had a 1929 Chevrolet truck, a 1938 or 1939 farm truck, and a 1942 Chevrolet truck that he had purchased for his ranch foreman, Murphy Marrs. The Judge himself drove a 1942 Chevrolet business

---

16. Zoe E. Smith e-mail to the author, August 28, 2001. She provided information found in *Windmilling: Swisher County, Tennessee, 1876–1977*.

17. Ibid. Further, along with a listing of the names listed in the telephone directory of Tulia, Texas, in 1926, as compiled by Zoe Smith of Tulia, Texas.

18. Judge Dinwiddie informed Junior Talbott during a drive around the ranch that he bought the third Caterpillar tractor simply for parts. It cost him approximately the price of two such tractors to use replacements parts rather than just take them from the "parts tractor." In other words, the whole was cheaper than the sum of the individual parts.

coupe. Indeed, for a young man from Finger, Tennessee, this seemed a rather large affair.

The cattle business was a booming agricultural asset of Texas in those days. Junior once asked Judge Dinwiddie why the folks back home in Tennessee didn't get in the cattle business. He explained that land was much too expensive there. According to Junior, land averaged about $10.00 per acre in Tennessee whereas land in Texas averaged about $2.00 to $2.50 per acre. Such cheap land prices made cattle farming far more practical in Texas.

Junior often wondered about the Judge's sons. The old man mentioned them on occasion, but during his stay at the Dinwiddie ranch, Junior could never recall a single visit by any of them. It was not until 2001 and early 2002, during Junior's old age, that he actually learned anything of substance about the sons of William Charlie and Ida (Borden) Dinwiddie. They were married in Jack County, Texas, in November 1895, and had six sons: Mongo Lyman Dinwiddie, Otto D. Dinwiddie, Jack D. "Doggie" Dinwiddie, Rondo Dinwiddie, and two young boys who died in early childhood.

Mongo Lyman Dinwiddie was the oldest of the sons. He was born in Justin, Denton County, Texas, on June 30, 1897. The young man was apparently very beloved by his parents as his obituary relates. His death was attributed to diphtheria.[19] Incidentally, Mongo Dinwiddie would become one of the first burials in the Rose Hill Cemetery.

Otto Dudley Dinwiddie was born in Swisher County on March 7, 1899. He was a 1918 graduate of Tulia High School and a 1922 graduate of Texas A & M University. Otto was a schoolteacher in Panhandle and Stratford and served as the superintendent of schools in Happy, Texas. When he was thirty years of age, he moved to Hart, Texas, where he joined Judge Dinwiddie in business at the Farmers Grain Company. He remained there until his death in 1969. Like his father, Otto was involved in the banking business as well. He served as an inactive vice president of the Farmers State Bank in Hart. He was tragically killed in a horrendous automobile accident outside of Hart on May 1, 1969, and was buried in the Hart Cemetery.[20]

---

19. Tulia *Herald*, July 14, 1910.
20. Ibid, May 8, 1969.

R.F. Dinwiddie was born on October 22, 1900, and died on September 30, 1906, perhaps of some childhood disease. Afterwards, Jack D. Dinwiddie was born in Tulia on November 2, 1903. He attended the Allen Academy and North Texas A & M University before moving to Laramie, Wyoming, to complete his studies at the University of Wyoming. In 1928, upon his graduation from the university's college of agriculture with a Bachelor of Science Degree in agriculture with a major in animal husbandry, Jack moved back home to assist his father. Newly married in 1928, Jack and his bride settled in Tulia where he managed the Dinwiddie Ranch. From 1932 until his entry in the U.S. Army Air Corps in 1941, he ranched with his wife's father, Oda Mason, in Albany County, Wyoming. He built a successful ranching career and attained great stature in his adopted home. Jack served in the Air Corps throughout the duration of World War II and attained the rank of Lieutenant Colonel. It was Jack about whom Junior heard much from Judge Dinwiddie during their time together.[21] Jack died in 1986.

Willie C. Dinwiddie was born on April 1, 1909, and died that fall on September 30, 1909. Thereafter, Rondeau "Rondo" Dinwiddie was born in Tulia in 1911. He married Nella Vee Anderson, the daughter of Mr. and Mrs. A.M. Anderson, Sr., of Swisher County. The couple had one son, Borden Dinwiddie. Rondo lived during his lifetime in Tulia, Hart, Lubbock, and Decatur, Texas. He died in 2008 at the age of 97. His son, Rondeau "Borden" Dinwiddie, born 1937, died on August 2, 2011, in Decatur, Texas, at the age of 74. He had no children. In regards to the sons of Judge Dinwiddie, Junior always thought that at least two of Judge Dinwiddie's sons were in the service during World War II. This other son was most likely Rondo.

During Junior's days in Tulia, he learned many things and made many acquaintances. One of his favorite stories regarded a Dutchman and his odd approach to farming. There was an old schoolhouse that adjoined Judge Dinwiddie's ranch. After the school was closed, the county (or a subsequent owner) sold the property, the building and ten acres, to a man who was referred to as a "Dutchman." Junior thought he was probably one of the Amish sects. He moved his family of sixteen, which

21. Ibid, July 10, 1986.

included an older couple, into the schoolhouse and began to farm the ten acres. The older couple was believed to be the parents of either the Dutchman or his wife.

The Dutchman and his family performed various work in town, primarily mowing and tending to other people's yards. They would gather the clippings, carry them back to their place, put the clippings in their furrows, and turn them back into the soil. They also cut bean and corn stalks and turned them back under the soil as well. These practices added to the quality of the soils they were farming. It was apparent to Junior that this "Dutchman" was very intelligent in the ways of gardening and feeding his family. Still, Junior found him quite peculiar for that time and place.

The Dutchman planted all the ground he owned but the drive leading from the schoolhouse to the main road. All else was in cultivation. One day in town, an old drunkard summoned enough courage or consumed enough whiskey to ask the Dutchman about his farming methods. "How do you plan to make a living on just ten acres of land?" The Dutchman responded, "Well, I don't know if I can. But, I'll tell you what I'll do if I can't make it on ten. I'll sell half of it, because I know I can make a living on five acres." The Dutchman recounted this exchange to Junior during a conversation one afternoon and could not help but laugh while telling Junior.

One day while working on one of Judge Dinwiddie's fences that divided his ranch from the Dutchman's land, the Dutchman asked Junior about using some of the Judge's property for crops. The large equipment the Judge used on his ranch could not reach the corners of the fences when planting. Those fairly large areas went completely unused and unproductive. Junior told him he would discuss it with the "old man" when he returned to the house for lunch. The Judge had no problem with the arrangement and Junior conveyed the message back to the Dutchman. He planted those corners and produced all kinds of foods. One day, the Dutchman asked Junior to tell the Judge they could have anything they wanted. This would be a form of repayment for the use of the land. Junior recalled that the areas brought forth amazing amounts of vegetables as the ground had been fallow so long and was rich in nutrients.

Junior told the story of another one of Judge Dinwiddie's neighbors. This older man owned a cattle herd composed largely of run-of-the-mill scrub cattle or "junk cattle." The Judge raised pure bred registered cattle and naturally did not want his neighbor's cattle mixing with his own. The Judge's cattle were well-bred, having been carefully designed by him. He determined which bulls and cows would be used to produce the young calves which then grew into valuable cattle. The old neighbor did not use such care in his beef production enterprise. He had an old bull that kept getting out and onto the Judge's land. The Judge had repeatedly told the old fellow that if the bull kept getting out, he would "take care of it." Finally, after repeated warnings, the old mixed bred bull escaped again. The Judge tracked down Junior and Murphy Marrs and asked them to come with him. The three men ran the old bull down the fence line and into a pond through a spot where a barbed wire fence ran. The old bull became tangled in the fence and that's where they left the bull to drown. The Judge had finally had enough!

Murphy Marrs was a man who captured Junior's respect and admiration. He was kind but tough. He worked hard and had seen much in his life to that point. Marrs, always called "Murphy" by Junior, was the manager of Judge Dinwiddie's ranch. He was a widower, his wife having died several years before 1941. He had several grown children.[22] Murphy was a hardworking individual who seemed to have no great interests other than managing Judge Dinwiddie's ranch and making sure it was operated efficiently. He showed no great interest in any women after his wife's death. His children were grown and independent, so he had time and energy to act as a mentor to Junior and other young men who worked for the Judge.

Murphy always advised Junior when he thought the young ranch hand was in danger of stepping over the line with Judge Dinwiddie. Junior always spoke affectionately of Murphy and thought highly of his abilities. He was one of many influential mentors Junior had when he was young. Murphy took opportunities to help him learn his way around as a ranch hand and as a man. Like his affection for Judge Dinwiddie, Junior held Murphy Marrs in the highest esteem. He was a rugged man in many ways, accustomed to hard physical work and wise in the ways of

---

22. Since Junior Talbott's death, research has uncovered a little information regarding Murphy Marrs' family. From newspaper notices in The Tulia Herald, we know that he and Mrs. Marrs had at least two children. They had a son born on April 8, 1920, and a daughter born on February 18, 1923. Tulia Herald, April 9, 1920, Vol. 11, No. 15, and February 23, 1923, Vol. 14, No. 8.

the ranching and cowboy life. He and Junior shared many days working and talking about things important to them. They became close out of common interests and often rode around the ranch deep in conversation while checking fences, the herd, and the pastures.

Murphy was just one of many interesting and complex characters who Junior met during his years in Texas. In addition to Blaine Barnes and Ms. Townsend, he also became acquainted with Sheriff Hugh White, a legendary lawman in the 1930s. He had been responsible for solving a high-profile murder. His brilliant investigative work became the subject of an article in a pulp magazine that specialized in detective stories. Hugh White was working in the wholesale oil business with his brother-in-law, Claude Kilcrease, who owned a Gulf Oil distributorship in Tulia.[23] It was while working in the oil business that Hugh did undercover detective work for Swisher County Sheriff John C. Moseley. Upon Moseley's death in 1933, White became more interested in law enforcement. He ran for sheriff and was elected in 1938.[24] The man was a real athlete and cut the figure of a real Western sheriff. His stride was long and large and Junior always had great respect for him. White was always friendly with Junior. He often saw the sheriff around town and enjoyed talking him about his experiences as a lawman.

Junior also became friends with a drunken chuck wagon cook named Bailey Dyer. He was the cook for the Dinwiddie outfit and quite the character. Bailey was a Cajun and he had a sister down in Louisiana. These types of characters appealed to Junior's sense of adventure and played a part in weaving the fabric of his own personal character.

Junior often said he first started getting an education when he traveled to Texas. He learned much from Judge Dinwiddie and Murphy Marrs.

23. Zoe E. Smith e-mail to the author, April 18, 2002. She procured the information from an uncredited source, but it may have been from the book *Windmilling*.

24. White served as Sheriff until January of 1955. At that time, he was appointed Probation Officer for the Sixty-Fourth (64th) Judicial District. He then served in this capacity until his retirement on December 31, 1973. White turned down many enticing offers to work beyond the boundaries of Swisher County. He was offered positions with state government in Austin, the Federal Bureau of Investigation in Washington, D.C., and the Texas Rangers. He also boxed and wrestled to remain in good physical shape and was active in the American Red Cross and the Texas Sheriff's Association.

These men tutored him in the ways of rural Western ranch life and the world itself. They provided a paternal influence while he was away from his own father. Working on a fence one afternoon, the Judge mentioned to Junior that he had built "these bodark (pronounced *bō-dock*) fences" when he had arrived in Texas.[25] That meant the fence posts they were inspecting had been split and installed in approximately 1897 or 1898. On this occasion, the Judge also mentioned that he had not returned to East Tennessee since his arrival in Texas in 1897, but he always wanted to make a return trip. The Judge's background always provided a fertile ground for Junior's mind to wonder about his employer and the man's past. No doubt it was interesting. Junior and the old man shared a common experience—both had come to Texas from Tennessee as young men to search out a new experience and a new life. This alone gave them a common bond.

Junior often talked about various aspects of the ranch and the ranching life.[26] Having no extensive personal contact with them back home, he was fascinated by the horses he rode while at work. He was amazed at their intelligence, intuition, instinct, and ability to guide themselves and their rider along a given path or through the motions of a cattle drive. A well-trained and experienced horse took Junior through the herd, almost

25. Bodark is another name for the Osage orange or hedge apple. It is a tree whose habitat is largely confined to the Southwestern United States, including the states of Arkansas, Oklahoma, and Texas. According to Junior Talbott, the Judge said to him, "I put these fence posts up back in '97 when I came out here."

26. L.E. Talbott interview, June 1992. The author interviewed Junior Talbott regarding the layout of the ranch. His wife Faye D. Talbott joined in the questioning. That interview/dialogue is as follows:
JET: How was the ranch laid out?
LET: The cookhouse was a dugout. Half of it was below the ground level; the other half was above it. The walls stand about, I guess, around four feet above the level of the ground. When you go in, you walk down some; it's like going into a storm house.
FDT: How big was it?
LET: It was about forty feet long, twenty feet wide, something like that. It was two rooms: a kitchen and dining room, I'd guess you'd call it, was all one.
FDT: Where did you sleep then?
LET: In the other room, it was twenty feet square; it was two beds in it.
JET: It was just the foreman and the cook that stayed in it?
LET: Yeah.
FDT: Where did you and the other ones stay?
LET: We stayed up at the old man's house. A few years before that, they had a regular bunkhouse down there; it rotted down or something.

doing his job for him. A horse once guided him through a western dust storm. Junior was working and cutting the cattle per the Judge's instructions when a sudden dust storm arose. His visibility was badly hindered by dense clouds of dust amidst a confused and panicked herd of cattle. In retelling this story, Junior recalled the sudden fury of a dust storm. The heavy dust cloud appeared far off and then suddenly seemed to engulf everything. It roared and raged intensely, the sand infiltrating everything in its reach. Such storms could even blot out the sunlight for a while when they were especially large. He could see nothing. He was in danger of choking and being blinded from the fine dust swirling around him. Finally, the storm settled down and died away.[27] More importantly, the horse was still there, a friend and an ally throughout the difficulty, guiding the young ranch hand through the tempest and back to the house.

The concept of a dust storm seems foreign today, but it was a common occurrence during the Dust Bowl years of this nation from 1934 to 1940. They were the result of severe drought in the American Plains and the failure of Plains farmers to apply the proper dry land farming methods. This failure to prevent soil erosion from the great winds that swept across the Plains resulted in tremendous dust storms. The Plains held their topsoil through the deep rooted native grasses. But when farmers applied deep plowing methods to the prairie soils, there was nothing to keep the strong and steady winds from blowing the topsoil away. The droughts turned the topsoil to dust and then the strong winds blew the dust across the land. Although the term "Dust Bowl" was meant to describe the region affected by the dust storms, it eventually became synonymous with the series of storms themselves. The dust storms of the Texas Panhandle were a new and foreign experience to the young ranch hand from Finger, Tennessee.

Junior was also fascinated by the differences between the ways certain work was done in Tennessee as opposed to Texas. These differences seemed strange and foreign to him, but he quickly adjusted. He found himself interested in the workings of a windmill, the history of the West, and the western diamondback rattlesnake. These were all new subjects for his fertile and active mind. A great sense of curiosity allowed Junior to enjoy the experience rather than dread it or face it with anxiety. He readily embraced new experiences.

27. Luther E. (Junior) Talbott interview, no date.

During his days in Texas, Junior became familiar with the workings of the windmill, an apparatus not seen very often in Tennessee. He found it interesting and studied its working parts while he worked around windmills in the pastures and wheat fields. The fact that wind could operate the machinery of a well-pump by turning the vanes or blades fascinated him. He had seen no such thing in Finger. Other priorities forced the laborer in the West to make sure certain chores were easy to carry out. There was a herd to care for and dangers lurking in the brush or up in the sky. If allowing the wind to pump water while a man dealt with these responsibilities, why not? He appreciated this attitude toward labor-saving methods that prevailed in the Panhandle.

Because the American West was a foreign land to him, Junior was anxious to learn of its history as directly as possible. He listened to old timers and asked them questions when time allowed. Although Judge Dinwiddie and Murphy Marrs kept the young man busy on the ranch, he sought out local characters when he could and absorbed their tales and lore. He later realized that some of these sidewalk historians were probably better qualified to be sidewalk folklorists. Still, their accounts were the things that American culture of the West was made of. They were grizzled men with weathered tan faces and worn-out bodies in dusty clothes, but their conversation and expressions were lively and entertaining. They sat on benches outside the stores and shops, spat on the sidewalks or into the street, and were always ready to spin a yarn.

Many years before, these old timers had been young men living when many of the famous gunfighters were still alive and building their reputations. They enjoyed telling and retelling their old stories about the outlaws and desperados who once roamed from town to town and territory to territory. Junior, himself destined to be an old man and storyteller in his own right, thoroughly enjoyed listening to them. He sat beside them on the wooden plank sidewalks as they recounted such famous personages as Frank and Jesse James, the Clanton brothers, and Billy the Kid. Whether or not these old men ever crossed the paths of these outlaws made little difference to Junior. They were contemporaries of these reprobates turned legends and just hearing about the times in which they lived made for fascinating conversation. These old timers would teach the eager young man much and added to the fabric of his developing life.

Junior's education and mind were broadened with each new experience. He gradually became more sophisticated and broad-minded about the world that still lay before him. One of the more humorous stories he told regarded a lady rancher who lived near Tulia. She drove up to the Dinwiddle ranch one afternoon in a fancy car and asked to see the Judge. Junior told her that he had gone to town on business. She wanted to look at some bulls and the Judge's absence did not deter her from her mission. Seeing her determination, Junior told her that he would round up some young bulls and bring them up to the house so she could inspect them. That wouldn't do. The lady rancher told him there was no need for that much trouble. Instead, she instructed him to saddle up two horses so they could ride out to the herd together to examine the bulls. In a little while, they reached the herd and began separating the young bulls. The lady rancher didn't hesitate to begin cutting the cattle and Junior recalled years later, "She was better at it than I was, because she'd been doing it longer."[28] As she scrutinized them, she noticed one particular bull that appeared to have only one testicle. The lady cut that particular bull out of the herd in order to examine it more closely. She dismounted from her horse and approached the young bull. Junior himself picks up the story from there:

> Then she shoved her whole arm up that bull, feeling around. Finally, she said, "I can only feel one nut. He's probably got another one up there and I can't get a hold of it. But I don't want to take any chances on buying him." Anyway, she got all the best ones there and the Judge had shown up when we got back to the house. She asked him [the Judge] if the deal he'd give her was the best he could do and he said yes. So, she took it and said she'd send her truck out to get them the next day.
>
> About a week later, a big ole' cattleman named J. Polk Osborne, who owned two ranches, one at Miama [Miami], Texas, and one at Canadian, Texas, came up to the ranch to buy some bulls. Me and the old man took him out to look at them and when he saw them he hollered, 'Goddamn! That

---

28. Luther E. (Junior) Talbott interview, 2001.

damn woman's been here!' I said, "What woman?" He said, "the only woman around here; she's got the best damn ones!"[29]

Junior always laughed at this story. Of course, he knew "what woman" the prosperous cattleman was railing about. The lady rancher had indeed gotten the best young bulls, but Polk Osborne bought some young bulls anyway. As Junior recalled, those were good bulls as well, but Osborne knew that the lady rancher had beaten him there again. Apparently, there existed a good-natured rivalry between the two ranchers.

Junior's stories and recollections of life in Texas ranged from one end of the spectrum to the other. He often chuckled about some skunks. In fact, he had several skunk stories. He talked about the sorghum harvest and seeing the sorghum stalks that were stacked in a teepee fashion. These were commonly called "shocks." Skunks would create dens in the hollows of these shocks and make homes of them. On the Dinwiddie ranch, however, the skunks had an adversary. Bailey Dyer, the drunken cook on the ranch, liked to sell their skins and hides. The Judge had a couple of dogs that often accompanied Junior on his rounds. One was a collie dog and the other was a shepherd. The shepherd dog would root around in the sorghum and kill the skunks. Still more often, the two experienced canines would flush the skunks out and Junior would kill the scented mink with his Smith and Wesson .22 pistol. Afterwards, Bailey would skin them and cure out the hides so he could sell them.

Usually, Junior would kill two or three skunks at lunchtime and about that many more at night. On one occasion, when he and Murphy were shooting at them, they got more sport than they had planned. The Judge sometimes hired Mexican labor for specific seasonal jobs. They were not a mainstay on the Dinwiddie ranch, but there was occasional need for them and they were inexpensive. Often they would stole away to catch a siesta when the Judge wasn't looking. A small group of Mexican laborers was sleeping behind one of the large sorghum stacks when Junior and Murphy began firing at the fleeing skunks. The laborers started running as well. They were not sure who was shooting or why, but they ran chattering and yelling as fast as their legs could carry them. Junior continued to get a laugh out of the sight of the fleeing and confused Mexicans for decades.

29. Ibid.

He also talked about a woman who had two skunks that followed her around like kittens. She was very eccentric and apparently an old maid. She dressed in an older fashion with petticoats and a large decorative hat. The woman would come to town and walk regally on her errands with the little skunks close behind, abiding her commands and instructions. According to Junior, she was nice and polite but strange and very unconventional. The woman was gentle and talked to her little skunks. She seemed quite an interesting character to the young man and he never forgot her eccentricities.

Junior, Murphy Marrs, Bailey Dyer, and sometimes Judge Dinwiddie traveled into town about every two weeks. Most trips were for simple routine matters. Some were recalled by Junior for unusual or memorable moments that occurred. On one trip to town, Junior recalled going to the barbershop for a haircut and shave. He sat in the barber's chair and after getting the hot towel/steam treatment, the barber turned toward to Junior with a straight razor to begin his shave. Suddenly, Junior noticed that the barber, an elderly man, had a pronounced tremor in his hands. As he neared Junior with the straight razor, Junior decided immediately in his mind to forgo the shave. Reading the look on Junior's face, the barber explained that he always settled down once the straight razor touched the skin. Still, Junior's faith in the man's ability to cease his tremor was not that strong. He decided to skip the shave on that trip. Even a friendly straight razor seemed frightful in the hands of a shaky barber.

On another occasion, Junior visited the store of a local merchant. It was a dry goods store of the variety that existed in those days with all types of clothing and accessories for sale. On this day, he picked out some nice khakis, both shirts and work slacks. The merchant carried them to the back storeroom, wrapped them, and brought them back bundled in brown paper wrapping. The first time he wore them, the shirt and slacks both came apart. They were torn and Junior looked like he had tangled with some sort of wild animal. He examined the clothing more closely and found they were dry rotted. They were not the same clothes he had chosen. He had been cheated by the merchant.

Junior put on good clothes and returned to the store. He laid the worthless clothing on the counter. The merchant began to protest that he didn't give refunds. Junior spoke up and said he did not purchase those clothes. He had bought good quality clothing and was given this rotten "crud" instead. Eventually, the merchant admitted that he had tried to cheat Junior. He took the actual clothing that Junior had selected and began walking toward the back of the store, but Junior stopped him. He wanted to *see* the right clothes being wrapped. He didn't want any more surprises from this merchant.[30]

On occasion, Junior was invited to special events that gave him a good taste of Texas cow town life. Tulia hosted an annual "Pioneer Days" type of festival on July 17 that included a large picnic.[31] Around the first of June of each year, the town fathers would impose a ban on selling or importing whiskey into the town until after the festival. A fellow had to get a prescription from his doctor just to get a pint of whiskey in Tulia.[32] This was a holdover from the Prohibition days when doctors and pharmacists had to issue prescriptions for folks to indulge in drinking whiskey when it was otherwise outlawed. Business for local pharmacists and doctors was brisk every July.

On the day of the big event in 1941, Junior, Murphy Marrs, and Bailey Dyer went to town for the festivities. It was a time when the wild old West was still alive. Cow towns still meant wild times and big celebrations. After procuring two prescriptions, i.e. two pints of whiskey each, they began to drink whatever else they could get their hands on. They found more than they could handle; Junior ended up with a bottle

30. Junior Talbott also recounted that this was a Jewish merchant. It was his contention that Jewish merchants were willing to sell shoddy merchandise at top dollar prices. Junior took a negative view of these small-town Jewish merchants because he felt that they possessed few scruples. Certainly, this is not a view that would be palatable to many today, but in the early 1940s, many people in the South and the Southwest shared this view. Junior also spoke with a Jewish merchant with whom he was friendly and on good terms. His friend knew the merchant with whom he had the trouble over the work clothes. According to him, this crooked merchant came to Tulia with only a bundle of new pencils and built his general merchandise store up from the ground up, starting with just that bundle of pencils. Junior recounted that this friendly Jewish merchant also told him that in the smaller communities, members of the Jewish merchant class assisted each other financially. Any particular merchant or other type of businessman was given three chances at success. He would be funded or assisted otherwise through the second business failure but the third attempt at commerce would be any given businessman's last opportunity.

31. Near the center of downtown Tulia was a street known as Dip Street. It was called such because of the dips in the road to slow down the traffic. This festivity seemed to center around this street.

32. This type of arrangement was prevalent during Prohibition and afterward in rural Southern towns.

of "Slo Gin." The three spent the day ambling through town taking in all the activities, competitions, exhibits, and sights of the festival. Junior, Murphy, and Bailey left town on foot in the direction of the Dinwiddie Ranch, badly inebriated after a long day and night of celebrating.

The next morning, Junior woke up in a horse trough with a horse nudging him. After several minutes and just as many nudges from the offended and otherwise very unappreciative animal, he managed to climb out, get properly to his feet, and stumble away. His head was killing him and he figured he had to find Murphy and Bailey. He wandered down to a livery stable where he found his friends asleep, lying in a stable on a bed of hay soundly passed out from the drunken spree. Junior managed to awaken them and told them to get up so they could get going. He was sure the Judge would skin them all. As Murphy and Dyer hastily got to their feet, Murphy asked Junior why he wasn't already at the ranch. He told him that all he knew was that he had woke up in a horse trough. Murphy said, "Well, we watched you 'til you got around the corner of the building." Junior told Murphy that he had apparently stopped when he got to the trough.[33]

The three men made it home to the ranch as fast as they could. Junior had to work out in a distant field. It kept the Judge from finding him in such a condition. After a while, Junior got hot from his work. He was dry and went to the closest windmill and grabbed a tin peach can stored there and filled it with water.[34] After a full can of water, Junior got sicker and "drunker" than ever. He managed to make it back to the truck where he lay down for a while. After a short spell, he got sufficiently well to drive back to the dugout, where he told Murphy about his condition. Murphy took one look at Junior and could tell that he was not in good shape. It was evident to anyone that Junior had pulled off a hellacious drunk. Knowing the Judge's distaste for drinking and his intolerance of drinking by his hired hands, Murphy was concerned. He told Junior that he needed to stay clear of the Judge for a few days and he managed to do

---

33. Junior Talbott often used this incident to point out the bad effects of drinking. He laughed that should he ever saw a drink called Slo Gin, he would run from it as fast as possible!

34. The Dinwiddie Ranch had ten windmills. Its purpose in western states such as Texas was to power water wells on the plains, which in turn produced water for the cattle. Usually a can or container of some sort was kept at the windmill so a worker could keep himself hydrated while working out on the ranch.

just that. He recovered fine, but never drank another drop of "Slo Gin." In the decades after the incident, Junior made a disgusted face when even talking about gin.

Another memorable occasion was a Cattleman's Dinner and Dance held at the Amarillo Hotel. J. Polk Osborne, the Miami and Pampa millionaire cattleman, invited Murphy and Junior to go with him and enjoy the festivities. Osborne had been visiting the ranch and originally invited the Judge, then decided to ask Murphy and Junior instead. The two ranch hands explained that they didn't have any good clothes that would be fit for that kind of occasion. Osborne told them that didn't really matter. He instructed them to wear their best denims. Such invitations from men as important as Osborne weren't everyday occurrences, so they weren't about to turn him down.

Junior vividly recalled the night. He spoke of a brightly lit ballroom with tables full of good food. They were heavy laden with old-fashioned Texas cuisine fit for such an event. His senses came alive with the sight and sounds of a talented band playing festive music and pretty women dancing with cowboys. It was something out of an old Western movie, but not black and white, instead vivid with color and not just color, but also sounds and smells. Junior remembered the festive atmosphere, the sound of the music, and the smells in the air. Both ranch hands had a good time. Junior danced with every young lady available. He saw one of them later and she pretended to hide her feet, indicating Junior's ability—or lack thereof—to navigate the dance floor. The girl laughed and pointed at him with good humor. Junior always got a laugh out of his apparent inability to dance. He never mentioned attempting to dance again.

When talking about the young lady he had danced with, Junior also recalled other women he encountered in and around Tulia. He saw many beautiful young Mexican and Hispanic women who were quite something in the eyes of a young man. But one of two things always seemed to happen as they grew older and kept him from courting them. According to Junior:

> Those girls either dried up like a prune and got all skinny and shriveled up or they got all fat and greasy. They sure weren't much to look at once they started putting on the years. You'd

look at one and think she sure was pretty and then you'd see her Momma or another of the older ones and figure what that pretty one would look like in a few years.[35]

While in the Texas Panhandle, Junior realized the difference in attitude about work and what constituted thorough work. The Judge once told him to mend a section of the barbed wire fence separating a certain one of the old man's pastures. Junior began replacing and straightening up fence posts and re-nailing the barbed wire. After he had gotten quite a bit accomplished, the Judge came out to where Junior was working to check on him. The old man got out of his vehicle and stood there watching his young ranch hand hard at work. It was then that he fully saw what Junior was doing. The Judge walked up and down the section of fence, inspected it, and smiled. He complimented Junior on his work, but told him that he and his fellow Texans' idea of "good" was just making certain the fence posts were still standing and the barbed wire secure enough to keep the cows inside the fence. Still, the Judge was impressed with Junior's work ethic. Being a native Tennessean, he knew that the young man's ways were deeply ingrained and taught from youth.

Texas in 1941 was still remotely close to the days of gunfighters, cattle drives, and the days of the Wild West. When Junior was working for the Judge, there was occasionally the need to work some cattle on horseback. Sometimes a horse would get spooked by the presence of a rattlesnake. It was an unknown danger to him until he went to Texas. This deadly venomous snake was not a concern to boys like Junior growing up in Finger, although he was familiar with other deadly snakes such as cottonmouths and copperheads. Now Junior had to learn of the deadly ways of the rattler. Usually he saw them while out working the cattle, but once in a while one would be spotted elsewhere. As part of his gear, Junior often kept a revolver on him. During his time in Texas from 1941 until 1942, he killed a good eight to ten rattlesnakes with his pistol. To the day of his death in 2007, Junior kept the rattles from these long-dead

---

35. L.E. Talbott interview, June 1992. The attitudes and beliefs that formed the impressionable young Junior Talbott in the 1930s and 1940s may seem unpalatable in today's carefully planned and, frankly, whitewashed media world where old ways and thoughts are presumed intolerant and therefore not worthy of tolerance. In fact, such colorful views created colorful characters with differing viewpoints on the world and allowed young men like Junior to flourish and grow beyond the small towns in which they were raised.

snakes in a small box in his bureau. He took great pride in showing them to his grandchildren. The presentation of these ancient relics from his youth was usually accompanied by an interesting story.

Junior recollected details of the ranch. The men who worked there either stayed in the old bunkhouse or the basement of the Judge's house. Mrs. Dinwiddie would change their bed sheets and blankets and keep the place tidied up for them. She stripped Junior's bunk every Monday morning. She was a kindly old woman whom he greatly respected. On one occasion, Junior had been sick and was nursing his sickness with a pint of whiskey he kept under his pillow. While out working the cattle with Murphy, it occurred to him that he had left the bottle under his pillow. He told Murphy, "Do you know what I did? I left a pint of whiskey under my pillow this morning and when Ms. Dinwiddie strips the bed, she's going to find it." After a few minutes, Murphy shook his head and thoughtfully responded, "Well, he'll [the Judge] be letting you go now." As stated earlier, the Judge did not like his hands drinking under any circumstances or for any reason. Murphy was absolutely certain that Junior would be fired. He had seen the situation before and just knew in his heart how the old man would handle it.

As it happened, the Judge didn't fire Junior. Nothing was ever mentioned specifically about it, though Mrs. Dinwiddie stopped stripping Junior's bed. Instead, on Fridays, she would just lay out the folded, fresh sheets as it was now Junior's duty to strip and dress his own bed. Junior was a good hand on the ranch and because of this and his affection for him, the Judge probably hated to let him go. But that didn't mean the old man was happy about it or willing to let it pass without a word of advice. One day not too long afterwards, while he and Junior were out riding around the pastures, the Judge turned to him and declared, "Kid, whiskey and wild women have ruined many a good man."[36] He said nothing else but instead just let this bit of advice sink in with Junior. Thinking seriously on his words, Junior took them as fatherly advice and heeded as best he could. He later imparted the same advice to his grandsons.

36. Junior Talbott often recounted his stories and gave quotes from many of the characters. These quotes were written down as he told them. Unfortunately, too often the dates of the conversations and interviews were not recorded along with the information. At the time, this work was not contemplated and these conversations were recorded simply for family purposes.

When contemplating Judge Dinwiddie's aversion to drinking hard liquor and alcohol, Junior often laughed at his strong constitution against it. There was no question that he was tough on those who worked for him when they were caught drinking. Junior simply assumed the old man opposed alcohol across the board. However, one very cold day, while delivering some cattle to the Judge's friend, J. Polk Osborne, Junior observed something quite interesting to him. Because of the bitterness of the cold weather, Osborne offered Junior and Murphy a shot of whiskey to "warm them up." They left the Judge and Mr. Osborne to do business. Junior looked back and the Judge had the bottle of whiskey turned completely up and was participating in the "warm-up." Junior told Murphy, "I want you to look there at the Judge." Murphy replied with a broad knowing grin, "I knew he would!" Both found it very amusing that the Judge would indulge in alcohol given his strong vocal objections to the use of it by his employees. Such human frailties and obvious inconsistencies did not diminish Junior's attitude toward the old man. They only warmed his feelings toward him even more because they made the old man seem as vulnerable to temptations as everyone else. To Junior, being human always seemed the best of all qualities.

Despite the Judge's strict rules about drinking and indulging in strong liquor, the old cook seemed to be exempt. Bailey Dyer had been an engineer for the Rock Island Railroad but was fired for drinking.[37] In fact, he was in jail when the Judge hired him. Swisher County Sheriff Hugh White told the Judge that he would have to keep Dyer out of town or otherwise he would stay drunk all the time. The Judge told the sheriff he and the boys would only bring Dyer to town every two weeks. They thought they could better handle of him in that manner. Dyer was a small man, not very big or tall, and always cooked up a hearty meal for the gang. The first meal he fixed for Junior and Murphy after being hired included a pan of eighteen biscuits. Both men ate them before they had time to cool and asked Dyer to cook another smaller batch. When they finished the second batch, Dyer told them, "I didn't know I was cooking for a bunch of hogs!" He often cooked up various edible varmints the

---

37. The Rock Island Railroad operated in Texas. It intersected two other railroads, the Cotton Belt Railroad and the Texas and Pacific Railroad, in Dallas. See S. Kip Farrington Jr., *Railroads of the Hour*. New York: Coward-McCann, 1958, 168.

boys killed while out working the cattle. Often cantankerous and full of opinions, still his cuisine was great and Junior enjoyed his company.

Junior's old friends from the Finger area, Hobert and Cora Patterson, also were occasional migrants to Tulia. Junior and Cora shared some common relations. Junior's aunt, Ada (Talbott) Barton, was married to Mr. Thaddeus "Thad" Barton. He was the brother of John Barton, who was Cora's father. In other words, Junior and Cora had common first cousins. One afternoon while working and talking, Junior and Murphy realized they both knew Hobert and Cora. Thereupon, Murphy related the following story. Cora had gone to visit her parents, John and Dora Barton, while she and Hobert were living in Tulia. While she was gone, Hobert and Murphy decided to make a batch of "homemade brew." They put the brew in glass containers and had them in the trunk of the car when the two went to the station to get Cora upon her return. The beer was still "green" and as the car hit potholes, the containers began exploding in the trunk. Upon the first explosion, Cora asked, "What was that?" Hobert responded, "Something popped when we hit those potholes." After the third explosion, Cora bluntly stated, "Something we hit, yeah! You boys have been making home brew again." Murphy laughed over the incident and Junior found it funny as well.

Hobert and Cora were of the same grain as Junior when it came to their wanderlust and desire to see America. Like others, they went to Texas during the Great Depression to procure steady employment and decent wages.[38] This couple did not let grass grow under their feet; they were always on the move or so it seemed. At various times, Hobert and Cora could be found working in Tulia. Hobert first took his family to Tulia in 1927, where he worked on a dairy farm for his half-brother, Blaine Barnes, a friend of Junior's. In 1929, Hobert left Texas and returned to McNairy County where he purchased a farm at the head of Tar Creek near Mount Peter in 1933 and farmed there until 1945. The couple continued to move and find work as the years passed on.

Many of Junior's memories demonstrated the ways and customs of a time now passed forever. The boys working on Judge Dinwiddie's ranch carried their laundry into town to be laundered. There was a local

---

38. The information regarding Hobert and Cora Patterson was furnished by Luther E. Talbott and published in *Reflections: A History of McNairy County, Tennessee, 1823–1996*. Marceline, MO: Heritage House Publishing Company, 1996, 568–570.

launderer who did it for a very reasonable rate. The boys carried their dirty clothes to town and dropped them off with the laundryman and his family, who washed it and returned it in brown paper packages. This was a foreign concept to Junior until he moved to Texas. It only cost him a small amount of pocket change to have his clothes washed and pressed. It was a service he appreciated. Junior also spoke of the Judge's old kerosene refrigerator. It was a refrigerator that had a kerosene powered motor. The fuel went into the tank at the back. It was the first such refrigerator Junior had ever seen.

 As stated earlier, Junior bunked in the Judge's basement rather than the bunkhouse. This proximity to Judge Dinwiddie and his wife gave him a good opportunity to become close to the older couple. Indeed, he viewed the Judge as a second father. He respected and loved him as one would a father. The Judge's sons choose not to continue his ranch after his death. Perhaps the Judge sensed this early. They were very busy men and never visited him during Junior's one-year stint on the ranch. Perhaps Junior's own responsibilities and service to the country in the years to follow precluded such visits.

 As the Second World War was raging across the European continent and the Japanese were behaving savagely in the Pacific, the Judge made an unusual offer to Junior. He had considerable influence with the Swisher County Draft Board and decided to do everything possible to keep Junior out of the war. He wanted him to stay and help him and Murphy run the ranch. Judge Dinwiddie realized that men would become scarcer and that labor would come at a premium as an entire generation of young men was going off to war. Those left behind would have to engage in other necessary wartime activities.

 Yet Junior did not feel it was right for him to remain safely insolated on the Dinwiddie ranch while others of his generation faced the dangers of war. He was genuinely appreciative of the offer, but something about the whole proposition bothered him greatly. The Judge's sons were fighting in far-flung places throughout the world. Junior simply did not think it right for him to use his influence to keep him out of the war when apparently he did not do the same for his own sons. Junior respectfully turned his mentor and friend down. Seeing potential in the young man, the Judge even offered to sell him the ranch over a period of time. Again, Junior gently rejected the proposition.

In his old age, Junior would smile and muse on the possibility of having stayed out west. He often said he might have become quite the cattle rancher and done well at it. In fact, the Judge's own sons did not take over his operation. Eventually, the ranch was sold and the property used for other purposes. Junior never let these ideas and suppositions cloud his judgment or cause him any true regret. He always answered his own questions on the subject with a grin and a chuckle and changed the subject.

With mixed emotions, Junior left Texas in March 1942 and returned to Finger to help his father and await his own call to serve his country in the Second World War. There was much to consider and much still to be experienced. His adventures were only beginning.

Luther "Junior" Talbott as a school boy

Junior's parents Newton P. Talbott and Varham (Matlock) Talbott, Junior, and sister Vonnie Mae about 1925–1926.

Junior and Vonnie Mae about 1925.

Junior's grandfather, Henry Thomas Matlock

Junior, his aunt Belle (Matlock) Martin, mother Varham (Matlock) Talbott, and sister Vonnie Mae.

Junior Talbott and Vonnie Mae Talbott, about 1925.

Cassie (Matlock) Herring and her sister Belle (Matlock) Martin

The small town of Finger, Tennessee, as it looked when Junior grew up there in the 1920s and 1930s.

Newt Talbott and wife Varham (Matlock) Talbott in their grocery store in Finger, Tennessee, about 1930.

The Finger School where Junior was a student from 1927 until about 1938.

Hugh Allen Basham, teacher, coach, and principal at the Finger School. with whom Junior did not get along.

Logan McCaskill and wife Alice (McIntyre) McCaskill

Earl McIntyre and Vonnie Mae (Talbott) McIntyre

This photo was taken shortly after Junior returned to Finger from Tulia, Texas. Left to right: Jewel Durbin, Hayes Hayre, Junior Talbott, and Frank Walker.

Like Junior, Hobert Patterson (who was also from McNairy County) journeyed to Tulia, Texas, to find work during the Great Depression. He is pictured with his wife Cora and their young son.

5

A World in Turmoil

In early March 1942, Junior Talbott returned home to Finger, Tennessee. He came back with mixed emotions. He thoroughly enjoyed his time in the Texas Panhandle and wanted to stay. Judge Dinwiddie offered him exceptional opportunities and had taught him a great deal about ranching and cattle. Staying in Texas meant adopting a different world and a different career from what he would have back home. He would carve out a new life in a distant place, more distant because of transportation limitations at that time. It also meant he wouldn't be close to those he loved the most.

Junior was hesitant to return, but war was imminent. It was a conflict that had drawn in almost every nation in the world. He knew his time to enlist was coming. It was a matter of either being drafted or voluntarily choosing a branch of service. Being of an independent mindset, he wanted to make his own choice. "I sure didn't want to spend the war marching," he recalled. "I never did." His preference was to avoid the Army and see the world from somewhere other than an infantry unit.

While Junior was in Texas, the United States tried remaining neutral as events unfolded in distant lands. It had not been politically popular or expedient to support intervention. The "America First" movement had yielded great influence with figures such as Charles Lindberg and Henry Ford, who urged the country to refrain from waging war against Germany. President Franklin D. Roosevelt had narrowly won reelection to an unprecedented third term over Republican Wendell Willkie, a political novice from Indiana, by promising to keep American boys out of "any foreign wars." On October 30, 1940, he promised voters: "I have seen war and I hate war. Your boys are not going to be sent into any foreign wars!"[1]

However, Roosevelt knew he couldn't keep that politically charged promise. In fact, he was already working quietly with British Prime Minister Winston Churchill to find ways for the United States to assist the beleaguered British Isles in their lonely battle against the Third Reich. The surprise Japanese attack on the U.S. naval base at Pearl Harbor in Hawaii changed everything on December 7, 1941.[2]

There were other issues on Junior's mind than those in the headlines. His father's health was in question. Newt Talbott needed help at home before his only son was caught up in the war. The elderly merchant's health was slowly but surely failing. Although it was not known at the time, he was suffering from heart disease. He often found himself sweating profusely and hurting in his left arm and chest after any slight exertion. His eyesight was also failing. Junior was needed by his father and would prove helpful while he awaited the call to serve his country.

---

1. Mrs. Eula Kirkpatrick served as the local chairwoman for the Willkie presidential campaign in McNairy County in 1940.

2. Like many of the more conservative Americans at the time and especially later after the war, Junior Talbott always believed that Franklin Roosevelt had foreknowledge of the Japanese attack on Pearl Harbor. Junior died believing that Roosevelt had been provided intelligence regarding Japanese plans to cripple the U.S. Navy. He allowed the attack to ensure that the country would become actively engaged in the war, thus evaporating the opposition of the American First movement.

A WORLD IN TURMOIL

On March 16, 1942, business and activities in town were as busy as always. A funeral was going on. Thomas Naylor, a longtime resident of Finger and the town's well-known coffin maker had died and was being buried in the Finger Cemetery that very day. Naylor was a well-liked man and could work wonders with a piece of wood. His wife was known as "Aunt Mary Tom." Another relative was known as "Aunt Mary Lum." Both women were kindly old people who had long been fixtures in the small town. They were beloved by local children, including Junior.

On this day, Junior was putting up a partition wall for his father in the store. It was needed to divide the public portion of the store where folks shopped from the back area where Newt stored feed and stock. Mashing his thumb while hammering a nail, Junior walked out of the store and into the street, cursing and nursing his sore thumb. He saw a strange sight in the distant sky. The clouds were heavy and roiling, unsettled. Junior and the other men in town saw the great forces of a tornado blowing up to the south and east of town. The cycle of storms had already devastated Mississippi and would eventually tear through six more states, killing 156 people and injuring 1,105.[3] Junior went back into the store and grabbed his father. He guided him up the street to Albert Weaver's store. They were preparing to jump into a culvert behind the building when Junior and everyone else realized the storm was not going to strike the town itself.

Less than a mile up the road, Junior's childhood friend, Faye (Davree) McIntyre, was huddled with her family and three neighboring families inside Hartle Hayre's storm house. Hartle and Alma Hayre and their two sons, Hayes and Billy Lee, were already there when the others joined them. John Robert and Ollie Pearl (McCann) McIntyre and five of their six children—Helen, Lessie, Vivian, Faye, and J.R.—scrambled across the road and into the storm house. In no time, they were joined by an elderly couple, Fonzo and Ella Young, who lived just below Mount Carmel Cemetery.[4] Faye remembered well the moment. Mrs. Young was claustrophobic and all but refused to enter the storm house. The elderly neighbor kept saying she would "smother" and stayed just outside the shelter. The

---

3. An account of the tornado of 1942 may be found in John E. Talbott, *Let's Call It Finger! A History of North McNairy County and Finger, Tennessee and Its Surrounding Communities*. Dickson TN: BrayBree Publishing, 2015, 288-293.

4. The Youngs lived in the farm house that is now the home of the Bryan L. Talbott family.

others crowded inside. John Robert stood in the doorway of the shelter keeping an eye on the path of the storm. He watched the sky and the roiling clouds. After a moment, John Robert turned to Ollie Pearl and told her, "It got your Poppa's place."[5]

The quick moving storm moved further northeast and struck the homes and farms of Walter Smith, George Calvin Holmes, and Junior's old friend, Bud Smith. The Nelius Young residence, actually owned at the time by John Tedford, was badly damaged. The home of Newell and Lexie Cone was razed. The Cones survived by taking refuge in a nearby culvert. The Ervin Deaton place, which was also known as the old Carroll place and was occupied by Major McCaskill, was completely destroyed.

As the storm moved toward the Hopewell community, the Robert Bailey and Harmon Naylor places were demolished. Farther out, Inez (Walker) Moore, the young wife of Millard Moore, was killed. With his pelvis completely broken, Millard pushed her body and his injured young daughter, Sandra Kay, up the steep hills to seek help.[6] They were brought to Finger to see Dr. Tucker and taken to Bishop & O'Neal Funeral Home next door to Newt's store. Guy Bishop sent for Junior to pull Millard's work boots from his feet. Others had tried and failed, only causing him more intense pain and further injuring his pelvis. Because Junior had worn them in Texas, he knew better how to remove Millard's boots than anyone else in town.

Many friends and people whom Junior had known since he was a child were having their worlds turned upside down. There was much destruction in the old Bullman Store community. Many houses and barns owned by members of the Bullman family—Bud, Elvis, George, and Otis—were razed or badly damaged. Bud Bullman's store had been destroyed and Elvis Bullman injured.

Junior recalled the huge amounts of timber that were downed, gnarled and twisted. He remembered the livestock and chickens that were completely wiped out in the countryside. Sheets of tin from roofs

---

5. These stories were taken from oral histories conducted by the author in 1997 with Hayes Hayre, Faye (McIntyre) Talbott, Vivian McIntyre, and Lessie McIntyre. In referring to her Poppa's place, John Robert McIntyre meant the old home place of Arthur Marion Douglas "Whig" McCann, which was indeed destroyed. Living there at the time were Whig's widow, Celia (Weaver) McCann, and their son, Dell McCann. In the same neck of the woods, the cyclone hit and destroyed the Virgil and Arnelia Smith house and the old Dan Griswell homeplace.

6. Inez Walker Moore was the daughter of Murray F. Walker of Finger.

were wrapped around trees and, in one case, a tin sheet had sliced into an oak tree. He heard about a piece of straw embedded in a fence post. Such sights were common in storms that fierce.

Back from Texas, Junior assisted his father in the store and worked at the Finger Gin Company, of which Newt Talbott was a minority stockholder. Working with good men like Lawrence "Red" Robison and others, Junior learned much. He often told an interesting story about the majority stockholder, local Finger banker John R. Harris. A farmer arrived at the gin to have a cotton sample graded. He asked to see Mr. Harris. The gin manager asked Junior to take the farmer up the street to Home Banking Company to see the crotchety old man, who was also president of the bank. The vice president and cashier, Leonard Rankin, told them that Mr. Harris was sick and recovering at home. The farmer was seeking a loan to put in a crop and the amount was above Rankin's loan limit. Rankin directed Junior to walk the farmer up the street to the Harris home, which was located only a short distance from the bank.

Junior and the farmer walked up the hill and made their way to Harris' relatively new brick home. They were shown into his home office where the farmer made his case for a crop loan. Harris, ever a good model for Ebenezer Scrooge or old Jacob Marley, thought about the loan request for a few moments. He leaned back, looked at the man, and finally approved the loan. But Harris quickly added to the terms. He told the farmer, "But now I remember an unpaid balance at my store from a few years ago. I guess we can add that in...with interest, of course." Harris put his pencil to his pad and totaled the final principal amount of the loan. The farmer accepted the terms and he and Junior left. On the way back to the gin, Junior asked the farmer about the terms of the loan and the exorbitant amount of interest tacked onto his old grocery bill. The farmer told Junior, "In these times, you do what you have to do to get your crop in."

As the months wore on, Junior continued to work at both the cotton gin and the family store. His father's eyes had deteriorated to the point that he had to rub the edges of coins and feel their size in order to accurately count change.[7] The time and day in which Newt was running the store was much simpler. He closed his store at 11:00 A.M. and walked

---

7. After Junior's marriage to Faye McIntyre, Newt's eyesight had deteriorated so much that he could no longer write checks. Therefore, he had Faye write his checks.

home for lunch. If anyone was in the store when Newt closed it, they were invited to join him. Sometimes there would be two or three extra people at Newt's and Varham's dinner table. Junior's sister recounted there was always someone extra at the table. Nearly every Sunday, they had company for dinner or the entire weekend.

After several months and much anticipation, Junior learned that he was likely to be drafted into the army. Accurate or not, he felt it was imminent. He was nervous about being drafted and had no desire to be a "foot soldier" or "spend the war marching." So Junior and his boyhood friend, Hayes Hayre, decided to go to Memphis and join in the Coast Guard.[8] The officer on duty at the Memphis office told the two anxious young men to return to Finger, inform their local draft board in Selmer about their enlistments, and then await their call.

No more than a week after their visit to Memphis, they received the dreaded letter. Men across America received identical letters that began with a greeting from the President of the United States. Both Junior and Hayes were ordered to report to Fort Oglethorpe in Georgia to join the U.S. Army. This, of course, wasn't what either man wanted. Fortunately, Hayes found an opportunity to join the Army Air Corps and ended up in Arizona for the duration of the war, helping train new airmen in some capacity or another.

Junior took another chance to avoid the Army. He and another friend, Belver Hutcherson, traveled to Nashville to join the Navy. At the recruitment office, a naval officer questioned him about his status. Junior truthfully told him that he was to have reported to Fort Oglethorpe that very morning. Rather than chastise him as was probably in order, the officer

---

8. In his old age, Junior Talbott laughed heartily at this attempt to avoid the potential consequences of being drafted into the Armed Services. He was glad to have eventually entered the U.S. Navy, but he was never ashamed of making every reasonable effort to avoid the Army. Service in the U.S. Coast Guard was certainly no guarantee of safety in a world where German Wolf Packs were prowling the waters of every Allied nation and sinking ships. In fact, German submarines were sinking American cargo ships in Mobile Bay and prowling the terminus waters of major American rivers as well as many bays and harbors. In 1942, it was reputed that the waters from Mobile Bay to Corpus Christi, Texas, constituted the single most dangerous shipping lane in the world. For an American man to serve in the Coast Guard or the Merchant Marine rather than some other branch would not have been a shame to him or his family. Such service was more than honorable.

ordered him to wait where he was. He returned in a few moments with another officer, who instructed Junior to raise his right hand. He was sworn into the service of the U.S. Navy there on the spot, September 22, 1942.

There was a flurry of paperwork over the next two days. The young volunteer who had no desire to march or live what he saw as the drudgery of the Army began signing more paperwork than ever had in his life. On the day of his induction, Junior signed an Age Certificate in the presence of C.F. Armstrong, Chief Specialist, United States Naval Reserve, certifying his birthdate and place of birth.[9] On September 24, he was formally enlisted into the United States Navy for a period of two years with a rank of Apprentice Seaman, General Service and Specialists. His First Enlistment record and Identification record provides a detailed picture of Junior as a young sailor. He stood 5'9" tall, with a ruddy complexion, blonde hair, blue eyes, and weighed 145 pounds.[10]

At Nashville's Union Station, Junior met a lively young fellow named Grady Middleton, who hailed from Henderson County, Tennessee. The two had never met before and probably never guessed they'd meet again. They introduced themselves and as it turned out, both were there for the same purpose. Grady laughed quickly when Junior told him he was from a small town called Finger. Grady bellowed out, "Who the hell ever heard of Finger, Tennessee?" That statement would prove a little unintentionally prophetic. Grady would be the first of many young men whom Junior met along the way. He would served in the Navy throughout the war.

Following his impromptu swearing-in ceremony, Junior was told to remain in Nashville until ordered otherwise. He bided his time at the Maxwell House Hotel for a few days, simply waiting. Finally, on September 28, he received orders to report for training and duty at the Naval Training Station in San Diego, California.[11] He was assigned service number 641-24-05, a number he would never forget. He underwent a number of examinations. He was given instructions for using a gas

---

9. Luther Edward Talbott Compiled Service Record, FC2d, Division F, U.S.S. *Arkansas*, *Age Certificate*, National Archives, Washington, D.C. This document is somewhat confusing. The address for C.F. Armstrong is Jackson, Tennessee, but Junior never mentioned visiting a recruiting office there, only the effort to join the Coast Guard in Memphis and the last ditch (but successful) effort to avoid the Army at Nashville.

10. Ibid. *First Enlistment Record* and *Identification Record*.

11. Ibid.

mask and put through the gas chamber, a standard training tool of the day. He qualified in recruit swimming, having demonstrated the ability to swim fifty yards, tread water, and float on his back with motion.[12] Upon his arrival in San Diego, he also experienced what hundreds of thousands of other sailors experienced, the explanation of his legal rights under the Soldier's and Sailor's Civil Relief Act of 1940 and his application for National Service Life Insurance.[13] Even in war, business had to be addressed.

After two or three weeks in boot camp, Junior was called in for an aptitude test. There he met a lifelong friend, Philip Wilcox of Oklahoma. Both young men tested out as being particularly fit for fire control duty. However, neither they nor the other men in their group knew what "fire control" even meant. One suggested that perhaps they were going to fight fires should one break out on the ship. Others couldn't venture a guess. Finally, an old officer who overheard the discussion laughed and told them that a selection to fire control meant they had scored at a high aptitude. He explained that fire control meant work in the gun turrets, including firing, maintaining, and repairing the circuitry of the heavy and complex gun systems.

To better understand the duty that Junior would perform throughout the war, one must understand the concept. The fire control rating was relatively new when he was assigned the rating. It only came into existence in 1941, the same year that radar was introduced to the U.S. Navy. Essentially, there was a "marriage" of radar technology and gunnery to create its offspring, the fire control system. Its purpose was simple: to increase targeting accuracy. It is important to understand the significance of this history. The technology was only a year old when the young sailor from Finger was selected for the task. Men were chosen from the gunners' mates rating and designated as fire controlmen. This meant that Junior Talbott was among the first or second generation of sailors responsible for this new and innovative fire control technology.

Like his comrades, Junior was trained to both operate the fire control system and repair and maintain it. He underwent training in electronics as the system became more developed. One of his duties included helping to develop targeting solutions. This insured accuracy so the fire from

12. Luther Edward Talbott Compiled Service Record.
13. Ibid.

the guns of his assigned vessel, the U.S.S. *Arkansas*, would hit the enemy from the beginning of the shelling. Like other men in the fire control division, Junior either operated deep within the bowels of the *Arkansas* or from a tower far above deck. Other newer ships possessed combat information centers deep within their interior. The *Arkansas*, however, was a retrofitted old ship with alterations made to it as best as could be accommodated. The duties vested in Junior and his fellow sailors made them responsible for successfully carrying out surface-to-surface combat. The fire control systems, like the one installed on the *Arkansas*, functioned to allow the ship to better and more accurately conduct "over-the-horizon" targeting. The fire controlmen became key individuals in the naval bombardments during the battles of the Second World War. One of Junior's assignments was to spot enemy surface combatants using fire control radar who were far out of view otherwise. After he determined the identification of an enemy target, he had to calculate the firing distances and options and actually place the shots.

Junior often used the term "gun director" to describe his battle station. But it seems clear from his remembrances that he also worked as a rangefinder. Therefore, a discussion of the typical fire control system, like that installed on the *Arkansas*, is needed to better understand the system with which Junior worked. The basic components of a fire control system included the gun director, the rangekeeper, the stable vertical, and the gun turrets.[14] The gun director, Junior's usual battle station, was located in one of two places on the *Arkansas*. According to him, the ship contained two gun directors. One was located in a tower on the ship's superstructure. Its placement was simple. The position atop the highest place on the battleship allowed for as distant a horizon as possible. In essence, the operator of the director needed the best view he could get.

The *Arkansas* was far older than most ships fighting in the Second World War. This was a pre-World War I era vessel designed and built between 1910 and 1912 that was outfitted with state of the art electronic equipment designed for modern ships. Discrepancies were expected in how such equipment was utilized on the *Arkansas* as compared with newer battleships, destroyers, and cruisers built after 1940. When operating the gun director, Junior used optical equipment and radar to track

---

14. *Fire Control Fundamentals*. Rating Specialization Training Series. Bureau of Naval Personnel, 1953.

his targets. Once tracked, he measured the target's range, bearing (the direction from the *Arkansas* to the target), course, and speed.[15] All of this information was transmitted to the rangekeeper and stable vertical. These two components were located in the plotting room far below decks.[16]

The rangekeeper received the information and combined it with data regarding the *Arkansas*' course (i.e. information taken from readings of the gyroscope)[17] and speed (information provided by the pitometer log, the device used to measure the ship's relative speed to the water)[18]. The predicted target position was continuously computed by the rangekeeper. At this point, orders are relayed to the gun turrets that were equipped to automatically train and elevate the guns in keeping with the orders given by the rangekeeper. The stable vertical measured the inclination of the deck and supplied that information back to the director and the rangekeeper, who in turn incorporated the necessary corrections into their computations.[19]

From this explanation of the process it took to ascertain and fire upon an enemy target, a great amount of aptitude was required to understand and achieve these functions. Junior was always inquisitive and a highly intelligent young man. One can understand a little more why he was chosen for fire control school.[20]

15. Ibid. General information regarding the functions of the gun director and its operator.

16. Ibid.

17. The gyroscope is the device for measuring and/or maintaining orientation. It is based on the old principles of angular momentum, a physics principle whereby the measure of the amount of rotation an object possesses is computed by taking into account its mass, shape and speed. Technically and practically speaking, a gyroscope is a spinning wheel (or disc) in which the axle is free to assume any orientation. The orientation will not remain fixed for it will change in response to an external torque (the tendency of a force to rotate an object about an axis, fulcrum or pivot) much less and in a different direction that it would otherwise with the large angular momentum associated with the wheel's high rate of spin and moment of inertia (the mass property of a rigid body defining the torque needed for a desired change in angular velocity about an axis of rotation). The gyroscope's orientation remains nearly fixed, regardless of the mounting platform's motion (which on the oceans could be constant at times and varying greatly) because the mounting of the gyroscope in a gimbal (a pivoted support that allows the rotation of an object about a single axis) thereby minimizes the external torque.

18. *Fire Control Fundamentals*. Rating Specialization Training Series. Bureau of Naval Personnel, 1953, General information regarding the rangekeeper and its operations.

19. Ibid.

20. At the end of his service, Junior Talbott was offered two potentially rewarding opportunities. First, the Navy offered him the chance to re-enlist and enroll in an officer training program,

Junior completed his initial training on November 2, 1942. As a result of his exceptional aptitude tests, he was required to attend additional special schooling in both Newport, Rhode Island, and Norfolk, Virginia. At Newport, he was enrolled in both the Naval Training School and the Fleet Service School, where he trained for service in fire control.[21] His course of study began on November 9 and took sixteen weeks.[22] Classes included various forms of mathematics such as algebra, plane geometry, and calculus. He was scored on such abilities as mechanical aptitude, English, spelling, and radio aptitude. Junior didn't recount much about his actual schooling other than the courses were challenging and he worked diligently to get on an even plane with his peers. He had not studied such advanced courses in mathematics at either Finger High School or Chester County High School and felt far behind his fellow sailors. It took a while to catch on to such complicated subjects that were new and foreign to him, but he did relatively well before he finished. He completed Fire Control School with an 80.00 average, graduating 77th in a class of 138 sailors. While not spectacular, it was only the beginning of his training. He qualified as striker for Fire Control Third Class and on November 6, 1942, his rating changed from apprentice seaman to seaman second class by order of Lieutenant N.E. Walker.[23]

While stationed in Newport, Junior was going through the mess line in the cafeteria one morning and picked up a cup of coffee. After a quick taste, he put it down just as fast. The chief commissary officer noticed his apparent dislike of the coffee and questioned him about his sudden reflex. Junior explained that he did not like sugar in his coffee and couldn't stand drinking any that had been sweetened. Taking mental note of it, the commissary officer told him to go on through the line. When he got to the kitchen door to go back inside, he could get his coffee the way

---

but he had no desire to continue in the Armed Services. Second, the Sperry Gyroscope Corporation offered him a position with their company and the incentive to attend college and obtain his degree in engineering. He had the desire and was very tempted by the offer, but his fidelity to his aging and ill father stepped in and he rejected the offer in order to return home, help his father, and be near his family and that of his wife Faye.

21. Luther Edward Talbott Compiled Service Record. *First Enlistment*, National Archives, Washington, D.C.

22. Luther Edward Talbott Compiled Service Record. *Service School Record*, National Archives, Washington, D.C.

23. Ibid.

he liked it. He even offered to let him eat in the kitchen if he wanted. Junior recounted that the chief commissary smiled and told him he did not like sugar in his coffee either. Junior soon learned that your fellow sailors would look out for you.

During the same period, the temperature at Newport was stuck at around minus 40°. In the Navy, each day brought a different dress combination and differing uniform of the day.[24] On one particularly cold, brutal winter day, the dress of the day was announced and Junior and a few friends chose to supplement their uniform with their "watch caps." The watch cap was a heavy woolen cap with long thick flaps that could be pulled down to cover a sailor's ears to keep them from frostbite. On this day, a watch cap was not part of the sanctioned uniform. The slightly rebellious but very resourceful young sailors slipped out of their quarters with their watch caps hidden in their overcoats. They remained hidden until they disembarked from the ship. Once on the grounds and safely out of sight, these watch caps were slipped out and worn between the walk from the *Arkansas* to the men's destinations in town. Once safely in town and close to warmth, the sailors slipped the watch caps from their heads and back into their overcoats to be concealed.

After returning to the *Arkansas*, Junior and his friends were called into the office and questioned by a senior officer. He began by asking the young sailors "what they had done." In other words, he was seeking a voluntary admission of their guilt. However, the young sailors professed both an abundance of innocence and ignorance. The officer then expounded upon the issue of frostbite. He informed the young men that they were the only sailors who had returned to the ship without some form of frostbite. Many of their comrades had lost portions of their ears, including quite a few ear lobes, due to the extreme cold. As Junior recalled six decades later, the boys continued to claim their ignorance as to what the officer was seeking from them or what the problem might possibly be. The officer grew somewhat exasperated. "Look, there's no problem," he told them. "You're not going to get into any trouble. I just need to know what you fellows did to keep from getting frostbite. You

---

24. This story was recounted by Junior Talbott at his home late on the evening of Friday, December 17, 2004. The Newport *Daily News* of February 17, 1943, recorded temperatures as cold as minus 50° Fahrenheit. Local residents said their breath "froze audibly" and more than a dozen deaths occurred. Again, a contemporaneous source corroborated his memory.

must have done something different from the other boys. Just tell me what you did." Finally, one of the boys admitted they had done something. Junior spoke up and admitted they had worn their watch caps. The officer thanked them and said hopefully this would help lots of other boys. The next morning, the announcement for the uniform of the day came and included the words, "Watch caps!"

Junior's schooling in Newport, Rhode Island, lasted from late 1942 until February 27, 1943. His studies had been intense and grueling, but ultimately rewarding. He was a dedicated student and wanted to earn his rating. On February 27, 1943, he received his actual certification from Fire Control School there at the U.S. Naval Training Station, with an overall mark of eighty percent. Between October 1942 and this point, he'd seen more of the country than he'd ever known beforehand. Now he was now ready to see the world beyond the waters of the United States. The world that he had read about and studied in school was now at war. The oceans of which he had read did not contain mines and enemy submarines but his world now did. The history and geography books of his schooling did not teach him about fanatical armies and nationalists who saw death in combat as honorable. So many things were about to take on new meaning and make memories which would haunt and remain with the young sailor until his death as an old man.

There is a photograph of the new young sailor taken at the Electric Studio while in Newport. One can see the fresh young face of a boy from the countryside of Tennessee who had not yet heard the awful shrill of the angry gun or the whirring, winding engines of a suicide plane bearing down on his ship. He had not yet smelled the stench of battle or tasted of the ports of Europe or Africa. He had yet to lie awake at night worrying over German U-boats deep below him or floating mines waiting to be touched by the broadside of the ship. He was yet to be marked with the dark dreams of an experienced sailor on the front lines of the naval war. He was still the young kid easily recognizable on the streets of his hometown back in Tennessee.

On February 15, 1943, Junior was qualified as a stereo operator, with above-average marks, having outscored sixty-seven percent of his class.[25] Lieutenant N.E. Walker, USNR, noted five days later of him:

25. Luther Edward Talbott Compiled Service Record.

Complete(d) course of instruction in Fire Control School and recommended for striker for FC3c. By direction of the Chief of Bureau of Naval Personnel [,] this man must be assigned duty where his specialized training may be fully utilized. The attention of commands to which this man is transferred is particularly invited to this directive.[26]

On February 27, Junior was officially transferred to service aboard the U.S.S. *Arkansas* by order of Captain C.W. Magruder. He traveled from Newport, Rhode Island, to New York City for his assignment. There his particular skills would be utilized.[27]

Junior once remarked that his skills in targeting and fire control improved with use and practice. Still, it appears from the outset that his innate skill was there already. A restricted report from Office-in-Charge E.H. Kincaid at the U.S. Naval Training Station in Newport remarked on the training of all men trained on the Mark V Stereo Trainer. It pointed out that Junior Talbott was an "above-average operator" who outperformed sixty-six percent of his colleagues.[28]

Upon finishing fire control school, Junior, like his fellow sailors, was waiting around for his assignment. A bunch of the fellows pestered the executive officer's office and they were finally sent to Pier 92 in New York Harbor. Junior too was sent there to await his own orders. Finally, he was given orders by the office of the executive officer to transport a prisoner to the brig aboard the U.S.S. *Arkansas*. The prisoner happened to be a fellow from Maine also named Talbott. Junior boarded the *Arkansas* and informed the officer that he had a prisoner and was himself reporting for duty. Once the prisoner was processed, Junior was taken by another sailor to be processed and get settled in on the ship. The sailor assisting Junior was a Polish fellow who told him that all new sailors aboard any ship were expected at some point to do mess duty. Junior said he preferred

26. Luther Edward Talbott Compiled Service Record. *Professional Qualifications, Conduct, and Marks*, National Archives, Washington, D.C.

27. Ibid.

28. Luther Edward Talbott Compiled Serice Record. *Restricted Report*, February 15, 1943, National Archives, Washington, D.C.

to go ahead with mess duty and get it behind him because it would allow him time to study for his rating. He was detailed as a messman from April 1 until June 30, 1943, by order of Commander W.E. Lankenay.[29] This down time served him well. He was already aboard the *Arkansas* when he earned his third-class rating.

During his first days aboard the battleship, Junior was sitting trying to figure out a particular problem. Someone walked up behind him and asked, "Are you having trouble?" He responded, "Yes, sir," and looked behind him and realized it was Captain Carleton F. Bryant, who was the ship's skipper from 1941 to May 1943. Junior quickly jumped to his feet and saluted. After Captain Bryant returned the salute, he took Junior's papers and figures, showed him the problem, and helped him work it.[30] Bryant was an able officer whose career would take him even further up the ranks. According to Junior, Bryant was "one more good captain." He always had great respect for the skippers of the *Arkansas*. In his own opinion, he was fortunate to have served under very able and considerate officers.

It is important to understand the careers of the men under whom Junior and his fellow sailors served. Captain Carleton Fanton Bryant was a native of New York City, born on November 29, 1892. A 1914 graduate of the U.S. Naval Academy, he served five years on the battleship, the U.S.S. *Wyoming*. He later served three years of sea duty on the destroyer U.S.S. *Stribling* and the battleship U.S.S. *Pennsylvania*. From 1927 until the mid-1930s, Bryant served aboard the aircraft carrier, the U.S.S. *Saratoga*. He served in the Far East commanding three different vessels in the 1930s: the gunboats U.S.S. *Ashville* and U.S.S. *Oah* (which themselves have an interesting history in pre-war China) and a destroyer, the U.S.S. *Stewart*. The late 1930s and early 1940s found him commanding the U.S.S. *Charleston*, also a gunboat, and in Washington, D.C., working in the office of Naval Intelligence. In April 1941, Bryant was assigned to the *Arkansas*. It was he who commanded the old battleship across the

---

29. Luther Edward Talbott Compiled Service Record.

30. After Junior and Faye Talbott's deaths, their son, Ronald, found one of Junior's notebooks in their papers. The notebook contained examples of the mathematical problems and equations that he constantly studied in order to remain prepared for his vital duties aboard the *Arkansas*.

Atlantic Ocean for many of its convoy escort voyages. It was during this period that Junior met Captain Bryant.[31]

In late 1942, at age 21, Junior had never traveled abroad. In the words of the legendary American author, Mark Twain, he could certainly be an innocent abroad. At the time of his planned voyage out to sea, his farthest journey had been to San Diego, California. All he knew about foreign lands was what he had learned in school and read in books as a boy and a young man. He could not have forseen the sights and scenes that awaited him in far-flung foreign places and mysterious ports. His first few voyages were down the eastern seaboard from New York to Norfolk, Virginia. Likely he reached Newport, Rhode Island, by bus or train and came south. He never elaborated on the mode of transportation he took, just on the weather.

Like almost any sailor on any ship, Junior held not just great admiration and near reverence for the *Arkansas*, but also a perceptible love. This is not unusual. Most sailors held a great affinity for the vessel on which they served. Junior often referred to this old battleship as the "Arky" and referred to it generically as "she" and possessively speaking as "her." To understand these feelings, one must better understand the history of this venerable old battleship. The U.S.S. *Arkansas* (BB-33) had an interesting history prior to 1941, when the United States entered the war.

The U.S.S. *Arkansas* was the third *Arkansas* in the U.S. Navy's history. It was a Wyoming Class battleship and at the time of its construction was designated as Battleship No. 33. The ship was laid down at Camden, New Jersey, on January 25, 1910. It was constructed by the New York Shipbuilding Company and commissioned at the Philadelphia Navy Yard on September 17, 1912, with Captain Roy C. Smith commanding. She was launched on January 14, 1911, and christened by Miss Nancy Louise Macon. She was 562 feet or 171.2 meters long and her beam was 93 feet one inch or 28.3 meters long. Her draft was 32 feet or 9.7 meters. Her displacement was 26,100 long tons and 27,243 long tons at full combat load. In 1942 she possessed twelve 12" inch guns, six 5" guns, and eight 3" anti-aircraft guns.[32] The *Arkansas* was powered by four-shaft Parsons

---

31. All information pertaining to Admiral Bryant in this section may be found at https://www.history.navy.mil

32. The statistics regarding the U.S.S. *Arkansas* are found on the Maritime Quest website, http://www.maritimequest.com. These same statistics may be found in a number of sources and

steam engines and twelve coal-fired Babcock and Wilcox boilers rated at 28,000 shaft horsepower capable of 20.5 knots. In 1925, it underwent modernization at the Philadelphia Navy Yard and her twelve coal-fired boilers were replaced with four oil-fired boilers.

During its first month in service, the *Arkansas* participated in a fleet review by President William Howard Taft in the Hudson River at New York City in October 1912. Afterwards, the president boarded the vessel and she sailed to the Panama Canal Zone. At the time, the Canal was still unfinished and President Taft was conducting an inspection of the work. Eventually, the *Arkansas* returned him to Key West, Florida.

Beginning in late October 1913, the *Arkansas* began her first European tour, which was memorialized in a scrapbook of photographs and captions. In April 1914, following an earlier coup in Mexico that found dictator Victoriano Huerta in power, President Woodrow Wilson ordered the Navy to Veracruz, Mexico, to prevent the delivery of a shipment of arms for Huerta. The *Arkansas* was a part of that mission and landed troops (bluejackets) at Veracruz who took part in the street fighting that secured the city.

Among her early callers and guests was Franz von Papen, later Chancellor of Germany and afterwards Adolf Hitler's Vice-Chancellor, Ambassador to Turkey, and a celebrity defendant at the Nuremburg War Crimes Trials. During the Great War (now known as World War I or the First World War), the *Arkansas* was attached to Battleship Division 7 and carried out patrol duty on the East Coast, including the York River in Virginia, and trained gun crews for service on merchant marine ships.

In 1917, young cadets from the Naval Academy at Annapolis including the class of 1919 participated in what was term a "Youngster's Cruise." Among these young sailor cadets was a future *Arkansas* skipper, Cadet Wade DeWeese. A camera buff, DeWeese recorded the cruise in a lengthy photo album with typed captions entitled U.S.S. *Arkansas Youngster Cruise Album*. This original artifact is in the personal collection of the author as a part of the Captain Wade DeWeese papers and artifacts. This century-old album contains invaluable photographs of a young crew on a new battleship going about the business of manning a

---

may similarly be found on other internet websites on naval history and the histories of battleships including www.navsource.org/archives/01/33a.htm and http://rasputin.physics.uiuc.edu/~wiringa/Ships/Period3/ UnitedStates/Battleships/Arkansas.

battleship, sailors at play and relaxation, and the ports they made while on the cruise.

In July 1918, the *Arkansas* was ordered to Scotland to relieve the U.S.S. *Delaware*. Until the end of the war, she served with the British Grand Fleet as a part of the Sixth Battle Squadron. Immediately following the German surrender, the *Arkansas*, among other battleships, escorted the U.S.S. *George Washington* to Brest, France. The *George Washington* was carrying President Wilson to France for the beginning of his treaty negotiations, a very eventful and historic trip. Between 1919 and 1940, the *Arkansas* performed interesting and varied service.[33] Prior to the Second World War, she never fired a shot in actual combat.

The *Arkansas* sailed to Casco Bay, Maine, in the summer of 1941 and was present as the heavy escort for the U.S.S. *Augusta* in August. The *Augusta* carried President Roosevelt and British Prime Minister Winston Churchill as they participated in the Atlantic Conference. During this famous first conference between the two leaders, the *Arkansas* housed Undersecretary of State Sumner Welles and career diplomat and later Ambassador and New York Governor Averill Harriman. With the onset of war in December 1941, it would dedicate herself to duty as escort for troop and cargo transport.[34] The rest, as they say, is history.

Junior's first "over the ocean" voyage was a convoy escort to Morocco. That first long voyage was never forgotten. The young sailor was in awe and amazement at the size of the ocean before him. The unimaginable breadth of the Atlantic waters and the openness of the sky were in stark contrast to the small creek waters, woods, and fields he was long accustomed. Suddenly, the depths of the ocean seemed real as the large ships of the convoys—these "floating cities"—were underway. His big

---

33. A relatively detailed but overall brief history of the U.S.S. *Arkansas* (BB-33) may be found at http://www.warships1.com/US/USbb33-history.htm

34. The U.S.S. *Arkansas* served as what was known as an escort ship. An escort ship did just that. It escorted troop and supply convoys across the Atlantic Ocean to keep them safe from Axis navies and the scourge of German submarines. The *Arkansas*, among other such convoy escort ships, protected the convoys and engaged in battle when necessary to protect the precious cargo of supplies and men. Eventually, she would be called upon to directly participate in such campaigns as the Normandy Invasion, the assault on Cherbourg and Southern France, Iwo Jima, and Okinawa.

adventure was beginning, with all of its tragedies, triumphs, toils, and troubles to come.

It was also Junior's first sight of a great naval convoy. On this voyage, the *Arkansas* was acting as a command ship for a troop transport convoy to North Africa. The fresh troops aboard the convoy ships would be supplied as replacement troops to the Allied Forces under the command of British Field Marshal Bernard Montgomery. At that time, the North African Campaign of Montgomery and Rommel had already ended with Rommel's defeat at El Alamein in November 1942.

The voyage began when the *Arkansas* left New York City on April 2, 1943. The route to Casablanca lay between the 30° and 40° parallels. For a young man accustomed to such small streams as Huggins Creek, Hogwallow Creek, and Bushel Creek, suddenly moving through New York Harbor into the great wide Atlantic Ocean was an experience to remember. His first recollection was of a body of water that seemed to stretch out before his eyes forever. The *Arkansas*, the grand old lady she was, made her way across the dangerous waters of the Atlantic Ocean and eventually to the northwestern coast of Africa to Casablanca, Morocco. The sight of first entering a foreign port, especially as exotic as one in North Africa, was especially exciting for the young sailor.

Upon arriving in port, the *Arkansas* stayed for about seven to eight days. Usually the ship remained long enough for the sailors in each section to have time to go ashore on liberty leave. Shore leave and liberty leave are often used interchangeably. Still, the concept is the same: it is the leave which sailors enjoy on dry land. In much earlier days, sailors were often renowned for their raucous and drunken sprees while on such reprieves.

As was customary, the commander would send shore patrol to keep military order. Volunteers were usually called for; if none did so, a sailor would be ordered ashore for such duties. Junior preferred to take shore patrol upon his first time at any port. There was a very practical reason for this choice. While on shore patrol, he could educate himself by learning the cities of port, their streets, the hot spots, the night spots, points of interest, and places to avoid. He could learn the location of the local markets, the local watering holes, the various neighborhoods, and get a feeling for the characters. Armed with this knowledge, Junior could take greater advantage of his liberty call and better use his time while in that particular port.

Junior often commented on various aspects of shore patrol. A sailor was entrusted with a .45 caliber handgun while carrying out his patrol. After shore patrol was completed, he was typically required to return his firearm. Interestingly, an officer issuing the .45 caliber handgun to Junior grew tired of going through the motions in regards to issuing and collecting the gun. He told Junior just to keep the pistol and return it at the end of the war when he was to be discharged from the Navy. When his service time was nearing the end, Junior tried returning the weapon as instructed. Apparently, it had been listed as missing and lost. The officer told Junior he could just keep the pistol and no one would know otherwise. He was afraid to keep it and instead returned it as a precaution.

Often on shore patrol, Junior and most sailors would find some nice young lady with whom to spend time while working. It was not difficult to find a date in port. Young ladies made themselves available to sailors and soldiers and provided company. Once, Junior and a fellow sailor hooked up with a couple of young ladies in a European port. As the four young people walked along, the two sailors told the girls, "If you see an officer approaching, drop back behind us a little." As it happened, they ran into a junior division commander. The young ladies took their cue and fell in behind a few steps and took on a nonchalant air. The officer passed by, and saw the two young sailors doing their jobs efficiently. When he was out of view, the young ladies stepped up their pace and returned to their sailor companions without causing them any trouble.

Morocco seemed both mysterious and fascinating to Junior. He quickly developed some opinions about his first port of call. Parts of Casablanca were decent, but others were deplorable. According to Junior, the ports of Morocco were filthy places. Although not a palatable opinion by today's standards, he viewed the people as little more than savages. Many memories became indelible to the young sailor and were carried with him throughout his life. He recalled that the natives of the North African nation bought mattress covers from the sailors. They would cut holes in the covers for their head and arms and slip them on. Once adorned with these covers, they were worn until they practically rotted off their backs. A lack of understanding of this foreign culture certainly did not help matters.

However, it was a bit much to expect from a rural West Tennessee boy experiencing such sights for the first time. The native population lived in a manner to which he was not accustomed.

In a related manner, Junior often recounted a story relayed to him by one of his relatives, Perry Barton, regarding island natives that he encountered. According to Barton, who was stationed in the vicinity of New Zealand, he and his colleagues grew tired of seeing the native women's bare breasts and so they gave them T-shirts in order to cover them. The next day, the boys discovered that the native women had modified the T-shirts by cutting holes out for their breasts. Junior found Barton's account very humorous. The poor guy tried!

As for Casablanca, there were plenty of open air markets. In the streets and alleyways, Junior saw many things being peddled: linens, handmade trinkets and jewelry, rugs, foods, pottery, and other goods. The markets were really bazaars. They were crowded and filled with people of all types. There were soldiers and sailors of all nationalities passing through the markets, walking past tents and tables with native men and women selling their wares. The Allied fighting men weren't the only ones milling around; there were also other Moroccans and Europeans living in North Africa. Junior recalled these strange sights but even more, he remembered the sounds and smells of these places: food cooking, cigarettes, cigars and pipes smoking, incense burning, the sounds of vendors and customers haggling and bargaining, and music being played by street musicians and beggars. These were sights and sounds he had never heard in his life.

Junior was fascinated by the butcher shops he saw in Casablanca. They were operated out in the open or at best in some cavernous metal building that was exposed in many places. The ceilings were approximately twenty feet tall and the fronts were open with the sides closed. There appeared to be no form of refrigeration. With temperatures during the summer months easily reaching 100°F or more, the butchered meat was pungent and could easily be smelled as the flies buzzed constantly. The winter temperatures were no better, still reaching levels in excess of 80°F. The smells were awfully strong and far different from anything Junior experienced back home. He often spoke of passing through the open-air markets and seeing large carcasses hanging out which he always believed to be the carcasses of camels. Junior once proclaimed, "They were hellacious animals!" He thought the large animals must have been dressed at night. Indeed, he never saw one being dressed but he saw the carcasses hanging large and heavy, flies and all.

Speaking of the city and these areas of the city, Junior declared, "It was pitiful!" He believed the back alleys and marketplaces alike were dirty and full of sketchy characters, men and women of questionable motives who were mysterious and strange. Still, they were characters and he never forgot them or their appearances. The women wore dresses and head coverings. The men wore coverings and often headdresses of their own or colorful woven caps. Outside official buildings stood men in white uniforms and in the doorways of ancient buildings often sat the elderly. There were parts of the city where the buildings had a modern feel and the streets were broad. In other parts, the buildings were decaying and the alleys could vary from very narrow to very wide. In the bazaars, the merchants and farmers peddled their goods from wooden crates and boxes and oftentimes from large woven baskets. Pack animals and camels could be seen in these areas milling around or standing awaiting an opportunity to serve their masters.

There was a brig in Casablanca used for jailing unruly and lawbreaking servicemen. Sometimes visits to the local wet spots resulted in an overnight stay. A sailor could sit on a barstool in the bars of the city all day and drink his whiskey, beer, and wine and it wouldn't bother him at all. However, the minute he walked out the door and into the street, he would pass out almost immediately. "It would just hit you in the face, just like a board," Junior recalled with mirth and laughter. The bars were usually cooler than other places in Casablanca and they were fairly dark inside. The difference in light and temperature caused a sailor to get an unexpected rush when he walked out onto the hot, dusty streets. Down at the dock, there were areas where the drunken sailors were placed. Their sober comrades would file by, pick them up, and carry them back to their respective ships.

Junior recalled the bars and dives of Casablanca as he experienced them. They carried on their business in many of the customary ways that any such place does. Some were very small, just a "hole in the wall" with enough room for a bar and a few stools and tables. They were grimy and littered with local characters, dark men in fezzes sitting quietly or talking in low tones to one another.[35] Others were a little more grand, maybe nothing like "Rick's Café Américain" in Casablanca, the movie based on the port city, but still nicer than a speakeasy. These nicer bars included some entertainment and were clean. The soldiers and sailors of the Allied powers more readily congregated in these places. One must remember that Casablanca was only liberated after Operation Torch in November 1942. Before then, it had been in German and Vichy French hands. It was still a place of intrigue and certainly full of mystery for young sailors and soldiers from rural America.

Casablanca had fairly wide streets and even the alleys were often somewhat wide. On one hot afternoon, while on shore patrol, Junior and another sailor rushed down an alley to assist a fellow sailor who was being robbed by native Moroccans. Apparently, the sailor was not as drunk as his thieving assailants originally thought and was putting up a pretty good fight. The thieves weren't going to abandon their robbery attempt until Junior and his fellow patrolman readied their guns. Upon hearing the familiar noise of an automatic firearm ready to open fire, the native derelicts fled, leaving the bewildered but quickly sobering sailor with his colleagues. Indeed, the dangers of a North African port city were real.

Morocco was an old French colony. Junior's arrival in Casablanca constituted his first encounter with French culture, the Islamic culture, and the mixture of both. These people were not like anything he had ever seen or encountered. The men were dressed in some form of robes and often wore turbans and beards. They could have been herders or farmers or street vendors. Junior watched them all carefully and concerned himself of all his own movements. He certainly didn't want to wander off in the wrong direction and wind up a non-battle casualty. Danger abounded in this port city.

The city was full of intrigue and that was evident even to a young man from West Tennessee. Because it had only been a short time since the coastal country was liberated by Allied forces, there was still uneasiness about the place. Despite the times and circumstances, Junior found

---

35. In his war dispatches published in *Once There Was a War*, novelist John Steinbeck (1902–1968) gave a colorful and apt description of the North African port city of Algiers. He described the sights and sounds of that city which were not unlike those seen and heard in Casablanca and other North African port cities. John Steinbeck, *Once There Was a War*. New York: Penguin Books, 2007, 105–108.

the introduction to North Africa's mixture of French and native culture very interesting. His experience with various cultures was mixed. With the Italians, he could half understand them because of his studies in Latin and foreign languages back at Chester County High School. He understood these people better than the Irish or the English. He sometimes found the native tongues of the British Isles more difficult to understand than others of which he had no experience. The Irish, he once said, "chopped it up and used all that slang." He found the quick and easy brogue of the Irish to be interesting but extremely hard to listen to because of its oddities.

When the sailors were on shore patrol in North Africa, they carried one canteen of water. They were told that if they exhausted their supply of water, they were to buy wine. Under no circumstances were the sailors to drink the water in Morocco. The sewage problem there was one worthy of alarm. In some parts of the city, the side ditches were full of raw sewage. Drinking wine would prevent terrible disease and possible epidemic on the ship. It was the sewage and filth that turned Junior's stomach and nose against Morocco.

It wasn't only the stench that bothered him in Casablanca. The place was dangerous. Like most cities, it had areas that the men were discouraged from visiting. For example, one quarter of the city, the Bousbir Quarter, was renowned for prostitution. Then there were the outlying villages. There were strict orders from the ship's officers to stay away from those outlying villages and the natives. These were places of mystery and intrigue to outsiders. They were certainly a peculiar people to young men from rural areas and even some cities. One young sailor from the *Arkansas* strayed out into the villages of the natives, whom Junior called "Arabs." It was assumed he went there looking for female companionship. Perhaps the sailor had other reasons for walking the dusty paths branching off these foreign streets, but that will never be known. Unfortunately, the young man never returned to the ship. After the *Arkansas* had been out to sea a day or so, a message was received via radio that the young man had been found. He was not AWOL (absent without leave); he was dead. His throat had been cut. Junior understood that the young man's body was sent home for burial. Because he did not die at sea, he could not be buried at sea.

In regards to burials at sea, this subject was very personal and evoked great emotion in Junior. There were few occurrences or events that he could hardly bear to discuss when it related to his naval service. However, one he found extremely difficult to discuss was the death and burial of Peter Paul Konosky, a coxswain and shipmate of Junior's aboard the *Arkansas*. Junior did not know him personally; at least he claimed no such relationship. But they served together and were brothers in arms, and that's all that mattered. Konosky underwent an appendectomy on board the ship. Somehow, he was poisoned by noxious fumes and died during or shortly after the surgery. Coxswain Konosky was buried at sea with full military honors.

Junior always recalled the actual ceremony with tears and became choked in his words. The officer of the deck called for "all hands bury the dead!" The *Arkansas* had stopped to a halt and was floating with its flags lowered to half-mast. The crew was assembled on deck along with a firing party, a bugler, and the casket bearers. The crew stood at parade rest as the ceremony began. The flag-covered casket of Coxswain Konosky was carried feet first to the deck and placed overboard. The *Arkansas*' chaplain, Commander D. S. Robinson, an older fellow, performed the ceremony. Afterward, the firing party was ordered, "Firing party, present arms!" At that point, the eight casket bearers tilted the platform and Coxswain Konosky's body slid into the ocean.

A three-volley salute was fired and the bugler played Taps. After the flag that covered the casket was folded, the ceremony ended. Coxswain Konosky had been laid to rest in the depths of the ocean. Junior said that a burial at sea was indeed the most touching and emotional of all experiences in the Navy. It was one of the saddest things he ever saw. Although he knew it was a great honor for a sailor to be buried at sea, he often wondered about Coxswain Konosky, his death, and the fact that he never got to enjoy the peacetime. It did not matter that Junior did not personally know him. Again, he was a fellow sailor and comrade in arms—a fellow human being—and another young man serving his country who wanted one day to go home.

6

Adventure and Peril in the Navy

The *Arkansas* left Casablanca on April 19, 1943, and sailed back to New York City to dock in the Brooklyn Navy Yard on April 28. The voyage became a familiar one. The destination was usually Pier 92 in New York Harbor or the Brooklyn Navy Yard. Junior often recalled the approach to the world's busiest shipping ports, the great ships that came in, and the busy nature of these ports. They were large cavernous places full of warehouses and loading docks. The berths were long and relatively narrow. Men and cargo were moving briskly and the great powers of commerce and business were busy at work as war activities kept the ports teeming with life.

The longshoremen and dock workers were interesting people who spoke a language all their own. Their accents were new and very different to the young sailor from West Tennessee. They were tough, weathered, experienced men. He could easily see the New York skyline in the distance. It was a far different sight from the plains of Texas or the hills of north McNairy County. Commerce and industry were everywhere and moving in tandem together to win the war.

At New York City, the *Arkansas* took on supplies and underwent minor repairs and alterations. During that period, old battleships like the *Arkansas* had to be altered to allow for continued use in modern times. On May 26, 1943, it left the Brooklyn Navy Yard and sailed for Norfolk, Virginia, arriving the next day. The trip up the eastern coast was never particularly memorable. It was usually very peaceful and gave young sailors time to think about home and more pleasant things than what darker possibilities lay ahead of them. At Norfolk, the ship took on a number of young midshipmen whose purpose on board was to complete their training.

During that time, Junior was enrolled in Fleet School in the Portsmouth/Norfolk, Virginia area, studying the repair and operation of fire control equipment. This was a vital component to the work of a sailor in the fire control section. It was important for a fire control officer to know the technology. Junior became a talented technician as well as a dependable man sighting and firing during the heat of action. Versatility, technical knowledge, and skill, were vital to successful fire control.

While in Fleet School, Junior received a postcard from his friend, Philip Wilcox. The two had grown close. He had given Junior the nickname "Hillbilly." Philip had a pass home to Oregon while Junior was "stuck" in school studying harder than he ever had in his life. Knowing full well where Junior was, Philip wrote him on August 30, 1943:

> Hi, Hillbilly,
> Sure am enjoying myself here in my old stomping grounds.
> Am going on to sweet home tonight so will write you then.
> I sure would not trade places with you now.
>
> As ever,
> Philip

The little postcard adorned with Indians in full headdress was formally addressed to L.E. Talbott, S 1/c, Fleet Services School, Fire Control Division, Norfolk, Virginia.

While he was enrolled in Fleet School, Junior spent much of his time studying, reading, solving mathematical equations, working trajectory problems, and sharpening his skills. He was expected to calculate a trajectory problem or solve a complicated mathematical equation in his head under stressful circumstances. Still, Fleet School meant a reprieve from dangerous Atlantic passages. On dry land or in dock, the young sailor was momentarily free from the worry of unseen mines or lurking submarines.

Junior's academic endeavors at Naval Fleet School were likely taxing, especially after a four-year absence from secondary school. He entered Elementary Fire Control School on July 24, 1943, just one day after his twenty-second birthday. His studies were intense and far more advanced beyond anything he had studied to that point. His courses included: mathematics, electricity, fundamentals of fire control, rangefinders, rangekeeper (Mark 7), stable elements and Thyratron, rangekeeper (Mark 8), radar, spotting and identification, director system (Mark 37), hydraulics and gun instruments, torpedo director (Mark 27), and director systems (Mark 45 and 51). Junior persevered through ten intense and exhaustive weeks and graduated on October 2, 1943. He finished eighth in a class of twenty-four achieving a GPA of 3.456. Upon his completion of Fleet Service School and Elementary Fire School School, he was assigned the rank of Fire Control Third Class.[1]

On October 4, the *Arkansas* left Norfolk and sailed back to New York City, arriving the next day. The ship's crew took on supplies and received their next assignment. They departed for Bangor, Ireland, on October 17. It was another convoy, another chance at unseen warfare—and possibly a watery grave in the oceans deep. Fortunately, the *Arkansas* arrived safely, along with her charges, and remained in Ireland until December 1, 1943.

This lengthy stay in Ireland provided Junior with a number of memories. He and his fellow sailors went ashore every fourth night. Usually the boys got at least one liberty, sometimes two, while docked on the Emerald Isle. He recalled that Ireland was "real nice" and the people

---

1. *Change in Rate or Reserve Class*, September 28, 1943. Luther Edward Talbott Compiled Service Record, FC2d, Division F, U.S.S. *Arkansas*, National Archives, Washington, D.C.

were very friendly. The country was as clean as "you could expect to be bombed and everything like that."

Both Belfast and Bangor had been bombed by the *Luftwaffe* (the German air force) in April 1941. These blitzes from above were not readily forgotten by their victims. Junior was always amazed at European efficiency and the ability of its people to endure bombardment in the morning and begin cleaning, recovery, and rebuilding efforts by the afternoon. Once the fires died out and the skies were clear of enemy bombers, the residents of European cities, towns, villages, and hamlets—whether they were British, Irish, or German—began stacking bricks, lumber, and other building supplies and salvaging furniture and furnishings to rebuild.

Junior recalled that the street buses had a very large bag resembling a balloon on the roof that carried the fuel needed to power them. Many of these resembled the popular two-tier vehicles. They were operated on a system of compressed coal/gas systems as a result of wartime petrol rationing. A hundredweight of burning coal enabled a bus to travel approximately 100 miles, allowing them to stay on the road and in business.

Ireland was an ancient land with buildings that were older and quite different from anything Junior had ever seen. His noticed that the villages were old and the buildings were well-worn and appeared to be low slung, not tall. Nothing looked new or refurbished. The green and lush lands stuck in his mind as well. He observed the sheep that were a mainstay on the Irish landscape. Seen from afar, they formed little white dots as they grazed on green, ancient fields. The young sailor was impressed by the flax market that flourished there. He took note of the agricultural and economic pursuits in the counties and territories where he visited.

While in Ireland, the *Arkansas* docked in Bangor and Belfast. Junior recalled the good Irish rye whiskey of which one could partake while on liberty. The pubs served no greater purpose than for one to walk in, begin drinking, and absorb the local flavor. There were certain hours that were busier than others and there were always plenty of locals leaning on the bar who were happy to see the sailors. Junior recounted that many good old stories, tales, and folklore were told and retold in these old Irish pubs. As a storyteller himself in old age, he relished memories of the old Irishmen telling their stories and anecdotes.

The romance of the warm old pubs was not lost on the young sailor from Tennessee. He visited them for all of the usual reasons. They were old with low ceilings and a well-worn and lived-in feeling about them. Space was tight and the old tables were occupied by men whose faces full of "character." The bar was usually full of the same types of characters, leaning into their drinks and trading talk with the barkeeper. They were laborers, farmers, tradesmen, local professionals, and men of many walks in life who gathered to pass the time with one other.

Interestingly, it was in a pub that Junior got a "lesson" in Talbott family history. He was visiting an establishment in Plymouth, England. As he sat at the bar, his cap lay on top with the inside facing up. The bartender saw that the name tag read "L.E. Talbott." He himself was a Talbott and could have been as young as thirty-five or as old as middle-aged. The bartender told Junior that his own grandfather of some degree had three brothers who had left the British Isles and ventured to the new world of North America. This account was in keeping with similar stories Junior had earlier heard regarding three Talbott brothers who had migrated to America. Of course, to hear it often told, every family had three brothers who came to America. Although it is possible, one may never know the actual origins of the family.

Ireland was one of the *Arkansas'* ports of call during the war and played a role in the ship's history. The U.S.S. *Arkansas* (BB-33) served as a command ship in transport convoys that carried supplies, men, and equipment to the European theater. Prior to the fall of 1944, the major path of transport with which the *Arkansas* was concerned was the Atlantic Ocean. It would eventually become the cold, watery graveyard for thousands of sailors and ships great and small, as well as the permanent dumpsite for inordinate amounts of needed supplies that would never be utilized for the war effort. Needless to say, the convoys that dared cross this ocean—which author James Joyce called a "bitter bowl of tears"—were constantly the target of and under the threat of the dreaded German submarines, the U-boats.

Junior's recollections of the quiet nights and tense days crossing the Atlantic Ocean are likely representative of many sailors serving on convoy escorts in the early 1940s. Like his fellow shipmates, he often found himself in deep thought and reflection as the old battleship powered its way across the ocean and between the continents. It is important to understand the nature and structure of Atlantic convoys during the first years of the Second World War and their involvement in that greater campaign known today as the "Battle of the Atlantic." The Battle of the Atlantic was itself the longest running, continuous military campaign of the war. The campaign was multi-faceted in that Allied Naval Forces had blockaded Germany and the German Navy, in turn, with its U-boat fleets, were making every effort to starve Britain by sinking commercial and cargo shipping. That phase of the war lasted from 1939 until 1945.

The Battle for the Atlantic was to be Junior's first real experience with the dangers of war. The importance of the effort being made to protect Allied shipping cannot be underscored. Winston Churchill himself set forth its importance afterwards, stating:

> The Battle of the Atlantic was the dominating factor all through the war. Never for one moment could we forget that everything happening elsewhere, on land, at sea or in the air depended ultimately on its outcome.[2]

Indeed, Churchill's reflection was correct. The British Isles could not survive without the provisions being shipped across the Atlantic Ocean from North America.

Escorts such as the *Arkansas* protected cargo ships carrying steel, iron, coal, fuel, foodstuffs, munitions, and arms, as well as manufactured goods and raw materials. The ships carrying war materiel to Britain did so in convoys in an effort to achieve safety in numbers. Ships traveling alone were easy prey for German U-boats, the warships of the German Navy (called the Kriegsmarine), and the German Air Force, the famed Luftwaffe. Therefore, they traveled in convoys protected by battleship escorts and contingents of faster, lighter destroyers.

The dangers encountered by Junior and his fellow sailors, American or otherwise, cannot be understated. The waters of the Atlantic Ocean were absolutely treacherous. According to Churchill, between January 1940 and April 1945, German U-boats caused the loss of 300,000 tons or 600 million pounds of cargo. Between January 1944 and August 1945,

---

2. John Costello and Terry Hughes, *The Battle of the Atlantic*. London: Harper Collins, 1977.

218 Allied ships were lost, resulting in the loss of 969,331 gross tons of shipping or almost 2 billion pounds of ships and materiel.[3]

According to Commander Walter Karig, USNR, the most important task before the U.S. Navy was to ensure the effective and safe delivery of war materiel to the United Kingdom and the Soviet Union. It became more difficult when troops had to be transported to North Africa, Italy, and France. There was also the problem of protecting shipping right off the coast of the United States.[4] There were no safe waters for American ships during the course of the war.

Junior described the convoys as a large operation with everyone very coordinated and knowing their duties so well that they were second nature. This may be over-simplification, but essentially every man implicitly knew his job and went about it efficiently under the ever-present fear of a silent enemy and a potentially fiery and ultimately watery death lurking below the hulls of their ships. Still, Junior recalled the grandness of these convoys, saying they were a "hell of a sight to see" that meant all the more when you were aboard one. He also described the overwhelming sense of relief and emotion one felt upon seeing the shoreline of a friendly port. This meant not only had you survived a perilous journey across rough seas and survived hostile powers, but your mission was accomplished and the war in Europe would and could continue.

Perhaps no one epitomized the Trans-Atlantic convoy better than historian Samuel Eliot Morison. In his work *The Two-Ocean War: A Short History of the United States Navy in the Second World War*, he described the grand spectacle:

> A convoy is beautiful, whether seen from a deck or from the sky. The inner core of stolid ships in several columns is never equally spaced, for each has her individuality; one is always straggling or ranging ahead until the commodore becomes vexed and signals angrily, "Number So-and So, take station and keep station!" Around the merchant ships is thrown the

---

3. Winston S. Churchill, *The Second World War, Volume 6: Triumph and Tragedy*. Boston: Houghton Mifflin Company, 1950, 545, 724.

4. Commander Walter Karig, Lieutenant Earl Burton, and Lieutenant Stephen L. Freeland, *Battle Report: The Atlantic War*. New York: Farrar & Rinehart, Inc., 1946, 91.

ADVENTURE AND PERIL IN THE NAVY

screen like a loose-jointed necklace, the beads lunging to port or starboard and then snapping back as though pulled by a mighty submarine elastic; each destroyer nervous and questing, all eyes topside looking for the enemy, sound gear below listening for him, radar antennae like cats' whiskers feeling for him. On dark nights only a few shapes of ships a little darker than the black water can be discerned; one consults the radar screen to ascertain that the flock is all there. To one coming topside for the dawn watch, it is a recurring wonder to see the same ships day after day, each in her appointed station, each with her characteristic top-hamper, bow-wave, lift and dip; the inevitable straggler, the inveterate smoker, the vessel with an old shellback master who "knew more about shipping forty years ago than any goddam gold-braid in a tin can," and whose sullen fury at being convoyed translates itself into belated turns, unanswered signals and insolent comebacks. When air cover is furnished there are darting, swooping planes about the convoy; upon approaching port, the stately silver bubble of a blimp comes out, swaying in the breeze and blinking a cheery welcome.

There is nothing beautiful, however, about a night attack on a convoy, unless you see it from a submarine's periscope. A torpedo hit is signaled by a flash and a great orange flare, followed by a muffled roar. Guns crack at imaginary targets, star shell breaks out, a rescue ship hurries to the scene of the sinking, and sailors in other ships experience a helpless fury and dread. If the convoy has a weak escort it can only execute an emergency turn and trust that the rest of the wolf-pack will be thrown off or driven down; if the escort is sufficient a "killer group' peels off, searching relentlessly with radar and sonar, while everyone stands by hoping to feel underfoot the push of distant depth charges that tells of a fight with a submerged enemy."[5]

---

5. Samuel Eliot Morison, *The Two-Ocean War: A Short History of the United States Navy in the Second World War*. Boston: Little, Brown and Company, 1963, 106-107.

This description of the convoys and the adventures experienced by them is an apt description that gives insight to Junior's own comments. He once described a well-conducted convoy itself as a "beautiful sight!" "You did not want lose a ship," he said. Extra care was taken to do your "damnedest" to fulfill your duties in order to keep the convoy's "machinery" well-oiled and operating without a hitch. He spoke of the blackouts of the convoys and the orders to keep quiet when it appeared a threat lurked nearby. He found humor in the behavior and attitude of non-military skippers who felt they knew the seas and oceans far better than their allied Naval counterparts. In fact, in those years, old sailors and skippers were often very earthy and cantankerous types who'd seen the world from one rust bucket or another in and out of far-flung ports across the globe. One must wonder though how humorous Junior viewed things in 1942 to 1945 and if his humor was gained when a young man becomes old and somewhat cantankerous himself.

To keep merchant and commercial shipping afloat—and thus England afloat—the convoys were well protected by British transports and a heavy American escort of battleships, destroyers, and cruisers. The battleships provided the heavy firepower while the cruisers and destroyers afforded speed where needed. Upon approaching their destinations, the convoys were given further protection by air escorts that could strike within miles of reaching shore.

One area of extreme activity by the German Navy's submarine fleet was the region of the Azores, a group of islands in the Atlantic Ocean's sub-region known as the Mid-Atlantic Ridge. The archipelago of the Azores is one composed of nine volcanic islands located approximately 930 miles west of Lisbon, Portugal. In 1943, the Portuguese leased bases in the Azores to the British government. The activities of the British in the Azores, code-named Operation Alacrity, were crucial to the Allied war effort. The British bases there allowed the Allied forces to provide aerial coverage in the region. This assisted in hunting U-boats which in turn helped protect the Allied convoys. Yet enemy submarine activity persisted in the waters off the Azores. The reason for the great concentration of German naval forces was the decision of neutral Portugal to allow the British and the United States to use these islands for such bases. An examination of voyage maps of the *Arkansas* shows a complete avoidance of these islands during the war. However, in order to better understand the reasons for the *Arkansas*' avoidance of the Azores and their role, a more complete discussion is required.

In April 1941, both British and U.S. Naval chiefs were concerned with U-boat activities around the region of the Azores. British Prime Minister Winston Churchill recalled in his history of the Second World War that Allied commanders strongly suspected the Germans of planning to seize the Azores as a base for aircraft and the German submarine fleet.[6] According to Churchill:

> These islands (the Azores), lying near the centre of the North Atlantic, would in enemy hands have proved as great a menace to our shipping movements in the south as Iceland in the north. The British government for its part could not tolerate such a situation arising, and in response to urgent calls from the Portuguese Government, who were fully alive to the danger to their own country, we planned and prepared an expedition to forestall such a German move. We had also made plans to occupy Grand Canary and the Cape Verde Islands, should Hitler move into Spain. The urgency of these expeditions vanished once it became clear that Hitler had shifted his eyes towards Russia.[7]

The great issue facing U.S. and British naval forces was the ability and endurance of the Allies to survey convoy runs that required passage anywhere from Freetown on the coast of Sierra Leone northwest to the Cape Verdes and northward to the Azores. This approximately 2,400-mile voyage was extremely dangerous. In a confidential letter to President Roosevelt on April 24, 1941, Churchill touched on this difficulty by stating, "We cannot route our convoys very far to the west owing to the endurance of the vessels on this run."[8] Churchill told Roosevelt that the only way to make the passage was to reduce cargo and take on extra fuel.

---

6. Winston S. Churchill, *The Second World War, Volume 3: The Grand Alliance*. Boston: Houghton Mifflin Company, 1950, 142-143.

7. Ibid, 142-143.

8. Ibid, 143.

Although Britain provided escorts for their convoys in this region, they required American assistance in the form of air reconnaissance.[9]

As one examines the Azores problem from the perspective of the Allies, it cannot be forgotten how important these islands were to the Germans. In 1941, Grand Admiral Erich Raeder was concerned with the flow of Allied supplies and materiel.[10] He urged Hitler to seize the Azores or extend the existing blockade, thereby stepping up attacks on American warships and the merchant ships they were protecting. This included ships like the *Arkansas*. The Azores were so important that the U.S. State Department put great pressure on the Portuguese government to allow for U.S. facilities in order to neutralize the Azores. In turn, there was concern that such pressure would turn the Portuguese in favor of the Germans.[11]

Having explained the importance of the Azores in the naval war, attention should be given to the problem of the common torpedo. If a ship spotted a torpedo, it was reported to all other ships in the convoy—its angle, direction, and path. This was accomplished through the use of the radio or signals, if no other way was safe or possible. Upon hearing or otherwise ascertaining the information, the ships then, in concert, changed their positions sufficiently to dodge torpedoes. Unfortunately, such evasion tactics were too slow. One can only imagine the speed of such a torpedo and the narrow window of opportunity the convoy had to avoid it.

During one trip to Ireland, a German U-boat fired a torpedo, sank quickly, and slowed its engines. There it remained eerily quiet down deep. On this mission, the sailors of the *Arkansas* were told by their commanders that there was only enough flour left in all of England and the British Isles to last another day. As Junior laughed and recounted, he doubted the veracity of the claim, but it provided him and his comrades great inspiration to continue without delay.

It's difficult to exaggerate the circumstances of the British people at that point in the war. There was want and scarcity all over the British

---

9. Ibid.

10. James MacGregor Burns, *Roosevelt: The Soldier of Freedom*. New York: Harcourt, Brace Jovanovich, Inc., 1970, 105.

11. Ibid.

Isles. They had to "make do" with whatever they could find as substitutes for even the basics. These convoys sailing under the protection of the *Arkansas* and her sister ships were essential for their survival and absolutely necessary for the prosecution of the war against Hitler, Tojo, and Mussolini. It's difficult for those who did not live through this period to understand the dire, desperate conditions under which this war was fought and won. The sacrifices that led to the great and costly victory over the Axis powers were rendered by common boys from farms and cities all over the world, including Finger, Tennessee.

One approach to discovering and neutralizing the threat of the German U-boat was to drop an "ash can." This was a method about which Junior often spoke. At a minimum, the ash can was a depth charge about thirty inches long and about fourteen to sixteen inches in diameter. The technicians would set the charge to activate when the charge sank below the submarine. Once the ash can fell to this depth, the charge would ideally ignite and force the U-boat closer to the surface so that it could become a more readily available target. Once sighted, the destroyers, or "tin cans" as the boys on the battleships often called them, would attempt to take out the U-boats. It was a very dangerous and risky game of cat and mouse. These convoys were carefully structured with the ships being about one thousand yards apart. Cruisers both led and tailed the convoy with destroyers sailing out in front and to the sides of the convoy itself. The command battleships, like the *Arkansas*, sailed proudly in the center of the convoy.

The *Arkansas* left Ireland on December 1, 1943, and sailed for New York City, arriving on December 11. Junior spent Christmas at the Navy Yard in New York and out and about in the city when time and leave permitted. It was during this extended visit that an interesting event occurred, one not unusual during this war.

Junior was sitting in Grand Central Station awaiting his orders from the Naval Office located there. While waiting, he met another fellow in the service and they ran around for a while just to keep each other company. The two never bothered to introduce themselves. After all, they were fellow Navy men and that was enough for each man to trust the other, even if a stranger. They ate dinner together, talked about their experiences, and went to a movie. At the designated time, the pair returned to the office and picked up their orders. As the two sailors turned to say their goodbyes, they suddenly recognized each other. Leonard Patterson and Luther E. "Junior" Talbott, both from Finger, realized they had an unexpected reunion.[12] After the shock wore off, the young men laughed about the whole affair, visited a moment more, and went their respective ways.

One might wonder how two childhood friends could spend an afternoon in New York City and not recognize the other. The answer is simpler than one would think. The two had not seen one another since 1941. In Junior's case, he went in with quite a youthful "baby face" appearance. He even admitted himself that he did not have to shave very often but was ordered to do so upon his entry into the Navy. Comparing photographs of him in October 1942 and again in late 1943 and early 1944 show two different individuals. Junior had aged considerably; he no longer resembled a young kid, but instead every inch of a man.

One can only imagine the age progression of Leonard Patterson, who had survived Pearl Harbor. It's no wonder that they did not recognize each other. Leonard was the son of Junior's longtime friends, Hobert and Cora Patterson, who had moved from Finger to Tulia, Texas. He was born on June 15, 1921, a little more than a month prior to Junior's birth. He entered the Navy prior to the outbreak of war and survived the Japanese attack on Pearl Harbor on December 7, 1941. Leonard was serving aboard the U.S.S. Tennessee, which was heavily damaged during the cowardly sneak attack on the Pacific Fleet. He saw considerable action in some of the major sea battles of the war, but he did not survive long after its end. Leonard was killed in an automobile accident just east of Wichita Falls, Texas on August 4, 1948.[13]

This very experience calls to mind the words of Ernie Pyle, the "G.I.'s reporter," when he described the changes that took place in America's young fighting men:

> They were young men, but the grime and whiskers and exhaustion made them look middle-aged. In their eyes as they passed

---

12. The information regarding Leonard Howard Patterson was provided by Luther E. Talbott and from an article entitled "Hobert and Cora Patterson" written by Charles O. Patterson, the son of Hobert and Cora Patterson, and published in *Reflections: A History of McNairy County, Tennessee, 1823-1996*. Marceline, MO: Heritage House Publishing, 1996.

13. Ibid.

was no hatred, no excitement, no despair, no tonic of their victory—there was just the simple expression of being there as if they had been there doing that forever, and nothing else.

Junior experienced many aspects of life in the Navy during the Second World War. He came into contact with interesting and colorful people from across the country. All had to adjust to this new adventure. Young sailors like Junior had to forsake their privacy and personal space. Old battleships of the pre-World War I era such as the *Arkansas* were too small to accommodate the social mores of small-town rural young men turned sailors. Six men were confined to sleeping quarters that measured approximately six feet by seven feet and seven feet high. Each had a mattress that could be no thicker than six inches. As many as forty to forty-eight men typically slept in a confined space. Young men who were used to wide open spaces on the prairies or in the small towns and back roads of America learned to assimilate.

When the sailors ate their meals, it was at designated times in minimal cafeteria space. They filed through lines past the serving stations and collected their meal on a cafeteria tray. Under a low ceiling, the men sat on metal benches that seated four sailors at a metal table accommodating eight sailors. There was no luxury in these accommodations. Officers enjoyed a little more comfort with individual chairs (barely cushioned) and ate from proper china and silverware. Black stewards in white coats belonged to the ship's "S Division" stood nearby awaiting the orders of the dining officers.

Junior and his fellow sailors learned to be resourceful while living in close quarters on a battleship. Occasionally, they wore their foul weather coats down to the ship's bakery. The baker would turn his back on the boys and give them a chance to take some hot bread, usually about four loaves, and a healthy amount of the officer's butter stores. Concealed under their coats, they took them down to their workshop and had a little feast. This was not uncommon among enlisted men. While it may seem unpalatable to us today, it was a common practice among these boys. Sailors often endured certain privations because of the limits on the military structure to provide adequate provisions on the battleships at sea for long periods.

Junior enjoyed relating another story regarding a breakfast he and his buddies prepared early one morning. They raided the officer's mess and made off with real eggs, bacon, and other "delicacies." Apparently, an officer got wind of their transgressions. Junior always believed it was Executive Officer P.M. Boltz, a man he neither liked nor respected. In any event, Captain F.G. Richards, a man whom Junior respected greatly, paid a personal visit to the boys' quarters while they were cooking their meal on a hot plate. The boys tried to concealing their activities, but Captain Richards instantly smelled the scent of the officer's supplies being cooked. He turned and closed the door, smiled at his boys, and asked them to pull up a chair for him. He ate with them and gently admonished them to refrain from getting themselves in trouble in the future. He seemed rather amused at the resourcefulness of his young sailors.[14] Junior never forgot the memory of sitting in the small room with Captain Richards eating bacon and eggs. With a smile and nod of the head, he often said, "Captain Richards was something. A good officer."

Captain Frederick Gore Richards was a native of the state of Arkansas. A career Navy man and a graduate of the U.S. Naval Academy, he was a smart navigator and a compassionate officer. He understood the young men from rural backgrounds who served their country on his ship. Richards had a rugged personality. He was beloved and all but revered by his sailors, a gentle man who had a wide toothy grin and found humor in most things. Commanding the ship on D-Day, Junior never forgot the sight of his skipper under pressure. He was cool and calm. He did not seem to ever really rattle or get ruffled. According to Junior, he was an unassuming fellow with an easy bearing. On that fateful day, Richards was very much in command and his men knew that.

The *Arkansas'* Executive Officer was Philip M. Boltz, a fellow from the northern United States. Junior despised Boltz and had no use for him.

---

14. In the modern U.S. Navy, it might seem strange that a captain would have such close contact with sailors, but such was not the case aboard the *Arkansas* in the early 1940s. It was a small ship and Captain Richards was a very kind and interested person. He took a keen interest in his boys. He was regularly spotted all over the boat visiting and talking to sailors as he went about his own duties. Junior Talbott often recounted that Captain Richards seemed to relish interaction and contact with "his boys." He was not aloof like many senior officers. Junior placed Richards in high esteem above all officers under whom he served.

He often described him as a genuine "smartass." His northern, urban background clashed with the young men from the rural South and West.

During Captain Richards' tenure aboard the *Arkansas*, an African-American sailor was rumored to be stationed in fire control by the Executive Office. This action during a time of racial segregation in much of the United States angered many sailors in fire control.[15] It was almost certainly just a rumor. Many of these boys were from Southern states and the border states like Kentucky, Missouri, and Oklahoma. They were not accustomed to such comingling of the races and were incensed by a forced integration of their division.

The young sailors put in a request for a "chit" to see Captain Richards. Normally, one had to be given a chit to officially see the Captain.[16] The request was denied, but the boys were determined to see him regardless. As they walked into the office to see Captain Richards, Executive Officer Boltz jumped from his chair and demanded to know their business. By this time, the captain came out and inquired as to the problem. The young men calmly explained their dilemma. Assuming the truth of the rumor, they said, "We're not used to this. If you don't keep this man out, we will." Further, they told the captain that the African-American sailor could "accidentally" end up overboard if he was forced upon them.[17] Captain Richards was sympathetic to the men's position. He smiled and told them, "Boys, I know how you feel. I'm from Arkansas. You boys

---

15. One must keep in mind that in the World War II era, the U.S. Armed Forces were still segregated. They would not be integrated until President Harry S Truman did so in reaction to the nomination of Strom Thurmond of South Carolina by the States' Rights Party in 1948. These rumors of a black sailor being stationed among F Division were probably rumors. No officer would have dared contradicted the official policy of segregation in the U.S. Armed Forces. However, it is entirely possible that rumors were occasionally circulated among non-black troops to gauge their reactions.

During the 1940s, many states in the United States practiced various forms of segregation. This practice was not confined to the South alone. The public schools of Boston, Massachusetts, were not integrated until the mid-1970s, which led to riots. In fact, many Northern states practiced a de facto segregation as insidious as any other form while their elected statesmen argued against Southern segregation and Jim Crow.

16. A chit was a small voucher, certificate, memorandum, or other document stating the favor or request granted. The use of chits were common on the *Arkansas*.

17. While it is often difficult for Americans in 2019 to understand such sentiments, it should be considered that the young men of the 1940s, at least many of them, were not accustomed to integration and had the institution of segregation ingrained in them.

shouldn't have come down here, but I don't blame you for it." He would do his best to ensure the unfortunate sailor wasn't placed amongst them. Captain Richards understood the upbringing and social mores of these young men. They were the products of their times, customs, and beliefs. Still, it is almost impossible that such a promotion would have officially occurred prior to 1948, though the idea was already being floated in some military circles.

Junior could never disguise his obvious disdain for Commander Boltz. He must have had a demeanor or way about him that quickly put off the young sailor. Junior did not like him from his earliest exposure to him. There may have been many reasons, some legitimate, others exaggerated. Commander Boltz did not survive the war by many years. He was eventually promoted to the rank of Captain but died on August 21, 1948. He was buried at Long Island National Cemetery in Section C, Site 277.

Although Junior and his fellow sailors objected to the potential integration of their quarters with a black sailor, this was not to say that he did not experience or otherwise appreciate certain diversity while serving in the Navy. The *Arkansas* had plenty of nationalities represented among the ranks. Hispanics (often referred to by Junior as the Spanish) and Italians were well represented. Junior had encountered Hispanics during his time in Texas as well. In the Navy, he had befriended a fellow by the name of Martinez from New Orleans.

One event that occurred on the ship brought Junior a great degree of mirth and laughter. There was a white sailor whose wife was expecting a baby. Like all expectant fathers, he was excited and talkative whenever the subject came up. When the child was born, it was quite dark-skinned. The new father exploded and wrote his wife claiming she had been messing around with a black man. Indignant, the wife demanded a blood test and that her husband help her get to the bottom of this mystery. After much investigation, including talking to people on both sides of the family, it was determined that one of the parents had African-American ancestry—the father! Needless to say, the sailor had much crow to eat. Junior never ceased to get a chuckle out of the matter.

Another officer about whom Junior spoke was Lieutenant Commander William F. McLaren. He recounted a couple of stories regarding him. Air raids were common on the high seas and especially in the Pacific Ocean.

On one particular raid, just off Okinawa, Junior and a fellow sailor, T.J. Drazdowski, Fire Control Third Class, were helping pass the ammunition. Another sailor with them who was of a slighter build manned the phones while Junior and Drazdowski worked.

Under the stress of the kamikaze attack, Junior instinctively lit up a cigarette and quickly began smoking as he worked.[18] A young officer, a lieutenant junior grade, became unnerved himself and left his battle station. As he walked around, he spotted Junior with the cigarette protruding from his mouth and proceeded to "throw a fit." In response, Junior was fairly smart to the young officer and rather short of temper. He let the officer know that he did not really care what the officer saw. In the heat of battle, Junior told him that he was too busy to deal with it at the time. After all, there was an attack to fend off.

Following the exchange, the indignant young officer reported the incident and Junior's misconduct, that of smoking a cigarette during an engagement, to the gunnery officer, Lieutenant Commander McLaren. Fortunately, Junior and McLaren "stood in together" very well.[19] Commander McLaren called Junior into his office and asked him about the situation. Junior explained that he was extremely busy at the time and under extreme stress and forgot about the smoking ban. After a few moments of reflection, Commander McLaren turned to the young officer and sternly asked, "Where was your battle station at the time?" The younger officer stammered for a moment and was forced to explain that he had walked away from it. The commander rebuked him. "Well, you had better keep your mouth shut, Lieutenant," he said. "You deserted your station in time of battle." Nothing more was ever said about the incident.

On another occasion, Junior went to see Commander McLaren for a chit to seek a release for alcohol from the medical office. The purpose of the alcohol was to clean the points on the gunnery machinery. When Junior asked McLaren for the chit, the commander smiled and asked, "What kind of juice do you want to go with it?" Junior responded that

---

18. There is no doubt that it was unwise to smoke cigarettes while passing ammunition and loading the heavy guns of the U.S.S. *Arkansas*. Even Junior Talbott, in his dotage, would laugh and cringe at the same time when recounting this story. He knew his hasty actions were not particularly wise but just pure reaction in the heat of battle.

19. Junior Talbott used the phrase "stood in together" when describing a friendly or close relationship.

it did not matter. In all honesty, he wasn't quite sure what Commander McLaren meant. Before Junior and the other sailors could get into the alcohol, which was pure grain alcohol (PGA), Commander McLaren got to it first. He had too much to drink and passed out in one of the boy's bunks. As one man would come off duty, he would pull the commander out of his bunk and place him in another bunk and retire to his own.

One of Junior's officer friends was a man by the name of Catildas. This older officer encouraged him to apply for officer training school. As Junior often explained it, attending officer training school ensured that he would finish with the rank of ensign. But certain academic qualifications were required to qualify for officer training school. These ensigns were called "ninety-day wonders" and were the least of the commissioned officers. While docked in Boston, Catildas spotted Junior repairing an electrical motor while he worked the switchboard. Impressed by Junior's work ethic, Catildas instructed him to procure a "special duty" chit for himself at the Executive Office, get his dress blues, and head for the beach. Sailors could not figure out why Junior was off duty with Officer Catildas watching the switchboard.

Catildas took a special interest in the young man from Finger, Tennessee and put him on scullery detail. A man on scullery duty had literally nothing to do between meals. That might seem a questionable honor, but there was a reason for this assignment. Catildas thought it would give Junior time to study for officer training school. However, Junior never tried to enroll. His interests simply didn't lie in that direction.

Junior related a number of other stories over the years. He often discussed matters related to the weather and its role in naval affairs. During one trip from Ireland back to New York City via the North Atlantic Ocean, the *Arkansas* encountered a storm that produced choppy waters and such tremendous swells that the sailors had to strap themselves in their bunks to keep from being thrown out of bed while sleeping. The Queen Mary, a British luxury cruise liner turned transport ship, was traveling with the *Arkansas*. They were traveling at the battleship's full-speed of sixteen knots, but both vessels were losing ground. Finally, the Queen Mary sought permission to proceed alone. It arrived at New York Harbor three or four days ahead of the *Arkansas* because they were capable of traveling about thirty knots at full speed.

The wintertime saw massive icebergs floating around the North Atlantic Ocean, creating their own natural obstacle course. Junior remembered:

> These icebergs were huge. You've always heard you only see the tip of the iceberg so it made you wonder what the rest of it looked like and how damn big it really was. Seeing these things and knowing they could make things dangerous for you made you realize how dangerous your duty really was. Not just from German subs and mines, but the weather and nature too.[20]

During these winter months, the sailors wore dungarees, a blue jean or denim type of material, and foul weather gear filled with a material that Junior believed to be feather down. He referred to this gear as "good stuff." Sailors like Junior would be put on watch and often stationed on a gun mount. The ocean spray would hit them and freeze. After their watch had ended, they would break the ice from their gear and shake it off. Junior often grew a beard under his mouth and chin. It would become so cold, his beard iced over after a period of time on deck in the open weather. Interestingly, the sailors wore this same insulated foul weather gear in Algeria to keep the heat out.

One of the reasons for the Navy's use of the North Atlantic Ocean as a course of transport was its cold, rough, and choppy waters. Enemy submarines couldn't function efficiently in such adverse conditions. The submarine commanders found it more difficult to extend their periscopes with any accuracy and see anything of consequence. They were forced to patrol the calmer, warmer waters to the south. By the time the *Arkansas* traversed the Pacific Ocean, most of the submarines in the Japanese Fleet had been destroyed.

Junior told a number of stories regarding the rough seas of the world. This was the environment in which the *Arkansas* and her crew operated. The waters affected the work that the sailors were called upon to do. Junior had to learn to plot coordinates of his targets despite the roll and

---

20. Luther E. Talbott undated interview regarding the North Atlantic Ocean and its effect on the voyages of the *Arkansas*.

pitch of the ship. He had to learn to accurately scout and site his target despite constant movements and rolls of the ship's hull from side to side with the waves. Junior could carefully hit a target without a single miss. He took great pride in his ability to adapt to his environment. It also made him somewhat indispensable when seas were rough and battles were raging in those rough, choppy waters.

Junior was often pulled half-asleep from his bunk to reclaim his duties at fire control. His replacement was a good man and a good sailor, but he could never master the waves. The relief man could not adapt to the roll and pitch of the ship as he plotted a target's coordinates and therefore often missed the target by overshooting or undershooting. So when highly effective targeting was absolutely necessary and not delivered, Junior was pulled from his bunk, briefed, and sent back to his station to resume targeting. This happened to him at Normandy, Iwo Jima, and Okinawa. He once said:

> Well, it was one thing to be able to plot coordinates and target a position; it was another to hit it. The ship wasn't going to sit still for you to hit your target. Once those big guns of ours got to firing and those around us were too, the waters got awfully choppy. The ship would pitch forward and roll backwards. If you didn't take that into account when you were aiming, you'd miss the target by a mile. I learned to plan for the roll and pitch of the ship and take those degrees and angles into account when aiming for my target.[21]

Junior once experienced the furies of a typhoon. The *Arkansas* was anchored in Buckner Bay (the American nickname for Nakagusuku Bay) on the southern coast of Okinawa Island in the Pacific. He was working on a circuitry board in the tower, an alternative fire control station. He received a warning that a typhoon was about to hit and he should vacate the tower. But he was so close to completing his work that he hesitated to leave. The storm hit and the ship rolled and became very unsteady. Junior rode out the typhoon in the tower. Angry swells washed over the ship. A photograph was taken of the waves obscuring its view of the nearby

---

21. Luther E. Talbott conversation notes, 2002.

U.S.S. Nevada. The typhoon rocked the *Arkansas* and other ships in the vicinity. Of the event, Junior recollected:

> It was hellacious! I didn't want to leave the tower 'til I was done and I almost was. I kept thinking I'd finish my maintenance on the gun directory and then I'd get the hell out of that tower. But I didn't get the chance. She hit before I could get out the tower. She just came on. There's was this big solid wall of water hit the broad side of the ship. I just knew I'd get sick but I didn't. But she shook me up and I was never so glad to get the hell out of a tower in all my life.[22]

Junior never admitted to getting sick in the tower, but he learned not to hesitate when a storm was approaching. To avoid damage, the *Arkansas* sailed out in the East China Sea. It returned to Buckner Bay three days later with only superficial damage. There were less fortunate ships and men who were lost to the waters and the storm.[23]

In regards to the sea and its occasional disturbances, Junior remembered experiencing sea sickness only once. While at San Pedro, off the coast of California, between November 27, 1944, and January 20, 1945, the waters of the Pacific Ocean became extremely unsettled due to swells. These swells cause the *Arkansas* to become unsteady and he became quite seasick.[24]

Junior also talked about the calmness of the water and more enjoyable times spent on the great oceans and seas of the world. One memorable event occurred many times over. It was the crossing of the Atlantic Ocean. Despite the concerns and dangers, there were opportunities to stand on deck, smoke his pipe, and soak in the sunlight. He recalled such

22. Ibid.

23. Lt. H.A. Wilson, *U.S.S. Arkansas: Pacific War Diary, 1945*. Washington, D.C.: United States War Department, Department of the Navy, 1945.

24. The author always found this fact to be quite interesting and more than a little entertaining. Here was a man who had sailed aboard a great old battleship in both rough and calm seas for more than two years by November 1944. He had ridden out a typhoon inside the confines of a tower high in the air and had endured other harrowing weather events afloat all over the world. Yet he got sick while off the coast of California less than a year before finally coming home. Even Junior Talbott took pause to laugh at this one while telling and retelling it!

quiet moments atop deck late in the evening when a sailor could clear his mind, think about past experiences behind him, and what could lay ahead, all the while worrying about what lay beneath him.

On December 27, 1943, the *Arkansas* departed New York City for Norfolk, Virginia, arriving on the 28th. The ship left Norfolk on January 14, 1944, and returned to New York the next day. She escorted a convoy across the Atlantic Ocean to Bangor, Ireland, January 19-28 and returned on February 14. The *Arkansas* remained in New York for quite some time before sailing to Portland, Maine, on March 28. The ship and crew remained in Casco Bay performing gunnery exercises until pulling out for Boston, Massachusetts, on April 8, 1944, to undergo repairs.

The *Arkansas* and her crew remained in Boston for a week. They departed on April 18, bound once again for Bangor, arriving on the 27th. There the crew started training for their new role of providing shore bombardment at Normandy. Junior often recounted bombardment practices in both Ireland and Scotland. The cliffs and terrain along both seashores were close enough in appearance to those of Normandy to give the men sufficient experience and practice in preparation for the invasion of Nazi-occupied France.

During the first couple of days in Ireland, Junior sat down and wrote a letter to his sweetheart back home, Faye McIntyre. It was commonplace for a sailor or soldier to write his girlfriend or wife when time allowed. In the case of Junior and Faye, they wrote each other on average one letter a day. They once estimated that they had written between them about 1,500 letters. The couple made the decision to burn their letters many years later to forever protect the privacy of their courtship. The letter that follows is only one of three known to survive:

        L.E. Talbott, F.C. 3/C
        U.S.S. Arkansas F Div.
        c/o F.P.O. New York City
        April 29, 1944

        Miss Faye McIntyre
        Finger, Tenn.

Dearest Faye,

How do these few lines find you? Fine, I trust. I am just fine myself. Having a nice time. How is everything around the old town now, kindly dull I guess.

Well, Honey, I am still missing you as much as ever and still more than I thought that I would. I sure am missing hearing from you but I guess it won't be long before I begin to getting mail. I sure hope it isn't. Say, I can't write very often now for a while or I mean not as often [as] I have in the past. But I will write every chance I get. So don't worry any if you don't hear so often. You know the old saying, "No news is good news." Well, I will close for this time.

Love
L.E.T.

While in the British Isles, the *Arkansas* sailed to Scotland, arriving in Greenock on May 13, 1944. The purpose of the journey was target practice. The cliffs at Greenock looked very similar to those at Normandy, the site of the invasion of northern France. At some point during the trip, Junior made his way to Glasgow. Visiting the city and soaking up the environs, he had a photograph made of himself wearing the traditional Scot wardrobe of kilt and matching accessories. It was done as a sort of lark. The photographer's studio was cold. Junior felt it was too cold to remove his pants while being photographed in the traditional kilt, so he devised an alternative. He rolled up his pants legs until they were far above his knees and then slipped on the kilt. He propped his foot up on a fake rock in front of a painted Scottish country scene and smiled for the camera. He sent this striking photograph home to his folks who, of course, always eagerly awaited any news of his activities, adventures, health, and safety. It was intended to be a present for his mother on Mother's Day.

Scotland was a land that always fascinated Junior. Some of his ancestors were from these regions and he found its history rich and interesting. He enjoyed the landscapes and countryside outside of the gritty industrial cities like Glasgow. Still, the cities and port towns like Greenock held an attraction for him. He found the old dirty industrial port cities to be full of character and color. The waterfronts were a mixture of adventure, danger, and lore. This world of ships and sailing held his interest even as he experienced it firsthand every day.

During the course of the war, Junior's father, like so many other parents across the country, worried about his son's safety and whereabouts. Newt Talbott eagerly sought information about the U.S.S. *Arkansas* and its expeditions from any potential source he could. When his failing eyesight prevented him from reading the newspapers, others read to him. At his store, he kept a small radio on a shelf. It hung on the partition wall that Junior had built for him before he left in 1942. Newt was unable to do as much work as he used to and business was rather slow, so he had ample time to listen for news. His wife Varham tried keeping as much information from him as she could about the war and their son's whereabouts. But Newt once told his future daughter-in-law, Faye McIntyre, "I may be blind, but I hear plenty." Despite attempts to shield information from him, he seemed to have an amazing knowledge of what was happening in the world around him, both at home and abroad.

Newt had to rely on newspapers and news broadcasts on the radio. It was a different world in the mid-1940s. Television and the Internet did not exist with twenty-four hour access to information about the events of the war. In fact, the War Department, with the cooperation of the major radio networks and newspapers, controlled the information (always positive) that was coming back from the front. Newt remained remarkably well-informed by listening carefully to Junior's letters being read to him, though they were censored by Naval Intelligence like all such letters written by sailors during the war. He also followed the news as presented in the Memphis *Press Scimitar*. This major newspaper carried relatively detailed reports and dispatches complete with artists' maps of the battle areas. Newt found the *Press Scimitar* to be very helpful to his understanding of the war.

Like all parents, Newt and Varham Talbott wrote to their son on occasion. Junior spoke often of receiving letters from his parents, but few remain. One found after Junior's death was an undated letter from his mother:

ADVENTURE AND PERIL IN THE NAVY

Finger, Tenn.

Hello Junior

How are you this bad day? We are just fine. The air is cooled off some. I thought I would write a few lines. I don't know whether you will get this before you leave or not. Faye went home yesterday. Will be back tomorrow. Buford Brock came in yesterday The other Brock is with Frank Walker. Will be at home Saturday. Hope to see you soon. So write if you can.

Lots of love,
Mother & Dad & Vonnie

Letters exchanged between parents and sons were important. Faithful sons all over the world sent lines home almost constantly to let their fretful parents know that all was well under the circumstances. They gave servicemen like Junior information about childhood friends and relatives. Letters and postcards from home also kept young men from feeling forlorn and forgotten while so far away from their loved ones. They were small reminders that someone still cared about them and wanted them to feel proud of their sacrifices.

As important as such communications were, it was the letter from a sweetheart that gave the serviceman something to live for, come home for, and plan for the future. Junior was no different. He too had been fortunate enough to catch the eye of a lovely young woman. His sweetheart's name was Faye McIntyre. Their romance, one that would last more than six decades, began in the early 1940s. She remained faithful to her sailor as she awaited news from him while doing her part to support the war on the home front.

7

His Sweetheart

The McIntyre family of Finger, Tennessee, had a long, colorful, and fascinating history by 1924. Where they were once prosperous and well-connected, they had struggled due to circumstances beyond their control. Yet this was not an abnormal situation for many families in the years following the American Civil War and prior to the Second World War. The McIntyre family had originally come to McNairy County from Mecklenburg, North Carolina, in the 1830s. There the family was known for its patriotic involvement in the Revolutionary War.

In October 1780, the family name was enshrined in North Carolina history when troops on reconnaissance for Lord Charles Cornwallis decided to pillage the John McIntyre Sr. farm in the Beatties Ford community near Charlotte. The battle of McIntyre's Farm (or McIntyre's Skirmish) pitted the family and their neighbors against the British Army. A heated attack from the cover of the woods surprised and shocked the British troops while they pillaged the family's home, smokehouse, outbuildings, stock pens, and farm. They upset McIntyre's beehives and the bees began to sting the offending troops. The British fled from the farm as several soldiers were felled by the bullets of the colonial patriots. Young Isaac McIntyre was six years old and witnessed an event which would be passed down in his family for generations.[1] Two of John McIntyre Sr.'s sons had joined the Revolutionary cause and were fighting in the Continental Army. One, Robert McIntyre, would die; the other, John McIntyre, Jr. would survive.

Isaac McIntyre was raised by his grandfather, John McIntyre Sr., and his aunts. His father married sometime after the war and had another family. Eventually, Isaac married Elizabeth Thompson, a spinster who had previously had a daughter out of wedlock. Both were older at the time. The couple had four sons of their own before Isaac died in 1826. From then until she left for McNairy County, Tennessee, Elizabeth raised her four sons by herself. She fought the battles necessary to ensure she could take care of her children, including suing her brother-in-law for support from her late husband's estate. Eventually, she prevailed and used her judgment to purchase land further west.

In and around 1835, Elizabeth led her family to north McNairy County, leaving their established life behind to start anew in a territory that still had aspects of a frontier. She and her sons Robert Thompson McIntyre and William Cogbourne McIntyre remained there while two other sons moved on. In 1858, old and tired, Elizabeth died and was buried at Mount Carmel Cemetery. William Cogbourne McIntyre moved on afterwards, but Robert Thompson McIntyre remained.

The family under the leadership of Robert Thompson McIntyre (1814–1902) took a leading role in developing the area into a viable thriving commercial town. It would come only after great loss and the trauma of a civil war. He established a grist mill close to the banks of Huggins Creek near present-day Finger and prospered. By the outbreak of the War Between the States, McIntyre had amassed considerable

---

1. A children's book entitled *Bees and Bullets* was written in 1975 by Sally Barry Dodd and published by the Charlotte Junior Woman's Club of Charlotte, North Carolina. This book was written from the perspective of a six-year old Isaac McIntyre. The battle was more particularly covered in LeGette Blythe and Charles Raven Brockmann, *Hornet's Nest: The Story of Charlotte and Mecklenburg County*. Charlotte NC: McNally of Charlotte, 1961, 86–87. Nearly a half dozen histories of North Carolina include accounts of the Battle of McIntyre's Farm.

wealth and influence. In 1858, he was elected to the McNairy County Quarterly Court and served his district as a magistrate on the court. He was active and a fervent Republican and Unionist leader in the northern section of the county. During the war, he sent one son to fight in the First West Tennessee Cavalry (later known as the U.S. Sixth Tennessee Cavalry). That son, Isaac McIntyre, named for his grandfather, was killed at Bolivar, Tennessee, in 1864. Robert Thompson McIntyre sent another son, John Absalom McIntyre, who was 14 years in 1862, to Nashville in Washington County, Illinois, to work at a munitions plant serving the Union cause. He acted as first Chief Presiding Justice of the McNairy County Quarterly Court when the war ended in 1865 and remained into the 1880s. He was a miller and farmer by trade and dabbled greatly in real estate. He helped establish his sons as successful men, but they remained largely self-made men. In fact, both were men on the make, part of a new thriving community.

John Robert McIntyre was born in 1893 to John Absalom McIntyre. When the War Between the States ended, John Absalom McIntyre came home and began farming and accumulating land. By 1896, he owned in excess of 1,000 acres and had the farm enclosed by a split rail fence. His interests also included a general merchandise partnership. He was happily married to Miss Mary Roberta "Robertie" Coleman and they had six children—three sons and three daughters. John Robert and his siblings were born into a relatively wealthy family for the day. However, all that changed too soon. While still a young man in his forties, John Absalom became ill with skin cancer and died in 1897.

His widow Robertie worked diligently to keep the family moving forward. However, she too died just ten years later of typhoid fever. The illness robbed the family of four of its immediate members. At age fourteen, John Robert McIntyre was left an orphan. His life would be a good one, but never easy. In 1911, he married Miss Ollie Pearl McCann. He was fond of saying of his bride, "Ollie Pearl, the prettiest girl in the world." She was the daughter of Arthur Marion Douglas "Whig" McCann and Parthenia (Tacker) McCann. The couple had been married in a buggy at the home of Squire I.C.B. Naylor. They were a shy couple. A Sunday wedding had been planned, but they learned that a large crowd wanted to greet them and attend. John Robert and Ollie Pearl snuck away to the Squire's house and were married a day early.

Much like Junior and Faye, this earlier couple had known each other since known childhood. They had both lost parents while young. Ollie Pearl always recalled standing near John Robert at his mother's grave on the day of her funeral in 1907. The very sad fourteen-year-old boy wrapped in a blanket stared off into the distance as his last living parent was committed to the cold winter ground. Young John Robert was lost and forlorn and had no one left to really love him but his sisters Zulphia and Sarah until he married his childhood friend, Ollie Pearl.

The couple struggled like all young people. They made their home in the old family seat, a log cabin on a hill just outside the relatively new bustling town of Finger. They farmed and kept a large garden to feed themselves. John cut crossties in the woods on the farm he inherited to make the ends meet. By the time Faye was grown, his major supplemental income came from making brooms. In the early years, John and Ollie Pearl struggled but they were happy from all accounts. In 1911 or 1912, John came across the water wheel from his grandfather Robert Thompson McIntyre's old grist mill. He pried from it a long cross plank made of chestnut. From this single board, he made his new bride a kitchen cabinet.

[2]By 1924, the couple had three daughters and a son. On March 10, 1924, the couple had a fourth daughter. They named her Faye Davree McIntyre. She was a healthy child and her father's favorite daughter. She adored her parents and they felt a particular affection and closeness to her. She would become the only of their daughters to marry and have children. This fact set her apart in their minds. She was born at the family home. It was here at the old McIntyre homestead that Faye would spend her first eighteen years. She was a smart and astute, though shy, young lady.

Faye attended the Finger School for the first through the tenth grades. Her father believed girls should receive no less than a tenth grade education. The Finger School offered this level of schooling and so all of John Robert McIntyre's daughters' formal educations ended with the completion of the tenth grade. Faye was a good student, quiet and obedient but smart and very inquisitive. Her teachers included Lorraine Bishop, Burleen Orr, Inetha Bishop, and Cecil Clayton. She particularly enjoyed the study of geography. One of her most vivid memories was witnessing a trial of a man who killed another in a wreck. According to Faye, the

---

2. This cabinet remains in the McIntyre family and in use at the home of the author.

trial was held at the school for some reason and conducted on the stage of the school. She recalled the man's last name to be McKenzie.³

Faye worked in the school library and was able to purchase her own winter coat with the proceeds paid to her. She studied hard and was a favorite of her teachers. Her parents had to buy her schoolbooks and she carried her lunch in a pail each day. Each student in those days had an investment in their own education. Faye took her schooling very seriously and dedicated herself to the task. Many of her teachers commended her and tried to reward her for a job well done. One of her teachers, Inetha Bishop, gave her a simple little wooden plague with the portrait of a European noblewoman or maiden covered in a decorative foil cover. It was not much by modern standards, but the little plague meant a great deal to Faye.⁴

Growing up on the farm, Faye had many memories. Some were pleasant and others were not. Most of her more unpleasant ones regarded her relationship with her sisters. They were jealous of her close relationship with her father. She remembered wet years and dry years, good crops and bad ones. The old home place was something out of a century already past. It was a log cabin home with a loft and a kitchen built on the back, various outbuildings made of hewn logs, an old-fashioned garden full of heirloom variety vegetables and a packed dirt yard that was swept clean at all times. The old hill had fruit trees and roses, baby's breath bushes, Forsythia, climbing vines, walnut trees and flowers innumerable. The family grew old varieties of fruits and vegetables including multiplying onions, speckled beans and plum grannies.

Every patch and field on the old farm had a name. There was the Rounding Patch, the Sandy Patch, the Indian Mound, the Watermelon Patch, the Lark New Ground, the Steve New Ground, the Cantaloupe Patch, and the Briar Patch, among others. The farm was worked by the parents, the children, and the old work horses, Nell and Sorrell. When Faye was just an infant, her mother put her in a washtub and carried her

---

3. Depending upon the nature of the charge or tort, it could have been heard by a local magistrate or justice of the peace. This was not an unusual occurence before the creation of the local county general sessions court.

4. The little plague remained in Faye (McIntyre) Talbott's possession until her death in 2011. It is now in the possession of the author, bearing a label written in her own handwriting: "Inetha Bishop gave to Faye Mc. Talbott when about 10 yrs of age."

to the cotton fields. Life on the farm included kinfolks coming out to stay for a spell, eating watermelon, visiting other kinfolk, and wonderful meals at Miss Ollie's table.

Faye recalled well her grandfather Whig McCann's visits to their home. He loved to sit in the front room and play his fiddle. He played tunes like "Pop Goes the Weasel" and "Dog Tree'd A Possum" and played his fiddle hard. Her grandfather often played so intensely he would break out in a sweat. Her mother often accompanied him on the guitar, mandolin, or juice harp, all of which she knew how to play. Her grandfather also loved to eat Ollie's home cooking. Faye relished memories of her grandfather sitting at the family table and twirling the ends of his long mustache after eating a helping of Ollie Pearl's sweet potato pie. He would declare, "More tater pie, Ollie!" Faye enjoyed the memories of visits from family. She recalled hiding from her uncle Truman McCann, whose wooden leg mortified her. She also adored her aunt Sarah (McIntyre) Fowler, who would visit from Abilene, Texas. She found small ways to indulge her nieces and nephews. Once she brought Faye a pair of shoes. They were tight and hurt her feet, but they were a gift from someone she loved dearly. She never forgot the kind gesture.

Faye learned about loss and grief even as a child. She never forgot her first cousin, Audrey Roberta McIntyre, the daughter of her uncle Hubert McIntyre. Audrey was a very mature little girl for her age. She was younger than Faye but the two were best of friends. They were born within a short walk of one another. In fact, a photograph exists of the family that shows Faye and Audrey eating watermelon. These two photographs were taken on the same August day in about 1934. In 1935, Audrey became ill with diphtheria and was treated by Dr. W.M. "Mark" Barnes, a local physician in Finger. Dr. Barnes was said to have the ability to either "kill you or cure you." According to family history, when he approached little Audrey Roberta with the shot, she dramatically declared, "If you give me that shot, I'll roll over and die." She was going to die, it is likely, but indeed she died shortly afterward. It was likely inevitable, but a young Faye never stopped blaming Dr. Barnes for the loss of her cousin.

Faye's childhood memories included holidays, special events, local characters, and ordinary events on the farm. She recalled vividly the day her brother, J.R., was born. She had been to school and when she arrived home, Ms. Lizzie Wharton was at the foot of the hill. She told her and her sister Vivian that they would have to come home with her. This scared Faye for she was afraid her father would punish them for not coming straight home as was the normal rule. So Faye cried and cried, fearful that she was going to be in trouble. Ms. Lizzie had to promise that they could listen to her phonograph to get her to go along. Ms. Lizzie loved children. At one time, she had given Faye a little colored glass with a bubble (an imperfection) in the glass. Faye treasured this little glass until it was broken, but she remembered it the rest of her life. Incidentally, it was when she returned home that she learned her mother had given birth to a baby boy. Her sister, Vivian, fainted when her mother pulled back the covers and revealed the infant.

One memory of Faye's that remained with her was a particular visit from her Aunt Sarah Fowler. Faye's class was going on a field trip to Shiloh National Military Park. Her father did not want to let her go as he was very protective of his children. Sarah prevailed upon him to let her go and let her see something aside from the normal everyday things on the farm. In the end, John Robert allowed her to go and she had a fine time.

Memories of the farm were, on the whole, warm and fond. Faye learned to work and the importance of industry and thrift. She learned to hoe and pick cotton and corn as well as how to grow about anything in a garden. She would retain a green thumb throughout her life. She also worked in the broomcorn patches with her sisters and her parents. Her father and mother were skilled broom makers who grew their own broomcorn. Faye's recollections of the scratchy, irritating broomcorn would never fade, but her memories were never bad or tinged with any bitterness. Her sisters' recollections of life on the farm often were.

During Faye's school days at Finger, she got to know a young Junior Talbott. She was a friend of his sister, Vonnie Mae. Faye and Junior became good friends. She grew into young womanhood while Junior was ranching out in Texas. She had finished the tenth grade at Finger School by 1940-1941. She turned eighteen in 1942 and was no longer just his little sister's friend. She began thinking about getting off the hill upon which she was raised and wanted a life and adventures of her own.

Around 1942, Faye moved to Jackson, Tennessee, to work at the Fox Café. At the time, old Mrs. Fox still ran the place and was very strict about the conduct and appearance of her waitresses. The young ladies had to appear well put together in their crisp uniforms with stockings, their posture erect while at their stations. The Fox Café was a full-service restaurant of the old order that retained an air of formality. All manner of meals and desserts were served. Businessman, sales ladies, professionals, and others took their meals in this first-rate local restaurant. Mrs. Fox expected her staff to behave professionally at all times and provide first-rate service to her patrons. The desserts were kept in glass covered pie and cake platters and were of the highest quality.

Faye came into contact with all types of people while working in downtown Jackson. She became friends with the secretaries of prominent men, regular folks, younger people, and all kinds of individuals she never would have met on the farm. Growing up on the farm, Faye's influences were tightly controlled. Her father was very peculiar about the things and experiences to which his daughters were exposed. He would not even keep bulls or boars on the farm to breed his cows or sows for fear his daughters would see something inappropriate. John Robert could be stern and his daughters especially saw his conservative side. Dinner time at the table required the children to be very quiet and very reserved. They were to remain relatively silent and eat without comment and humor. Faye once recalled her first cousin, Earl McIntyre, coming to visit with her brother Roy. Earl was a character and he enjoyed making people laugh. The children almost got into trouble because they were laughing, giggling, and picking at one another during a meal.

Faye lived at a boarding house where her roommate was one of the Wharton girls from Finger. This was altogether a new experience from her days at home with her sisters. She made friends at the boarding house. One was a medic named Brown Carter, who also sang in a quartet. Faye became an independent young woman, a far cry from the timid farm girl who had come to Jackson from Finger. Even then, certain things spooked her in the city. One night while sitting in her room at the boarding house, she looked up and saw a "peeping Tom" looking in her window. She was quite scared by the incident. Her landlady thought it might have been the fellow working on the telephone earlier. Regardless, it gave her quite a scare.

After working as a waitress, Faye decided to find a better job. She decided to seek employment at the Milan Army Arsenal. This would give her the opportunity to participate in the war effort in the role of a

"Rosie the Riveter." Unfortunately, she had to have a high school education to qualify for a position. She knew the secretary of Roger Murray, an attorney in Jackson who was a powerful Democratic political operative and brother of Congressman Thomas Jefferson "Tom" Murray. The secretary helped her complete her employment application. When they came to the requirement that the applicant possess a high school education, Faye confessed that she only had a tenth grade education. The secretary, being quite resourceful, replied that they could mark she had a high school education. "Well, you went to high school," she told Faye. "It doesn't say anything about graduating."

Faye got the job at the Milan Army Arsenal and began her own service to the country. Her boss was a German man who knew all of his employees by name. She remembered meeting him and he greeted her by saying, "Good morning, Miss McIntyre." He was a good man but very strict and very professional. She worked hard and paid attention to the details of her job. She knew some of her co-workers since early childhood like longtime neighbors Eddy C. Peeples and wife Oma Peeples. She enjoyed her job and felt she was contributing to the war effort.

One day while working at the arsenal, Faye was called upon to inspect some bombs packed in grease. She used her knowledge attained on the job to carefully and correctly identify the type of shells/bombs. Her expertise earned a promotion to inspector. This allowed her to advance over people who were senior to her. Faye enjoyed being an inspector. The shifts were long, but the work was interesting as well as vital. It was far different from waiting on patrons at a local café. However, she became allergic to the stenciling ink used on the ammunition crates and eventually had to quit her job at the Arsenal. By this time, Faye had been writing frequently to Junior Talbott, who was now her boyfriend, with thoughts of marriage on her mind.

She had started writing to Junior simply wanting to keep him company. She felt sorry for him and wrote to him so he wouldn't be so lonely. At one point, when Junior was home on leave and saw Faye, he remarked, "You've grown up!" Slowly, the couple fell in love and hundreds and hundreds of letters passed between them. Faye came back home to the farm after her service at the Milan Arsenal. But she often went to Finger and helped Junior's father at his store. As the young couple wrote one another, their bond became stronger. Faye's parents wanted them to wait until after Junior came home from war, not wanting her to be a war widow should he be killed. Faye and Junior were insistent, eager to be married as soon as they could.

Soon, the sailor and his sweetheart announced their plans to marry. It would begin a partnership that lasted over 62 years, through good times and bad, lean times and prosperity, heartbreak and happiness. Faye was just beginning to show the steel of her character and the strength of her loyalty to Junior. But for him, there were battles still to fight and adventure yet to experience. His most challenging times were just ahead, in a war that would remain with him the rest of his life, one that would define his own character.

8

Fighting the Germans in France

For Junior Talbott and his fellow countrymen, the month of June 1944 brought many new challenges and great dangers. The *Arkansas* had left Greenock, Scotland, on April 18, and arrived back in Bangor, Ireland, that same day. Remaining in port for more than two weeks, the old battlewagon, once scheduled for mothballs and the scrap torch, sailed for Normandy on June 3, for the big showdown—Operation Overlord, D-Day!

However, the preparations and the build-up began much earlier. Junior related many memories about the historic experience. It would be the first full-scale battle that he would participate in and the largest amphibious invasion in world history. There had been a great deal of secret preparation to lay the plans and the groundwork for a successful and effective invasion of Nazi-occupied France. Aside from the vital but mundane planning regarding logistics, weather, men, and materiel, a number of cloak and dagger style missions were planned and carried out beforehand to provide superior intelligence for the invading Allied armies.

Leading up to D-Day, the planners did everything they could to obtain intelligence about the region. This required secrecy and discretion. Possible targets and their positions were determined as well as the layout of the coastal towns and villages. Each battleship and destroyer had objectives that had to be met to allow the men to land. That meant the gunnery and fire control teams on these ships needed accurate information.

Junior described the opportunity to be part of such a secret operation in France.[1] Its purpose was to provide the gunnery and fire control teams of the *Arkansas* with information needed to make their firepower on D-Day and D-Day Plus deadly accurate and effective. Why he was chosen and given such an opportunity, he never knew or speculated. However, such an assignment seems fitting for one with a high aptitude for spotting and locating targets.

Junior only explained that two sailors from the *Arkansas* were chosen for the assignment. One was the primary agent and the other was an alternate. The first phase was to study the available intelligence to give the Allied Armada information regarding potential targets. The next phase included training in the skills needed once the sailor landed in Nazi-occupied France.

After thorough study and training, the agent would be placed in the interior behind enemy lines to gather intelligence for transmission back to his superiors. This would be used to assist the invading forces during the Normandy campaign. Junior was given a map to memorize of a small town on the northern coast of France. This map included every building, bridge, road, side road, alley, ditch, and possible landmark known there. It was crucial that his knowledge of the town and its infrastructure be as thorough as if he had lived there his entire life.[2]

---

1. There are no records or documentation to prove this claim by Junior Talbott regarding a secret mission. He was a very low-key person who made no claims to extraordinary activities or accomplishments that were not his own. He was even humble about those normal activities to which he could easily be connected. Being one so humble, careful consideration and credit should be given to this claim.

2. Junior Talbott had a very close and constructive relationship with his officers. He was an industrious and curious sailor, always eager and willing to learn. This combined with his aptitude and good performance may have been reasons for consideration of him for a special project.

Once their training was complete, Junior and the other agents would be parachuted and dropped at a safe point. Each man would make his way to the village or town to which he was assigned. From the point of drop, Junior was to make contact with a local agent and live "underground." His job was to collect information and intelligence regarding German occupation forces and return all information back to the appropriate authorities. Junior always said that he didn't mind the operation, its purposes, or even the dangers at that point in his life. But he was very apprehensive about air travel and having to parachute out of a plane.

Like all participants in the mission, Junior had a well-prepared substitute in the event that he was unable to serve. As it happened, his substitute was much more anxious to fulfill the assignment. Their superiors approved the two young men trading positions and Junior shifted to the role of substitute. After Operation Overlord and D-Day, his replacement returned to the *Arkansas* extremely mentally unstable and quite mad. Junior recalled, "That boy came back crazy as a betsy bug!" He remembered vividly that the man returned with a bag full of gold teeth and valuable watches. Apparently, the strain had been too much and the man lost his sanity. It was assumed that the replacement had extracted the gold teeth from the mouths of German soldiers and the wrist watches from their arms. The disturbed young man was sent back home to the States and Junior counted himself fortunate that he had remained on the ship after all.[3]

Secrecy and intrigue were intertwined throughout the war, but Junior noticed these elements were especially present during the days and weeks leading up to Operation Overlord. As the *Arkansas* prepared for

---

Talbott had to learn very specific information and study maps to effectively knock out targets on D-Day. Incidentally, his targeting during the campaign were superb, thanks to the additional training and information he received.

3. Junior Talbott never identified the operation by name or gave any specific details other than those described above. However, many years after this account was related by Junior, the author learned of the operation known as "Operation Jedburgh." It was a clandestine operation composed of U.S., Dutch, and Belgian military personnel, the British Special Operations Executive, the U.S. Office of Strategic Services (OSS), and the Free French Bureau Central de Renseignements et d'Action. The operatives were dropped by parachute into enemy territories such as occupied France, Belgium, and Holland. A thorough and engaging account can be found in Lt. Col. Will Irwin, *The Jedburghs: The Secret History of the Allied Special Forces, France 1944*. New York: Public Affairs, 2005.

FIGHTING THE GERMANS IN FRANCE

her voyage to the English Channel and the invasion of northern France, she picked up equipment stored in crates and approximately four to six men in Boston and New York City. The contents of the crates and the mysterious men escorting them intrigued Junior and his fellow sailors.

The veil of secrecy was lifted about three miles out of port. The equipment taken from the crates were used for jamming the radio signals of V-1 rockets launched by the Germans. The men were the technicians who operated them. They were assisted by the sailors of the *Arkansas* stationed in radar. Once the signals were jammed, the massive and deadly rockets—instruments of great destruction and greatly advanced technology for the times—would malfunction. There were rumors that the Germans would use the V-1's in defense of occupied France during any Allied invasion of Europe. Junior heard through the ship's grapevine that the jamming equipment was not used after about the third and fourth days of the invasion because a V-1 rocket's signal had been jammed and fell from the sky onto a destroyer, exploding and sinking the ship.[4] This proved not to be true.

The V-1 rocket was a long-range rocket. Though it proved troublesome for the Germans to perfect, it still caused considerable angst and upset to the civilian population of Great Britain.[5] Hitler did order the V-1's into action on June 6, 1944, but it took six crucial days to transport the rockets to the Channel coast.[6] In the end, only ten of the bombs were utilized—three hit open fields, one destroyed a London railway bridge, four crashed upon launching, and two vanished without a trace.[7] The German Minister of Munitions and Chief Architect, Albert Speer, admitted the project was "bungled" but claimed that five rockets reached London.[8]

---

4. The author has sought to corroborate this rumor as recalled by Junior Talbott. It was recalled by him some sixty years after D-Day and based on items he had learned from others on or after D-Day, June 6, 1944. There still remains room for error. In the case of this rumor, it was indeed false.

5. Churchill, *Second World War*, 49–50. Albert Speer. *Inside the Third Reich: Memoirs by Albert Speer.* New York: Macmillan Publishing Company, 1970, 356.

6. Speer, 356.

7. Stephen E. Ambrose, *D-Day, June 6, 1944: The Climatic Battle of World War II.* New York: Simon and Schuster, 1994, 482.

8. Speer, 356.

Junior's recollection of the radar and rocket jamming equipment and the specialists sent to install them were independently verified by the *Daily War Diary* of the U.S.S. *Texas* as referenced by author John C. Ferguson in his work *Historic Battleship Texas: The Last Dreadnought*. According to Ferguson, communications experts from the U.S. Army installed this special communications equipment, radios, transmitters, and receivers. Their purpose was primarily to jam German radars and German radio guided missiles.[9]

Even as D-Day approached, there were still mundane duties to perform. Junior served on guard mail duty in Europe just before the Operation Overlord invasion. This involved the transport of orders and communiqués that could not be relayed on the wire for security purposes. It was absolutely vital. Certain items had to be carried from ship to ship by personal courier to avoid the accidental divulgence of important information just prior to the invasion. This was accomplished through the use of the Captain launch, a small motor boat that ferried the courier from ship to ship.

Prior to the invasion of France, on May 19, 1944, Junior was given command of the Captain's launch which brought the overall Allied commander, Dwight David Eisenhower, to the sailors of the *Arkansas*. The men were allowed to come together in normal wear. This was an interesting fact of his service that he seldom mentioned. What little he spoke of was quite understated. He recounted that Eisenhower was a seemingly nice but serious Midwesterner with little personality. Such reactions and low-key reminiscences were common from veterans who saw so many great men and events despite their small-town backgrounds.[10]

Inclement weather, the threat of V-1's (or flying bombs), and the withdrawal of the American battleships and craft after the invasion

---

9. John C. Ferguson, *Historic Battleship Texas: The Last Dreadnought*. Abilene TX: State House Press, 2007, 102–103.

10. According to Frank LoPinto on the blog, "The Cool Blue Blog": "[O]n 19 May, the *Arkansas* along with the other battleships in her task force, the *Nevada* and *Texas*, were inspected by Dwight D. Eisenhower and deemed ready for action. Together, these were the oldest ships in the fleet and according to Stephen Ambrose, Eisenhower along with the top military commanders fully expected to lose one or more of these ships during the battle." Frank LoPinto, "Omaha Beach and the U.S.S. *Arkansas*," *The Cool Blue Blog*, June 5, 2004, http://coolblue.typepad.com/the_cool_blue_blog/2004/06/omaha_beach_and.html.

were primary concerns for the Allies. In fact, Eisenhower's Naval Aide, Harry C. Butcher, recorded the following in his diary on Wednesday, June 21, 1944:

> The persistence of bad weather is the major worry of headquarters. This is the third day that unloadings on the far shore have practically ceased. Everyone takes more than the usual interest in weather these days because of their intense personal concern in air attacks against the sites of the flying bombs and the rockets. I used "flying bomb" this time because this name seems to be most prevalent. Whatever the name, they give no one satisfactory peace of mind. We have yet to receive the rockets.
>
> Ike had been awakened during the night by an urgent phone message from the Prime Minister, who was upset because Admiral Stark had requested authority to withdraw the *Nevada*, *Texas*, and *Arkansas*, battleships; the *Tuscaloosa* and *Augusta*, cruisers; twenty-six destroyers, and assorted supporting craft, both transport and antiaircraft generally, by July 1. The purpose of withdrawing the U.S. naval vessels was to send them to the Mediterranean to hasten Wilson's amphibious assault in southern France. Admiral Ramsay, the Naval C-in-C, had reported on the situation and considered that it would be unwise to withdraw the American battleships and heavy cruisers until the Cherbourg Peninsula is captured.
>
> During the day Ike sent a message to General Marshall to cover the general situation but primarily to ask Admiral King not to withdraw his ships at this critical stage.[11]

One can only imagine the strains and stresses placed on the Allied commanders with so many intricate plans to develop and personalities with whom to deal.

---

11. Captain Harry C. Butcher, *My Three Years with Eisenhower: The Personal Diary of Captain Harry C. Butcher, USNR, Naval Aide to General Eisenhower, 1942 to 1945*. New York: Simon and Schuster, 1946, 589.

As stated earlier, the *Arkansas* was docked in Bangor, Ireland, for some weeks prior to the Normandy invasion. One of Junior's fellow sailors, Richard Kelly, recounted the following:

> We left Bangor on 3 June. The invasion was to be on the morning of the 5th, as you probably know. The ship was sealed. No one could go ashore after, oh, I'd say about 31 May. They sealed the ship. We were all anchored off Bangor, the whole invasion fleet. Only the high-ranking officers that had business were permitted to shore for any reason. We were shown detailed maps and everything off the Omaha beachhead where we were based. I would say we were shown the relief maps probably 1 or 2 June, because the ship was sealed and no one could go to shore or come and go.[12]

The *Arkansas'* departure from Bangor on June 3, 1944, opened the curtain for the venerable old battleship's entry onto the stage of battle for the first time in its history. From the naval history for the *Arkansas* and the naval history blog previously referenced:

> On 3 June, the *Arkansas* left Bangor in her wake, sailed to join Rear Admiral Carleton F. Bryant's fire support force 'O', which was parked nearby such famed battleships as the *Nevada* and *Texas* and the British *Warspite*, *Rodney*, and *Nelson*. In the pre-dawn darkness of 6 June, U.S.S. *Arkansas* took up position 4,000 yards off Normandy's Baie de la Seine beaches.
>
> Slave labourers [*sic*] under the direction of Nazi technicians had made of Normandy's shores an adequate rampart for Fortress Europe. High-calibre [*sic*] guns were sheathed in thick concrete emplacements. Machine-gun nests and pill boxes dotted the countryside, together with slit trenches, tank traps and anti-tank ditches. Between the high and low water levels on the beaches were several rows of underwater

---

12. This Richard Kelly is most likely R.E. Kelley, MM3c, M Division. His comments provide yet another perspective on the invasion itself. LoPinto, "Omaha Beach and the U.S.S. *Arkansas*," *The Cool Blue Blog*, June 5, 2004.

obstacles—hedgehogs, tetrahedrons and pole ramps interconnected by barbed wire and liberally sown with mines. Allied planes had hammered these defences [*sic*] but a heavy barrage was needed to cut a swath, through which the invaders might pour.

Behind the *Arkansas*, the gigantic invasion armada filled the channel to the horizon. She had remained undetected, even with the great clanking of her chain as she lowered anchor.[13] Officers in the *Arkansas* CIC [Combat Information Center] anxiously penciled charts, gun crews sprawled at their stations and lookouts peered at the shadowy shoreline until their eyes ached. In the distance the rumble of the pre-invasion aerial assault was audible. At 0530 the surface around battleship *Arkansas* began erupting with near misses from unseen shore batteries. Turrets buzzed as their electric motors swung them into position; ammunition passers formed their queues. Twenty-two minutes later Skipper Richards ordered his guns into action. For the old *Arkansas*, Operation Overlord was underway.[14]

One historical fact that truly amazed Junior was the fact that the Germans were unaware of the Normandy Invasion until that morning. He could not understand how the Germans could be so ignorant of the greatest invasion force in world history, of the approaching Allied armada, and the onslaught from the air on its way over the English Channel. Interestingly, despite our historical knowledge, Junior believed the Germans knew of the invasion, but they thought it would occur in Denmark or one of the other Nordic countries. One must keep in mind that the sailors and soldiers knew details that average civilians often didn't. They never forgot those impressions and often carried them into their old age.

---

13. This veteran's memory conflicts with that of Junior Talbott. As Junior remembered, the clanking of the anchor chain brought the hills over the beach at Omaha Beach alive with German artillery fire.

14. Ibid. LoPinto, "Omaha Beach and the U.S.S. *Arkansas*," *The Cool Blue Blog*, June 5, 2004.

In fact, the Germans did not know of the plans and preparation for the invasion.[15] It remained probably the greatest secret ever conceived. Because knowledge of it was so carefully protected, the Germans had no E-boats patrolling the waters and reconnaissance planes were unaware of the presence of the greatest invasion fleet in naval history. It wasn't until 0309 on the morning of June 6, 1944, that German radar picked up anything in the Channel.[16]

Junior recalled well the sensation of first knowing that German artillery in the hills above the beach was firing on them. It was a peculiar feeling to know that large shells were being hurled at the *Arkansas* and that death was certainly possible. For the first time in his naval service, death would not come from a silent cold mine planted to kill anonymously but from the sights of German artillerymen training their sights and concentration on the *Arkansas* and her crew. In this case, death was personal and meant to be intentional and that was a peculiar feeling for him. It would not be the last time he felt that sensation. He recalled:

> I knew how I felt down in the ship so I could only imagine how the boys on the beaches felt. It was sure enough close to them. They were seeing death up close. My thoughts were more on who I was killing because I knew the firepower I was throwing at them. The chances I was going to hit them was far bigger than them hitting me. And I'm sure I killed plenty.[17]

Junior touched on another aspect related to this *Arkansas* veteran's memories. He too spoke of the turrets coming alive as they threw shells at the pillboxes and gunnery emplacements along the hills overlooking the beach at Omaha. As the need to defend the invading troops and the Armada arose, the turrets became electrified with activity and action. Men were passing powder bags and ammunition and hurriedly but efficiently performing their duties. Junior received constant calls and messages about the sighting of targets and the locations of potential targets.

---

15. Morison, *The Two-Ocean War*, 394.
16. Ibid, 394.
17. Luther E. Talbott conversation, 2001.

FIGHTING THE GERMANS IN FRANCE

The Allied Forces were supposed to land on June 5, but the seas were too rough and choppy. The entire operation had to be delayed for a day. Weather delays provided great anxiety for the fighting men and their commanders. Junior himself recalled the torture of the delays. According to him, they deeply frustrated everyone. They had reached the point when they were ready to bite the proverbial—and perhaps literal—bullet and begin the invasion. He described it as a great build up only to be almost let down. "Everyone seemed to know that we were going to do this," he recalled, "but putting it off just made the whole thing worse."[18] In fact, it was this delay of a day that Junior often said was more nerve-wracking than the actual day of the invasion. As he often put it, "Once you're in the thick of battle, you aren't so nervous anymore because you're too busy to think about your nerves anymore." He dreaded the wait of the extra day because he knew what was coming. A delay just added to the frustration.[19]

At this juncture, history and an old man's memory become wonderful collaborators. It is often the bad habit of younger, less experienced men to question the motives and memories of old men. People tend to believe that old soldiers and old men of all rank and station exaggerate their own involvement or that of their colleagues in the course of great events. Their loved ones are usually the guiltiest of parties. All of this to say, Junior's recollections of the morning of June 6, 1944, would be repeatedly reaffirmed by the succeeding generations' greatest and most accomplished historians.

According to General Eisenhower's own estimates and information, there were more than 6,000 landing craft, merchant ships, and naval fighting vessels present for the D-Day invasion, not including "ducks" or "swimming tanks." Of these 6,000 plus vessels, only six were battleships, of which the U.S.S. *Arkansas* was one.[20] The three American battleships present for the invasion were the *Arkansas*, the U.S.S. *Nevada*, and the

---

18. Ibid.
19. Ibid.
20. Dwight D. Eisenhower, *Crusade in Europe*. Garden City NY: Doubleday & Co., 1948, 53.

U.S.S. *Texas*. The other three battleships present were either Royal Navy or Royal Canadian Navy.[21]

Interestingly, the role of the aging battleships was being questioned at that particular time. The experts and the Navy Department itself gravely doubted the ability of the *Arkansas*, *Nevada*, and *Texas* to perform in battle. It would be up those very battleships and their crews to prove them wrong. Normandy gave the old battlewagons and their boys just that chance.

At this juncture, it is appropriate to let the crew of the *Arkansas* pick up the story and the history leading up to it:

> About mid-afternoon, Tuesday, September 17, 1912, a brand new battleship, the pride of the Fleet, was commissioned amid much ceremony and speechmaking. Many fine things were said about her and many fine things were predicted of her. Thirty-two years later, after a flawless career, though still more or less unstained by the rigors of war, and despite the pessimistic predictions of "Doubting Thomases" and armchair strategists, the U.S.S. *Arkansas* entered active combat and received her Baptism of Fire. After more than a quarter of a century, the "Arkie" made those fine predictions come true.
>
> It was early Spring, the eve of the greatest invasion of all history and the *Arkansas* was an important part of that greatest Armada involved. As one privileged to have been a part of that gallant ship's crew, let me relate here a small part of what I saw.
>
> When we started into the channels leading ultimately to the landing area, we were all keyed up to a high pitch; and then, when D-Day had to be postponed for a day because of unfavorable seas and weather, we were left hanging high and dry in an emotional pitch, having steeled ourselves for what was to come. As the weather opened up and, once more, we

---

21. Samuel Eliot Morison, *History of United States Naval Operations in World War II, Volume II – The Invasion of France and Germany, 1944-1945*. Annapolis MD: Naval Institute Press, 2011, 56.

FIGHTING THE GERMANS IN FRANCE

began to move toward the landing area, gathering ships as we went; we became accustomed to the electric tension in the air. We were in a constant state of alertness those few hours previous to H-hour, for we were passing through heavily mined waters all the time.[22]

As H-hour drew nearer, there was a marked quietness about the ship, for it was still very dark, and every turn of the engines brought us nearer to, we knew not what.[23] Over in the east, there was only the faintest hint of approaching dawn. At last, what had appeared to have been an unusually high horizon, and toward which I had been steadily training my binoculars, began to take on definite shapes and outlines, and I realized that it was not more water, but the coast of France—Normandy.

When the sky finally began to get lighter, it did so quickly. The old saying, "The hour is always darkest before dawn," is certainly true, and I believe that particular hour is the darkest I have ever witnessed.

During the blackest hours just prior to early morning light, our bombers began to come over in droves; so that there was a steady hum of engines overhead. Though we could not see them, the sound was a comforting one. There were hundreds of them. They had been bombing the beachhead area heavily for twenty-four hours prior to our arrival.[24]

The night, black as pitch, would be pierced periodically by tracer fire from the beach—German AA fire, visible from quite a distance. Ignoring this and heavy AA bursts that threw flak among them, however, the bombers came on, dropped their "sticks" and went back for more. As the bombs hit the

---

22. H-hour was the name assigned to the airborne assault during the D-Day invasion of northern France. This bombardment took place approximately three hours prior to the landings on the beaches at Normandy. It was carried out by the American 101st Airborne and 82nd Airborne Divisions and the British 6th Airborne Division.

23. It was this quietness that Junior Talbott spoke of. Most certainly, there was plenty of noise going on in the clouds prior to the German batteries opening up on the *Arkansas* and the rest of the Armada. For Junior, sitting in a turret, the sound would have been blunted or muffled.

24. This was the action contemplated prior to and carried out during H-hour.

beach, the entire horizon would come ablaze with light, like the bright red sun coming up. Time after time the bombers hit, mercilessly, steadily, unerringly, till it seemed there was not a square inch they had missed.

All this was not confined to the beach alone, for we witnessed dogfights in the air, not being able to see the planes, but by watching the straight, then arching, then sharply-falling lines of horizontal tracer fire. Many times we witnessed a plane go down in a spectacular mass of flames, then the subsequent blinding explosion as the fireball struck the ground. One marine standing near me, watching the bombers' work, said fervently, "If anyone even makes a crack about a "dogface" again, he'll have me to whip!" And that was representative of all our feelings, particularly after the troops began to hit the beach. During those long, tiresome, sleepless vigils we were to keep, when normally grousing would have been at its best, there was a marked absence of fatigue. We had only to think of those heroes so few yards away fighting the toughest kind of battle, and the gripe was killed at the outset.

By the time we had gotten within five thousand yards of one firing position, the sky was bright enough to see the beach clearly, and make out the cathedral spires and larger buildings.[25] When we reached our firing position, the sky was quite bright, though the sun had not yet made its appearance. The high cliffs to our left loomed ominously nearby, and to our right, the beachhead was still caught in shadows. We had not yet had our "Baptism of Fire." However, it was soon to come.

No sooner had we reached our anchorage when a large well of foam appeared just off our port quarter, about six hundred yards out; from which arose a high column of water. Shell splashes! We had begun to receive fire from the beach. Judging from the size, the guns firing at us must have been seventy-five millimeter cannon. Shortly after the first splash appeared, the report came up, "Splash off stern!" I looked back and saw a white circle of water settling back into a maze of concentric

---

25. These were likely the structures and the cathedral that Junior Talbott had to target.

circles, with a small cloud of black smoke hovering about it. Regularly, then, the splashes were reported all around us. It was quite plain that we were being straddled, and we were more or less apathetically waiting for the "third" salvo that would spell a hit. About the time I was getting ready to give voice to the query "Why don't we fire?" a tremendous blast from our port secondary battery answered my unspoken question. I remember then passing the word down through the phone circuit that the *Arkansas* had at last fired her opening salvo into this war of Shickelgruber's.[26]

Through my binoculars, I could see occasional gun flashes from the crests of the cliffs just aft the port beam. As I trained the glasses over to the area of one flash, I saw a great cloud of dirty gray smoke and flame burst, which I later learned spelled the doom of that battery. We were to see all of them blasted one by one out of existence.[27] Later, as we moved nearer to the beach, we could see the twisted remains of the guns and the piles of rubble that were the shattered pillboxes.

I happened to glance at the main battery and noted that they were training at port. I moved the crews to the leeward side and shortly after heard the word passed, "In one minute the main battery will fire to port!" A few seconds later, the entire ship shuddered as the big guns thundered their reply to the paperhanger's boast, "...Tomorrow the world!" We were prepared for a shock, having experienced main battery firing in practice. However, we had neglected to take into consideration the extra powder charge that accompanies service ammunition and we were indeed literally raised off our feet.[28]

Our target was a heavily fortified gun emplacement, After the first spot, the word came back from the spotting plane that

---

26. *Shickelgruber* was a derisive slang term for the German soldiers, much like the term "Jerry." Interestingly, Junior Talbott never referred to them in such a negative manner.

27. Junior Talbott often spoke of the target of their fire: the notorious German pillboxes. He spoke with pride of the Allied Armada and troops on the ground taking out these nests of deadly German fire one by one.

28. Junior Talbott often discussed the concussion and power of the big guns and the loud and familiar boom they made.

the target was destroyed, and so it was to continue throughout our firing—mission accomplished. A small coastal village, bristling with enemy ammunition dumps, anti-aircraft batteries, tanks and troops was to feel the impact of our fire.[29] An inland city was to be fairly blasted out of existence for harboring enemy troops and supplies. Deadly accurate was our fire, and devastating to Nazi troop concentrations, tank columns, fortified houses, and ammunition and fuel dumps which we were called upon to destroy. So accurate, in fact, that from our radio transmitter room, where the operators had been monitoring German broadcasts, came word that a Nazi broadcaster had dubbed us the "Devil Ship," and that the Luftwaffe were out to "get us." We were to later learn that they were quite serious in their threat, for the repeated air attacks made upon us were quite often the cause of some hair-raising experiences.[30]

I never shall forget a little sideshow that was performed before our admiring eyes by a plucky little destroyer that had chosen a war all of her own with an enemy observation post and gun emplacement just at the crest of the cliffs off our beam. The "can" was incredibly close to the beach, moving parallel with it like a scrappy little dog, stalking back and forth, looking for a fight. Each time the shore battery would open up, the can would reply with everything she had, from five-inch batteries to twenty millimetre machine guns. Someone, watching the scrap, said he would bet even the skipper was even on the bridge, shooting with forty-five, and it looked just like that. The shore battery scored several near misses around the can, but still she fought on. At last, upon orders from the group commander, the can was obliged to move out and let the larger ships take care of the target. This the destroyer did

---

29. It is believed that this anonymous coastal village was home to the cathedral that Junior Talbott was forced to destroy because it was being used as an ammunition dump.

30. The Devil Ship moniker would be well-known. Junior Talbott often discussed this status with the author. The ship's activities and great record during the Second World II brought it attention. Even Tokyo Rose gave it homage (of sorts) during one of her broadcasts. Junior recalled with pride that his ship gave the Germans and later the Japanese such fits.

most reluctantly, it seemed, and even then she continued to spot for the big guns, pointing out the target with tracer fire.[31]

During D-Day, the anti-aircraft gun crews were spectators, little more. However, the first night they well-earned their pay shooting at representatives of the Luftwaffe. Just at evening twilight, our alert was high-lighted by a JU-88 dropping out of the sky, across our port bow.[32] A few seconds later, the ship was shaken by a near miss just off the starboard beam, estimated to have been a thousand pound bomb. Our guns and those of ships around us were blazing and few of the planes lived to return to tell any tales. It was this night that we downed the two planes generally accredited to us.

One of the most awesome sights I believe I witnessed during the operation was that of the underwater mine fields near the beach being exploded.[33] It looked like solid areas hundreds of yards square were being cast up from the sea amid a pall of smoke and flame, accompanied by hundreds of sharp, staccato explosions. After the mine fields had been set off, and the beachhead area heavily bombarded by naval gunfire and aerial bombing, a dense, heavy pall of dirty gray smoke clung to the shoreline. It was under and through this dirty-gray cloud that our first troops hit the beaches. From then on, the multi-varied assortment of landing craft moved past in a steady stream. Off to seaward, the big transports and supply ships, with their many barrage balloons, or "rubber cows," hovering above them, continued to move toward the beach, until by the fourth day they had by-passed us and were fast becoming emptied and sent back for more.

---

31. The author wonders if this is the little destroyer that requested the twelve-inch guns of the *Arkansas* to fire over her.

32. A JU-88 was a Junkers JU-88, a Luftwaffe aircraft during World War II. This aircraft was used by the Germans as a dive bomber and even a flying bomb. It was a twin-engine German plane.

33. The underwater mine was the stealthiest of all silent killers whose presence the sailors were always aware. Like the submarine and its deadly torpedoes, the mine lurked beneath the surface of the dark waters, waiting to cause death and destruction.

Invariably troops passing close aboard would wave friendly and shout remarks like "Give 'em hell!", "See you in Berlin!" and "Save a few for us!" They are great fighters and gallant heroes, and deserved the well-earned ovations paid them.

It was dusk of the ninth day that we experienced one of the most harrowing experiences of the entire operation, and here the officer and crew unanimously averred, "There are no atheists in foxholes—or on battleships, either!" Just as the sky was growing dim, a spine-chilling sound, difficult to adequately describe, filled the air all around us, terminating in a large splash just off the starboard beam. It sounded like an ear-filling whistle, sans the shrill whistle sound; or like a gigantic rush of air. Unconsciously, we all hit the deck and hugged it, bracing ourselves for the explosions.[34] At last, a thousand years later, when it did not come, we cautiously looked up and saw thousands of tons of water settling back down. Needless to say, the crew were painfully alert the remainder of the night, and not at all in vain, for no more than an hour later, we were dive-bombed. What an uncomfortable, uncertain feeling that is! Hearing a diving plane come closer by the second until its engine reaches an ear-splitting intensity, and still not be able to see it, is not recommended for relaxation. Such was the case of "our" dive bomber. He dropped his bomb, missing us by just a scant few yards off our starboard fantail.

Each night we were regaled by displays of tracer fire and AA bursts described best, I suppose, as being a Fourth of July celebration. Almost every night Jerry came over and dropped flares all around us, many uncomfortably close.[35] We witnessed Jerry's "pathfinder" tactics, and could see the tracer fire of our

---

34. Such memories must have remained fresh in the minds and dreams of the sailors of the *Arkansas*. After returning to peacetime Finger, Tennessee, Junior Talbott one day hit the ground when some mischievous kid threw a cherry bomb or other form of firecracker. The offending firework whistled and made shrill noises as it went off. As soon as Junior heard it, he dove for cover. This was a common reaction for war weary veterans returning home whose nightmares and long years to recovery were just beginning.

35. "Jerry" was the derisive term used for German, just as "Jap" was the term identified with the Japanese.

FIGHTING THE GERMANS IN FRANCE

destroyers in the outer screen firing at Jerry's "E-boats," with the tracers describing slow, lazy arcs across the water.[36] And there were submarines, for we could sometimes feel the ship shudder as she sensed occasional depth charges dropped by the destroyers.

One impressive sight was a very large Tricolor flying from a shell-blasted building in the little coastal village whose name I may not yet reveal.[37] I wonder if I fully appreciate how these Frenchmen, so long denied the right to fly their beloved standard, feel upon once again seeing it fly over their homeland. It was a very fitting picture and a nice one to remember as we left the scene of the invasion coast for other parts where we could again strike at the enemy.

Our wait for another opportunity was not a long one, for soon after we left the Baie de la Seine, we were called upon to assist in the bombardment of the port of Cherbourg and thereby assist in the capture of that city. The task was a brief one, but not without excitement. Many near misses struck quite near us, and we were regaled by demonstrated of smoke-laying by plucky destroyers that moved uncomfortably near the coastline. Two ships of our company were hit and suffered personnel casualties. When we withdrew, the harbor batteries had been silenced, and we received a heartfelt message of congratulations from the doughboys for another job well done.

Yes, the "Arkie" made all the predictions come true, and she will continue to do so until the final battle is won. New, finer predictions are being made for her. We, of her crew, feel infinitely closer to her and endeared to her for having gotten us through safely.[38]

---

36. The term E-boat was an Admiralty term used by Allied navies for any small, fast water craft belonging to the enemy. As a general rule, an E-boat was a 105-foot Schnellboot, which was similar to the American PT boat or the British MTB. The boat could also be called an R-boat, an inshore minesweeper. Morison, *History of United States Naval Operations*, vol. 2, 174.

37. The reader must remember that this was written in 1944. Thus the rules of discretion and secrecy were carefully guarded.

38. *U.S.S.* Arkansas, *1944 Pictorial Review*, published by the U.S. Naval Department. The ship is referred to as the "Arkie" rather than its common nickname "Arky."

Although there was some confusion in the gathering together of the invasion fleet, the planners were fortunate because the fire support vessels (such as the *Arkansas*) got in ahead of everyone else and out in front of the confusion itself. According to naval historian Rear Admiral Samuel Eliot Morison, the fire support ships arrived in the transport area around 0220 and then divided into western and eastern groups.[39] The British light cruiser, the H.M.S. *Glasgow*, led the column to the western fire support area, followed by Admiral Bryant's flagship, the U.S.S. *Texas*. The *Arkansas* led the procession to the eastern area. In her youth, the *Arkansas* had served with the U.S.S. *Texas* as part of Admiral Rodman's famous Sixth Battle Squadron in the Grand Fleet. The *Arkansas* was followed by the French light cruiser, the *Montcalm*, the flagship of Contre-Amiral Jaujard, and by *Georges Leygues*, a ship known to American signalmen as "George's Legs."[40]

There are two distinct memories of Junior's that the author has, in recent years, had the fortunate experience of proving accurate. Further, there is one historic event that the author suspected and which Junior would not affirm, but historian John C. McManus indeed affirmed, which should make the families of every *Arkansas* family even more proud. The first matter involved the beginning of the actual battle for Normandy. According to Junior, the *Arkansas* cut her engines at midnight on the morning of the sixth. She drifted toward the coast so that she might arrive around 0600 hours.

Junior always maintained that everything was as quiet as one could imagine, given the fact that an entire flotilla of ships—the whole of the Allied invasion fleet—was drifting toward the shore and planes full of parachuting troops were in route. The silence was broken, he remembered, when the *Arkansas* dropped her anchor. As he recalled, "when they [the German troops] heard the sound of that heavy old chain dropping anchor, all hell broke loose on us." It was also Junior's contention that the first shots fired by the German troops in the hills above Omaha Beach at Normandy were fired on the *Arkansas*. This recollection would be easily explained by the phenomenon of a sailor earnestly engaged in the activity around him but not fully realizing that he is witnessing only part of

39. Ibid, 118.
40. Ibid.

the action and is unaware of what is occurring in the greater theater. In other words, he sees the trees around him but not the forest beyond him. Therefore, all events seem rather personal.

That reasoning would make it sensible that sailors on other ships experienced the same feeling as Junior—that *their* ship broke the silence and therefore was the first to be fired upon. However, they would be wrong. Junior was indeed correct. The U.S.S. *Arkansas* received the first enemy fire upon the Allied armada on the first day of the greatest amphibian invasion in world history. This fact would carry with it even greater consequences for him and his fellow sailors upon the Arky, the venerable old battlewagon of the American fleet. This long-held belief of being the "first" to receive enemy fire was corroborated by John C. McManus in his work, *The Americans at D-Day: The American Experience at the Normandy Invasion*.[41] According to him, the "shooting" at Omaha Beach began shortly after 0530, which was approximately twenty minutes before sunrise.[42] This information fully affirmed Junior's recollection that the fighting began just before sunrise.[43] The invasion troops were churning toward Omaha Beach in their landing craft when a German battery located near Port-en-Bessin to the east of the beach "opened up" on the *Arkansas*.[44] The *Arkansas* immediately responded in kind. McManus's work gives the impression that the *Arkansas* was the first of the Allied fleet and forces to fire upon the Germans at Normandy. This fact has rather large implications.

To understand the facts as set forth by the historians of the Normandy invasion is to understand that Junior and his colleagues operating the guns of the *Arkansas* that fateful morning fired the first Allied shots on the first day of the greatest amphibious invasion in world history. That fact was not unbeknownst to Junior, but he chose to never make an issue of it or assume it gave him and his colleagues in fire control aboard the *Arkansas* some degree of bragging rights. He understood well what had

---

41. John C. McManus, *The Americans at D-Day: The American Experience at the Normandy Invasion*. New York: Forge Press, 2004. McManus' treatment of the subject begins on page 254 with Chapter Eleven, entitled "The Naval Bombardment."

42. Ibid, 254.

43. According to Junior Talbott, it was still somewhat dark when the Germans opened up on them. He always thought it was roughly thirty minutes before sunrise.

44. McManus, *Americans at D-Day*, 254.

occurred in those first minutes at Omaha Beach. When recounting his memories of that morning, his face told of a long-held sadness of that day as well as of the triumphs of that campaign. What he could not see with his actual eyes on D-Day, he could see in his mind's eye as he went about his duties in those first hours. He knew well that many young men just like himself were wading ashore only to be mowed down by German fire. He also knew that just as many young men were drowning under the weight of their gear before they ever got ashore. Ever-present in his mind were the sacrifices given up to the gods of war for the gift of victory over the Axis Forces.

The retelling of those first few hours in the waters off Omaha Beach brought a wide array of reactions from an old and reflective man. If a question was asked or a point raised, the first reaction was often a look outside his window in front of his chair. After a moment, one could easily tell both the mind and heart were working to muster the courage and strength to revisit those anxious hours. Then the story would begin to slowly and laboriously roll off the tongue. Sometimes, there was laughter over some long remembered humorous second amidst the terror and rush of war. There would be a pause and the story would continue. Occasionally, there was a grimace and a pained look at the thought of a difficulty or moment of supreme uncertainty. More often, there was a quiet recounting and eyes that welled up and a moment was needed to recover before the story would continue.

Incidentally, there is other documentation regarding the circumstances of the opening shots at Normandy. According to Admiral Morison, the first enemy gun, which fired from a light battery near Port-en-Bessin, opened up on the U.S.S. *Arkansas* at 0530.[45] Again this substantiates Junior's own memories of the early morning hours of June 6, just prior to sunrise. This was at a point in the morning about as early as a ship could be seen from the shore.[46] Approximately five minutes later, other batteries along the east flank fired on the Allied destroyers.[47] As air spot had arrived, the destroyers replied promptly and in kind and thereaf-

---

45. Morison, *History of United States Naval Operations*, vol. 2, 122.
46. Ibid, 121.
47. Ibid.

ter the *Arkansas* followed. By 0552, these batteries had been silenced, at least momentarily.[48]

At 0552 on D-Day, the U.S.S. *Arkansas*, after counter-battery fire on the German guns placed on the eastern flank, shifted her fire to Les Moulins.[49] The actions of the battleship in those early morning hours were very significant. It is important to acknowledge that this was the U.S.S. *Arkansas*' first engagement with an enemy in the whole of her career. Despite being in service since 1911–1912, the old battleship had never engaged in any conflict to this point. While this may seem inconceivable, other than the First World War, there were no wars or major military engagements in which the *Arkansas* could participate and it had not participated in any during the Second World War. This is not to say that she had not participated in some missions, but they were limited.[50] According to Admiral Morison, the "old gal" neutralized a radar station, a machine gun position, and a fortified house.[51] The H.M.S. *Glasgow*, at the same time, fired 219 rounds on the bluffs above Les Moulins.[52] Around 0630 or shortly thereafter, the *Arkansas* was preoccupied with a battery two miles inside the British zone that had been assigned to her.[53]

Writer Cornelius Ryan adds to our knowledge of the activities of the *Arkansas* in his legendary work, *The Longest Day: June 6, 1944*. According

48. Ibid. It is important to note that Junior Talbott was at the controls of the *Arkansas*' twelve-inch guns on the morning of June 6, 1944. He remembered well those first shots fired. Despite the fact that they were likely among the first fired on behalf of the Allied Forces after those of the destroyers, Junior Talbott never spoke of them as such. Whenever discussions were initiated by the author regarding such implications, he simply ventured that all of his colleagues that day were heroes. Morison differs from McManus as to which Allied ships fired first.

49. Ibid.

50. The *Arkansas* did participate in the landings at Veracruz, Mexico, during the American-Mexican border incidents in 1914. During World War I, her involvement in active engagement was limited to a questionable incident in July 1918, as she was about to arrive in Scotland. The *Arkansas* opened fire on what was thought to be the periscope wake of a German submarine or U-boat. The destroyers escorting the *Arkansas* dropped depth charges but made no hits. The *Arkansas* saw no further incident during this war. She did not see any other hostile activity until June 6, 1944. This information was taken from an article entitled "U.S.S. Arkansas BB-33 History" found at https://web.archive.org/web/20061121203108/http://www.warships1.com/US/USbb33-history.htm.

51. Morison, *History of United States Naval Operations*, vol. 2, 122.

52. Ibid.

53. Ibid, 123.

to Ryan, the *Arkansas*, along with her sister ships, came steaming majestically toward the French coast with all its battle flags flying.[54] Once settled off Omaha Beach, the *Arkansas* and *Texas* (together mounting 10 fourteen-inch, 12 twelve-inch, and 12 five-inch guns) pumped 600 shells onto the coastal battery position atop Pointe du Hoc in an attempt to clear the way for the Ranger battalions.[55]

The *Arkansas* remained actively engaged throughout the day of June 6. At 1238, with the destroyer *Emmons* acting as a spotter, Junior and his colleagues aimed their twelve-inch guns and fired on an artillery emplacement east of Port-en-Bessin.[56] Noticing German troop movements, the *Arkansas* strafed these troops with shell fire.[57] At 0800, a Spitfire pilot provided the *Arkansas* with a report regarding a mobile antiaircraft battery on the Bayeux-Isigny Road and reported a successful shoot.[58] At that point, she turned her guns on the German batteries at Port-en-Bessin and between that port and Colleville, using both plane and top spot. The *Arkansas* expended some three hundred fifty rounds of 12-inch ammunition, which Admiral Morison stated was "pretty good for a thirty year old battleship."[59] Junior often spoke of that eventful first day of the invasion. He and his colleagues were worn out, but adrenalin and a healthy amount of fear allowed them to remain very alert.

While fighting to take Omaha Beach, the bridge on the *Arkansas* received a call from the commander of a destroyer that was directly in the firing path of the *Arkansas*. The target was communicated to Junior down in the turret. The destroyer requested that the *Arkansas* fire a shot directly over and above the destroyer so a pill box could be knocked out. Junior intentionally put off carrying out the command because he didn't feel safe firing above a sister ship. He knew if one of the powder bags wasn't up to par, it could cause the shell to fall short and possibly onto the destroyer itself. He didn't want to be the one who "pulled the trigger" that caused the death of many of his own countrymen. Finally, Junior

---

54. Cornelius Ryan, *The Longest Day: June 6, 1944*. New York: Simon and Schuster, 1959, 90.
55. Ibid, 198.
56. Morison, *History of United States Naval Operations*, 145. L.E. Talbott interview, undated.
57. Ibid, 146.
58. Ibid, 148.
59. Ibid.

and the crew were forcefully commanded to fire at the target. He placed four or five twelve-inch shells and destroyed the pill box.

On June 7, D-Day plus one, the *Arkansas* had plenty of business to conduct. There were four calls for targets to destroy a railway train, tracks, and overpass at La Plaiseon on the Caen-Cherbourg line, which she accomplished.[60] Other targets included a battery southeast of Trévières and troop concentrations on the main road south of Vierville.[61] The big guns of the Arky remained hot all that day.

As D-Day plus two dawned, on June 8, the *Arkansas* and her sailors continued to support the troops on shore. She anchored off Port-en-Bessin that morning and answered calls from her shore fire control party (s.f.c.p.), who was seven miles inland.[62] Throughout the day, she poured 138 rounds of her twelve-inch shells on German troops, vehicles, tanks, and batteries.[63] These were busy and anxious days for the sailors aboard the *Arkansas*.

Generally speaking, from June 6 through the 18th, Junior and his colleagues worked to soften up the Western Sector beachheads of the Baie de la Seine ("Bay of the Seine") river. It is a bay in northern France characterized by its wide rectangular shaped inlet approximately 100 kilometers by 45 kilometers. The *Arkansas*, along with the *Texas* and the *Nevada*, were referred to by historian Richard Goldstein as being the "mightiest ships" in the U.S. fleet.[64] The official histories, while thorough, still

---

60. Ibid, 158.

61. Ibid.

62. A shore fire control party is a specially trained unit for control of naval gunfire in support of troops ashore. It consisted of a spotting team that adjusted fire and a naval gunfire liaison team that performed liaison functions for the supported battalion commander. Sybil P. Parker, ed. *McGraw-Hill Dictionary of Scientific and Technical Terms*. New York: McGraw-Hill Companies, Inc., 2003.

63. Junior Talbott often discussed these calls from the shore fire control party (s.f.c.p.). He recalled vividly being in the heat of battle, trying to think clearly as he sighted and fired the Arky's twelve-inch guns, all while receiving instructions, calls, and information from the s.f.c.p. During the telling and retelling of these reminiscences, Junior often seemed to go back in his mind to those days. The tone of his voice was grave as he recalled the hectic activities of sitting in a gun turret, firing, and receiving information that was changing his course of actions constantly as he struggled to keep up with events.

64. Richard Goldstein, *America at D-Day: A Book of Remembrance*. New York: Delta Trade Paperbacks, 1994, 76.

lack the perspective of the common sailor like Junior. Fortunately, their recollections of the bombardment at Normandy have been preserved.

Junior recalled many stories about his targets there. Reports came back to the *Arkansas* that a cathedral just over the hillside in a village near the coast was being used by the Germans as an ammunition dump and storage facility. Coordinates were radioed back and given to him as he attempted to eliminate the target. After a few tries, one of the twelve-inch shells found its target. According to Junior:

> When I hit that cathedral, she went sky high. You could see it blow. There was no doubt it was full of German ammo. We knew it was and I hated to blow it, but it had to be done. You know, I've often wondered how many men I probably had to kill blowing up that place. I'm sure there were plenty of German boys [i.e. soldiers] working in and out of that cathedral handling the ammo. I'm sure I killed a few. But it was one of those things. You have to protect your own boys.[65]

Such ruminations about having killed enemy soldiers always caused Junior to pause and appear sad and often emotional. He would have to gather his thoughts for further conversation. It was a cost of war that he had come to accept, but it still never quite stopped haunting him. As he grew older, his mind drifted toward the subject of the war and the price for victory. He knew that but for the war, he and any German soldier or sailor might have been friends.[66] The Germans he was fighting were in many ways no different from him. His thoughts on the subject were reminiscent of the Thomas Hardy poem, "The Man He Killed":

Had he and I but met

65. Luther E. Talbott interview, 1998.

66. On the other hand, he never thought he could be a friend to the Japanese soldiers. Perhaps the memory of Pearl Harbor, the knowledge of Japanese atrocities in the Philippines and the Pacific Theater, and their wholesale cruelty toward American military and civilian prisoners were among the factors that prevented the same sadness in Junior Talbott that he felt toward the Germans.

By some old ancient inn,
We should have set us down to wet
Right many a nipperkin!

But ranged as infantry,
And staring face to face,
I shot at him as he at me,
And killed him in his place.

I shot him dead because—
Because he was my foe,
Just so: my foe of course he was;
That's clear enough; although

He thought he'd 'list, perhaps,
Off-handlike—just as I—
Was out of work—had sold his traps—
No other reason why.

Yes; quaint and curious war is!
You shoot a fellow down
You'd treat, if met where any bar is,
Or help to half a crown.[67]

Hardy's poem aptly describes Junior's emotions and feelings about German enemy troops. He often wondered about what their lives might have become had they lived. Strangely enough, he never seemed to wonder about the Japanese soldiers whose deaths he may have been responsible for. Again, he seemed to have little or no sympathy or empathy whatsoever for the Japanese.

Junior also worried about civilian casualties and the cost incurred by the woman and children behind enemy lines. In one incident, some of the spotters noticed a woman walking in the hills above the beach. This was a most unexpected sight. Given the gravity of the invasion taking place, it is hard for us to imagine. The spotters saw the woman plainly.

---

67. *Harper's Weekly*, Vol. 46, November 8, 1902, 1649.

She was spotting for the German artillery. The twelve-inch guns of the *Arkansas* alleviated the woman of her duties and obligations permanently. Junior could not believe such a possibility when the coordinates were given to him. Duty bound, he coordinated the hit. Again, he speculated:

> It was a strange thing. It wasn't the kind of thing we would usually see, a woman walking around on a hillside during an invasion. There wasn't any question why she was up there. She was spotting for the Germans. So there wasn't any choice but to take her out. There couldn't have been anything left of her after we hit her. A twelve-inch shell could do a hell of a lot of damage to a building or a pillbox. But a woman, God Almighty, I'm sure you couldn't have found anything left of her. It was a shame.[68]

The large guns of the *Arkansas* had a distinctive sound or boom. They could be identified by those with a trained or discerning ear. Many old veterans of the U.S. Army or Marines who were fighting to take a position with the support of the *Arkansas* remembered well the sound of these big guns. More significantly, they recalled the reassuring presence these guns brought. In other words, these fighting men felt reassured when they heard the *Arkansas* was at work pounding away at enemy defenses and installations.

Interestingly, one man who felt compelled to describe these distinctive guns was none other than the grand old man of American literature himself, Ernest Hemingway. In an article in Collier's entitled "Voyage to Victory" dated July 22, 1944, Hemingway wrote of the experience of riding through rough seas in a Landing Craft, Vehicle, Personnel (LCVP), a craft more famously known as a Higgins boat, with troops ready to land at Normandy. Hemingway described the LCVP rising to the crest of a wave where he and the troops could see the "line of low, silhouetted cruisers and the two big battlewagons lying broadside to the shore."[69]

---

68. Luther E. Talbott interview, 1998.

69. Ernest Hemingway and William White, ed. *By-Line Ernest Hemingway: Selected Articles and Dispatches of Four Decades*. New York: Charles Scribner's Sons, 1967, 340. Hemingway began wrote of his activities on June 6, 1944, and of seeing the grand old ladies of the Navy, the U.S.S. *Arkansas* and U.S.S. *Texas* at work.

Hemingway described the "heat-bright flashes" of the guns of the *Arkansas* and *Texas* and the brown smoke those guns belched forth as it was pushed out against the wind and then blowing away with the wind.[70]

Hemingway recounted how the steel-helmeted troops were in awe of the large fourteen-inch guns of the *Texas* as well as the large guns of the *Arkansas*. Despite the job ahead of them, these nervous G.I.'s were silently admiring the size of the guns in question as well as the destruction they were wreaking on the cliffs and hills above the beaches of Normandy. Hemingway himself marveled at the intensity of the fire of the *Texas* and *Arkansas* and the noise around him. He wrote of the experience:

> I found if I kept my mouth open from the time I saw the guns flash until after the concussion, it took the shock away.
>
> I was glad when we were inside and out of the line of fire of the *Texas* and the *Arkansas*. Other ships were firing over us all day and you were never away from the sudden, slapping thud of naval gunfire. But the big guns of the *Texas* and *Arkansas* that sounded as though they were throwing whole railway trains across the sky were far away as we moved on in. They were no part of our world as we moved steadily over the gray, white-capped sea toward where, ahead of us, death was being issued in small, intimate, accurately administered packages. They were like the thunder of a storm that is passing in another country whose rain will never reach you. But they were knocking out the shore batteries, so that later the destroyers could move in almost to the shore when they had to come in to save the landing.[71]

Hemingway's account of the guns of the *Texas* and the *Arkansas* is in keeping with other popular ideas and recollections about the firepower of these two old battleships. The *Arkansas*'s large guns had a distinctive large "boom" about them. At their firing, the guns emitted a loud explosion heard and recognized easily. More than once, upon hearing the familiar boom of the *Arkansas*' guns, an excited or otherwise exhausted

---

70. Ibid, 340.
71. Ibid, 342–343.

sailor on another ship would breathe a sigh of relief and utter a common phrase, "It's going to be okay now, boys! The old 'Arky' is here!"[72] These reassuring utterances were apparently commonplace and the presence of the old battlewagons delivered some measure of much needed peace during otherwise tense and troublesome days.

An anonymous soldier on the beach commented on seeking the assistance of the Navy as he and his fellow soldiers made their way across the beach and inland. He picks up the story:

> I remember one night we got the Navy's 16" shells coming in.[73] The U.S.S. *Arkansas* and the U.S.S. *Texas* were out there in the channel. By accident our radioman got a hold of them. And the Germans were moving stuff up to blow us off the high ground. We made contact with them but we didn't know who they were. We wanted artillery support. We gave them our location, where we were according to their map. They got all that and the guy on the radio said, "Fire for place" to see how close they were to us. They were too close. That old boy said, "Boy, you're too close." From where we were, we were up so high that you could look out to the channel and see them firing.[74] You could see the flash. Boy, it looked like a house coming at you.[75] That old boy said, "Raise it up about 200 yards and fire for effect." You couldn't see the ships but you could see the flashes and then all hell would break loose.[76] This was near Ste.-Mère-Église. I could see the shells coming in. They were traveling. They fire a far piece. I liked it. We

---

72. The *Arkansas* was often referred to by others as the "old Arky." She was the oldest battleship in the fleet still afloat during World War II. She belonged to an earlier age when battleships were much smaller. These factors led many to call her one of the fleet's grand "old ladies."

73. The author is uncertain what ship—if any—would be firing a sixteen-inch shell. The *Arkansas* fired a twelve-inch gun while the other battleships fired fourteen-inch guns.

74. The *Arkansas* and the *Texas* made a magnificent sight when firing their big guns sitting out in the English Channel.

75. Hemingway recollected that it was like the battleships were throwing entire locomotives across the water towards the Germans.

76. Junior Talbott often recollected about the concussion and rock of the *Arkansas* as she fired off a round from her guns.

sent patrols out to see what happened. Boy, they blew those Germans all to hell. They really did a number on them. They went "whir-r-r-r" as they passed overhead.[77]

Regarding the concussion caused by the intensity of the large guns' firepower, Junior personally experienced the pain and harsh shock of being too close to one of the large twelve-inch guns when it went off and while he was himself not in the turret. He experienced a horrendous shock or concussion to the ears, experienced momentary bleeding, and some small measure of permanent hearing loss in one ear.

The Normandy invasion was about more than one or two days' activities. This greatest of all amphibious invasions required the crews of the *Arkansas* and her sister ships to remain at their battle stations for weeks with little rest. By June 13, D-day plus seven, the *Arkansas* was still engaged, but had shifted to a position off Grandcamp les Bains.[78] Fire control was in touch with its s.f.c.p. but had only one call that particular day.[79] The *Arkansas* had to fire upon tanks at a position southwest of Isigny.[80] The next day, Quinéville fell and thereafter a new line was established on the ridge behind it. The *Arkansas* was active all of that day and again on June 15.[81] Thereafter, her activities and attentions shifted toward Cherbourg and the upcoming fight to take this crucial port from German hands.[82]

It is difficult to underscore the role of the *Arkansas* and her sister battlewagons in the Normandy invasion. Although their contributions seem somewhat minimized by some of today's revisionist historians, the men who planned the invasion understood the importance of their endeavors. In direct reference to the *Arkansas* and the *Texas* specifically, Vice

77. LoPinto, "Omaha Beach and the U.S.S. *Arkansas*," *The Cool Blue Blog*, June 5, 2004, http://coolblue.typepad.com/the_cool_blue_blog/2004/06/omaha_beach_and.html.

78. "U.S.S. *Arkansas* BB-33 History." http://www.warships1.com/US/USbb33-history.htm

79. Morison, *History of United States Naval Operations*, vol. 2, 167-168.

80. Ibid. A more detailed account of the military activities in and around Isigny may be found in John C. McManus, *The Americans at Normandy: The Summer of 1944—The American War from the Normandy Beaches to Falaise*. New York: Forge Press, 2004.

81. Ibid, 167.

82. On June 24, 1944, the *Arkansas* was with an accompanying minesweeper squadron, at Plymouth, England. See Morison, *History of United States Naval Operations*.

Admiral Samuel Eliot Morison quoted the First Division's Chief of Staff who, when writing to Rear Admiral J.L. Hall, remarked, "Without that gunfire, we positively could not have crossed the beaches [of Normandy]."[83] This statement has tremendous importance. Sailors like Junior and his colleagues understood their role was vital and they made the best of their efforts, as proven on that early June morning and in the days thereafter.

The Normandy invasion left an indelible mark on Junior as it did every soldier present. The reader must ever bear in mind that he, like his comrades, was participating in the greatest amphibious assault in world history. Never before—or since—had there been an invasion force like it. Sailors in fire control knew that every target, pillbox, and artillery position they eliminated was one less source of injury and death to the men on the beachheads. Despite the pressure of the mission and the indelible images burned into their minds that resurfaced in dreams and nightmares, these men, including Junior, felt a sense of pride and satisfaction in their old age. Long after the nightmares ended and the pain had somewhat subsided, he would look back on these events with a measure of understanding and satisfaction that he did his small part to rid Europe and the world of the menace of dictatorial Fascism. He further ruminated that so many young men never lived to be old and never saw the results of their sacrifice.

Interestingly, Junior never commented on or alluded to the fact that it was his twelve-inch guns that were returning that first fire back upon the German positions in the hills above Omaha Beach. Perhaps he chose not to think about it or make much of it. Yet he was on duty and discharging his fire control duties on the morning of June 6, 1944, when those first shots were fired from the guns of the *Arkansas*. Junior's ability to hit targets was well-respected by his superior officers. He often was given the opportunity to be the man on the spot in the heat of battle.[84] Still, his willingness to understate his involvement is normal for his generation and his own personal nature.

It was during the time of the invasion that Junior parted ways with a friend with whom he had been acquainted since the first days of his

---

83. Ibid, 403.

84. His old friend and colleague, Philip Wilcox of Oklahoma City, Oklahoma, alluded to this ability in an interview with the author in 1994.

service. Junior and Philip Wilcox of Oklahoma first met on board the *Arkansas* and went through fire control school together. Philip called Junior "Hillbilly" even though both shared rural backgrounds. They were inquisitive and curious young men who yearned for adventure and travel. Though quiet by nature, each had a hearty sense of humor. They developed a warm and genuine friendship. Philip was reassigned from the *Arkansas* to a destroyer escort based out of a naval base in Florida.

Following the initial invasion in June 1944, the *Arkansas* was charged with further action off the French coast. From her hard fight at Omaha Beach, she would take part in the battle for another important German stronghold in France—Cherbourg. Her presence was needed almost immediately. The Allies had to soften the German defenses as the Nazis tried to stave off the onslaught of the invasion.

The battle of Cherbourg and the justification for that campaign are difficult to describe to one who is not a student of military history or the Normandy campaign. The author often wondered why Junior placed so much significance on an obscure battle compared to Omaha Beach. Upon further study, the importance of the Cherbourg campaign—and why he felt this way—can be better understood.

Cherbourg is a coastal port in northern France close to Normandy. The Germans considered it essential and were absolutely determined to defend it.[85] Hitler himself ordered General Gerd von Rundstedt and Field Marshall Erwin Rommel to hold Cherbourg "at any cost."[86] Fortunately for the Allies, the Germans blundered. Conflicting field orders resulted in a confused and poorly executed defensive deployment and the German defense of Cherbourg was compromised.

According to Lieutenant General Omar N. Bradley, the D-Day invasion as described in its broadest terms included the following steps. General Miles Dempsey would land his British Second Army on the left with Bradley's First Army on the right.[87] Once these forces landed on shore, the goal was for Dempsey's men to move ten miles inland and

---

85. Omar N. Bradley and Clay Blair, *A General's Life: An Autobiography*. New York: Simon and Schuster, 1983, 258. Bradley, who was General of the Army, provides a very personal yet objective account of the campaign for Cherbourg in his autobiography.

86. Ibid, 262.

87. Ibid, 233.

capture Caen, France. Caen was a major road center on the Orne River and the most likely route through which the counterattacking German forces would pass. Bradley's First Army would then start their inland trek and cut the Coentin Peninsula. From there, the Allied forces would pivot to the right and seize Cherbourg. The port city would be an entry point for their supply lines.

As these objectives were being accomplished, General Henry D.G. Crerar's Canadian First Army would wade ashore to provide reinforcements for Dempsey's British Second Army. General George Patton's army would come ashore to reinforce General Bradley's First Army. All of these movements would set the stage for what the Allied commanders called the "breakout."

The Canadian and British forces under the command of British Field Marshall Bernard Montgomery (popularly known as "Monty") would draw the fire of the counterattacking Germans in order to provide cover and protection for Bradley's troops. The American First Army would then turn in a movement like a giant arc reaching as far to the southeast as the Loire River. In the converse, as General Patton's men of the Third Army proceeded inland and wheeled westward, they were to capture the Brittany Peninsula. This campaign was designed to establish an Allied line that would be 140 miles in length on a North-South line or front which faced eastward toward Paris and the Seine River. Certainly, the Allies expected the Germans to put up a stiff resistance along that front in order to protect France from further Allied invasion.

Aside from the German viewpoint that Cherbourg was vital, General Bradley himself recounted that he turned his full attention to the Cherbourg campaign during the weeks leading up to the Normandy invasion. According to him, the campaign turned out to be "one of the classic actions of the war."[88]

Given these opinions by the high command of the both the German and the American armies, Junior's opinion and reminiscences of the importance of the actions at Cherbourg are justified and vindicated. It is important to remember that veterans often didn't study the histories of the campaigns in which they were engaged. Instead, they carried with them the contemporary knowledge and reminiscences from their actual

---

88. Ibid, 262.

days in the field. The two World Wars were really the first conflicts in which American soldiers and sailors were provided sufficient information during their service to understand the purpose of their missions. These men fought with an understanding of their greater goal, even if they did not know or understand the details of the missions.

As with D-Day, the weather continued to cause angst among the Allied commanders as they planned the Cherbourg Campaign. Rough weather would make for disastrous results if not properly considered. The Allies needed every port and path of passage they could take. Following the Normandy invasion, the weather did indeed turn foul. June storms made landing supplies, equipment, vehicles, and troops an almost impossibility. The heavy surf crashed upon the beaches, forcing the stoppage of work and resulting in the destruction of mulberries, which were artificial harbors built by the Allies and towed to northern France for use in getting war materiel from their ocean worthy carriers to the beach.[89]

Weather difficulties made it clear to the Allied high command that their hold on Normandy was rather precarious and fraught with uncertainty.[90] They would be reliant upon the unpredictable weather of the English Channel until the city of Cherbourg could be captured. It would give them a port from which to safely debark their men, materiel, and supplies.

Hitler and his High Command were adamant that Cherbourg be held. Over 40,000 German soldiers were garrisoned at "Fortress Cherbourg" with orders to make the city "impregnable." The Fuehrer was under no illusions. He knew perfectly well that the Allied armies needed a port from which to supply their men. Hitler was determined to deny them Cherbourg at all costs.

At midnight on D-Day plus 12, June 18, the assault beaches were pelted by heavy rains and strong winds.[91] As the day wore on, the winds increased. Unloading on Omaha Beach had to stop because of rising tides. Heavy surf hammered the beaches for the next two days. All work had to stop. When the winds and storms abated, Omaha was a mess. Stranded crafts, Mulberry wreckage, and coasting barges and vessels littered the

---

89. Morison, *The Two-Ocean War*, 408–409.
90. Ibid, 409.
91. Ibid, 408.

beaches. During this period of bad weather and destruction, there was no unloading being done.[92] This type of delay caused obvious problems. The storms and foul weather demonstrated to all that the Allies' hold on Omaha was precarious and tenuous. This made the capture of Cherbourg a serious and urgent goal. Until it was taken, they would continue to be at the mercy of the unpredictable weather of the English Channel.

On June 22, General Lawton Collins' VII Corps was ready to advance on Cherbourg. Three of his divisions lost more than 2,800 killed and 13,500 wounded before liberating the port city. But it was the U.S. Navy that acted decisively in assisting Collins' armies on June 25, with the *Arkansas*, the U.S.S. *Texas*, and several destroyers pounding the German's coastal guns placements.[93] Each ship or group of ships had an assigned target or group of targets. This form of militaristic multi-tasking allowed the Allies to overwhelm the Germans at Cherbourg and to continue the tide of victory that would force the Germans' continued eventual retreat back to Berlin. The *Arkansas* had her place in that formation.

Admiral Morton L. Deyo commanded the naval bombardment forces. They were comprised of the Utah fire-support vessels and a few of the fire-support ships from the Omaha force, including the *Arkansas*.[94] A coastal defense battery at Querqueville was silenced by carefully placed air-spotted fire, allowing American troops to advance. Battery Hamburg, consisting of four 11-inch, 280 mm artillery pieces, was taken with the assistance of the *Arkansas*, the *Texas*, and a contingent of destroyers.

At 12:08 P.M. on June 25, the *Arkansas* was the first to fire upon the German positions at Cherbourg. The Germans waited until the *Arkansas* and the *Texas* were within firing range of their batteries. The *Arkansas* escaped injury and destruction. The naval battle for Cherbourg was relatively short and ended within the day. It fell rather fast in contrast to other naval battles in which the *Arkansas* would participate. Still, the battle stood out in Junior's mind as ever important and a major accomplishment for him and his fellow sailors. Interestingly, Junior's twelve-inch guns were the only ones on the *Arkansas* that fired at the Battle of Cherbourg and

---

92. Ibid, 409.
93. Ibid, 410.
94. Ibid.

unleashed only fired 58 rounds. These rounds were carefully and precisely placed, however, in order to make the destruction efficient and effective.

Junior also recalled the battle for Cherbourg because of an interesting incident that occurred upon a sister ship, the *Texas*. It and a couple of the destroyers were hit by German batteries. The impacts were significant but not disastrous. In fact, the *Texas* was hit twice. The first shot rendered considerable damage to the old battleship. That first shell, a German 240 mm (9.4 inch) shell, struck the *Texas* at 13:16 P.M. It skidded across the top of its conning tower, tore off or sheared off the top of the fire control periscope, and proceeded to hit the primary support column of the navigation bridge before exploding. The explosion caused the deck of the pilot house to be blown approximately 4 feet high, wrecking the interior.

However, it was the second shot to the *Texas* that would marshal Junior's attention and give him pause to think for the next six decades. At 14:47 P.M., an unexploded German 240 mm (9.4 inch) shell crashed through the port bow directly below the Wardroom and lodged in the wall of a stateroom. It was this unexploded shell that Junior discussed for years after, not the first one that actually exploded and caused damage and injury. Shortly after the battle, he and a contingent of his *Arkansas* shipmates from fire control were ferried over to the *Texas* to inspect the lodged and unexploded shell. Their assignment was not to disarm it, but instead to study the effects of an artillery shell upon an aging battleship only one year younger than their own beloved *Arkansas*.[95]

Junior remembered this unexploded shell and described it in some detail many years later. According to author John Ferguson, the 240 millimeter high-capacity shell was found lodged in the port side of the ship some twelve feet down from main deck and the unexploded shell came to a rest in a stateroom.[96] Although Ferguson does not document the inspection by men of the *Arkansas*, he does document the aftermath,

---

95. Many years later, a man named Mark Pope, who once worked for Junior and Faye Talbott at their grocery store, told their grandson, Bryan L. Talbott, about Junior's account of this incident. Pope had visited the U.S.S. *Texas* in San Jacinto, where it is harbored as a museum. He related to Bryan Talbott that while touring the ship, he carefully reviewed an exhibit that explained the story of the unexploded shell. He saw a photograph of sailors from the *Arkansas* inspecting the shell. In the photo was none other than his old employer, Junior Talbott.

96. Ferguson, *Historic Battleship Texas*, 125.

inspection, and defusing of the shell in the days following the action at Cherbourg.[97]

It was widely recognized on both sides that naval firepower from the *Arkansas* and the *Texas*, with assistance from the destroyers, was largely responsible for the fall of Cherbourg, Hitler's vital port. The naval onslaught amounted to a "naval bombardment of a hitherto unequaled fierceness." Although a number of forts and units remained under German control, the Navy eventually helped deliver them to the Allies as well. This campaign would continue to be a source of pride to Junior as the years passed.

Junior's service record, dated June 26, 1944, noted the following:

> Participated honorably in the Naval Bombardment Support for the Allied landings in the Western Sector beachheads of the Baie de la Seine, France from June 6 to June 18, 1944. Also participated in the Naval bombardment of the Cherbourg fortifications on June 25, 1944…Participated honorably in the Naval Bombardment Support for the Allied Landings in the Gulf of Frejus, Southern France, from August 15 to August 17, 1944.[98]

Thus, the campaign in Europe ended for Junior and the U.S.S. *Arkansas*. The anxiety and feelings aroused by the action in the English Channel were only a prelude to the severity and ferocity of the campaigns that lay ahead in the Pacific. For their heroic and faithful service from June through August 1945, he and his fellow sailors were authorized and entitled to wear "one star in the European-African-Middle Eastern Area Service Ribbon for participation for Bombardment and Invasion of the French Coast 6-25 June 1944" and "one star in the European-African-

---

97. The author viewed this unexploded shell aboard the U.S.S *Texas* on June 2, 2019. Interestingly—and unbeknownst to both parties until the next day—the author's aunt and the daughter of Luther E. "Junior" Talbott viewed the shell aboard the ship a day later.

98. Service Record dated September 28, 1943. Compiled service record, Luther Edward Talbott, FC2d, Division F, U.S.S. *Arkansas*, National Archives, Washington. D.C.

Middle Eastern Area service ribbon for participation in the Invasion of Southern France 15-17 August 1944."[99]

---

99. The Normandy Campaign star was authorized in September 1944 and the Southern France star was authorized by the Commander in Chief, U.S. Fleet Ltr. Ser. 13 of January 2, 1945. Service Record. Compiled service record, Luther Edward Talbott, FC2d, Division F, U.S.S. *Arkansas*, National Archives, Washington, D.C.

9

Lively Days Before Transfer to the Pacific

Following the invasion of Normandy on D-Day and the collapse of Cherbourg, France, there would be intense days ahead for Junior Talbott and the crew of the *Arkansas*. Much travel and preparation lay ahead. But their work in the European Theatre was not quite finished.

On July 21, 1944, prior to the invasion of southern France, the *Arkansas* sailed into the port of Taranto, Italy, where she remained until August 6. Italy had surrendered to Allied forces at this point and was no longer an Axis power. Benito Mussolini had been the head of an exiled Italian puppet government, a reward from his old friend, Adolf Hitler. Not all Italians were grateful for the fall of their Fascist government. Sailors of the *Arkansas* returning from shore were waiting on the dock for the Liberty Launch to pick them up and return them to the ship. Suddenly, a group of Fascists (also called "rebels" by Junior) began firing on them. One Italian sniper was perched in a window firing an automatic weapon. Luckily, a handful of British Marines eliminated him. These were

LIVELY DAYS BEFORE TRANSFER TO THE PACIFIC   209

the dangers posed to American fighting men and the Allies in a quickly changing world.

The *Arkansas* belonged to Battleship Division Five. It joined the Eighth Fleet in the Mediterranean Sea in July 1944. Though there had been no ship-to-ship combat, enemy fire and attacks from German pillboxes and other shore positions were a constant danger. The men of the *Arkansas* would later discover the terrible threat from the kamikaze. Other experiences were yet to be known, some that were enjoyable.

Junior recalled activities in which he and his fellow sailors engaged while on their way to various points in the world. About four days out of New York City, they would sunbath out on the decks of the ship in nothing but their shorts. Junior first discovered sunbathing while on shore patrol at Pier 92. He saw sailors as "brown as Negroes." Usually the sunbathing activities depended upon the presence of submarines.[1]

Following the battle of Cherbourg, the *Arkansas* made its way to North Africa. Junior first visited Oran, Algeria, between July 10 and July 18, 1944. It was a place that fascinated him. While there, the sailors were given three hours of liberty per section. In order to reach a good section of beach, they had to travel over the mountains. Some of the Army boys coming off active duty from Italy or the North African campaign acted as drivers for the Navy boys. They picked them up in open bed trucks with seats on each side in the back. These Army boys drove wildly, accustomed to wartime obstacles and conditions. Coupled with the fact that the road to the beach was narrow, winding, and over the mountains, it was a short but harrowing trip.

The sailors of the *Arkansas* preferred traveling to the white beaches over the mountains because the port in Oran, according to Junior, was "not fit for a hog to swim in." The scum, filth, and garbage made the water unhealthy and wholly unattractive for recreational activities. They didn't stay in town any longer than necessary. The native people were light-skinned and more Mediterranean in appearance than African. According to Junior, they were of an olive complexion that he described as a "high yellow" variety. They seemed to be a relatively intelligent people.

One of the more colorful anecdotes that Junior remembered about Oran involved trading with the locals. Once the sailors disembarked,

---

1. This was a memory often shared over the years by Junior Talbott.

they would sell bed sheets to them. The locals would cut holes in them for their heads and arms. When the bed sheets became filthy and nearly rotten, they would simply put on a new bed sheet over the old one. American cigarettes—high quality or even cheap ones—were used as currency to buy anything. Chocolate bars and other American luxuries served the same purpose. They could take a GI or sailor a long way in a North African port city. Junior enjoyed observing the native population—their clothes, architecture, and customs. North Africa particularly fascinated him.

Between trips to Oman in 1944, the sailors engaged in activities aboard ship. There were USO (United Service Organizations) shows, dinners, and plays that warded off boredom and kept their minds occupied from the mundane day-to-day toil of war. The boys of the *Arkansas* saw live performances of the Jack Haley Show and the Irving Berlin Show. Jack Haley (1898–1979) was a vaudeville song and dance comedian who was best known for his portrayal of the Tin Man in the 1939 film *The Wizard of Oz*. Irving Berlin (1888–1989) was a well-known songwriter, composer, and lyricist who wrote numerous Broadway scores. To have had either man on board for a show would have been quite a big event. Having both celebrities perform in the same year gave the servicemen variety. Berlin held his show aboard the *Arkansas* on July 25, 1944.[2]

The most memorable performance for Junior was that of the famous funny lady Martha Raye. Known as "The Big Mouth," she performed in USO shows during World War II, the Korean War, and the Vietnam War. Junior always laughed when recalling this USO show. Raye got the boys to really "hooting and hollering." The officers thought they were getting out of hand and tried to quiet them. "Leave these boys alone!" Raye shouted. "They're doing just what you fellows wish you were down here doing!" The officers left the boys alone to cheer for her. Junior never failed to laugh and shed a joyful tear at the memory of this lively diversion.

Following the lengthy and complicated invasions of Normandy and Cherbourg, the *Arkansas* sailed into the waters off the coast of Southern France in the region between Toulon and Cannes. She would be called upon once again to assist the ongoing invasion. The amphibious assault was

---

2. Ray Hanley and Steven Hanley, *Arky: The Saga of the U.S.S. Arkansas*. Little Rock AR: Butler Center Books, 2015, 101.

originally known as Operation Anvil, but it was later renamed Operation Dragoon by British Prime Minister Winston Churchill.[3] For a number of reasons, including the insufficiency of troop-lift and gun power for two French invasions at one time, the invasion of Southern France did not occur until August 15, 1944.[4] General Eisenhower insisted on the invasion in part because he knew the Allied armies would need another major port, namely Marseilles, to handle the logistics supply. Antwerp had not yet been secured.[5]

There was plenty of politics swirling around the invasion. Churchill and the British Chiefs of Staff opposed the invasion outright because it would require taking troops from the British Army's Italian Campaign. Their preference was to conduct an amphibious operation at Trieste in the Mediterranean.[6] Churchill continued to push for the Mediterranean invasion at Trieste right up until the actual Normandy campaign.[7]

The primary objectives were the ports of Marseilles and Toulon. Both were well-protected by 240 mm coastal defense batteries. The invading forces needed all the naval support they could get. The yellow sand beaches located between pine-covered rocky terrain on the Provence Coast were formidable. These coasts were fortified by heavy coast artillery and large French guns as well as land mines and underwater obstacles.[8] The German Army had thirty thousand troops in the assault zone and another two hundred thousand in the vicinity.[9]

The Eighth Fleet, including the *Arkansas*, was sent down from the English Channel to conduct the naval bombardment of the coast. Joining them were the American battleships *Nevada* and *Texas*; the British battleship H.M.S. *Ramillies*; the French battleship *Lorraine*; three heavy cruisers—the *Augusta*, *Quincy*, and *Tuscaloosa*; and numerous destroyers and

---

3. Samuel Eliot Morison, *The Two-Ocean War: A Short History of the United States Navy in the Second World War*. Boston: Little, Brown and Company, 1963, 411.

4. Ibid.

5. Ibid, 412.

6. Ibid.

7. Ibid, 413.

8. Ibid.

9. Ibid, 414.

cruisers.[10] This invasion was fairly complicated. The Allies performed a 400-plane parachute drop and Commando raids by moonlight.[11] Admiral and historian Samuel Eliot Morison penned a very thorough explanation of the preparations and planning for the invasion of Southern France in his work, *History of United States Naval Operations in World War II, Volume XI: The Invasion of France and Germany, 1944–1945*.[12]

Junior and his fellow sailors knew they were being tracked by the Germans. Seaman David Roberts recorded in his journal on August 12, 1944, that the *Arkansas* would "again be the target ship" and "move to within 6,000 yards of [the] assigned target which is four 6-inch guns encased with 16 ft of concrete."[13] He was concerned that the *Arkansas* would be within 9,000 yards of the Germans' 9-inch guns. The same guns would be targeted by the *Texas* and the *Nevada*. These battleships were staying some 15,000 to 20,000 yards away. Seaman Roberts noted on August 14 that "Nazi Search Radar has picked up." Later that day, three more Nazi search radars" had picked up the *Arkansas*.[14] The German focus on the old battlewagon was not unusual. They called it the "Devil Ship."[15]

Junior recalled the cat and mouse game between the *Arkansas* and her German enemies. As the battleship moved down the French coast, the men knew they were being tracked. This fact added an ominous edge to the mood aboard the ship. As Junior explained it, they were already on edge because the fighting they had engaged in along the coast of France had varied from Normandy to Cherbourg. No one knew exactly what to expect. The Germans gave much credit to the *Arkansas* following the Allied victory at Normandy. Indeed, Junior himself took great pride in the merit given the old battlewagon by the German Armed Forces.

In August 1944, Allied forces began the terrible work of softening up German defenses along the coast of Southern France. The repeated bombings effectively knocked out vital guns and radar stations along the

10. Ibid.
11. Ibid, 415.
12. Morison, *History of United States Naval Operations* 6, 219–292.
13. Hanley and Hanley, *Arky*, 101.
14. Ibid.
15. Luther E. Talbott interview, 2003, regarding the German view on the *Arkansas*.

coast for at least ten consecutive days from August 5–15.[16] The Germans were expecting this invasion and concerned about their weakened defenses and forces.[17] The Allied invasion was aided by factors that could have proven more positive than they were. During the last couple of days of the Allied bombings, their accuracy and effectiveness were the result of good timing and execution. They were further enhanced by the fact that little opposition was encountered from antiaircraft and none from the German air force, the Luftwaffe.[18] Unlike the invasion of Normandy, the invasion of Southern France was aided by perfect weather during the actual air bombardment. The amphibious landing, however, was far less ideal with a heavy mist over the land.[19]

Night landings occurred in the Provence region of Southern France August 14–15 prior to the main landings. They were well documented in Admiral Morison's narrative *History of United States Naval Operations in World War II*.[20] On the morning of August 15, at 0730, the aerial bombing of the coast ceased and the Navy began its onslaught. The naval bombardment was indeed rough. Allied destroyers delivered withering fire and LCT's fired rocket missiles onto the beach. By 0801, assault troops were landing on the beaches.[21] By nightfall, there were approximately 16,000 troops and more than 2,000 vehicles on the shore.[22]

The *Arkansas* was engaged fully in supporting the invading troops on August 15–17. At the time of the amphibious invasion, there was great concern about lethal mines in the coastal waters off Southern France. In fact, Junior vividly recalled the sight of the minesweepers doing their work. He was fascinated by the technology of both the German mine and the Allied minesweepers doing their damned best to keep Allied fighting ships from becoming German casualties. His curiosity was boundless when it came to technology and tools of warfare with which he was personally involved. He found the overall collective effort to land troops

---

16. Morison, *History of United States Naval Operations* 6, 243–244.
17. Ibid, 244.
18. Ibid.
19. Ibid, 244, 249.
20. Ibid, 248–254.
21. Morison, *The Two-Ocean War*, 411.
22. Ibid, 418.

on the beaches of France to be masterful and impressive. With the exceptions of General Douglas MacArthur and Executive Officer Philip M. Boltz on his own battleship, Junior found no fault with the Allied military leadership and his immediate superiors. He considered these men to be an impressive collection of minds and admired their ability to see the big picture while minutely managing the smallest details of the war machine.

Junior was grateful for the minesweepers. The *Arkansas* would be the battleship closest to the coast, making her susceptible to the shore batteries and the added danger of possibly floating into a sea of mines. The service rendered by the many minesweepers working back and forth across the waters of the Mediterranean Sea was crucial. These small, fast ships weaved in and out of the imaginary lanes set for them and detonated the deadly mines. Their hard work and bravery prevented possible mass destruction of Allied naval forces. Junior would never forget them.

In most respects, Operation Dragoon was a relatively easy objective for the Allies. However, not all elements of the operation were without difficulty. Task Force 87, Camel Force, did not have an easy assignment in the Southern France invasion. Neither did the Naval Bombardment Group under the command of Rear Admiral Morton L. Deyo that supported the Camel landing troops. One of the battleships under Admiral Deyo's command that comprised a part of Camel Force was the U.S.S. *Arkansas*. As usual, the Arky found herself in trying circumstances with the most difficult of tasks. She was the sole battleship in Task Force 87, Camel Force.[23]

Perhaps one reason Junior recalled the minesweeping activities so well was because this coastal section of Southern France was so strongly fortified. Unlike other invasion zones in Operation Dragoon, Camel Force and its supporting vessels were operating in an area that was truly well-defended and heavily mined.[24] The naval gunfire support group under Admiral Deyo included the *Arkansas*; the U.S.S. *Tuscaloosa*, a heavy cruiser; and five light cruisers.[25] Seaman David Roberts recorded in his journal the events of the battle. From their ship, the men of the *Arkansas*

---

23. Morison, *History of United States Naval Operations* 6, 341.
24. Ibid, 267.
25. Ibid, 268.

could see the Air Force, Army, and Navy carrying out bombing raids on the beach.[26] According to the men themselves:

> When the *Arkansas* left the Cherbourg Peninsula many believed that her role had been played in the European Theater and that she would gracefully retire from the combat stage. Such a suspicion was soon dispelled as she set out for the Mediterranean area seeking new conquests and Nazi objectives. It was mid-August. Again she headed another armada-parade. The destination was the coast of Southern France.
>
> The show was a good one, following the pattern of the Normandy invasion—moving up to the coast in the night closely trailed by an impressive armada of invasion ships and landing craft from many Allied nations—watching our roaring swarms of heavy and medium bombers blast coastal defenses and enemy troop concentrations until our turn came to open fire.
>
> This time, however, we fired before we were fired upon, possibly because the coastal batteries which were our targets were too stunned by the shattering aerial bombardment to open up on us. The Arky's first target was a large battery of casemated heavy guns, at short range. She plastered it with a smashing barrage of twelve-inch shells until it was neutralized. Next came the landing beach. She drenched it with high explosive from her twelve and five-inch guns, frequently throwing in a twelve-gun salvo from her main batteries to pep things up ashore.
>
> Our last designated target was a good-sized coast town, an important harbor, and Nazi headquarters area. Again our twelve-inch shells quickly reduced much of it to rubble, fires and shattered buildings. Some Nazi prisoners we later took aboard said the naval bombardment was the worst experience they had ever undergone.
>
> Following D-day the Arky stood by to act as artillery for our troops ashore, but the Nazi "super-men" and their motley assortment of slave soldiers from conquered countries either

---

26. Hanley and Steven Hanley, *Arky*, 103.

surrendered or 'advanced' backward so rapidly we had no further opportunity to fire at them. Needless to say, the whole crew enjoyed this shoot. Getting shelled doesn't seem so bad when one can hand it back as we did on D-day. No enemy shells came close this time. Once again the Arky came through without a scratch. Although she was in the 'hot spot' and expected plenty. At night she retired from her close-range position and consequently was not bothered as much by enemy planes as she was at the Normandy beach. Our AA gunners got in a little target practice at the few planes that did not come over but they weren't lucky enough to bag them.

The whole show was beautifully timed and executed, clicking smoothly with perfect teamwork between the combining Army, Navy and Air Forces of several nations. A couple of thrilling sights—big squadrons of heavy Liberator bombers coming in at low level, dumping tons of explosive all over the beach within a few short seconds—watching the French cruisers and destroyers having a field day celebrating their big moment of triumph, slashing away at targets up and down the coast with every gun blazing almost continuously. New twist to the Arky's adventures was a considerable number of Nazi prisoners she picked up from one of our destroyers who, in turn, had acquired them from a landing craft. They trooped aboard, bedraggled, dirty and obviously happy to be out of war. We cleaned them up, fed them, and later landed them at a port where they were taken off to a prison camp.

The prisoners were interesting, as were the various ports the Arky visited, but as this is being written, the unanimous and most immediate interest of all hands is a new type of invasion – the invasion of a port in the U.S.A."[27]

This narrative tells little if anything truly about the involvement of the *Arkansas* in the invasion of Southern France. But it gives some insight on the perspective of sailors involved in the European Theater. The *Arkansas* provided heavy fire support during the difficult landings on both Red Beach and Green Beach on the Golfe de Fréjus. The main battery of

27. *U.S.S.* Arkansas: *Pictorial Review – 1944*. United States Navy, 1944.

their 12-inch guns, where Junior was engaged, fired 470 rounds during the invasion while the secondary battery of 5-inch guns shot 87 rounds and the ship's anti-aircraft battery 1,644 rounds.[28]

Thereafter, the *Arkansas* departed Southern France for Palermo, Sicily.[29] When Marseilles and Toulon fell on August 28, 1944, the goals of the operation were achieved.[30] Interestingly enough, Junior never mentioned any specific details of the campaign other than to admire the tenacity and hard work of the minesweepers. He simply and perhaps characteristically stated that the campaign simply kept him "awfully busy." In fact, the *Arkansas* fired a significant number of rounds at the coastal batteries and other targets during the invasion.

One of Junior's shipmates, Turret Commander Harold Clements, wrote to his parents about the eventful campaign. His comments reflect what he and his shipmates thought during the invasion of Southern France.[31]

> August 22, 1944
> U.S.S. *Arkansas*
> Dear Mom and Dad:
> The Allies struck a heavy blow in the invasion of Southern France several days ago and the American warship, as in the Normandy invasion, was present at the initial assault helping to blast a path for the first landings. Not long after we left port the captain spoke to us describing the task which lay ahead. Meanwhile, we were joined by men-of-war of both our own and other nations. As we plowed onward I wondered if the enemy realized when or where we were about to strike and would he be ready to "take it" and "dish it out."
> During the night many shapeless, obscure forms of transport and landing craft were overtaken and left behind in the

---

28. Lt. H.A. Wilson, editor. *U.S.S.* Arkansas, *Pacific War Diary, 1945*. United States Navy, 1945.

29. Ibid.

30. Morison, *The Two-Ocean War*, 420.

31. Howard H. Peckman and Shirley A. Snyder, editors. *Letters from Fighting Hoosiers*. Bloomington IN: Indiana War Commission, 1948.

darkness as we moved into our forward and final position. Angry rumblings of bomb bursts and flashes of fire came from the distant area as bombers unloaded their deadly cargo. Swarms of bombers, fighters and troop transport planes droned overhead passing to and from the engaged area.

When the skies began to glow just before dawn, we found ourselves surrounded with ships and landing craft of all descriptions while the shores of France loomed surprisingly near, shrouded with a haze of dust and smoke from the night bombing attack. We were then well within range of enemy coastal batteries and I for one hoped we would not long delay our opening fire. We had not long to wait, however, as the main battery was trained on an enemy installation of casemated guns and the sounding of the firing buzzer announced "standby for opening salvo." With a deafening roar we sent our salutation to Hitler's crowd on the beach. All around us ships of all nations were blasting away as we fired salvo after salvo while hundreds of landing craft moved shorewards.

As you know, the Army took the beach in stride and moved inland in high gear. We had a number of German prisoners aboard for a while. They didn't have the tough superman appearance the German propaganda experts would have us believe. A couple of nights we were sighted by JU-88 snoopers but a lusty barrage of A.A. [anti-aircraft] fire drove them off.

The gun crews really enjoy throwing the big stuff over here at the Germans and are getting worried for fear the war will be over for the Navy and we will be left out at the finish. Anticipating this possible situation, the gunners are trying to have the engineers install wheels on our ships so we can catch up with the Army and help chase Heinies through the streets of Berlin…

Yours,
Harold

The issue of prisoners of war being brought aboard during this time was seldom mentioned by Junior. In fact, German prisoners were housed on the *Arkansas* following the battle of Cherbourg. They had been transferred from American destroyers who picked them up from landing craft coming back from the beaches.[32] This duty was short-lived but nonetheless showed the multi-faceted assignments of the *Arkansas*.

Junior did recall the peculiar appearance of these men. American soldiers and sailors had heard so much about the invincibility of German soldiers that to actually see them in person was intriguing. They gave no appearance of being fallen "super-men" but simply what they were—soldiers from a defeated army wanting to be back home. Although he recalled the sight, he certainly did not revel in it. As he often stated about German soldiers and sailors, but for the war, any one of them might have been his friend. The common German soldier was essentially like himself, fighting for his country.

As it turned out, Hitler himself was determined that the Brittany ports be destroyed and his forces hold out to the end. This attitude only further reinforced Eisenhower's belief that Marseilles must be captured.[33] The business of weakening the German hold on France continued. However, the *Arkansas* was dispatched elsewhere and thus moved on to Sicily and afterwards to Oran.

Junior and the crew of the *Arkansas* spent the second week of August 1944 at Palermo, Sicily. His time there was not ideal, but it did leave an impression. Many times he said it was the "nastiest" place he ever visited. In villages and places around Palermo, there were open ditches laden with raw sewage. He saw more prostitutes and women of the night on its streets than anywhere else in the world he visited. Junior grimaced each time he talked about it. He truly held it in disdain. When asked to tell more about Sicily, he only ventured that the island "wasn't fit for a hog." He remembered:

> Without a doubt, Sicily was the filthiest place I'd ever been, then or since. It was god-awful! The women were willing to do anything. I saw more prostitutes in Sicily than anywhere else I'd ever been. The place [Palermo] was dirty. There was

---

32. Hanley and Steven Henley, *Arky*, 100.

33. Carlo D-Este, *Decision in Normandy*. Old Saybrook CT: Konecky and Konecky, 1994, 463.

sewage in the ditches and the streets. I'm sure there were more decent places on the island but from what I saw, you wouldn't know it. There wasn't anything on that damn island that really interested me at all. To tell the truth, it wasn't fit for a hog to live on. It was awful![34]

Nevertheless, Junior did a little souvenir shopping. He purchased a pewter ashtray with a horse head and horseshoe pattern and inscribed roughly with the words, "Sicily 1944." This was the only souvenir he wished to bring back from Sicily, though in his opinion, it was certainly possible for a sailor to bring back other more sinister souvenirs from the island.

While in Palmero, he took time to write a letter back home to his fiancée, Faye McIntyre. He was looking forward to going home and seeing his sweetheart. He wrote:

Aug. 9, 1944

My Dearest Faye:

Hello Honey, hoe does these few lines find you now. Fine I trust, and having a swell time. As for myself, I am O.K. and having as nice a time as I can expect being this far from you. But I keep thinking of the time when I can be back with you and I hope that it isn't as long as it has been till we can be together again.

Well Honey I wonder what you are doing these days. Nothing much I am guessing that it too hot there to work. Am I right? Well you haven't anything on me. I'm not doing much myself now. Just a little now and then. Except for a lot of thinking about you and the times we spent together and wishing I were there now.

Say Honey tell J.R. I said for him not to study too much and to be sure and not keep you too busy helping him with his lesson that you haven't time to write a few letters.

Say Honey, how is Lucille and Roy getting along? I guess they still like La. fine. Tell them I said Hello.

---

34. Luther E. Talbott interview, 2004.

Say Darling, are you getting my letters regular now or not. I have been wondering how the mail was from here to there. It is swell from you to me. I get your mail in about 7 to 10 days. I think that is purty good myself.

Well Honey, I will close for this time as I have run out of anything to write. So just remember that I will be thinking of you wherever I am and loving you more each minute that we are separated. So here is hoping to hear from you soon.

All my Love,
L.E.T.

Junior gladly sailed out of Palermo on August 19 and arrived in Oran, Algeria, on the 21st. The *Arkansas* docked off the coast until September 4. In stark contrast to Sicily, he always found Oran fascinating. The people interested him and the customs even more so.

Places that he saw only from the deck of the ship thrilled him just as much. The world is replete with destinations that he passed but did not set foot upon their soils. In some ways, they fascinated him more because he could not visit them. He could only see them from afar with the sea breezes blowing against his face.

One of these landmarks was Gibraltar, the site of the famous Rock of Gibraltar. The *Arkansas* passed through the famous Straits of Gibraltar on her way to the Mediterranean Sea; Palermo, Sicily; and Taranto, Italy. Another place he often discussed—but it cannot be ascertained whether or not he ever visited—was Tunis, Tunisia. He was very interested in Tunis and spoke of it often. There is no doubt that the *Arkansas* sailed directly past and within sight of the coast. The cruise books of the battleship do not refer to any portage in or off Tunisia. However, it is possible that Junior and his shipmates may have been given leave to go ashore at Tunis. But this is not known with any certainty.

The *Arkansas* was docked in Taranto, Italy, from July 21 to August 6, 1944. This time allowed Junior an opportunity to see and experience some of the old Italian culture that he had only read about in schoolbooks. This exposure was captivating in the greatest classroom of all—the world. He recalled being invited by a lovely young lady to eat dinner with her family in Taranto, an experience he never forgot. The little

Italian mother made a pizza pie, the first such delicacy that Junior had ever eaten. According to him, she had saved her leftover vegetables and cheeses throughout the week. She made a crust and a sauce and dumped the leftovers into the crust and baked it. The family was large and they dined at a long table. Junior enjoyed the pizza thoroughly. The dinner was also the first time he ever drank wine with his meal. He seemed to relish this memory and smiled greatly at its recall.

Another vivid remembrance involved a visit to an abbey in Taranto. Junior was not sure of its identity, but it may well have been the Abbazia di Santa Maria della Giustizia (Saint Maria of Justice), a medieval abbey built in the twelfth century. Regardless, it was a very old monastery and contained a burial vault, a large sarcophagus, and a burial area. He recalled the vault of a young lady who had died during the period of the First World War some thirty years before. She was entombed in a casket with a sealed airtight glass top. Junior could see her face, head, and shoulders through the glass. She looked as if she was only asleep. Despite being dead for more than thirty years, she looked as if she would awaken at any time. He found the experience touching and fascinating. He often thought about that long-dead girl and the things he had seen at that ancient abbey. He often wondered how it was possible that a young man like him could see so much in this mysterious old world.

Aboard the *Arkansas*, Junior sailed past the islands of Sardinia and Corsica and Messina, Italy. He found the Mediterranean Sea alluring and the terrain of the coast captivating. He also enjoyed the architecture of the Mediterranean regions that he visited. Being in Italy, the lessons learned in both Latin and history classes at Chester County High School suddenly came alive in a way he could not have otherwise imagined. The Mediterranean also made for a deeper swimming hole than Huggins Creek back home. He took the opportunity and swam in that renowned sea.

Junior also sailed in the region of the Canary Islands and the Azores. It was a center of activity for submarines, especially Germans. From December 1942 until December 1944, the approximate time of the *Arkansas*' transfer to the Pacific Theater, the battleship sailed a total of 67,629 miles. The majority of that time was spent in the Atlantic Theater and the Mediterranean.

By the fall of 1944, Junior and Faye wanted to be married. They would have done so much earlier, but her parents were hesitant to give their blessing. The reason was simple. John Robert and Ollie Pearl McIntyre were afraid their youngest daughter would marry this young sailor and be left a young widow. The couple reluctantly agreed, but finally decided they would wait no longer.

In September, Junior sailed home from Oran and arrived in Boston Harbor on the 14th. The *Arkansas* entered dry dock for repairs and to be updated with new tools and equipment in preparation for service in the Pacific Theater. She would remain for the next two months. The crew tells the story in the *Pacific War Diary*:

> After firing hundreds of full service rounds on the beach heads of Normandy, Cherbourg, and Southern France, the Arky's guns were replaced as part of the Boston Navy Yard overhaul. New fire control instruments were installed and necessary repairs and alterations were made to give the Arky additional offensive power for her forthcoming operations in the Pacific.[35]

The *Arkansas* received her largest retooling of the war. The *Pacific War Diary* showed photographs of the actual reconditioning work. The top plates were removed and a turret made ready for "regunning." Very large cranes hoisted the old rifles out of the turrets. According to the editors of the *Pacific War Diary*, it took patience and skill to handle the 50-foot guns that were "10 feet longer than a railroad boxcar."[36] Afterwards, with the muzzle first, the new rifle barrels were placed in the after ends of the turrets. Ships sometimes received a camouflaging paint for their next assignment.

The process of retooling the old battleship was lengthy and painstaking. The long interval gave Junior and Faye sufficient time to get married and enjoy their honeymoon. He arrived back in Finger, Tennessee, in late September 1944. By this time, he had survived three major battles in a much larger campaign and was preparing to engage a far more ruthless enemy in the Pacific Theater. Marriage would wait no longer. Junior

---

35. Wilson, ed. *U.S.S. Arkansas: Pacific War Diary, 1945.*
36. Ibid.

and Faye applied for their marriage license. On October 3, they went to the home of Brother Brody Henson, a Church of Christ minister in Henderson. Faye had been baptized into the church a few years before; Junior had not readily identified with any church. Regardless, they asked Brother Henson to perform the ceremony. The two young people stood in his front parlor with Mrs. Henson standing by to witness the event. As the elderly Brother Henson performed the marriage, Brody Henson Jr. and his good friend John A. "Buddy" McDonald waited outside and peeped in the window. Junior and Faye never ceased to laugh remembering the boys sneaking a peek at their wedding.

The young couple honeymooned seventeen miles northwest in Jackson. They stayed at the New Southern Hotel. Faye never forgot their honeymoon meal. While eating at the hotel restaurant, a couple of squirrely fellows approached them and asked Junior for money so they could go see their "sick mother." Junior harbored certain suspicions about the men that were probably correct. He did not believe they were brothers or that anyone was going to see a sick mother. His suspicions were all the more aroused when they insisted he step outside to talk with them. Junior expected the men to "roll" him or gang up and mug him. He didn't take the bait.

Junior and Faye stayed in town only a short period of time before making their way by train to Boston. The author has always been curious of the exact route taken from Jackson or Finger. Nevertheless, for Faye, it was an interesting trip. She had never traveled farther than West Tennessee. Junior had already been around the world but Faye had not seen any of it. One can imagine the rural countryside and the cities that she saw for the first time. Their honeymoon continued in Boston, a large metropolitan city like none she had ever experienced.

Junior and Faye spent close to a month there. For Faye, it was a period of firsts. For Junior, it was time spent with his new bride while still fulfilling his duties aboard the dry-docked *Arkansas*. They shared an apartment with a couple named George and Florence Johnson. Supposedly, George was an heir to the Standard Oil Company fortune. The author seems to recall that George was not in the service due to some reason that disqualified him. Florence's brother was the assistant district attorney of Miami-Dade County, Florida.

The couples quickly hit it off. They talked and got to know one another. Their worlds were different. George and Florence were city kids and Junior and Faye were country kids. Still, they bonded. One evening, Faye cooked up a batch of biscuits. George ate through the pan of biscuits and wanted more. Florence told Faye, "I wish you'd never made those biscuits. George loved them so much, I'll have to go on making them myself." Faye never forgot the incident. She often wondered if Florence indeed kept up the practice of making biscuits.

While Faye was in Boston, she visited a Catholic Church and was surprised by how quiet it truly was. As a member of the Church of Christ, she was accustomed to somewhat subdued services. The busy nature of the city itself was quite overwhelming for the country girl. She recalled the vastness of the train station that was far larger than the Finger Depot. While walking towards a crowd, she realized that she was hearing in person the voice of New York Governor Thomas E. Dewey. The Republican presidential candidate was delivering a speech as he campaigned against a fourth term for President Franklin D. Roosevelt.

While in Boston, Faye became friends with a sailor from Louisiana. He was a gentleman and a nice fellow. They got along very well and liked to cut up with one another and laugh. Playfully, the two debated who made the best molasses, Tennessee folks or Louisiana folks. The sailor called Faye by the nickname "Tennessee-lasses," and Faye called him "Louisiana-lasses." He was nice to her because she was now a Navy wife and he understood her plight. He died in service to his country when his ship was sunk a few months later. The author has no record of the sailor's name and with Faye's death, the man's name, if she recalled it, was lost forever to anonymity.

Another story that both Junior and Faye laughed about often regarded, of all things, the length of Junior's toes! One evening while still honeymooning in Boston, the couple retired to bed for the evening. At some point, Junior moved his foot over and pinched Faye's leg with his long toes. She screamed and thought something had gotten her. They laughed about the incident for the rest of their lives.

Faye learned the ways of the big cities: buses, train lines, passes into facilities, and meeting new people. She had the opportunity to visit a USO facility and was given a room for the evening. This was most likely on her return trip.

Junior left Boston aboard the *Arkansas* on November 7, 1944, sailing for Portland, Maine. Faye made the journey back home to Finger by herself. The train trip was memorable for one occurrence. Sitting in the dining car, it was noticeable that even in the Northern states, the whites sat on one end and the blacks on the other. As soon as the train crossed the Mason-Dixon line in Maryland, the porter drew a curtain in the center, separating the dining car into a white section and a black section.[37]

Interestingly, Faye wrote down on the back of a postcard the names of the cities and towns through which she traveled. They included Boston, Providence, Rhode Island; New London and New Haven, Connecticut; New York City; Atlantic City, New Jersey; Philadelphia; Wilmington, Delaware; Baltimore; Washington, D.C.; and the Virginia cities and towns of Charlottesville, Lynchburg, Bedford, Roanoke, Shawsville, Christianburg, Radford, Pulaski, and Wytheville. The postcard itself had been purchased in Boston. On the front were pictures of Pemberton Square and the new Boston Courthouse (1944). Never before had she traveled so far and seen so much.

As soon as Faye returned home, she resumed her regular correspondence with Junior and continued to help his father at the store. She ferried between the Talbott home and her parents' home on the old McIntyre farm. Life as a Navy wife began in earnest now that she was back and her husband was far away. There was no certainty that he would return. In fact, he was in greater danger now than at any time thus far in his military service.

---

37. At that time, the black or African-American section of a facility was known as the "Colored" section.

Luther Edward "Junior" Talbott, circa late 1942 or early 1943

U.S.S. *Arkansas*, BB33, circa 1942

U.S.S. *Arkansas*, BB33, circa 1944

U.S.S. *Arkansas*, BB33, ca. 1938, just prior to the outbreak of war in Europe.

Captain Wade DeWeese (*center*), the last skipper of the U.S.S. *Arkansas*, on board the battleship.

Captain Frederick G. Richards (*right center*) and Rear Admiral Carleton F. Bryant (*left center*), former skipper of the U.S.S. *Arkansas*, greet sailors aboard the *Arkansas*, which Bryant used as his flagship during the D-Day invasion.

Captain Frederick G. Richards was Junior's favorite skipper on the U.S.S. Arkansas.

Lt. (jg) L.L. Clardy inspecting damage to Japanese gun emplacements on Okinawa inflicted by the big guns of the U.S.S. *Arkansas* after island fell to Allied forces

(*Left*) Luther Edward "Junior" Talbott as a new graduate of the Naval Fleet Service School in Newport, Rhode Island, ca. March 1943.

(*Bottom*) Sailors of "F" Division (fire control) on board the *Arkansas*, ca. 1944. Junior is in the third row, fourth from left (*below*).

"F" Division (fire control) on board the U.S.S. *Arkansas*, ca. 1943. Junior Talbott is on the third row, seventh from the left.

Luther Edward "Junior" Talbott, while a cadet at the Naval Fleet Service School in Newport, Rhode Island, ca. January 1943.

Luther Edward "Junior" Talbott, shortly after graduating from the Naval Fleet Service School, 1943.

Luther Edward "Junior" Talbott in Glasgow, Scotland, May 1944, during preparations for the invasion of France (D-Day).

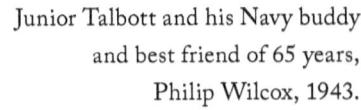

Junior Talbott and his Navy buddy and best friend of 65 years, Philip Wilcox, 1943.

(*Above*) The masthead of the U.S.S. *Arkansas* sailors' newsletter, *The Arklite*, announcing the action of Iwo Jima.

Executive Officer of the U.S.S. *Arkansas*, P.M. Boltz, an officer Junior neither liked nor respected.

(*Above*) The typhoon at the mouth of Buckner Bay which found Junior stuck in a tower to weather the storm and which forced the U.S.S. *Arkansas* to sail into the East China Sea to avoid significant damage. (*Below*) The burial at sea of Coxswain Peter Paul Konosky, an event which Junior witnessed firsthand that left him saddened and moved until his dying day.

Scenes from the U.S.S. *Arkansas* during the sail to Normandy for the D-Day invasion, June 1944.

The *Arkansas* in action at the D-Day invasion at Normandy on June 6, 1944.

(*Above*) The U.S.S. *Arkansas* delivering fire on Mount Suribachi at Iwo Jima. (*Below*) The battleship came within 1,700 yards of the shore in order to destroy the gun emplacements.

Cartoon from the U.S.S. *Arkansas* sailors' newsletter, *The Arklite*, depicting their efforts to goad the Japanese out of their foxholes at Iwo Jima.

Some of Junior Talbott's comrades ashore at Okinawa inspecting an old native tomb.

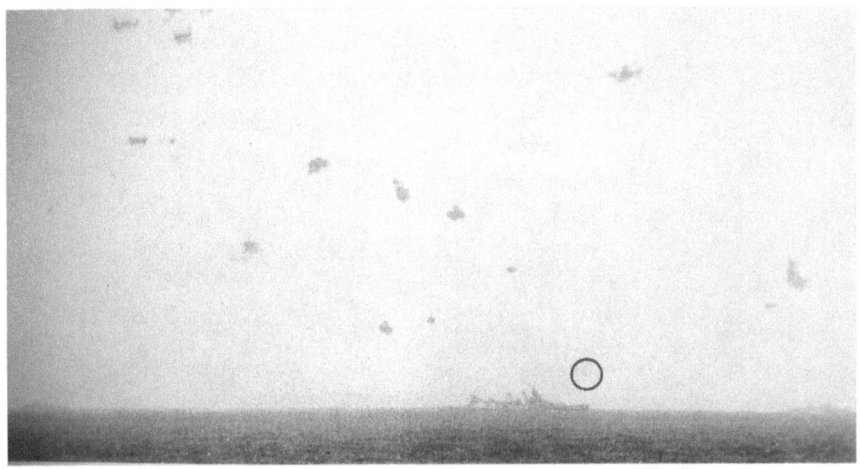

Photo taken during the Battle of Okinawa demonstrating the proximity of Japanese kamikaze planes to American naval battleships. The circled object is a kamikaze plane targeting a battleship.

Junior Talbott remembered the German prisoners of war who were transported aboard the U.S.S. *Arkansas*.

An old newspaper article depicting the invasion of Okinawa. It was a historic battle for many reasons, one in which Junior Talbott experienced and witnessed many terrible horrors. He kept this clipping for more than 62 years.

Grand Old Lady OF THE PACIFIC FLEET

U. S. S. ARKANSAS

The U.S.S. *Arkansas* was honored on Navy Day 1945 for her role as the U.S. Navy's oldest active battleship.

Junior Talbott's sweetheart of more than 63 years—
and his friend for more than 70 years—Faye (McIntyre) Talbott.

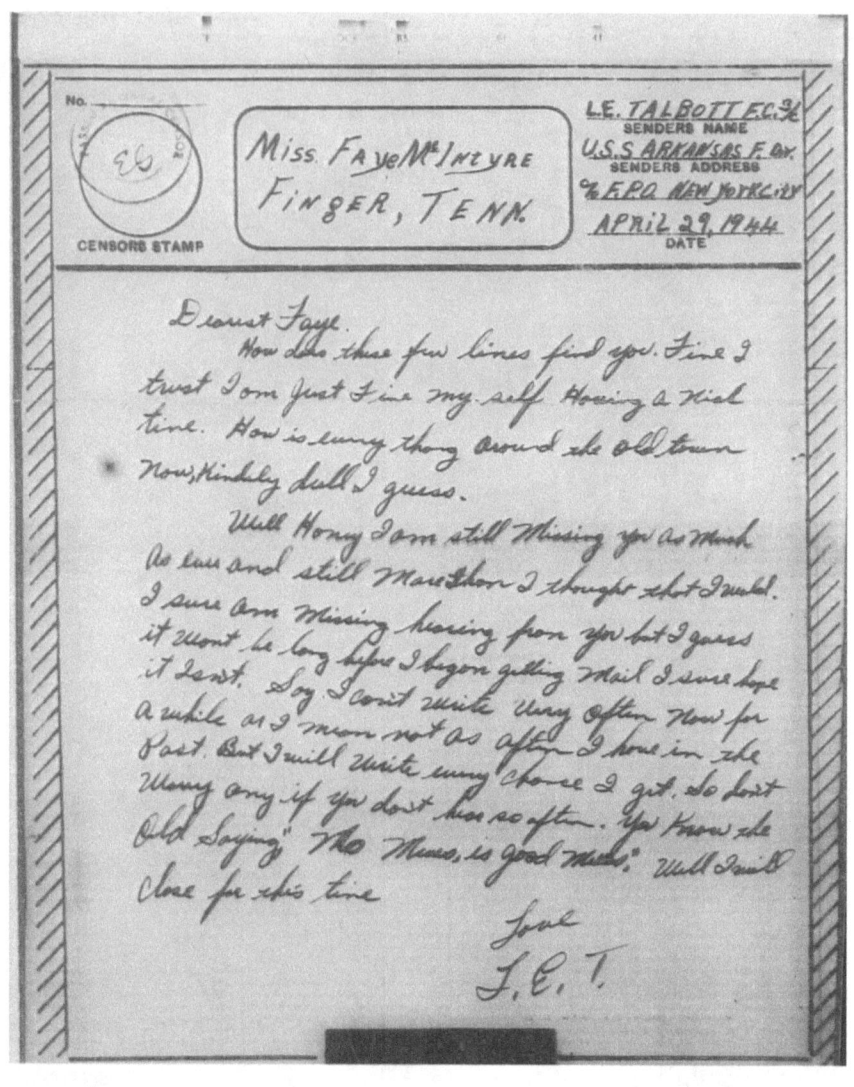

A V-mail between Junior and Faye during their courtship. It demonstrates the strong bond between them and the type of ties that kept sailors like Junior fighting and holding on during the biggest war in world history.

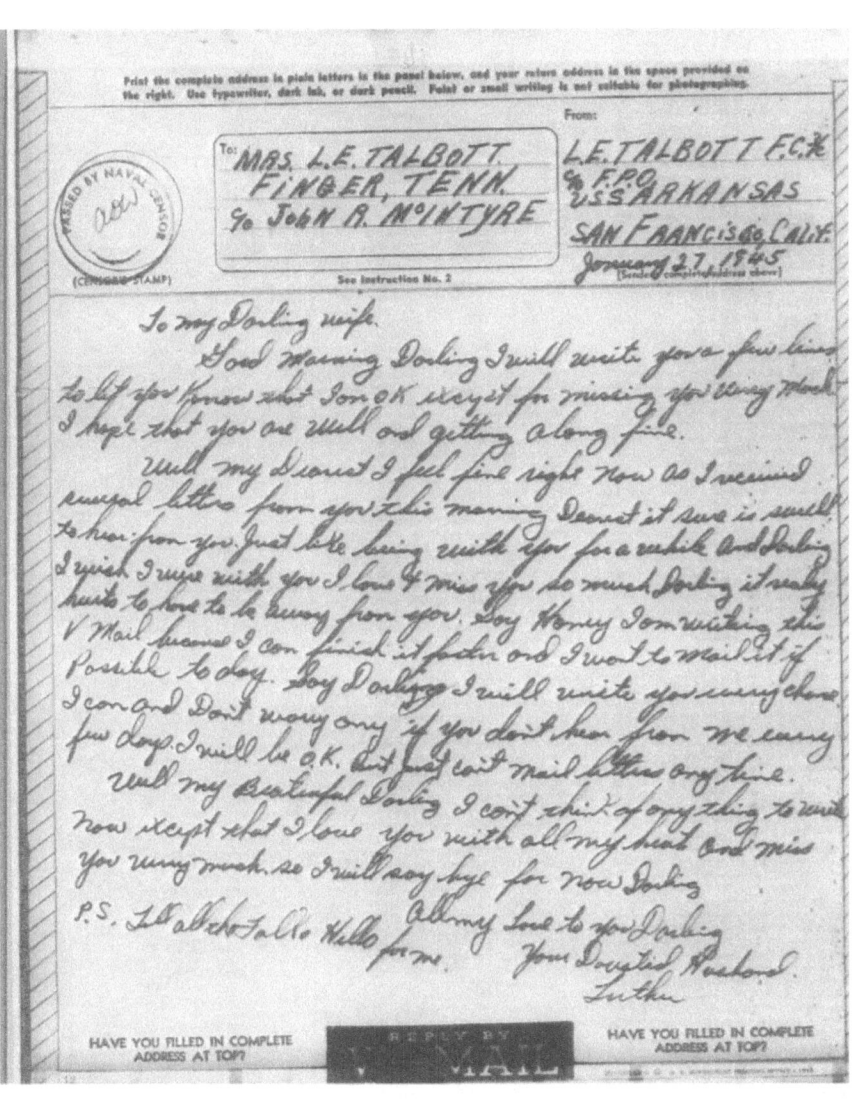

A V-mail between Junior and Faye following their marriage. These communications were all important to sailors and their loved ones during the war.

Faye McIntyre proudly holding a photograph of her sailor.

Faye McIntyre and future sister-in-law, Vonnie Mae Talbott, helping Newt Talbott in his general merchandise store in 1944. They were filling the shoes of Junior Talbott, who was far away doing his part in the war.

Newlyweds Junior and Faye Talbott, late 1944

Home from the war and happy to be back forever. Junior with Faye and his parents, Newt and Varham Talbott, ca. 1946.

(*Below*) An honorable and well-earned discharge from the United States Navy.

10

Breaking the Japanese Grip on the Pacific

The European war was over for Junior Talbott and his fellow sailors aboard the *Arkansas*. The powers that were had decided that the old battlewagon had performed so well in Europe that she could now perform valuable service in the Pacific Theatre. Given what the War Department knew about the fighting habits of the Japanese, it is no wonder the war planners made such a decision. After all, the efficient and effective firepower of the *Arkansas*, *Texas*, and *Nevada* would be very useful when attempting to take Mount Suribachi at Iwo Jima and later Okinawa.

The differences between the two theatres of war would soon become clear. The Germans, like most people, believed in some form of self-preservation in the face of defeat. Under similar circumstances, the Japanese accepted self-sacrifice and—more dangerously—taking the enemy with them. They could be quite fanatical.

In the Foreword to the *U.S.S.* Arkansas' *Pacific War Diary*, Lt. (jg) L.W. Hayman wrote the following, which seems very appropriate:

> There is no room in this book for such words as "brave," "gallant," or "heroic." These words have been so cheapened by ad-writers and the like that they have lost all meaning and proportion. Rather, describe the Arky and her men as an outfit that went to war and into battle afraid but willing, realizing full well the suicidal power of the Jap, yet determined to do their part to make the Allied victory final and complete. They were gripped with the terrible conviction that the more smashing the victory, the longer the future would keep the peace.
>
> For the man who re-reads these pages after the war, many things will be recalled: the prickly heat, the monotony, the dysentery, the long days and nights spent at General Quarters and Air Alert stations. He'll remember, too, the companionship and the silent understanding that comes only among men who have gone through great danger together. He'll remember how the beer tasted at Guam, how the gun crews played pinochle and acey-ducey during intervals between firing, how he sang and shouted himself hoarse on Aug. 10, the real V-J night, how the American girls in Honolulu looked.
>
> He'll remember how he felt that January morning when the ship sailed westward out of Long Beach Harbor, how he felt at Okinawa when he heard the news of President Roosevelt's death, how big the lump in his throat was when he first sighted Puget Sound on his way home.
>
> Above all, he'll never forget that he fought the war on his ship, in defense of his country and her ideals. He'll never forget that war is the dirtiest and most horrible business a man can engage in.
>
> And remembering all this, he'll always be a fighter…for peace, for his home, for his democratic rights, for his country and his fellow-man.

Many of these emotions were expressed and described by Junior during his later years. He remembered well the heat, the long days, and the Divine Wind—the Kamikaze. They were forever branded upon his memory. He recalled the green flies and blow flies lighting upon the dead ashore following the invasion. In the South Pacific, Junior contracted a skin disorder that caused his legs to become red and inflamed, the skin scaly, itchy, and irritable. This condition stayed with him until his death some sixty-two years later.

The Pacific Theater was an entirely different set of circumstances for the sailors of the *Arkansas*. The Atlantic and European naval campaigns involved the danger of Wolf Packs lurking deep in the cold Atlantic waters, the dangers of mines floating just beneath the surface of the water, and being the target of German batteries and pillboxes at Normandy, Cherbourg, or Southern France. Junior recounted the anxiety he and his shipmates experienced with every voyage across the Atlantic Ocean, knowing other vessels had fallen prey to the U-boats of the German Navy.

The challenges of the Pacific Theater were unknown to them. There was the potential of Kamikaze attacks and reports of the atrocities the Japanese committed, but they had not experienced the potential of those dangers due to their lack of proximity to the war with the Japanese. There was another aspect of the war with the Japanese that differed from the war which the sailors of the *Arkansas* waged with the Germans. The Germans were not disposed to suicidal missions and were known for generally humane treatment to enemy troops.[1] Of course, this was vastly different from the conditions of concentration camps, which were anything but humane.

The Japanese were a different set. For reasons of culture and military tradition, they treated enemy troops with great cruelty and could be quite sadistic in their methods of treating captured Allied soldiers and sailors. Further, there was always the concern of the Divine Wind, the Kamikaze attack. The young, but experienced sailors of the *Arkansas* had only heard of these dangers. They did not know personally of the experience. Soon they would learn and understand the true anxiety of the sailor waiting on the next surprise Japanese attack. That was the situation that the *Arkansas* was sailing into as she left the Atlantic and European

---

1. German prisoner of war (POW) camps were more humane by far than the Japanese POW camps; their treatment of POW's was far more humane than their treatment of Jews, Jehovah's Witnesses and other groups.

theater to enter the fight against the Imperial Army and Navy of Japan in an effort to bring the Second World War to an end.

No person less than the famed war correspondent, Ernie Pyle, said of the transition from the European Theater to the Pacific Theater:

> Covering this Pacific war is, for me, going to be like learning to live in a new city.
>
> The methods of war, the attitude toward it, the homesickness, the distances, the climate—everything is different from what we have known in the European war.
>
> Here in the beginning, I can't seem to get my mind around it, or get my fingers on it. I suspect it will take months to get adjusted and get the "feel" of this war.
>
> Distance is the main thing. I don't mean distance from America so much, for our war in Europe is a long way from home too. I mean distances after you get right on the battlefield.
>
> For the whole Western Pacific is our battlefield now, and whereas distances in Europe are hundreds of miles at most, out there they are thousands. And there's nothing in between but water.
>
> You can be on an island battlefield, and the next thing behind you is a thousand miles away. One soldier told me the worst sinking feeling he ever had was when they had landed on an island and were fighting, and on the morning of D-day plus three he looked out to sea and it was completely empty. Our entire convoy had unloaded and left for more, and, boy, did it leave you with a lonesome and deserted feeling.
>
> As one admiral said, directing this war is like watching a slow-motion picture. You plan something for months, and then finally the great day comes when you launch your plans, and then it is days or weeks before the attack happens, because it takes that long to get there.
>
> As an example of how they feel, the Navy gives you a slick sheet of paper as you go through here, entitled "Airline Distances in Pacific." And at the bottom of it is printed "Our

Enemy, Geography." Logistics out here is more than a word; it's a nightmare.

Here's another example of their attitude toward distances in the Pacific:

At Anzio in Italy just a year ago, the 3rd Division set up a rest camp for its exhausted infantrymen. The rest camp was less than five miles from the front line, within constant enemy artillery range.

But in the Pacific, they bring men clear back from the western islands to Pearl Harbor to rest camps—the equivalent of bringing an Anzio beachhead fighter all the way back to Kansas City for his two-weeks' rest.

It's thirty-five hundred miles from Pearl Harbor to the Marianas, all over water, yet hundreds of people travel it daily by air as casually as you'd go to work in the morning.

And there is another enemy out here that we did not know so well in Europe—and that is monotony. Of sure, war everywhere is monotonous in its dreadfulness. But out here even the niceness of life gets monotonous.

The days are warm and on our established island bases the food is good and the mail service is fast and there's little danger from the enemy and the days go by in their endless sameness and they drive you nuts. They sometimes call it going "pineapple crazy."

Our high rate of returning mental cases is discussed frankly in the island and service newspapers. A man doesn't have to be under fire in the front lines finally to have more than he can take without breaking.

He can, when isolated and homesick, have more than he can take of nothing but warmth and sunshine and good food and safety—when there's nothing else to go with it, and no prospect of anything else.

And another adjustment I'll have to make is the attitude toward the enemy. In Europe we felt our enemies, horrible and deadly as they were, were still people.

> But out here I've already gathered the feeling that the Japanese are looked upon as something inhuman and squirmy—like some people feel about cockroaches or mice.
>
> I've seen more groups of Japanese prisoners in a wire-fenced courtyard, and they were wrestling and laughing and talking just as humanly as anybody. And yet they gave me a creepy feeling and I felt in need of a mental bath after looking at them.
>
> I've not yet got to the front, or anywhere near it, to find out how the average soldier or sailor or Marine feels about the thing he's fighting. But I'll bet he doesn't feel the same way our men in Europe feel.
>
> —*Ernie Pyle writing from Honolulu, Hawaii, on February 16, 1945, prior to actually covering the Pacific War. This was in anticipation of the Iwo Jima campaign in which Pyle would be the victim of a deadly Japanese sniper.*[2]

Pyle's observations are telling in many ways. They were eerily reflective of the feelings of the typical sailor such as Junior Talbott. Pyle discussed the distances and the vast expanse of water between landmarks. This was an observation that Junior made more than once in his reflections. While a sailor could view long stretches of shore while coming into port in England or France or another European port, such was not the case in the Pacific. There would be hundreds of miles of nothing but water and finally a small island that might be only a mile or so in length. These small islands might provide the only stop along the way, the only respite from the Pacific deep. Indeed, Junior had sentiments and opinions similar to Pyle's regarding the Japanese.

One of the islands which provided the *Arkansas* with a break from the monotony of endless water was the tiny island of Ulithi. The Ulithi Atoll was desired by the Allied Fleet for its large, deep lagoon that would provide a "perfect" fleet base.[3] Admiral Chester Nimitz was the man responsible for ensuring the capture of Ulithi for Allied naval purposes.[4]

---

2. David Nichols, ed. *Ernie's War: The Best of Ernie Pyle's World War II Dispatches.* New York: Simon & Schuster, 1986, 366–367.

3. Morison, *The Two-Ocean War*, 428.

4. Ibid, 422.

Indeed, Ulithi became the fleet rendezvous and forward base for the Iwo Jima and Okinawa Campaigns and the site of the *Arkansas*' rearming, re-provisioning and refueling between campaigns.[5]

Although Junior and his fellow sailors aboard the *Arkansas* got the opportunity while anchored at Ulithi to enjoy some rest and recreation on Mog-Mog, there was still danger present even at Ulithi.[6] According to Admiral Samuel Eliot Morison, the naval historian and officer earlier quoted and referenced in this work, the only contribution of the Japanese Navy to the defense of Iwo Jima was submarine employing the use of the *kaiten*. The *kaiten* was a "human torpedo" carried and directed by one swimmer. On November 20, 1944, one of these kaitens sank a fleet oiler in the Ulithi Lagoon, but this Japanese success was not repeated in this form.[7] However, just off the shore of Ulithi and just four thousand yards off the bow of the *Arkansas*, Junior and his fellow sailors saw a Kamikaze "hurtle through the sky and smash into flames on the flight deck of the U.S.S. *Randolph*.[8] This initial view of the Kamikaze gave Junior and his colleagues a preview of what they were to later experience at Okinawa.

It was likely at Ulithi that Junior contracted a lifelong skin disorder that would plague him for the remainder of his long life. It was a dermatological disorder that affected his arms and legs, most specifically his legs. It resulted in an inflammation of the skin and flesh on the underside of the arms and on the shin of the legs. The condition resulted in an irritation that caused the skin to become scaly and itch. Junior often scratched his legs until they were blood red. The author asked about this condition and was told that it was a skin irritation that he, Junior, picked up on the islands of the Pacific.

Ulithi was heavily populated by coconut trees and primitive thatched huts, all set against an attractive backdrop of green sea and white coral.

---

5. Wilson, ed., *Pacific War Diary*, 1945.

6. It could not assumed that an island of strategic importance taken from the Japanese anywhere in the Pacific realm was safe from further attack. In the case of Ulithi, an important base for Allied naval and other military operations between the Iwo Jima and Okinawa campaigns, it became an important piece of dry land in the Pacific for the Japanese. Its importance to this prong of the Axis powers is reflected only by its importance to their enemies, the American and Allied forces. Incidentally, Mog-Mog is a tiny green island located in the Bikini Atoll.

7. Morison, *The Two-Ocean War*, 515–516.

8. Wilson, ed., *Pacific War Diary*, 1945.

Junior spent a considerable amount of time on the island. There he saw men climb coconut trees like monkeys and retrieve the tough coconut. He and his fellow sailors would pay the young native boys a nickel to climb the palm trees to retrieve a coconut. The little native boys, he recalled, climbed like little squirrels. While resting at Ulithi, Junior and his comrades enjoyed such activities as writing a letter home, drinking a little beer, getting in some swim time, or hunting for shells.

Still, such momentary relaxations were just that—momentary. It was not to last. The island was again a forward base, a staging area and a rendezvous for the Navy. The next great objective of the Allied Naval forces was the conquest for the tiny island of Iwo Jima and the first Pacific battle to test the mettle of the sailors on the *Arkansas* was indeed Iwo Jima. This battle would give these boys their first chance to fight the Japanese and understand the gravity of the situation in the Pacific.

IWO JIMA: THE FIRST REAL TEST IN THE PACIFIC

> *"Following the days of blasting by the heavy units, the assault waves hit the beach under cover of our fire. The Jap gunners are still potent and effective, but the amphibious craft never waver as they carry load after load of Marines from the transports to the beach."*[9]

Ulithi was a stop on the way to and from Iwo Jima. It was at Iwo Jima that Junior got his first taste of action against the Japanese Imperial Forces. The young sailor from Finger, Tennessee, would have respectfully disagreed with Ernie Pyle as to the monotonous nature of the Pacific Theater. Perhaps it was monotonous for some, but not for a floating city upon the open waters of the Pacific Ocean. Junior often stated that he and his fellow sailors worried as much about not making it back alive while sailing the Pacific as they had escorting ships across the Atlantic. Until the battle for the volcanic island of Iwo Jima, the horrors of war with the Japanese were still unknown to the boys of the *Arkansas*. What they knew had been read in newspapers and briefly glimpsed in newsreels of the day.

9. Ibid.

The *Arkansas* began its Pacific journey when it departed from Portland, Maine, on November 11, 1944. She sailed down the eastern seaboard and through the Bahamas. The vessel sailed between Cuba and the island of Hispaniola past Jamaica in the Caribbean Sea. She arrived at the great Panama Canal, one of the greatest engineering feats of the twentieth century, on November 17. One of Junior's most personally entertaining memories was the experience of sailing through the canal. He often laughed while reminiscing about the *Arkansas* carefully making her way through. The ship's decks were so close to the edge of the locks that sailors could purchase bananas from Panamanian vendors just by leaning over the railings and exchanging currency with the locals. An antique postcard belonging to the author illustrates the closeness of the "quarters" as the *Arkansas* made her way through the locks and channels of the Panama Canal.

They sailed from the Canal Zone on November 19 and arrived in San Pedro, California, on November 27. She remained at San Pedro until January 20, 1945. It was here that Junior experienced his only episode of sea sickness. Unfortunately, there is no information available regarding this lengthy stay off the coast of California. He never expounded on this period. It is assumed that little of consequence occurred other than his bout with sea sickness. However, we know that on November 29, 1944, the *Arkansas* was underway for exercises to be held off the coast from San Diego. On December 10, she returned to San Pedro for three more weeks of preparations.[10]

The *Arkansas* arrived at Pearl Harbor, Hawaii, on January 26, 1945. The sailors received a message from Fleet Admiral Chester W. Nimitz: "CINCPAC bids you welcome to Pearl and the Pacific Fleet."[11] Despite such a distinguished welcome, the *Arkansas* did not linger. The venerable old battlewagon departed Pearl Harbor and sailed for Ulithi on January 27. As the ship was preparing to sail out and just shortly prior to casting off, Junior sat down to write a few lines to Faye:[12]

---

10. "U.S.S. *Arkansas* BB-33 History," http://warships1.com/US/USbb33-history.htm.
11. CINCPAC was the acronym for Commander in Chief, Pacific Command.
12. This is the second surviving letter from Junior Talbott to his wife Faye (McIntyre) Talbott.

L.E. Talbott, F.C. 3/c

                                        c/o F.P.O. U.S.S. Arkansas
                                                  San Francisco, Calif.
                                                         January 27, 1945

Mrs. L.E. Talbott
Finger, Tenn.
c/o John R. McIntyre

To my Darling Wife,

    Good morning Darling, I will write you a few lines to let you know that I am OK except for missing you very much. I hope that you are well and getting along fine.

    Well my Dearest I feel fine right now as I received several letters from you this morning. Dearest, it sure is swell to hear from you. Just like being with you for a while and Darling I wish I were with you. I love & miss you so much Darling, it really hurts to have to be away from you. Say Honey I am writing this V Mail because I can finish it faster and I want to mail it if possible today. Say Darling I will write you every chance I can and don't worry any if you don't hear from me every few days. I will be O.K. but just can't mail letters any time.

    Well my Beautiful Darling, I can't think of anything to write now except that I love you with all my heart and miss you very much. So I will say bye for now Darling.

    All my Love to you Darling,

                                                  Your Devoted Husband,
                                                                 Luther

P.S. Tell all the Folks Hello for me.

During the cruise to Ulithi, the *Arkansas* crossed the International Date Line in the Pacific Ocean. It was an event that Junior recalled with great interest. As the ship approached the line, he was writing a letter to Faye. The letter was dated January 31, 1945. Once it crossed, he wrote another letter to her. Though written only a few moments later, he penned the official date of February 1. In the same manner, when Junior returned home for good in October 1945, he had the opportunity to repeat the same day twice. In other words, he "gained" a day by crossing the International Date Line sailing east.

The *Arkansas* first arrived at Ulithi on February 7, 1945. There the ship refueled and took on provisions. She departed on February 10 and sailed to Tinian, arriving the next day. A small island near Saipan, Tinian is one of the three principal islands of the Commonwealth of the Northern Mariana Islands. It had been a protectorate of the Japanese following the First World War. Tinian was sparsely populated but heavily garrisoned by the Japanese during the Second World War. American forces had captured the island following the Battle of Tinian in July 1944. Afterward, it became one of the busiest airbases of the war.[13]

Upon arriving at Tinian, the *Arkansas* engaged in shore bombardment exercises in preparation for the upcoming assault on the small volcanic island of Iwo Jima. The grand old lady of the fleet, the oldest battleship in the United States Navy, the mighty *Arkansas*, arrived at Iwo Jima on February 16, 1945. The Marines and their naval counterparts would learn that the Japanese were indeed the type identified above by Ernie Pyle. They had no intentions of quitting the war they started on December 7, 1941.

Iwo Jima was a significant target. Islands were few and far between in the Pacific region. With three airfields, it served as a bridge between the Allied controlled Mariana Islands and the mainland of Japan. Its capture was essential in a successful push toward Japan that would end the war.

On the morning of February 16, 1945, at 0600 hours, the *Arkansas* lay off the west coast of Iwo Jima and opened fire on specific Japanese strongholds.[14] Radio San Francisco issued the following statement to the Press Association on the 19th:

> United States Marines supported by heavy units of the U.S. Pacific Fleet and by shore based and carrier aircraft have landed on Iwo Island in the Volcano Islands. The landings were made by the Fifth Amphibious Corps—After heavy bombardment by battleships, cruisers and lighter units of the Pacific Fleet and sustained bombings—The Naval Forces which prepared

---

13. "Tinian," Wikipedia. http://en.m.wikipedia.org/wiki/Tinian.
14. "U.S.S. *Arkansas* BB-33 History," http://warships1.com/US/USbb33-history.htm.

the island for invasion with heavy bombardment included the following old battleships: U.S.S. Arkansas, U.S.S. New York, U.S.S. Texas, U.S.S. Nevada, U.S.S. Idaho and U.S.S. Tennessee.[15]

The combined firepower of the old Arky and her sister battleships would make a significant impact on the battle. As in previous engagements, their goal was to provide massive firepower to soften the defenses on Iwo Jima and give the Marines a better chance to take the island with minimal losses.

MOUNT SURIBACHI—THE ARKY ALTERS ITS FACE

"Our special target was Mount Suribachi, a dead volcano rising starkly at the southern tip of the island. The Japs had it fortified with railroad guns, AA guns, and observation posts peeped out of hundreds of pits and crevices."[16]

Junior remembered well Iwo Jima's prominent geographical feature, Mount Suribachi. It was the primary target of the *Arkansas* for the first few days of the campaign. He recalled with disdain the attitudes of the Japanese soldiers. Their tenacity was far different from that of the German. He heard stories of the entrenched Japanese soldiers who burrowed themselves into every nook, cranny, and crevice of the terrain and their stubborn refusal to surrender regardless of the odds facing them. Junior often spoke of the suicidal tendencies of these men. They viewed the defense of Iwo Jima as tantamount to the defense of Japan itself.[17] After

15. Wilson, ed., *Pacific War Diary*, 1945.
16. Ibid.
17. The author recalls well reading his first book about the Battle of Iwo Jima. It was in 1987. The book was from the library at Chester County High School. Sitting at the sandwich counter of the family grocery store, Junior Talbott walked up behind the author, looked over his shoulder, and saw the pages being read. The book was turned to page 168, "Iwo Jima: The Dramatic Account of the Epic Battle That Turned the Tide of World War II," by Richard F. Newcomb. The author was looking at the iconic photograph of the flag raising on Mount Suribachi. Junior spoke up with words recalled as follows: "That's not the first flag that went up. They raised a smaller one first. That's the one they raised for the reporters and photographers. I remember when our boys raised the first one." At this point, Junior had never discussed much with the author about his

all, this was the first American attack on the Japanese Home Islands, a significant event in and of itself. It proved that the Japanese were not invincible and their territory was not impenetrable. The very presence of Allied forces this deep in Pacific territory represented a disturbing potential for their defeat.

The *Arkansas* sailed close to the shores of Iwo Jima just as it had the coast of Omaha Beach and the beaches of Southern France. Although 1,700 yards may seem a great distance, it is much closer when fired upon by shore batteries and gun emplacements. They caused damage to several ships participating in the invasion. Both the U.S.S. *Tennessee* and the U.S.S. *West Virginia* were struck by shells. Luckily, the *Arkansas* escaped such mishaps despite the fact that she was closer to the volcanic shore more often than the other vessels.

Like their German counterparts, the Japanese used mines for defense in the harbors and outlying waters around the island. The Allies countered with minesweepers to avoid damage and destruction to their vessels. As he had during the assault on Southern France, Junior watched the minesweepers do their work. He saw a few mines set off by the sweepers during his three years on the high seas. He remembered the tall and wide columns of water and foam such explosions caused. They were quite the sight!

> The crew of the Arky had a grandstand seat when we moved in to within 1700 yards of the western beach of Iwo Jima. White bursts…were a familiar sight. The minesweeper…was one of many which cleared the water for landing forces.

---

experiences in the Second World War. The only other instance was a discussion on June 6, 1984. On that summer day, the author, then an eleven-year old boy, was helping his grandfather cut plastic for use in his garden. As the two crawled around on the ground measuring and cutting plastic, Junior said, "Forty years ago today, there was a lot of crawling going on at Normandy." Somewhat confused, the author asked further about Normandy. Thus began an impromptu lecture on the D-Day invasion and the involvement of the U.S.S. *Arkansas* in that invasion. Afterwards, Junior would occasionally open up and discuss his experiences. The author took great interest in the library book about Iwo Jima and began asking his grandfather about the battle. Junior seemed very pleased, which was somewhat surprising at the time. From that point, grandfather and grandson began talking regularly about his experiences during the War.

The *Arkansas* covered the Marines during their landing. Junior fired the twelve-inch guns while his shipmates worked the five-inch guns and anti-aircraft battery. He was asked to remain on duty and continue firing from the main battery on several occasions. Often when he was relieved, the younger, less experienced sailor would have trouble landing the shots. According to Junior, these boys would try in the "damnest way" to land their shots without as much success. After some degree of rest and sleep, he would be summoned back to his post to resume his duties. He had learned his equipment well and knew how to operate it under the most stressful circumstances. Junior learned to plot target coordinates in spite of the roll and pitch of the ship. He could carefully hit a target without so much as a miss even with rough seas and choppy waters. This ability made him a valuable member of Division F.

It was at Iwo Jima that Junior first experienced the true horrors of war and witnessed the tramatic sight of death. He saw blowflies and green flies lighting upon dead soldiers who had fallen. Their buzzing was so intense that it drowned out most other sounds. The gruesome sight haunted his memories. He once said it boiled down to the fact that he was unaccustomed to the scale of the slaughter at Iwo Jima. It made a lasting impression. Indeed, he would carry those sounds and sensations with him for more than six decades.

Mount Suribachi was taken on Friday, February 23, 1945. The point seemed impenetrable. But with the help of the battleships and other vessels, the pill boxes and blockhouses were ripped "from their roots" and the great objective was open to the Marines.[18] They started out at 8:00 A.M. to secure Suribachi and accomplished their goal at approximately 10:15 A.M.[19] Junior remembered the image of the scarred, battered, black mountain smoldering in the distance. He recalled the impressions he had of this island for which they were fighting:

> It was the worst looking place you ever saw. I mean it didn't look like anything. It was all so God-forsaken. You wondered what in the hell good this piece of rock was to anybody. You wouldn't want to live on it. We knew it was strategic but for

---

18. Richard F. Newcomb, *Iwo Jima*. New York: Henry Holt and Company, 1965, 164.
19. Ibid, 164–165.

what…we wondered. As you floated out there in the water, it was this big black mountain coming out of the water. Of course, you had no idea what was waiting on everyone out there.

It was at Iwo Jima that Junior saw one of the most famous events in American military history. He watched as the American flag was raised on Mount Surbachi. Yet this iconic moment—and the memorable photograph that resulted—was actually a staged, second flag raising.

The *Arkansas* received reports back from troops ashore about the targets, range, and activities on the ground. It was important to know the progress of the soldiers for whom they were providing cover fire. A patrol scouted the crater atop Suribachi, secured a pipe, fitted a flag to it, and raised the flag to signify its conquest. According to historian Richard F. Newcomb, "this was the flag raising on Iwo Jima that thrilled the troops. The one that thrilled the world was still to come, nearly two hours later."[20] Like the troops on the ground, Junior, floating off the coast and having helped rip those blockhouses and pill boxes from their roots, was equally thrilled.[21]

When the first flag was hoisted atop Mount Suribachi, Junior and his colleagues were being kept abreast of this historic event. It was a scene that he and his fellow sailors would never forget. It was unceremonious and rather perfunctory. It did not have the imagery associated with the second, staged flag raising. Still, the event held a special place in Junior's long memory. As he grew older, he often became emotional when discussing it. Seeing the flag flying above Mount Suribachi was a surreal and powerful moment. It sent a message to the war-weary sailors, Marines, and soldiers. They had finally triumphed over their grim and determined foe. The Allies were one step closer to their goal of defeating the Imperial Forces of Japan and ending the long and bloody war.

---

20. Ibid, 165.

21. Junior Talbott always thought it shameful that the men who raised the first flag did not receive the credit and fame they were due. However, historian Richard Newcomb recognized them in his work *Iwo Jima*. Those men were: Lieutenant Harold G. Schrier, Platoon Sergeant Ernest I. Thomas Jr., Sergeant Henry O. Hansen, Corporal Charles W. Lindberg, Private First Class James R. Michels, and Private Louis Charlo, a Crow Indian from Montana. Newcomb, *Iwo Jima*, 164.

The *Arkansas* continued her heavy bombardment of the island through February 19, 1945. She provided cover for the Marines during the evening hours. Junior knew that American G.I.'s were fighting desperately to take it. He often spoke about the sacrifices of those young men and his pride in supporting them while out in the waters of the Pacific.

> We gave Suribachi plenty of hell with our main battery for days. One of the biggest thrills of the whole Pacific war was the moment when the lookouts reported that the American flag was being raised at the top of the mountain—the now immortal scene of the U.S. Marines hoisting the colors.

The Marines fought relentlessly to take Surbachi and root out the Japanese resistance. Junior recalled that the *Arkansas* shot her big twelve-inch guns continuously. He and his fellow crew members fired 1,262 rounds from the twelve-inch guns of the main battery. The boys in the secondary battery fired the five-inch guns a total of 1,702 rounds. Though the anti-aircraft guns fired off fewer rounds (some 435 rounds), they would more than make up for it when they arrived at Okinawa.

It was during this battle that Junior realized how savage the Japanese soldiers could be. Reports and stories came back to the ship of their fervor and the atrocities they committed. Iwo Jima and other islands served as a buffer to the Japanese mainland and protected it from invasion by the Allied forces. They would hold the island at any cost. Junior understood why the Japanese wanted to defend their island. But he could never understand why they were so brutal and cruel to American prisoners of war and civilians in occupied lands. He insisted that Japan built its great war machine from scrapped American iron and steel sold to them in the 1930s. He held little respect for them because of what he saw during the war.

There was more significance to the battle of Iwo Jima and the *Arkansas'* participation. It marked one of the "last appearances of the 'Old BB's', the old battleships," the "old ladies" of the United States Navy. The *Arkansas*, an old coal burner converted to diesel, was the oldest battleship still on the waters. The era of the battleship was passing away. It had dominated the seas for generations, but new developments and technology were emerging that rendered these grand old ladies of the Navy obsolete. In fact, their appearances at Normandy, Iwo Jima, and Okinawa were among their last on the grand stage of world history. Yet to the men aboard these great ships, their places in history as well as the hearts of those who called them home during this war were secure.

The *Arkansas* continued her heavy bombardment of the island through February 19, 1945. She provided cover for the Marines during the evening hours. From February 19 to March 7, the sailors spent an eventful sixteen days shelling enemy positions on Iwo Jima to support the Marines in eliminating all Japanese resistance on the island.[22]

On March 5, 1945, Rear Admiral W.H.P. Blandy sent the following message to the Task Force battleships and cruisers, including the *Arkansas*:

> I wish to add my own congratulations especially upon the firing on D-1 Day. While all of us knew the limitation—It was the naval gunfire delivered with great accuracy on that day which was primarily responsible for destroying or heavily damaging the batteries, blockhouses and pillboxes on the landing beaches, in the rear and on the flanks of these beaches, thereby making the landing itself possible without great loss—.[23]

Taking Mount Suribachi did not end the battle. The Marines succeeded in cutting it off from the rest of the island. The Japanese defenders retreated into an extensive system of underground tunnels. Because the north end of the island was still under their control, the *Arkansas* remained until March 7, 1945. Iwo Jima was not declared secure until March 26. For the support they offered during the campaign, Junior and his shipmates received one star in the Asiatic-Pacific area service ribbon for their "participation in the bombardment and invasion of Iwo Jima, Volcano Islands, Western Pacific, during 16 February to 7 March 1945." Junior received a rating of 3.5 for "proficiency in rating," "mechanical ability," and "ability as leader of men." His conduct earned a 4.0 rating.[24]

The *Arkansas* had performed her duties and seen the thickest and most heated parts of the battle. She did not stay for the mopping up action.

---

22. Ibid, 67–68.

23. Wilson, ed., *Pacific War Diary*, 1945.

24. Service Record dated June 30, 1945. Luther Edward Talbott Compiled service record, FC2d, Division F, U.S.S. *Arkansas*. National Archives, Washington, D.C.

Instead, she withdrew to Ulithi to rearm, refuel, and receive provisions on March 10. It also marked Faye's twenty-first birthday back home in Tennessee. The 10-day stay allowed the war weary crew to get some rest and relaxation after their exhausting experiences. On March 21, the battleship departed for Okinawa. Junior and his fellow sailors had no inkling of the fear and terror they would soon experience. The fight would not be a conventional one; instead it would be a confrontion with the fierce "Divine Wind" that would blow around and through them.

At this point, the author wishes to detour for a moment and discuss the *Arkansas'* leadership during the period that they were engaged at Iwo Jima. As had been the case for some years, Commander P.M. Boltz was the Executive Officer. But the skipper of the *Arkansas* in the spring of 1945 was Captain George M. O'Rear. In the spring of 1945, the boys of the *Arkansas* published a newsletter called the *Arklite*. The March 15, 1945, issue included a column entitled, "The Arklite's Who's Who." It profiled "The Skipper," George M. O'Rear. The profile reads as follows:

The Skipper

"Who's the Captain? What's he like?" To answer these questions for the crow, the Arklite's interviewer called upon Captain George M. O'Rear in his emergency cabin on the Navigation Bridge and was received cordially and with many questions about the newly-revived ship's paper.

Looking bronzed and fit and showing little sign of the strain of the past month's operations, Captain O'Rear discussed his naval career.

"My Annapolis class was 1919, but because we were a maritime class, we were actually graduated on June 6, 1918. I was sent overseas to serve on destroyers based in Brest, France."

After the Armistice was signed, he was assigned to the ARIZONA which was then on Mediterranean Patrol. In 1919, the ship was in Turkey making a neutral observation of the Turko-Greek war.

His two years duty on the ARIZONA was followed by a year as navigator on a gunboat; then to submarines for ten years. During this time he also attended the War College at

Newport, R.I. 1927 saw him commanding the U.S.S. QUAIL, an armed minesweep which took an active part in the Nicaraguan Campaign as a gunboat and coast patrol.

The lines around the Captain's sea-blue eyes crinkled good-humoredly as he recalled those days. "I was then a lieutenant and was put in the delicate and somewhat precarious position of relieving a captain in charge of the west coast of Nicaragua and then being relieved myself by an admiral."

Following a tour of duty at the Naval Academy, the captain reported to the U.S.S. MARYLAND in 1933, on which he served a year as assistant gunnery officer and two years as gunnery officer.

The next four years saw him successively as officer-in-charge of the Naval Gun Factory in Washington; as C.O. of the U.S.S. SMITH (DD378); and as C.O. of the U.S.S. BOREAS, an auxiliary refrigerator ship, which he recalls affectionately as an "old meat box."

As the war clouds gathered, Captain O'Rear returned to Washington as a member of Admiral Bristol's staff and as prospective commanding officer of a submarine base to be established at Gibraltar. The plans for this base cancelled, the captain remained in Washington as submarine force representative on the staff of Admiral Edwards, then Commander Submarines, Atlantic.

His last duty before taking command on the ARKANSAS was in the War Planning Division under the Chief of Naval Operations. As officer-in-charge of the Ordnance Progress Section, he was cited by Secretary of the Navy, Forrestal, as follows:

"Displaying great resourcefulness and sound judgement (sic), Captain O'Rear determined the requirements for the production of munitions and supervised the development of new weapons and the allocation of various types of ammunition to the fighting forces of the United States as well as to foreign nations, thereby rendering invaluable service to the CNO.

On September 25, 1944, the captain bade goodbye to his wife and his daughter, Virginia (a real navy "junior," born in

Honolulu in 1925) and was welcomed aboard the Arkansas by Captain F.G. Richards, who turned over command to him.[25]

Captain O'Rear was one of the officers about whom Junior spoke some, but not very much. He respected and admired Captain O'Rear and saw him as a true spit and polish Navy man.

O'Rear's predecessor, F.G. Richards, was the one captain about whom Junior spoke often and affectionately. Richards was a native of Maine and had an easy bearing for a career Navy man. He was not of the "spit and polish" type to which most were sailors were accustomed. Captain Richards was a man with somewhat rough-hewn features and a wide, toothy smile. He was most comfortable in the dressed down casual khakis of an officer or a windbreaker in foul weather. Richards did not possess the usual bark and command personality of a naval captain. He was far more easygoing than most. He gave his sailors the benefit of the doubt and was understanding of their plight as young sailors away from home. Junior actually got the chance to develop a personal relationship with Captain Richards, who encouraged him. Junior's affection for him was genuine and lasted until his death. Yet Junior might have been surprised in later years if he'd known more about his beloved Captain Richards.[26]

As hellacious a battle as Iwo Jima had been, the bloodiest one in the Pacific Theatre was still ahead. Okinawa still stood and Japan was like a wounded animal—very much alive and dangerous.

---

25. A. Madden, ed., *Arklite: Arkansas Blasts Iwo*. Volume 2, No. 1, March 15, 1945.

26. See Epilogue for biographical information pertaining to Rear Admiral Frederick Gore Richards.

11

Okinawa and Home

Okinawa would prove a fateful testing ground and a final, horrible chapter for the *Arkansas* and her crew. It would be the last major battle of the Second World War and end Japanese domination of the Pacific region. It would present the final fiery farewell of ship-to-ship combat and mark the final appearance of battleships on the world stage and in warfare.

The battle would rage for over eighty days, involving more men and materiel than utilized the year before at the invasion of Normandy. It was also a terrifying experience for both landing troops and sailors, pitting young sailors like Junior Talbott against the terrifying waves of screaming, hurdling kamikazes determined to wreak mass destruction upon the Allied armada. Still, the *Arkansas* and her crew were prepared.

On March 25, 1945, the battleship sailed into the waters around Okinawa. Junior recalled the arrival:

> Well, we knew now what it was like to fight the Japs. We probably went into Okinawa feeling more nervous and unsure than when we sailed to Iwo Jima. There wasn't much unknown left anymore. We knew the bastards would fight like hell. Because this was it. There wasn't much between us and Japan now but Okinawa. We knew about kamikazes but still didn't have any idea about how deadly they were. Once they flew out at us it was like stepping into a hornet's nest. They were coming at you from everywhere. That was when I began to doubt making it home. It hit you.[1]

For the first time since October 1942, he had serious doubts he would ever see home again. He and his shipmates were now hardened veterans of tough and demanding campaigns. They were no longer idealistic young sailors hoping for adventure and excitement. They were men, realistic about their chances of survival and the likelihood of being casualties in a sad chapter of world history.

Once off the coast of Okinawa, the *Arkansas* began preliminary shelling of various Japanese positions. This began several days before to soften their defenses ahead of the invasion force. The assault troops would not wade ashore until April 1, 1945. The Joint Chiefs of Staff had chosen Okinawa as the "springboard" for the invasion of Japan. It was a sixty-mile long island belonging to the Ryukyu chain, located about 400 miles from the Japanese mainland.[2]

Junior and his comrades knew about the dreaded kamikaze. At Okinowa, the *Arkansas* and her companion vessels would face the first true test of battle against these Japanese pilots. This was by no means accidental or coincidental. Lieutenant General Mitsuru Ushijima, the Japanese commander in charge of planning the defense of Okinawa, deliberately allowed the American and Allied forces to "land in full" on the island and push inland. They would outdistance the range of the battleships providing cover and targeting from the aerial bombardment. Once the troops advanced beyond the bounds of their protection, Ushijima wrote,

---

1. Luther E. "Junior" Talbott interview, 2004.
2. John Costello, *The Pacific War, 1941–1945*. New York: Harper Perennial, 1981, 554.

"...we must patiently and prudently hold out fire. Then leaping into the action we shall destroy the enemy."

Junior knew the terrifying possibilities that awaited the Marines wading ashore. These young fighting men would have an easy way in, but once there, all hell would break loose. The Japanese wanted to distract the Allied naval forces with the terrifying "divine wind." If the naval fleet could be kept at bay, it would prevent them from taking out their defensive positions and providing much needed cover for the invading troops.

The Japanese strategy involved tying down the invasion force on land and forcing the naval fleet to remain off the coast to provide air support.[3] This would make them a perfect target for the Kamikazes. Despite the constant danger, the *Arkansas*, her crew, and her sister ships continued to discharge their duties. That was a source of pride for Junior. He spent decades talking about the bravery and endurance of his brothers in arms, both his fellow sailors and the invading troops running towards almost certain death. Despite his own humility, great pride developed over the decades in the knowledge and recognition that he and his comrades overcame great odds and carried out their duties.

Discussion of the Pacific Campaign was far more painful and difficult for Junior than the European Campaign. Any information gleaned from him about Iwo Jima or Okinawa was significant. There was a particularly painful memory that he only once or twice related. It occurred at Okinawa. Junior and his mates were providing fire support to the invading Marines. A pocket of men seeking cover needed a position knocked out above them. After some consideration and contemplation, Junior was instructed to direct fire toward the general vicinity where they were to eliminate the gun emplacements above them. He never could bring himself to finish the story without getting emotional. One does not know if Junior's shell fell short of its target and killed the Marines or not. Perhaps that was the conclusion to the unfinished story. He always had a fear of firing over Allied men or ships. A light powder load could cause a shell to fall short and result in loss of life from friendly fire.

During the battles of Iwo Jima and Okinawa, the main and secondary batteries were assisted in directing their fire by OS2U's. The Vought OS2U was a shipboard observation plane carried onboard a battleship

---

3. Ibid, 555.

such as the *Arkansas*. It was a catapult launched plane used for scouting. The pilot of the *Arkansas*' OS2U accurately spotted for fire control and gunnery. Because of that spotting, the battleship was far more accurate and efficient in its firepower. There was no way for the plane to take off from the deck like those on aircraft carriers. When it was ready to return, it had to land on the water and a flagman had to guide it to a recovery sled. This was possible because the OS2U was a form of sea plane. Once ready, the radioman left his cockpit and rigged lines to guide the plane aboard. It was then hoisted aboard the ship. Junior found the plane and the process fascinating.

During this period, the *Arkansas* rearmed and refueled at a collection of nine islands called Kerama Retto.[4] This staging area had been taken after she had "blistered the Keramas relentlessly" with her twelve-inch guns on March 26. Other vessels and carrier-based planes joined in softening up the Japanese positions there. The fighting on Kerama Retto and the resulting carnage among combatants and civilians was astounding. Junior recalled the horrors of learning about mass suicides by locals who feared what American soldiers and sailors would do to them if caught. He recounted stories of bodies floating in the waters off these islands, so thick the water they were floating in could scarcely be seen. It was at this final battle that Junior witnessed some of the most sickening of war horrors. It was at Okinawa that he learned of the awful horror of the green fly.

The intensity of Junior's memories of dead bodies floating off the shores led the author to determine what insect had haunted him for decades. The green fly was the common green bottle fly (Lucilla sericata), a blow fly with a metallic blue-green and goldish coloration and black markings. They are larger than the common housefly and live in warmer climates. They are prevalent along coastlines like that of Okinawa. These flies lay their eggs in and on corpses and dead animals. Certainly, the body littered coast was a vast breeding ground for them. An individual green bottle fly makes a loud buzzing noise. One can only imagine the level and intensity of the buzzing of millions of these flies swarming on the dead and decaying bodies floating off Okinawa.

---

4. Bill Sloan, *The Ultimate Battle: Okinawa 1945—The Last Epic Struggle of World War II*. New York: Simon & Schuster, 2007, 41.

The suicide of civilians on Kerama Retto and Okinawa was absolutely horrid. They had been indoctrinated by the Japanese for months, if not years, that Americans were monsters. It was an interesting practice in psychology from a cruel and ruthless enemy. Officers and soldiers told these pitiful natives that American G.I.'s and sailors would butcher and eat the men and children and rape the women. These poor misled people believed every word and took the only "sensible" alternative: suicide![5] Junior remembered well the stories and reports of what was occurring on Okinawa.

It is also important to understand the designation of Kerama Retto as the "Graveyard of Ships." It was among these islands that damaged and battered vessels, including destroyers such as the *Hyman, Leutze, Morris, Mullany,* and *Newcomb,* were towed and abandoned. During the opening days of the Okinawa campaign, many naval vessels were knocked out of further action and left there. These included the *Bush, Calhoun, Emmons, Rodman, Hobbs Victory,* and *Logan Victory.*[6] The amount of expended war materiel left for scrap always astounded and amazed Junior, a man very conscious of wastefulness. Even into old age, he marveled at what the cost must have been.

THE INVASION OF OKINAWA

The battle of Okinawa had been long in coming for Junior and his fellow seamen. In the dark of a Pacific morning, at 4:06 A.M. on the first day of April 1945, the order was given to land the invasion force on the beaches.[7] Within the hour, the terrific, horrific naval bombardment started in earnest. Ten battleships, most considered obsolete at the outset of the war, positioned themselves eight miles along the coast and began an amazing show of firepower.[8] These old girls of war, including Junior's beloved old *Arkansas,* were proving their advocates and disproving their cynics. These grand old ladies of the navy still had some snap left in their steel garters!

---

5. Ibid, 43.
6. Ibid, 103.
7. Robert Leckie, *Okinawa: The Last Battle of World War II.* New York: Penguin Books, 1995.
8. Ibid.

By 1945, there had become a habitual joke of people offering the chief engineer baling wire to fix up the *Arkansas*.[9] There was an old saying down in the engine room:

> By sweat and tears
> The engineers
> Have kept her running
> Through the years.[10]

The *Arkansas* was an old ship. She had mechanical eccentricities and needed constant help to keep going, but she could still handle herself. Junior revered and loved the "Arky." His reverence for her never waivered, even long after she lay deep under the ocean.

Her chief engineer, Lieut. Commander Frank A. Blackwood, was philosophical about the situation. He remarked:

> She's just about on her last legs…After 33 years she's done her time. I'd rather have an Arky engineer under me than any other man in the Navy, though. They've been through more breakdowns and repairs. They're really a skilled outfit…The only thing about this job that gets me is that wherever I go people start offering me baling wire.[11]

The author Robert Leckie expounded on the virtue and defects of these old battlewagons in his detailed but succinct history of the campaign, *Okinawa: The Last Battle of World War II*. They had varying histories: some were raised from the watery floor of battleship row at Pearl Harbor. Others like the *Arkansas* were saved from the scrap heap simply because of its destruction. These battleships could hurl powerful, spinning shells weighing from 1,200 to 1,800 pounds and in diameters of twelve to sixteen inches.[12] On that first day of April 1945, those lined up waiting included the *Arkansas, Colorado, Idaho, Nevada, New Mexico, New York,*

---

9. Unidentified newspaper article in the Captain Wade DeWeese Papers.
10. Ibid.
11. Ibid.
12. Leckie, *Last Battle*, 67.

Texas, *West Virginia*, and the *Tennessee*, which beared the honor as flagship.[13] Those battleships had one major drawback that made them ideal for shore bombardment. All were far slower than the more modern carriers, but their firepower from a distance made up for any deficiencies.[14]

Even their use for shore bombardment was a deviation from the traditional use of the battleship. The *Arkansas*, like her sisters, were built to fight other ships using armor piercing shells on flat trajectories. They had been altered and readjusted to achieve high angle fire of highly explosive shells capable of shattering enemy gun emplacements. Many of these gun emplacements were in hill sides, cliffs, and mountainsides.

But the era of the battleship was passing away. In fact, the battle of Okinawa would be the last engagement in which these vessels would wage war. This was an important historical event. Battleships, in some form or another, had fought one another for centuries, from the sail to the steamer to the modern oil burning battleship of the 1930s and 1940s. Nations rose and fell on the strength of their navies and battleships. Yet Okinawa would be the swan song for the great old lady of the seas.

Indeed, it is a mark of honor that Junior and his colleagues participated in not only one of the most heated of battles during the Second World War, but also the last in which battleships participated. This fact attached great historical significance to the Battle of Okinawa. They were also fighting the opening battle in the invasion of Japan. It marked the last great use of the kamikaze mission in warfare. In short, these fighting men were making history on every level.

The invading force and support ships at Okinawa included much more than the battlewagons like the *Arkansas*. Spaced between the nine vessels were nine heavy cruisers, all pre-war ships and veterans of previous Pacific bombardments. Twenty-three destroyers, three light cruisers, and dozens of LCI's (land craft infantry vessels) were also present. This gathering of men and materiel, including Naval vessels, was overwhelming.

Because the Japanese had moved their armies away from the beaches, they were unaffected by the bombardment.[15] The initial shelling fell

---

13. Iid, 67–68.
14. Ibid, 68.
15. Ibid, 68-69.

harmlessly on hills, beaches, and valleys.[16] The Allied landings proved relatively uneventful and seemingly too easy.[17] Yet the bombardments did have psychological impacts. First, it was a very impressive sight for the Japanese commanders watching from afar. They were satisfied that Lieutenant General Mitsuru Ushijima had foregone the idea of defending the island at its beaches. Second, the massive onslaught encouraged the troops and gave them a great psychological boost.[18] They enjoyed the sound and fury they were hearing.[19]

Over the next few days, the bombardment became stronger and more effective. The *Arkansas* and her sister ships maintained their incessant firing as the Marines continued the desperate struggle on Okinawa. Junior remembered well the forty-seven days he and his mates sailed off the coast. They received little rest. Because he had mastered the roll and pitch of the ship's hull while aiming the *Arkansas*' twelve-inch guns, he was repeatedly called back to duty. The young fire control mate who was Junior's relief was not as skillful as he. After a few hours, it was Junior who was summoned to relieve him. He once figured that he was on duty some eighteen hours a day during many of the 47 days the *Arkansas* was in action.

Junior's remembrance of Okinawa was very vivid. In fact, these memories were among his most troubling of the war. The carnage and death, like he experienced at Iwo Jima, troubled him greatly and haunted his dreams. He talked about the sight of bodies floating off the coast and washed ashore in piles. It was hot and the heat didn't help matters. Junior could recall the sight and smell of the decaying bodies. The stubbornness of the Japanese defenders amazed him. Though he seemed to admire their determination, he considered them barbaric and ruthless. He knew they were dug in at Okinawa as they had been at Iwo Jima. Their absolute refusal to capitulate resulted in the deaths of too many American soldiers.

Junior also recalled the tiresome fatigue he felt when discharging his duties. He remembered the determination of his fellow sailors and the

---

16. Ibid, 68.
17. Morison, *The Two-Ocean War*, 531.
18. Leicke, *Okinawa*, 69.
19. Ibid, 70.

fear they endured as the relentless battle wore on, especially during the kamikaze attacks. Any man who said he felt no fear during those long anxious days, he said, was a "damn liar." For Junior, there was plenty to fear in the prospect of a fiery kamikaze attack followed by a sinking ship and a watery grave. Those long days fighting to pave the way for the Marines and repulse the kamikazes created fatigue and endurance all at once. Junior recounted:

> Sure, you were scared. You'd been a fool not to be. On top of being scared, you'd get worn too. You worried about doing your job and then on top of that, you worried about what was going on around you and whether or not your friends up there were doing their job. You knew they were.

The battle of Okinawa saw the *Arkansas* performing extensive service. The old battlewagon fired more shots from her guns than at any other engagement she took part in during the war. She arrived at Okinawa on March 25 and remained until May 10, 1945. During those forty-seven days, the *Arkansas* fired 3,240 rounds from its secondary battery of five-inch guns and 2,835 rounds from its anti-aircraft battery. Junior and his mates fired 2,646 rounds from the main battery of twelve-inch guns.

Junior shared with the author in conversations over the years his experience with the deadly specter of the kamikaze suicide planes. It was a difficult job from the outset to deliver accurate and effective fire on Okinawa. That task became even more difficult, almost impossible, when sailors were being assaulted by desperate Japanese suicide pilots intent on hurdling themselves into the Allied vessels. He described the ferocious and blood-curdling scream of the engines as they came barreling towards them. They came in fast like swarms of hornets at low altitudes. The day he most remembered was April 12, 1945, when hundreds of kamikaze attacked the Allied Naval Fleet, the heaviest single Japanese air raid of the war.

Junior recalled that on days like those spent off Okinawa, the news from the rest of the world seemed of little importance and almost trivial. The only news that ever mattered to an enlisted man outside of military intelligence or plans was news from home. Still, when delivering a shelling like they were at Okinawa, all concentration had to be upon the task at hand. Moments to read letters from home or write ones back were precious few. There was simply too much going on. Still, like all sailors and soldiers on the front lines, Junior took such moments when he could to lift his spirits and keep hope alive for those back home.

During the campaign, Junior and his shipmates received news that shook the world, though it did not shake him personally. To be sure, neither Junior nor his father held any great respect for President Franklin D. Roosevelt. As Republicans, they had long labored under a liberal Democratic president with whose policies they did not agree. Newt Talbott had objected to the New Deal policies regarding business and commerce. Faye's father, John Robert McIntyre, also a staunch Republican, had disagreed with Roosevelt's agricultural policies of destroying crops and livestock to artificially bolster prices and markets. After more than twelve years of Roosevelt's presidency, everything changed in a heartbeat or, more properly, the lack thereof.

Junior and Faye both told of certain circumstances on the news of the sudden death of President Roosevelt. The President was visiting his Southern retreat, The Little White House, with members of his entourage, including his cousin Margaret "Daisy" Suckley, his former mistress and confidant Lucy Mercer Rutherfurd, and artist Madame Elizabeth Shoumatoff. His cottage was located just outside the small hamlet of Warm Springs, nestled in the piney woods and hills of central Georgia. The President's health had been greatly weakened by heart disease, hypertension, four years of long struggle during the Second World War, and twelve years in office. He had been living on borrowed time for many months. On April 12, 1945, while sifting through his correspondence in his cabin and sitting for a portrait by Madame Shoumatoff, he collapsed without warning and died very shortly of a cerebral aneurysm.

The news traveled across the world in a matter of minutes and hours. Junior was on deck and saw a young Lieutenant j.g. crying almost uncontrollably. About the time that Junior approached him, so too did a senior officer. This kind-hearted but practical fellow asked, "Good Lord, Lieutenant, what in the hell is wrong with you?" The young man looked up almost bewildered and replied, "Sir, haven't you heard? President Roosevelt has died!" The seasoned officer responded, "Of course I've heard, Lieutenant. Instead of squalling, you ought to be laughing. We'll be out of this war and going home in no time now!" Junior and the senior officer were of the same mindset. Both felt that Roosevelt's policies had helped put them where they were now. Junior also supposed this old officer could have been a diehard Republican, too. At last, Junior said he felt some hope that this long and bloody war would finally end. He was confident about the new President, Harry S Truman, known to be a feisty, earthy man who had himself known the war-ravaged battlefields of Europe during the First World War.

Meanwhile, back home, Faye was working at her father-in-law's store on the day the news arrived in Finger. Newt Talbott was sitting toward the back of the store. He was listening to his little radio that sat on a small shelf on the partition built by Junior in March 1942. Suddenly, the radio burst forth that the President had died. As soon as Newt heard the news, he jumped up, patted Faye on the back, and laughed. He truly felt happy and spry for a moment. He told Faye they had cause to celebrate. Her mother, Ollie Pearl McIntyre, told her they ought to be ashamed in taking such pleasure in the President's death. Still, Faye later said, the news meant to them they would soon see Junior back home.

Junior was always impressed with Roosevelt's successor, President Truman. He admired Truman's Midwestern simplicity and his feisty and fearless leadership of the nation. Junior could identify with him because of his own humble rural background as opposed to Roosevelt's patrician wealth and aristocratic air. He felt that President Truman would stand up to the other Allied powers in order to end the war more conclusively and in a more efficient manner. He never tired of comparing the two men. He was also certain that Roosevelt was the prime reason he and other boys had to leave their peacetime lives and shed blood on foreign soils and in foreign waters. He believed that Roosevelt intentionally involved the nation in the war to assist the British and the rest of Europe. In his heart, Junior always maintained that Roosevelt knew of the attack on Pearl Harbor before it occurred and allowed it as a way of coming to the aid of the Allied powers. Reasonable or not, accurate or not, it was his belief. He always credited Truman with bringing them home. Incidentally, academic arguments to the contrary mattered not to this old sailor!

During the latter part of the *Arkansas'* time at Okinawa, the world was shaken once again. On May 7, 1945, the inevitable—though what often seemed impossible—finally happened. The principle of attrition finally forced reality upon the German government and its army. A desperate and selfish Adolf Hitler had committed suicide and his successors saw fit to sue for peace with the Allies. Junior never forgot getting news of the surrender. While it brought a certain amount of happiness and knowledge that the Normandy Invasion was certainly worth the expense and bloodshed, its comfort was not all encompassing. Like his fellow sailors and other comrades in arms, Junior knew the determination of the Japanese. He had already experienced it at Iwo Jima and, at the moment, at Okinawa. They were a more determined foe than even the Germans. The Japanese had proven so barbaric that he believed it doubtful that an Allied victory would be a quick one.

Iwo Jima and Okinawa had proven to Junior, his mates, and their commanding officers that the Japanese would put up a desperate fight to protect their homeland. They had rebuffed all offers to surrender. When the battle for Okinawa concluded, there was no certainty that the *Arkansas* would not see further action in battle. Perhaps seeing the aftermath of Okinawa created this mindset. Junior declared:

> It was probably the worst I ever saw, worst I ever smelled. We went ashore (most likely on a LCVP or Higgins boat) and the boat engines were diesel and they were loud. It was hard to hear yourself over the engines. But when we got close the shore, we began to see the bodies. You couldn't see the water for the bodies floating in it. Some had been floating awhile. Suddenly you realized you couldn't hear the boat motors for the buzzing of the green flies lighting on the dead bodies. It was terrible. And these were the ones you could see. God knows how many were on the island. It was one of the worst things I ever saw during the war. I never forgot that sound. It stays with you.

Despite the horrors just witnessed, the battle for Okinawa ended for the *Arkansas* on May 10, 1945. She sailed for Guam for some rest and recreation. The sailors, including Junior, often headed for the beach upon arriving in port. The boys were transported to Hoover Beach aboard landing craft. According to the *Arkansas' Pacific War Diary*:

It was a long hike along the white coral sands of Hoover Beach to the recreation center, but the precious and long-hoarded beer at the end of the road tasted all the better for it.

Junior and his fellow sailors were entertained by local acts and shows while visiting Guam. These shows included dancing with everything from Chamerro dances to swing. They were often provided by a Mrs. Johnston and her students from Washington High School there on the island. As with all such shows, the boys were also entertained by their more talented fellow G.I.'s. One of these fellows was W.O. George Tweed, also known as "Robinson Crusoe, USN." The shows included pretty girls who each wore a lei of tropical flowers and a short print dress or grass skirt. Other naval outfits such as Seabee units presented shows for their fellow sailors. These included such characters as "Hashmark Harry" and the "49'ers."

These moments of happy rest gave Junior and his comrades an opportunity to clear their minds of what they had seen, smelled, heard, and experienced. He especially enjoyed these shows as he'd been raised in Finger which had no movie theater and few distractions other than the annual Finger Barbecue. These young men had experienced the invasion of Normandy (D-Day), the battle of Cherbourg, the invasion of Southern France, and the battles of Iwo Jima and Okinawa in the Pacific, all in less than twelve months. Junior spoke often of the sheer hell and stress of such battles, but he never really divulged that all were fought in a short time span. These moments of light-hearted entertainment kept his spirits afloat as did the hope of going home. The *Arkansas* remained at Guam until June 12, when she sailed to San Pedro Bay in Leyte Gulf, arriving on June 15, 1945.

The stopover in Leyte Gulf was somewhat bittersweet. By this time, the Allied forces had largely pushed the Japanese out of the Philippines. Junior himself stated they were there at the "tail-end of the mopping up." As a result, it was now safe for the boys of the "Arky" to explore the gulf and the local areas around it. One of their favorite activities was to hunt shells on the popular and crowded San Antonio Beach at Leyte Gulf. A trip through the local villages revealed much to Junior and his fellow sailors. Photographs of their trips to the town of Tacloban showed open-air markets in a wet, humid, tropical climate. Dogs, children, sailors, and native Filipinos mingled on dirt streets and lanes, ambling and shopping the wares being peddled. Filipino merchants or traders sat on a grass rug under a tree and drove hard bargains with the sailors. Junior saw thatch huts where more than one generation of Filipinos lived at the same time. As in Casablanca and other locales around the world, he found things of interest there as well.

There was also time for Junior and his friends to seek out relaxation and diversion in the Phillipines. Entertainment ranging from the normal music show to the more exotic was held on the ship's forecastle. Among them were the magic show of Professor Paz, a native magician and performer, and his troupe of talented daughters who sang and danced. Shows also featured slapstick comedy and musical performances by Coast Guard sailors based in Tacloban, including a Hawaiian guitar player. The boys also saw unusual animals such as monkeys.

Junior stayed busy during the last months of the war in July and August 1945. On July 1, he qualified as a Gun Director Pointer (P) first class and was stationed in that capacity.[20] Though the war was winding down, there was still work to do. The *Arkansas* was ordered to Leyte Gulf in the Philippines to provide assistance in any potential mopping up exercises.

The *Arkansas* remained in the Philippines in San Pedro Bay in Leyte Gulf from June 15 until August 20, 1945. The crew stood ready but performed little in the way of battle or military matters. They docked and remained there performing various supportive duties. On July 14, Junior and his fellow sailors on the *Arkansas* were authorized and entitled to wear the Philippine Liberation Ribbon without the bronze star. They also received one star in the Asiatic-Pacific area service ribbon for participation in the bombardment and invasion of the Karama Islands and Okinawa Island, Main Japanese Chain from March 25 to May 10, 1945.[21] Junior laughed about the propriety of this decoration. "It was good of them to award it," he said, "but honestly, we didn't do a damn thing in the Philippines to get it. We were just there and were around if needed. The mess had already been cleaned up."[22]

---

20. Service Record dated July 1, 1945. Luther Edward Talbott Compiled Service Record, FC2d, Division F, U.S.S. Arkansas, National Archives, Washington, D.C.

21. Ibid, Service Record dated July 14, 1945.

22. Luther E. Talbott interview, 2004.

Given the down time in the Philippines, the men spent these moments ashore, exploring the region. It also gave them time for reading and writing letters. Junior's mother wrote to him during this time, hopeful that the war would soon end. On August 11, 1945, Varham Talbott wrote:

> Sat'day 11 1945
> Finger, Tenn.
>   Hello Junior
>   How are you this hot day? We are doing very well. Your Dad is doing all right just now if he can hold it. I hope he can. Say, my blood is high. Now I have to take something all the time to keep it down. Hope you are well and having it good. Fay is ok. We sure feel good about the war. I think you will get to come home soon. I hope so anyway. Leonard Patterson was in town today. He was asking about you. He will have to leave Monday. Sure is dull today, everybody is gone to Selmer today. So be good and rite. We are getting your letters good. Now we are hearing every week Junior Gilbert is getting to come home sooner. He is on his way. So be good.
>   Lots of love
>   Mother & Dad & Vonnie

This letter was indicative of the types Junior received from his mother during the war. Interestingly, both Leonard Patterson and Junior Gilbert's names are found in Junior's wartime address book, along with a number of other family as well as friends serving in the military at the time including S.M. Peeples, Philip M. Wilcox, W.B. Moore, J.C. Moore, Ermon D. Matlock, H.A. Greening, Aaron Gilbert, J.E. Gilbert, Johnnie H. Hutcherson and Belver N. Hutcherson.

The *Arkansas* remained in Leyte Gulf until August 20. The Japanese had exacted terrible cruelties upon the people of the Philippines, both native and foreign. It was appropriate for Junior to still be there when the Japanese finally capitulated and surrendered to the Allied Forces. With the decimation of the cities of Hiroshima and Nagasaki by the new atomic bomb, they surrendered on August 10. The fighting at Iwo Jima and Okinawa had taken its toll on the nerves of many servicemen. It was no different for the sailors of the *Arkansas*. These boys had served gallantly in the European Theatre. Now they had seen and experienced unspeakable sights in the Pacific Theatre where the Japanese soldier fought with far more fanatical zeal than the Germans. It would be the Japanese soldier of whom Junior would speak with considerable disdain in his later years.

Junior recalled well V-J Day (Victory over Japan). He spoke of it with more emotion than V-E Day (Victory in Europe), though he and his comrades were directly involved in both outcomes. Yet, it was as he himself said:

> We knew on V-J Day that we were going home. We knew that we were now going to survive even though so many of our friends didn't. Unless an accident happened, we would see home now. That meant everything.[23]

Emotion always brimmed in Junior as he spoke of the knowledge of winning the war. He had missed home and worried constantly about his father. His only desire was to return to Finger and begin life anew. Junior had seen in the world all he ever wanted to see. The United States was big and wide enough with plenty left for him to see without ever crossing another ocean.

The end of the war with the Japanese brightened the outlook of Junior's fellow sailors aboard the *Arkansas*. One of his comrades wrote in the *Arkansas' Pacific War Diary*:

> V-J Night!! No Fourth of July demonstration could compare with the show of rockets, flares and searchlights the beach and ships sent up when we heard the first news of the Jap surrender on August 10th.

Before leaving the subject of Leyte Gulf, the author feels compelled to discuss Junior's view of the Pacific commander, General of the Army Douglas MacArthur. When others praised the legendary general, Junior laughed and shook his head. He felt MacArthur had an inflated personality with an overgrown ego. "A real blowhard, a put on," was how Junior described him. No doubt President Truman would have agreed

---

23. Luther E. Talbott undated interview.

wholeheartedly. Junior derided MacArthur for evacuating the Philippines with his closest aides and his family. He would not have thought so little of MacArthur had he quietly withdrawn. But his ostentatious declaration of "I shall return!" seemed awfully shallow to Junior.

Junior had an old-fashioned idea when it came to the duty of commanders toward their men. He truly believed the captain "ought to go down with his ship." In his mind, it was cowardly and selfish of MacArthur to evacuate. He felt strongly that the General owed it to his men to stay put and endure the deprivations and captivity with them. Junior didn't blame him for evacuating his family, but he damn sure blamed him for saving himself and abandoning his men to be starved and tortured. He believed MacArthur would have been a far more inspirational figure had he suffered with his men. Junior made it plain that any man with MacArthur's ego and self-confidence should have backed those traits up.

Junior remembered some of the emaciated survivors of the Japanese occupation. He admired their grit and determination to survive. General Jonathan Wainwright, who stayed behind and endured what his men did, suffered great privation and humiliation during his captivity. Junior often became choked with emotion thinking of the decency and courage of Wainwright. He bristled when others spoke with adoration of MacArthur. He was proud that President Truman fired MacArthur during the Korean War.

Whenever Junior saw film footage of MacArthur striding ashore the beaches of the Philippines with his corncob pipe, scrambled eggs cap, and sunglasses, he would call him a "damn old banty (bantam) rooster." The author thought this an odd comparison considering that MacArthur actually stood six feet tall. His ego, said Junior, stood even taller than he did. He once remarked:

> MacArthur was a coward. He didn't have to leave the Philippines. He could have stayed and took his with everyone else. He was a damn coward. Nothing more than a coward. Full of shit and all politics.[24]

---

24. Luther E. Talbott undated interview.

On August 20, the *Arkansas* left Leyte Gulf and sailed back to Okinawa, arriving on the 23rd. The crew had not been there since the long bombardment of the island that spring. This time, the *Arkansas* would launch a peaceful invasion of the island. The last time Junior had been to Okinawa, he had been busy firing twelve-inch guns at battery emplacements and dreading contact from kamikazes. Now he would see the results of his handiwork. Again, according to the *Arkansas' Pacific War Diary*:

> Relaxing amid the rubble of houses and gun emplacements, we wandered over the rolling green plains of Tsuken-Shima. On this second trip, we saw the deadly results of our main-battery pinpoint shooting.

In fact, during this second "invasion" of Okinawa in August, Junior and his fellow sailors spent a great deal of time exploring the island. They saw firsthand the devastation of their dogged bombardment. They saw the damage that the batteries, including Junior's guns, had inflicted on various installations, including the beacon lighthouse on Tsuken Shima, the coastal batteries, the tombs in the side of the mountain, the wrecked houses, and the Baka bomb installations. A photograph exists of one of Junior's officers, Lt. (jg) L.L. Clardy, inspecting a wrecked coastal rifle position that had been destroyed by Clardy's turret number three. It should be remembered that the main battery, Junior's 12-inch guns, fired 2,646 rounds at the battle of Okinawa.

The *Arkansas* remained in port at Okinawa from August 23 until September 23. In Junior's final month on board the venerated *Arkansas*, her mission shifted. On September 6, 1945, a Bulletin was issued to the officers and sailors of the *Arkansas* that exuded both a certain emotion and sentiment to be expected at the end of a terrible war. It reads as follows:

BULLETIN[25]
U.S.S. *Arkansas*, 6 September 1945—The U.S.S. *Arkansas* will operate as a unit of Vice-Admiral J.B. Oldendorf's Task Force in covering the occupation of the Japanese Home Islands.

---

25. This Bulletin issued to the men of the U.S.S. *Arkansas* stated that it was "NOT AN OFFICIAL NAVY RELEASE." This copy was the same bulletin issued to Junior Talbott in 1945.

The war in the Pacific will be climaxed by the signing of the final papers in Japan, and the Navy point system (to be revised soon, we hope!) is making it possible for many men to return to the United States and civilian life.

For many the parting will be a sad one. A large part of the crew has served in the *Arkansas* for several years and can testify to their happy days on board. Many can relate various experiences of this grand old ship in the Pacific; others can tell tales of her Atlantic Operation; and the old timers can go way back to the old days. If they all got together and wrapped their yarns into one story, it might sound something like this:

The U.S.S. *Arkansas*, known to all salty men as "The Arky" is not only the oldest battle wagon in the fleet today, but is by far the most distinguished. When World War Two was declared and the "Arky" was stripped of all but fighting gear, it was said that the removal of her trophies won in fleet competition actually lightened her by several tons. It is difficult today to find a naval officer with any length of service who hasn't served at least one hitch on the "Arky." Incidentally, this is the third hitch of Captain Wade DeWeese.

To begin with, the U.S.S. *Arkansas* was commissioned on September 17, 1912 at the Philadelphia yard. She and her sister ship, the U.S.S. *Wyoming*, were by far the most powerful warships in the world. That same year President Taft took passage to inspect the Panama Canal. In 1913 Turret Four established a record during target practice which has never been equaled. Admiral Henry T. Mayo, Commander in Chief, U.S. Fleet, flew his flag on the "Arky" in 1914 during the occupation of Vera Cruz. In this encounter one man was killed and seven wounded in the Battalion landed by her.

In 1918 the "Arky" left the States and joined the Grand Fleet in the firth of forth as a member of the Sixth Battle Squadron, relieving the U.S.S. *Delaware*. On August 4, 1918 she sighted and fired upon a submarine, and on November 21 of that year witnessed the surrender of the German Fleet.

After serving as reference vessel for the first Trans-Atlantic flight by naval aviators, she experienced a long period of relative inactivity due to our indifferent naval policy following the end of the First World War. During this period the "Arky" underwent a modernization program which was completed in November, 1926. Even the youngest sailor can remember or has heard of the story of the sinking of the U.S.S. *Nautilus* in 1931. It was the "Arky" who searched for and stood by the stricken submarine. In 1932 she proceeded to the West Coast and joined the Pacific Fleet for a tour of duty. The "Arky" became the flagship of the training squadron in 1934, directing the drilling and education of the men who were later destined to become key figures in leading our Navy through the dark days in the early part of World War Two.

When war flamed again in Europe, the "'Arky" was assigned the important task of protecting convoys to the United Kingdom. Though German submarines were sinking a phenomenal number of ships, running into many hundreds of thousands of tons monthly, the "Arky" never lost a single ship from all the numerous convoys she mothered.

With countless ship loads of men and weapons safely ferried to England, the time grew ripe for the invasion blow. Though she was once declared to be the most powerful warship afloat, she had grown old prowling the seas unchallenged. After an overhaul at the New York Navy Yard and with new equipment aboard she was ready to wage war in the enemy's own back yard.

In the early morning darkness of June 6, 1944, the "Arky" glided quietly to a pre-assigned position 4000 yards off the Normandy coast. The silence was broken when she dropped her hook with a great clanking of anchor chain. All hands topside sighed with relief as the old wagon remained undetected.

Allied bombers were keeping the shore batteries busy, but when the sky brightened the "Arky" was discovered and a couple of salvos splashed off her stern. Her five-inch guns answered first, promptly followed by her main battery, and the battle was on. Large caliber enemy guns in the vicinity were effectively neutralized. Then the "Arky," in conjunction with other supporting ships, laid down a devastating barrage on her sector of the landing beaches for troops who were now passing by in hundreds of landing craft for the initial assault. The barrage was lifted as troops streamed ashore to commence the long awaited assault on German aggression.

This was only the beginning of the "Arky"'s task. Spotters flying Spitfires from across the Channel directed her fire power by radio to neutralize artillery, break up troop concentrations and smash supply lines as our troops advanced. Each dusk brought enemy low flying bombers seeking to destroy the ships which had caused their troops so much trouble during the day. But the "Arky"'s luck held—several near misses were the best the bombers could do. For days the "Arky" cruised up and down the coast bombarding enemy positions wherever she could reach them, but eventually the enemy was pushed back beyond her range in all sectors.

After a few more days of standing by, in case the enemy was able to launch a successful counter-attack and get back within her range, the "Arky" sailed for England for supplies and minor repairs. After a few restful days in England, the "Arky" received a hurry-up call to support troops attacking Cherbourg. In company with the U.S.S. *Texas*, U.S.S. *Nevada*, U.S.S. *Tuscaloosa* and several destroyers, the "Arky" blasted the German defenders with numerous morale busters before retiring.

Later that summer she sailed into the Mediterranean, visiting Oran, Palermo and Taranto, in preparation for the assault on the Southern Coast of France. Here again the "Arky" proved herself by accounting for many targets, battering enemy coastal positions and enabling the Army to establish a beachhead. Late in the summer when the issue was no longer in doubt, the "Arky" sailed for home and a well-earned rest.

By the Germans' own admission, the might of naval gunfire could not be denied. The screaming high capacity shells thrown over the beachheads with their murderous devastation wrecked German defenses—and morale—beyond repair. Because she had contributed so much in the European Theater, it was a foregone conclusion that the "Arky" would soon be sent to the Pacific for a chance at the Japs.

The "Arky" completed a Navy yard overhaul period at Boston the first part of November 1944 and sailed north for Casco Bay off Portland, Maine. A few days later she joined a task force and headed for the Panama Canal—and the Pacific War.

Every man on board felt a tingle of excitement as the ship headed west for action. After joining forces commanded by Vice Admiral J.B. Oldendorf, USN, daily drills and practices readied all hands for the job ahead.

After a brief pause at Ulithi, the "Arky" steamed north with a large force to lay down the pre-invasion barrage on the mighty Jap fortress of Iwo Jima. On the morning of February 16 she poured shells into AA gun positions and pillboxes on the western side of Iwo Jima. Several hard days of firing followed as the ships prepared the beaches for assault Marine troops.

Many long days of almost continuous firing followed as the operation progressed. The "Arky"'s aviators directed her fire at many Jap positions while splashes of various sizes near the ship testified that the Japs were doing their best to damage our ships, but luck held. On March 7 the "Arky" steamed away, proud of the fact that she had played an important part in the successful occupation of Iwo Jima.

A short rest followed this operation, but the morning of March 17 saw her underway once again, headed for another Japanese stronghold—Okinawa. Kerama Rhetto, a small group of outlying island, was sighted March 26 and the "Arky"'s first firing assignment came the morning of the following day.

Many weeks of day and night firing followed for this trusty old battlewagon. Thousands of rounds from her guns plastered targets on the beach as all possible support was given to Army and Marine forces ashore.

Air attacks by Jap Kamikazes were an every night occurance [sic]. The largest raid of the Pacific War started the afternoon of April 12 as the "Arky" was steaming with a large force which was set to repel the attacks. Scores of planes made coordinated attacks on ships in the force, damaging several. One "Zeke" headed for the "Arky"'s starboard bow. Withering AA gun fire met the challenge and splashed the plane short.

Twice during the Okinawa operation shore batteries opened fire on the "Arky." Effective counter battery fire, rapid maneuvers—and luck—brought her away unscratched.

The "Arky" finally left Okinawa on May 10 and sailed to Guam for repairs and provisions. Summer found her operating in the Philippine area, and today she is standing by to help cover the occupation of Japan as a unit of Vice Admiral J.B. Oldendorf's invasion task force.

Time was winding down for both Junior and the *Arkansas* in the war. Like her crew, the battleship had performed her duties well and had earned her rest.

THE WAR ENDS AND JUNIOR HEADS HOME

The *Arkansas*' new mission was taking part in "Operation Magic Carpet." This mission may have been the happiest for the men to carry out. Its purpose was to ferry the troops home from the war. Perhaps no mission was more aptly named. As Junior and his fellow sailors prepared to sail home, they received the following memorandum:

U.S. NAVAL SEPARATION CENTER
STATION MEMORANDUM NO. 20
To: All Hands
Subj: Security of military information after separation from active service.
   1. The following message from the Chief of Naval Personnel is quoted herewith for the information and guidance of all hands:
The war is over and you have done your job well. However, in leaving the service you are reminded that each discharge and release carries with it certain responsibilities towards maintaining world peace. Some of you while in the service had access to certain secret and confidential equipment, Navy codes

and ciphers, or intelligence material, the status, technique, and procedures of which still remain highly classified in peacetime. To divulge this information not only endangers the national security, but also jeopardizes everything for which we have fought. We must therefore be prepared to protect this information in peace as we have in war.

To this end, the cooperation of each and every man or woman is requested. When you leave the service, those military secrets which you have learned should be left behind. Failing in this, you may have to return to do the job again. To you then goes this responsibility of helping those who remain to protect your nation.

G.D. Dickey/s/
G.D. Dickey
Commanding

Junior took this message very seriously. This was the reason he returned the service revolver he had been issued while on shore patrol.

During this period, the leadership of the *Arkansas* changed once again. Captain Wade DeWeese succeeded to the command of the *Arkansas* on August 18, 1945. He was different in some ways from Captain Richards. Although an equally friendly and approachable man, DeWeese was far more formal in his manners. He was born on February 3, 1899. He attended the Nichols School in Buffalo, New York, before his appointment to the U.S. Naval Academy in 1916. During the First World War, DeWeese served as a midshipman aboard the *Arkansas* during the summer cruise of 1917. An avid amateur photographer, he kept an original labeled photo album of the Summer 1917 "Youngster Cruise" of the *Arkansas*.[26] He had graduated from the Naval Academy with the Class of 1920 on June 6, 1919. DeWeese's naval career drew him to many ships, including the *Arkansas, Rhode Island, Siboney, Colorado, Converse, Reid, Hazelwood, Detroit,* and *Savannah*. Three terms were served on the *Arkansas* (Summer 1917, 1926–1928, and 1945). By June 1942, he rose to the rank of captain.

---

26. This album includes Captain DeWeese's personal papers, photo albums, scrapbooks, and the mahogany chest built for DeWeese by the carpenter's mate of the *Arkansas* upon his departure from the battleship in late 1945. It is now in possession of the author.

DeWeese would command the *Arkansas* until shortly before its destruction in the Bikini Atoll atomic tests.[27]

During the last days of August and early September 1945, both at home and abroad, everyone was ready for the war to be over and eager to see their loved ones. Junior and Faye Talbott were no different from any other young couple who had exchanged wartime wedding vows. They wanted to live a normal life in peacetime America. On September 13, Faye sent her husband a first anniversary card. Knowing it would take some time for it to reach him, she wrote simply:

> Oh Darling
> How I wish I were with you. Maybe we'll be in our home the next one.
>
> All my Love,
> Your loving wife Faye

The war had taken its toll on soldiers and sailors as well as their loved ones back home. Everyone was ready to get on with life.

On September 23, 1945, the *Arkansas* left Okinawa and set course for Pearl Harbor, Hawaii. She docked there for four days, then sailed to Seattle, Washington, on October 8. With this leg of the *Arkansas'* long journey, Junior was going home. He had seen much of the world except for the polar ice caps and Australia, though he came fairly close to Australia. He had traveled some 103,000 miles across the Earth and fought five major battles in both theaters of the war. He had seen unforgettable things, some of which he tried to forget. He saw the old order pass and a new one born in the fires of war he helped to fight. This last voyage seemed anticlimactic to Junior. Reaching San Diego, California, on October 15, he and his fellow sailors were processed and sent by train homeward. His ultimate destination was the receiving station at Memphis, Tennessee.[28]

Junior never signed up to be a hero or considered himself one. He enlisted to do his small part in a horrendous war. He didn't care for

---

27. All information regarding Captain Wade DeWeese was taken from his own copy of his U.S. Navy Officer Service Record, which is part of the author's U.S.S. *Arkansas* collection.

28. *Standard Transfer Order* dated October 5, 1945. Luther Edward Talbott Compiled Service Record, FC2d, Division F, U.S.S. *Arkansas*, National Archives, Washington, D.C.

anything but the fact that the Allied powers had won the war. He cared only that life would once again mean waking up every morning in his home at Finger, being near his loved ones, and enjoying small things like fishing, working, and starting his life with Faye. What had seemed like small things a few years before were now amazingly wonderful things.

One can only imagine the emotions that flooded through Junior's mind on that train ride home. He would never discuss it. The only mention of it was that some of the men became sick with a stomach disorder on the way home. Because he had not taken sick, he helped gather up sufficient medicine to treat his comrades. Following this diversion, the men resumed their trip. Until his death, Junior kept his thoughts upon returning home a secret. Perhaps the torture of the soul began with that journey home, one that would continue for decades. No one really knows. Some subjects remained buried in the layers of his heart and his long memory.

Meanwhile, the *Arkansas'* days afloat were coming to an end. Arriving at San Diego in October 1945, she was outfitted for service in Operation Magic Carpet and made three voyages to bring homebound servicemen to Pearl Harbor, Hawaii. Shortly thereafter, she was chosen to serve as a target vessel for Operation Crossroads and sent to Terminal Island, California, to be prepared for bomb tests. The *Arkansas* returned to Pearl Harbor for a while before departing again on May 20, 1946, this time for the Bikini Atoll. She was not the only brave old lady of the seas to be sacrificed at Bikini Atoll. The brave old *Nevada*, which had served alongside the *Arkansas* in the European theatre, pouring devastating fire on the Germans at Normandy and Cherbourg, was also chosen for the upcoming tests.

The *Nevada* was the target ship for the "Able" test. The *Arkansas* was moored off the *Nevada*'s port beam and was one of three major combatant ships located within one-half mile of the zero-point. Taking part in both the "Able" and "Baker" tests, she survived the former and was moored within 500 feet of the detonation point for the latter.

On July 25, 1946, the atomic bomb comprising the "Baker" test was detonated. After over thirty-five years of glorious service to her country, the *Arkansas* went to rest in a watery grave at the Bikini Atoll Lagoon. Sinking in such a manner brought with it a distinction unlike any other for a vessel sunk by conventional means. The *Arkansas* added to her many distinctions two final ones. She became the first battleship in history to be sunk by an atomic bomb and the first to be sunk by a bomb that never touched her.[29]

---

29. James P. Delgado, Daniel J. Lenihan, and Larry E. Murphy, *The Archeology of The Atomic Bomb: A Submerged Cultural Resources Assessment of the Sunken Fleet of Operation Crossroads at Bikini and Kwajalein Atoll Lagoons*. Santa Fe, NM: Submerged Cultural Resources Unit, National Maritime Initiative, National Park Service, 1991, 55.

12

Coming Home and Moving On

In October of 1945, Junior received his decorations, but these medals were not of any real importance to him. His government saw fit to bestow upon him the Combat Action Ribbon, the American Campaign Medal, the European-African-Middle Eastern Campaign Medal, the Asiatic Pacific Campaign Medal, the World War II Victory Medal, the Philippine Liberation Ribbon, and—best of all to him—an honorable discharge. In fact, Junior's service record contains the following statement:

> Man interviewed and stated unwillingness to reenlist in Naval Reserve or enlist in the Regular Navy.[1]

---

1. Service Record dated September 30, 1945. Luther Edward Talbott Compiled Service Record, FC2d, Division F, U.S.S. *Arkansas*, National Archives, Washington, D.C.

Junior was approached with the idea of continuing his education and going back to school to become a commissioned officer. His conduct, ability to lead men, and technical skills had been valued. Still, his interest did not lie in that direction.

Junior did just what he always set out to do. He came home. He never planned to do any different. He was, after all, just an ordinary young man who happened to live in extraordinary times. He loved his journey and his travels out into the greater world. But he was ready to come home and resume a normal life in normal times. There was an ailing father to care for, a business to take over, and a new wife to love. In some ways, it could have been very overwhelming. In fact, it probably was.

It is hard for most today to understand. Like his comrades in arms, Junior saw amazing sights and took part in historic moments. When sitting on the bank of Huggins Creek on late evenings, he surely never imagined he would be sitting on the deck of a battleship staring out at the dark waters of the Atlantic worrying about submarines. When traveling to the new dam at Pickwick, Tennessee, on the Tennessee River with his friend, Logan McCaskill in the late 1930s, Junior did not imagine traveling through the locks at the Panama Canal, trading American dollars for stalks of bananas and other local items. When keeping watch over the Judge's cattle in Tulia, Texas, he could not imagine keeping watch over foreign ports of call in Europe, North Africa, and the Mediterranean. Shooting at squirrels in the hills and bottoms around Finger, Tennessee, seemed so different from firing twelve-inch shells into enemy pillboxes, positions, and villages in France and later the Pacific islands. Now, he was back home.

How could a man play a role in the largest amphibious invasion in world history one year, only to return to stocking store shelves in a dusty little town just two years later? It was simple: that was life. Although Junior had seen a great deal of the world and was involved in some pretty impressive adventures, he himself was not all that impressed by any of it. He felt some of the places he saw were far inferior to his little spot in the world in West Tennessee. He basically lived by the words of Harry Truman, though Truman himself had not yet uttered them. Still, the sentiment was the same. It came down to this: "I tried always to remember who I was, where I came from, and where I'd be going back to."

At the same time, things were different at home. The little streets of Finger and everything around seemed smaller. Many people were not around anymore. Some had died, others had moved to large cities for work, and all were older. Nothing was the same anymore, including Junior. Because he had been exposed to malaria at one time, it required him to seek certain strong medical treatments on occasion. A few months after returning to Finger, he walked into Dr. Nathaniel A. Tucker's quiet, high-ceiling office and asked for medicine. The crusty old doctor eyed him suspiciously and asked, "What do you need with that?" Junior explained that he had taken these pills regularly while in the Navy and needed some now. Doctor Tucker instructed him to wait. After a few moments, he returned to his desk with a small white envelope. The doctor retrieved a large two-gallon glass bottle containing white tablets. He poured twenty-five into the envelope and handed it to Junior. Asking how much he owed, old Doctor Tucker gruffly replied, "Oh, about 25 cents." Finally, after an eventful three years trekking across the world, Junior was returning to a life of semi-normality.

This did not mean that Junior was unmarked, unaffected, or without scars from the war. Indeed, he was deeply scarred. The horrors of war, the impressions of mass destruction, and the knowledge of a man's own part in those events made him a haunted man. Like so many others who had served, he tried to bury his nightmares in hard work and by simply not talking about what he had experienced.

Junior concentrated on trying to make his way in a much smaller world. He ran the family store, established a peddling route, started a family, and worked at being a good neighbor to his community. He did all of this with the support and cooperation of his life partner, Faye. Though he kept busy, he still had his nightmares, both literally and figuratively. According to Faye, in the early morning hours, he often woke up with nightmares that left him shaken, temporarily lost, and sweating profusely. He would suddenly be sitting upright in bed calling out coordinates, ranges, or targets and be back on board the U.S.S. *Arkansas*. In his dreams, he was back in the bowels of the old battleship, firing on enemy positions. The images, sounds, and scents of war were still with him. These he could not so easily shake. Faye herself recalled the strain and worry on his face, the former sailor completely unconscious of the moment.

When some young boys set off some fireworks near him, Junior "hit the decks" by diving to the ground. The sound of fireworks and small rockets awakened in him the sounds of shells screeching across the bow of the *Arkansas* and landing somewhere beyond. These sounds could not be drowned out; they could not be buried. No matter how the horrors of war faded from the face of European and Pacific soils, those same horrors could not so readily be eradicated from the memory and heart of Junior Talbott. He would carry them all his years. Time helped—but could never erase—the scars of World War II.

According to Faye, these memories and recollections of war and Junior's struggle to deal with them were hard on them both. She divulged that he could not talk for years about these things in great detail. He probably dealt with them as best he could. Perhaps he vented through his temper at the wrong times on the wrong persons. At the same time, he might be too easy-going on the very persons he needed to really ride hard and with whom he needed to lose his temper. Still, he probably dealt with it all in the only way he knew.

Still, it is difficult for a man to know exactly what to do when he is still dealing with the torment and demons of his experiences. The stories are similar for veterans of all wars. Many of their children lament the fact that their fathers were distant, temperamental with them though tolerant with others, or simply disconnected. Junior Talbott's emotions, while very personal and singular in one sense, were quite commonplace. Like his comrades, he had seen enough of war and wanted so badly to be at peace, whether it be with neighbors, strangers, family, or even himself. Still, it would not be easy and sometimes not even manageable.

Yet, as with all things, time becomes a healer. Life takes its own course and both the strongest and weakest men are forced to adjust. He did not give in to mental distress. He did not turn to the bottle or spend his life poor mouthing or lamenting his lot in life. He did seek out a government disability check or claim to suffer from post-traumatic stress disorder (PTSD). Instead, he made the conscious decision to work extremely hard and make his life a success. He partnered with a good wife and built a world in which his descendants could thrive if they chose to do so. He made the most of what he was given in life and the most of what he earned.

Junior and Faye made their first home in a little shack of a house behind the Finger Church of Christ. They always referred to it as "the little black house." It was not much of a house. Because the walls were so thin, he tried to insulate them with pasteboard. Faye always recounted with a laugh a visit from her mother, Ollie Pearl McIntyre. Faye had the flu and was sick in bed. Junior tried to clear the soot out of the stove pipes by dropping a brick down them. When he did, the soot blew out and coated Faye's face with black ash. When her mother saw her sick daughter lying in bed with soot on her face, she went home and cried over the plight of her daughter. Luckily, the little black house was only temporary.[2] Junior and Faye soon moved into the house with Dave and Evelyn Alexander.

On July 13, 1947, Junior and Faye had their first child, Michael Edward Talbott. It was a very difficult birth. Junior, his father-in-law John Robert McIntyre, and Dave Alexander held vigil in the front yard of the Alexander house. When the time came, Dr. Nathaniel A. "Al" Tucker was grim and referred the worried parents to Dr. Webb at The Webb-Williamson Hospital in Jackson, Tennessee. Michael was born with intestinal problems and lingered for nine days before dying. Faye's mother, Ollie Pearl McIntyre, brought the poor dead child home in her arms for burial at the Finger Cemetery.

The birth was very hard on Faye's body and she was forced to endure a partial hysterectomy. The young couple put the tragedy behind them and on June 30, 1949, a second son, Ronald Lane Talbott, was born. By this time, they had purchased the Sally Young house. They raised a son and ran their business and engaged in small scale farming on a two-acre plot or less, where they would remain. A second child, Deborah Jean Talbott, was born on March 4, 1954. Their family was now complete.

Slowly, they built their own piece of the American dream. Two children were taught the importance and virtue of hard work. They were loved and their parents pushed them to get the advanced education they didn't themselves have. They were the Greatest Generation raising their Baby Boomers. The children grew and moved out into the wider world. They themselves married and the young parents, Junior and Faye, became middle-aged grandparents. As they aged, they became mellower

---

2. While this living arrangement seems very primitive, there was still little money and opportunity for a young couple in north McNairy County, Tennessee, in 1945.

themselves and learned to live with other people's imperfections as well as their own. Junior's mantra, basically of "live and let live," became stronger in his mind and in his ways.

More importantly, the ghosts and the nightmares had given way to acceptance. Slowly, the aging sailor began to embrace his history and find ways to live with his experiences. After four decades, he began to share some of those old memories with his grandson and others. Tears were shed and he struggled to get them out at times, but they slowly ebbed out and the trickle became a steady stream. The pall was lifting and the ghosts of his past were taking new life as stories of a fascinating life finally being told.

From that point forward, despite frequent moments of emotion, Junior began to discuss and explain the war, his own part in it, and share how he felt about what he had seen, heard, smelled, experienced, and done. He finally was able to embrace his own history and the remarkable past that had once been his life. Perhaps it was his own therapy, his own way to "lie down on the couch" and receive treatment. Each year after 1987 and for the next twenty years, Junior found himself talking more and more about the war and his past. If only his family had listened more intently and with more interest.

With advancing age, the memories were no longer the unbearably painful and burdensome relics of a former life. As the years quickly passed, Junior took comfort in his youth and the memories he had long retained. As his body failed, his mind remained sharp and he relished certain aspects of his youth. He seemed to retreat into the past as he neared the end of his life, but he did so voluntarily and in a way that would be constructive to understanding him after his death. He was now finding comfort in the memories of a strong, vibrant, and youthful self that no longer was. Yet that younger self could be conjured up in just a few seconds with a question or a photograph.

Retirement brought happiness for Junior and Faye. She accepted the man for all of his faults and shortcomings in light of his experiences and sacrifices. Had she not, their marriage would not have lasted 62 years. She loved him and expected her children and grandchildren to do the same. After they gave up the store and retired, they traveled and gardened. They pursued their hobbies and interests. They doted on their grandchildren and great-grandchildren. Both were gentle and loving grandparents. As he aged, Junior's body began to wear down, but his mind remained bright and sharp. At the end of his life, he seemed to know that his journey was coming to an end. In December of 2006, he was greatly weakened and expressed to Faye that he "hated to leave" her behind. In those final months, the primary concerns on his weary mind were his past and Faye. He worried about "all those people I killed," as he would say, troubled about the lives he personally brought to an end. He worried about Faye being alone, knowing he would have to leave her behind.

On the first day of January, 2007, Junior was full of life and talked philosophically throughout the day. He played with his great-granddaughter Ava, doted on his new great-granddaughter Claire, ate heartily, bragged about eating his first peanut butter and jelly sandwich, and talked about the brevity of life. He beamed and smiled broadly, enjoying his day. It was the perfect day and the perfect memory. That evening, he watched television with his bride of decades and picked at her for falling asleep in front of the television. These would be the last memories made or recalled by this very human man.

On January 2, 2007, in the early hours of the morning, Luther Edward "Junior" Talbott ended his long journey and passed into history. It was a quiet and peaceful death. As he fell back into a chair, his face turned toward a window and he passed without a fight. Indeed, the fight had gone out of him. As he made his way toward their bed, his last words to Faye were, "I don't think I'm going to make it." Perhaps in those last moments, he found peace in the past and in letting go of this life.

Junior had always laughed and said his family would have to hire mourners and pall bearers because he had outlived so many of his contemporaries and had been out of the public eye for so long after his retirement. Still, the people he had befriended and benefited did not forget him. On a cold, rainy January night, a line of mourners stood under umbrellas around the local funeral home and waited more than two hours in line to pass by the casket of an old man whose youth was decades gone. Still they came, roughly four hundred strong over two days, to pay tribute to a man they admired and whose character they respected.

Junior was laid to rest in the ground within sight of his home in the little town that he had known since youth. His family and his community mourned him, but it was Faye who had lost a life partner and best friend. She remained vigilant to his memory and his contributions to the wider world. Her heart remained with him and he was never far from her mind. She often expressed to her grandchildren that Junior was still there with her and that she could feel his presence with her at all times. Death could not break their bond.

Faye too grew faint of body, but her mind remained sharp. Her family increased and they prospered. She never lost her devotion to Junior. As her own health failed, he remained ever on her mind. Like Junior, she left this conscious world standing up. She had learned to "stand up" plenty in her life and for all purpose, she went out the same way. She died on October 16, 2011, and was buried next to her best friend, her only love, and her life partner, Junior, at the Finger Cemetery.

Their remarkable journey together in this life was over.

Epilogue

The life of Luther "Junior" Talbott was a pageant that crossed interesting intersections of world history and involved a fascinating cast of characters. A man with a remarkable memory for details, he carried them in his heart and mind for six decades until the day he died. Some went on to fame in their professions; others, like Junior, lived out a quiet life in peace. Some died early; others lived to see great changes in this country and world. These characters that passed before Junior's eyes in his formative years of the 1920s through the 1940s could be easily divided into two groups—his peers and his mentors.

Junior respected men of ability and knowledge. He was fortunate to follow in the footsteps and tutelage of several mentors, both prior to and during his naval service. Successful men had lessons to teach him or anyone wise enough to listen. Junior gravitated toward those who were self-made and understood the virtue of hard work and industry. He appreciated their success stories and the efforts they had put into their own goals. Among his mentors was his own father, Newton Perry Talbott; his boss in Texas, Judge William Charlie Dinwiddie; his foreman Murphy Marrs; and the commanding officer of the U.S.S. *Arkansas*, Captain Frederick G. Richards. He admired other naval officers, but none above Richards.

Junior returned home largely due to his love and affection for his parents. Newt Talbott remained active and engaged despite his deteriorating heart condition and failing eyesight. He stayed active in the family general store, going to work daily but getting help from Faye and his daughter Vonnie Mae. Newt and Junior formed N.P. Talbott & Son General Merchandise in Finger in 1945. Junior sent money home to his father each month to purchase the family store. He gave up opportunities to come back home. The two worked together and Junior got established in the mercantile business. Two years after coming home, Junior watched his father slowly become more and more ill. His heart was weak and he had suffered from advanced heart disease throughout the war years. His loved ones tried to shield Newt from news from the front. Letters to Junior from home detailed his deteriorating condition. Eventually, his heart gave out. Newt left the store one afternoon and went home complaining of flu-like symptoms. It wasn't the flu but his heart. Newt Talbott died of a heart attack in his sleep that December evening in 1947. Junior had lost his first and foremost mentor. His mother Varham lived on as a widow for almost twenty-three years. She watched after her grandchildren, spent time with her friends, and watched the once vibrant town of Finger wane and fall into decline. She died in 1970.

After he left Texas in 1942, Junior never saw or spoke to Judge William Charlie Dinwiddie again. "The Judge" continued ranching through the Second World War with the help of his foreman, Murphy Marrs. His sons served as officers in various branches of the Armed Services. Dinwiddie became ill in 1945 and lingered for another two years. He died in a Dallas hospital far from his beloved ranch at 5 o'clock on Sunday morning, March 23, 1947. The Judge was 74 years old. Junior once said that it was appropriate that both men, one of whom was his father by blood and the other who was almost like one, died in the same year. If not for his father, Junior would have stayed in Texas and worked for the Judge. He loved and revered Dinwiddie for more than sixty-five years.

The Judge's faithful wife, Ida (Borden) Dinwiddie, survived him by many years. The woman who discreetly left Junior's whiskey bottle under his pillow and let him change his own bed linens was born in Denton County, Texas, on July 26, 1875, near present-day Justin. She moved to Wise County in 1881, then to Jack County ten years later. After marrying the Judge in 1895, she moved from Denton to Swisher County in 1897. Mrs. Dinwiddie survived her husband by more than a decade, dying early one Monday morning, September 19, 1960, in a Plainview hospital where she had been a patient for two years. Junior always recalled how kindly both the Judge and his wife treated him. He carried affectionate memories of them in his heart to the day of his death.

Any conversation about the Dinwiddies usually included another mentor, ranch foreman Murphy Marrs. Junior had great respect for him. The older man spoke to him about ranching, work, and life. Junior returned to Tulia, Texas, while vacationing with his family out West in 1966. He found Murphy sitting in a drugstore. Seeing the middle-aged father of two, Murphy said, "Kid, is that you?" He had not forgotten his young friend, even after all those years. The two men had a brief reunion, but it would be the last time they saw each other. It would also be Junior's last visit to Tulia.[1]

The years spent on the U.S.S. *Arkansas* were an educational experience. They opened up a new world and new opportunities for Junior. Captain Frederick G. Richards was the most memorable of the naval officers under whom he served. Junior revered Captain Richards with an almost folk hero status. He was a man who could identify with young sailors. Junior erroneously believed that Captain Richards was from Arkansas and a rural Southern like himself. In fact, he was far more complex than Junior believed. When Junior last saw him, Captain Richards was relinquishing command of the U.S.S. *Arkansas*. His destination would have surprised Junior. In September 1944, he took charge of Princeton University's new Navy military government school. A month later, he commanded all Navy units there, succeeding Captain Roy Dudley.[2]

---

1. While working in Texas, the Judge, Murphy, Bailey Dyer, and all who knew Junior Talbott well called him by the nickname of "Kid."

2. *Princeton Alumni Weekly*, 45, no. 10 (November 24, 1944), 3.

EPILOGUE

According to the *Princeton Alumni Weekly* of November 24, 1944, residents of the Ivy League town learned that they had in their midst a man who had been in the "thick of the Normandy and Cherbourg naval operations" and a recipient of the Navy's Silver Star Medal. The honor was presented by Rear Admiral William M. Munroe, then commandant of the Third Naval District. The accompanying citation, signed by Admiral Harold G. Stark, commander of U.S. naval forces in Europe, declared:

> For meritorious performance of duty as commanding officer of the USS "Arkansas" during the approach and assault on the coast of Normandy, France, on June 6, 1944, and the bombardment of heavily casemated enemy installations at Cherbourg, France, June 25, 1944.
>
> While under accurate and persistent enemy fire from heavy, casemated coastal batteries, Capt. Richards displayed outstanding ability, initiative, mature judgment and inspiring leadership. He skillfully and efficiently handled his ship under the most adverse conditions, taking advantage of every opportunity to close the enemy and accomplished his assigned missions.
>
> Capt. Richard's cool, courageous leadership, his total disregard for his personal safety, and his tenacity of purpose were in keeping with the highest traditions of the offensive spirit of the United States naval service.[3]

In 1949, Captain Richards became the headmaster of the Hun School of Princeton, the private co-ed academy that produced and continues to produce notable alumni.[4] An actual native of Maine, he married Mary Ligon (1894–1962) and the union produced three children: Frederick Gore Richards Jr. (1918–1984), Charles Ligon Richards (1920–2017), and John Thorpe Lawrence Richards (1922–2013). Eventually, Captain Richards became a Rear Admiral and later owned the Historic Rideout House in Annapolis, Maryland, as well as the historic Portland, Maine,

---

3. Ibid.
4. *Princeton Alumni Weekly*, 49, no. 28 (May 13, 1949), 3.

home known as Kavanagh.⁵ He died in 1970 and was buried in Glidden Street Cemetery, in Newcastle, Maine.

To a lesser degree, Junior was influenced by Captains Carleton F. Bryant, George McFadden O'Rear, and Wade DeWeese. All three were competent and able naval commanders. Junior believed them to be good captains who were concerned about their men. He admired them all. Being on a small battleship, sailors were confined to close quarters and observed first-hand their leadership abilities every day.

Captain Carleton F. Bryant left the *Arkansas* in May 1943, having been promoted to Rear Admiral and given command of a battleship division. During this service, he was most active in the invasions of Normandy and Southern France. He was aggressive in the pursuit of his duties. Historian, Harvard professor of history, and Rear Admiral Samuel Eliot Morison described Bryant's actions at Normandy and Southern France in his work, *The Two-Ocean War: A Short History of the United States Navy in the Second World War*. Eventually, Bryant rose to the rank of Vice Admiral before retiring in May 1946. A recipient of the Navy Distinguished Service Medal, he enjoyed a long retirement until his death in Camden, Maine, on April 11, 1987.⁶

Captain George McFadden O'Rear, a native of Jamestown, Alabama, graduated from the U.S. Naval Academy in 1919. He served for over thirty-three years and retired from the Navy with the rank of Rear Admiral on June 30, 1949. O'Rear died on May 30, 1979, at Massillon Community Hospital, in Massillon, Ohio, at the age of 83. He was buried at Arlington National Cemetery in Arlington, Virginia.⁷

Captain Wade DeWeese was the last captain under whom Junior served. He was a Navy man through and through. An adventurous man thoroughly versed in Naval history, he left the U.S.S. *Arkansas* in 1946, serving as her last captain before she was sent to the bottom of the ocean. His career continued and he eventually became Director of the Naval Museum at the U.S. Naval Academy. He and his wife Catharine

---

5. *Annapolis Capital*, 73, no. 43, February 20, 1959. Evening Edition.

6. Information in this section pertaining to Admiral Bryant may be found at http://www.history.navy.mil, the Naval History and Heritage Command, as well as https://testvalor.militarytimes.com.

7. "Descendants of John O'Rear," www.tmgtips.com

Hillman "Kitty" DeWeese had no children but enjoyed a long marriage and comfortable life on the Academy's campus. He died there on January 28, 1972, just shy of his seventy-third birthday. Following his death, his wife established the Captain Wade DeWeese Memorial Honor Scholarship at the Naval Academy in his honor. It continues to benefit young Naval cadets to this day. Kitty lived another 28 years and died at the age of 99. They were both buried in the U.S. Naval Academy Cemetery in Annapolis, Maryland.

Upon Kitty DeWeese's death in 2000, a large mahogany trunk was discovered in her basement. It had been constructed by the carpenter's mates aboard the U.S.S. *Arkansas* in 1946 and presented to Captain DeWeese prior to him relinquishing command of the vessel. He kept photo albums of his and Kitty's travels to the Orient, his Youngster's Cruise Album from 1917 aboard the *Arkansas*, and other important photographs and papers. Today, the trunk and its contents are part of the author's private collection of U.S.S. *Arkansas* artifacts.

Those who Junior knew during his childhood and helped usher him into manhood were important to him. He kept them on his mind and in his heart through his youth, his service to his country, and in his dotage. He knew the hearts of these people who helped develop him into the person he became. Many remained close to him throughout their lives. Most of them enjoyed long and good lives; some died young and were never able to enjoy the fruits of their sacrifices.

Junior became very dedicated and devoted to his wife's parents, John Robert and Ollie Pearl McIntyre. They continued to make brooms and farm and made their home with their spinster daughters, Lessie and Vivian. They lost their elder daughter, Helen, in 1962, which seemed to rob Ollie Pearl of much of her vibrancy and enjoyment of life. Junior remained devoted to his wife's family and made every effort to be helpful to his mother-in-law and father-in-law into their old age. Ollie Pearl developed what was called "hardening of the arteries" and slowly lost her memory. Her health continued to deteriorate and she eventually died in 1980. John Robert lived on without the woman who grew up with him and looked upon him with sadness and sympathy in 1907 at his mother's graveside. He grew more feeble and finally became bedridden. John Robert died in 1989 at the age of 96. He was born in the administration of Grover Cleveland and died seventeen U.S. Presidents later during the administration of George H.W. Bush. He had lived through the years of the Spanish-American War, the Great War, World War II, the atomic bomb, the Vietnam War, and countless other historic events. Both were interred in the ancient family burying grounds at Mount Carmel, about a half-mile from their home.

As with all young men, those who came of age during the Great Depression and fought fascism and oppression during World War II grew eventually into old men. For the most part, friends and acquaintances of Junior's came home and worked hard, building families, productive lives, and communities. Those young men grew into middle age and raised children whom they sent off to college, trade school, and good jobs. They traveled the country they sacrificed to protect, grew into retirement, and enjoyed their grandchildren and great-grandchildren. The stories of the men who befriended Junior or grew up with him are as diverse as the men were themselves.

Hayes Hayre came home from Arizona never having seen a war zone. But he still rendered important service to his country, leaving the Army Air Force with the rank of Sergeant. He married Miss Stella Lynch of nearby Montezuma, Tennessee, and they spent their lives in Finger, just a short distance from where Hayes grew up. The couple raised a daughter and Hayes worked as a factory supervisor. His spare time was spent studying local history and relic hunting for Civil War artifacts. He remained a quiet and serious person with simple tastes, living a simple but studious life. He lost his wife shortly after their fiftieth wedding anniversary in 1996. Hayes himself served as mentor to the author and encouraged his interests in history and writing. Hayes died quietly in the presence of his family, friends, and the author on July 16, 2000. The author eulogized him and considered his loss a great personal one that he still feels today.

Grady Middleton spent his years as a Seabee in the Navy. For the man who first met Junior at Union Station in Nashville and wondered, "who in the hell ever heard of Finger, Tennessee," he returned home, married, and made his home there. He and his wife raised two children and lived a simple life farming and working. They stayed very close to their friends Hayes and Stella Hayre, enjoying a lifetime of friendship together. Grady was full of mirth, jokes, and good humor. He and his wife were present when their friend Hayes died. Grady himself passed away on November 1, 2001, and was buried in the cemetery of the small town he'd never heard of in 1942.

Leonard Patterson saw much action during World War II. He had survived the Japanese attack on Pearl Harbor, Hawaii, by the time that Junior had unknowingly bumped into him at New York's Grand Central Station. Leonard served on the U.S.S. *Tennessee* and following its repair after Pearl Harbor, he took part in the shore bombardments of Aleutian Islands, Tarawa; the Marshall Islands; the Marianas; the Philippines; Iwo Jima; Okinawa; and the battle of Suriao Strait. Leonard made it home after the war unharmed but war-weary. Tragically, he did not live after, dying in an automobile accident just east of Wichita Falls, Texas, in 1948. He was only 27 years old.

Joseph P. "Josie" Adams was born on September 17, 1918, and raised near Finger. He was the son of Estilee Adams and her elderly husband. Mr. Adams died an old man while Josie was still a teenager and Estilee raised him on her own. A pre-war photograph taken in the spring of 1942 shows Junior, Josie, Hayes Hayre, and other friends. This photograph shows young men before the ravages of war took its toll on them, especially young Josie Adams. He enlisted in the Armed Services, serving in the Coastal Artillery Corps. Severely injured during the war, he was never the same again, according to Junior and Hayes Hayre. His injuries or conditions appeared to be both physical and emotional. He did not long survive the war. Josie died on May 6, 1947, and was buried in the Finger Cemetery where he lies just a few yards from Junior himself.[8] The war that neither Junior nor his friends either foresaw or desired had essentially claimed young Josie's life. The sad young man was only 28 years old. His memory was one that regularly provoked tears in the eyes of an elderly Junior in his later years. He wondered why his friend could not have lived to enjoy the same fortune he had. Sometime following Josie's death, Lee A. Weaver, local banker, insurance agent, businessman and notary public, asked Junior and Hayes to accompany him out to Ms. Adams' house to witness her last will and testament.[9]

---

8. On the very few occasions that Junior mentioned Josie Adams, he would become visibly upset when discussing Josie's early death following the war. Likely, the memory of this young man gave Junior pause to remember his own good fortune.

9. Hayes Hayre (1921–2000) was the grandson of Lee Andrew Weaver.

Mary Frances (Brown) Robison was the daughter of Zannie and Mary Brown and the sister of Guy Brown. Born the same year as Junior, they spent their childhood together from 1927 until he went off to war. They skipped classes together and slipped behind the school to smoke cigarettes. They lived a happy childhood in Finger and retained their warm affection for each other, recounting their memories at every get-together and reunion. She married Noah Allen Robison and had two sons, both of whom became successful men. She seldom missed a Decoration Day at Mt. Carmel Cemetery or a Finger Barbecue. She always enjoyed those days and visited with Junior to happily relive their childhood days. She passed from this life on April 10, 2007, just three months after Junior died. She was buried in Oak Hill Cemetery in Huntingdon, Tennessee, the town she adopted for her home.

Others friends of Junior or those who made an impact on his life, either positively or negatively, went on to quiet, productive lives. The wide array of characters with whom he interacted was varied. Most remained close by and Junior saw them every day. The man who first told him he ought to go to Texas and seek work in 1941, Emanuel "Manley" Chandler, lived out his life just a few minutes' walk away from Junior's own home. Chandler had a large family. In his old age, he made daily trips to Talbott's Grocery to visit his old friend, reminisce, and pass the time. Chandler died in 1988 at the age of 82. It had been a long time and a lifetime ago since both men had worked for Judge Dinwiddie, their mutual benefactor and friend. His other Texas co-worker and childhood friend, Horry Young, never went back to Tulia. He enlisted in the Army as a private when he was in his thirties. After returning home, he moved to Selmer, Tennessee, where he worked for the city. He was frugal and lived simply. He died in 1986 at the age of 79 and was laid to rest in the Finger Cemetery.

Junior's childhood friend Clifford Young had been quite the rounder in his youth and witnessed much of Finger's heydays. He always had many tales to tell. A descendant of the McIntyre family and a cousin to Faye, it was his mother, Sally Young, with whom Junior and Faye lived for some years after the war. Eventually, Clifford and his siblings sold their parents' old home to Junior and Faye, which was the first home the young couple ever owned. Clifford enlisted in the Army during World

War II and lived out his years in the area around Cairo, Illinois. He returned to Finger for a visit occasionally and the author had the distinct pleasure of interviewing him in 1994 on the grounds of the old Finger School at the annual Finger Barbecue in 1994. It was an annual event that had been spearheaded for many years by Young's maternal uncle, Freelin Dickey. Clifford Young was spry and lively and continued so until his sudden death the next year in 1995 at the age of 90.

Logan and Alice (McIntyre) McCaskill were both friends of Junior's for many years. Alice had moved to Finger from Leapwood and walked Junior to school when he was six years old. As a young man, Junior was befriended by portly businessman and promoter Logan McCaskill. He was a popular and well-known man and was the owner of Logan's Lake Lodge. He and Junior remained friends and did business together, with McCaskill serving as his insurance agent. He died in 1960. His wife Alice lived a long and prosperous life. She carried on Logan's enterprises and remained in touch with her Finger friends and family even after relocating to Jackson. Interestingly, the couple didn't marry until 1948 when she was forty and he was fifty-two. They had only been married almost twelve years when he died. Alice corresponded with the author in the last five years of her life. She died in 2008, having almost reached the age of 99.

Junior's friends Arthur and Pearl Petty lived in Finger for many years before relocating to Illinois to be closer to their sons. Junior had great affection for them. Charles Haze Petty, one of their sons, shared memories and stories that his parents had told him about Junior. Arthur Petty died in 1975 in Peoria, Illinois, at the age of 71 and was buried in the Fon du Lac Township Cemetery. Pearl Petty survived her husband by many years and died in 1997 at the age of 93 in Lexington, Tennessee, where their son, Haze, had retired. Pearl was buried next to Arthur, both far from the little town of Junior's youth.

Finally, it's fitting that we discuss Junior's lifelong friend, Philip Wilcox. The man Junior met when he joined the Navy lived a long life. Philip Malachi Wilcox was born in Glasgow, Montana, on August 23, 1921. He was the son of Milton Earl Wilcox and Georgia Deliah (Carey) Wilcox. He graduated from La Grande High School in La Grande, Oregon and joined the Navy in 1942. During his service, Philip received the European African Ribbon, the American Area Campaign Ribbon, and the Good Conduct Award. Following the war, he attended Oregon State College and graduated in 1950 with a Bachelor of Science Degree in Electrical Engineering. He accepted a job in Alaska with the Civil Aeronautics Administration. Philip moved to Oklahoma City in 1956, where he remained as the Branch Chief with the Federal Aviation Administration until his retirement in 1978.[10]

Philip was married first to a woman named Ruth. Junior had a print of their wedding photograph. She and Philip married while he was still in the Navy and they had three children. Junior and Faye never knew why Ruth and Philip divorced, though they were very curious. Deeply respecting Philip and his privacy, they never questioned him. Later, he married a young lady by the name of Juanita and they had a daughter. Philip became an aeronautical engineer and enjoyed a successful career. On more than one occasion, he and his son Milton hunted rabbits on the John R. McIntyre farm while visiting Junior in Tennessee.

Junior and Philip's friendship endured for sixty-five years. During the 1960s, Philip visited him in Finger with his son, Milton. Junior returned the favor, traveling to Oklahoma to see him in 1966. Many years later, in 1994, Philip, now a widower, made his way back to Finger when both men were in their seventies. They wrote to each other at Christmas each year until 2006. By that time, Philip's mind had faded and Junior did not receive a card for the first time since the war. Of course, this was also Junior's last Christmas. Not knowing that he had passed in January 2007, Philip's daughter wrote him that her father was not well. Philip would live until January 2011. Interestingly, after years of wondering about the fate of Philip's first wife, Ruth Wilcox, it was learned that Ruth died in 2012.

Many friends passed throughout Junior's long and productive life. The fates of some were never known. Even now, there are still mysteries. Sometimes a name appeared but nothing else could be found. Perhaps the letters that passed between Faye and Junior would have revealed these secrets. But facts, stories, and words rose into the air as ashes and embers when they chose to seal those letters forever in flame. Junior's death in

---

10. Much of the information regarding Philip's background, education. and post-war career were taken from his obituary in *The Oklahoman* on January 22, 2011.

2007 and Faye's in 2011 also closed their mental and emotional libraries, so those stories have also been lost. And yet, we are fortunate to have what Junior left behind in an unconscious account provided to the author in long, substantive, and now treasured conversations.

So ends the story of a humble and quiet man who never saw his contribution as anything special or significant. Perhaps his grandson will be forgiven for thinking otherwise.

Bibliography

BOOKS

Ambrose, Stephen E. *D-Day, June 6, 1944: Th Climatic Battle of World War II*. New York: Simon and Schuster, 1994.
Blythe, LeGette and Charles Raven Brockmann. *Hornet's Nest: The Story of Charlotte and Mecklenburg County*. McNally of Charlotte, 1961.
Bradley, Omar N. and Clay Blair. *A General's Life: An Autobiography*.New York: Simon and Schuster, 1983.
Burns, James MacGregor. *Roosevelt: The Soldier of Freedom*. New York: Harcourt, Brace Jovanovich, Inc., 1970.
Butcher, Captain Harry C. *My Three Years with Eisenhower: The Personal Diary of Captain Harry C. Butcher, USNR, Naval Aide to General Eisenhower, 1942 to 1945*. New York: Simon and Schuster, 1946.
Churchill, Winston S. *The Second World War: Triumph and Tragedy*. Boston: Houghton Mifflin Company, 1953.

Churchill, Winston S. *The Second World War, Volume 3: The Grand Alliance.* Boston: Houghton Mifflin Company, 1950.
Churchill, Winston S. *The Second World War, Volume 6: Triumph and Tragedy.* Boston: Houghton Mifflin Company, 1950.
Costello, John. *The Pacific War, 1941–1945.* New York: Harper Perennial, 1981.
Costello, John and Terry Hughes. *The Battle of the Atlantic.* London: Harper Collins, 1977.
Delgado, James P., Daniel J. Lenihan, and Larry E. Murphy. *The Archeology of The Atomic Bomb: A Submerged Cultural Resources Assessment of the Sunken Fleet of Operation Crossroads at Bikini and Kwajalein Atoll Lagoons.* Santa Fe, NM: Submerged Cultural Resources Unit, National Maritime Initiative, National Park Service, 1991.
D'Este, Carlo. *Decision in Normandy.* Old Saybrook CT: Konecky & Konecky, 1994.
Dodd, Sally Barry. *Bees and Bullets.* Charlotte Junior Women's Club of Charlotte. Charlotte NC: Charlotte Junior Women's Club of Charlotte, 1975.
Eisenhower, Dwight D. *Crusade in Europe.* New York: Doubleday & Co., 1948.
Farrington, S. Kip Jr. *Railroads of the Hour.* New York: Coward-McCann, 1958.
Ferguson, John C. *Historic Battleship Texas: The Last Dreadnought.* Abilene, TX: State House Press, 2007.
Fire Control Fundamentals. Rating Specialization Training Series. Bureau of Naval Personnel, 1953.
Goldstein, Richard. *America at D-Day: A Book of Remembrance.* New York: Delta Trade Paperbacks, 1994.
Hanley, Ray and Steven Hanley. *Arky: The Saga of the U.S.S. Arkansas.* Little Rock AR: Butler Center Books, 2015.
Hemingway, Ernest and William White, ed. *By-Line: Ernest Hemingway: Selected Articles and Dispatches of Four Decades.* New York: Charles Scribner's Sons, 1967.
Irwin, Lt. Col. Will. *The Jedburghs: The Secret History of the Allied Special Forces, France 1944.* New York: Public Affairs, 2005.

Karig, Commander Walter, Lieutenant Earl Burton, and Lieutenant Stephen L. Freeland. *Battle Report: The Atlantic War.* New York: Farrar & Rinehart, Inc., 1946.
Leckie, Robert. *Okinawa: The Last Battle of World War II.* New York: Penguin Books, 1995.
McManus, John C. *The Americans at D-Day: The American Experience at the Normandy Invasion.* New York: Forge Press, 2004.
Merrill, James M., ed. *Quarter-Deck and Fo'c's'le: The Exciting Story of the Navy by the Men Who Served.* Chicago: Rand McNally & Company, 1963.
Morison, Samuel Eliot. *The Two-Ocean War: A Short History of the United States Navy in the Second World War.* Boston: Little, Brown and Company, 1963.
Newcomb, Richard F. *Iwo Jima.* New York: Henry Holt and Company, 1965.
Nichols, David, ed. *Ernie's War: The Best of Ernie Pyle's World War II Dispatches.* New York: Simon & Schuster, 1986.
Parker, Sybil P., ed. *McGraw-Hill Dictionary of Scientific and Technical Terms.* New York: McGraw-Hill Companies, Inc., 2003.
Peckham, Howard H. and Shirley A. Snyder, eds. *Letters from Fighting Hoosiers.* Bloomington IN: Indiana War Commission, 1948.
Reflections: A History of McNairy County, Tennessee, 1823–1996. Marceline MO: Heritage House Publishing Co., 1996.
Ryan, Cornelius. *The Longest Day: June 6, 1944.* New York: Simon and Schuster, 1959.
Speer, Albert. *Inside the Third Reich: Memoirs by Albert Speer.* New York: Collier Books, 1970.
Sloan, Bill. *The Ultimate Battle: Okinawa 1945—The Last Epic Struggle of World War II.* New York: Simon & Schuster, 2007.
Steinbeck, John. *Once There Was A War.* New York: Penguin Books, 2007.
Talbott, John E. *Let's Call It Finger! A History of North McNairy County and Finger, Tennessee and Its Surrounding Communities,* Henderson TN: Self-published, 2003.
Talbott, John E., J.D. *Let's Call It Finger: A History of North McNairy County & Finger, Tennessee & Its Surrounding Communities.* Dickson TN: BrayBree Publishing Company, LLC, 2015.

Tennesseans in The Civil War: A Military History of Confederate and Union Units with Available Rosters of Personnel, Part 1. Nashville TN: The Civil War Centennial Commission, 1964.
U.S.S. Arkansas, *1944 Pictorial Review.* U.S. Naval Department, 1944.
Webster's Unabridged Dictionary of the English Language. New York: Portland House, 1989.
Wernert, Susan J., ed. *North American Wildlife.* Pleasantville NY: Reader's Digest Association, Inc., 1982.
Wigginton, Eliot, ed. *Foxfire 6: Shoemaking, Gourd Banjos and Songbows, One Hundred Toys and Games, Wooden Locks, A Water-Powered Sawmills and Other Affairs of Just Plain Living.* Garden City NY: Anchor Press/Doubleday, 1980.
Wilson, Lt. H.A. *U.S.S.* Arkansas*: Pacific War Diary, 1945.* United States War Department, Department of the Navy, 1945.
Windmilling: Swisher County, Texas, 1876–1977. Tulia TX: Swisher County Historical Commission, 1978.

GOVERNMENT RECORDS

Compiled Service Record, Luther Edward Talbott, FC2d, Division F, U.S.S Arkansas, National Archives, Washington.
Death Certificate of Markus Dee Malone, Registration Number 27379, State of Tennessee, State Department of Health, Division of Vital Statistics.
McNairy County Death Book B, page 36.
McNairy County School Records: Finger School, 1927–1936.
McNairy County School Records: Leapwood School, 1925–1926.
McNairy County Register of Deeds
  Deed Book 21, page 7
  Deed Book 16, page 620
1910 U.S. Census for Swisher County, Texas

INTERVIEWS AND ORAL HISTORIES

Mandy Jamerson Amerson
  March 14, 2008 interview/conversation pertaining to Moore Family History

Hattie Lee Cone
    2002 interview/conversation pertaining to Talbott Family History
Hayes Hayre
    Interview/conversation, 1993
    Undated interview/conversation
J.R. McIntyre
    2007 interview pertaining to old Newton Perry Talbott homeplace
Charles Haze Petty
    October 28, 2014 interview/conversation
Luther E. Talbott
    Undated interview pertaining to Atlantic voyages
    Undated interview pertaining to the Japanese surrender
    Undated interview pertaining to Gen. Douglas MacArthur
    Undated interview pertaining to the German view of the *Arkansas*
    1992 interview
    1993 interview
    1994 interview
    2001 interview regarding acquaintances in Texas
    October 23, 2002 interview
    October 23, 2002 interview with he and Faye Talbott
    March 22, 2004 interview
    Innumerable conversations and discussions, 1992–2006
Clifford Young
    August 6, 1994 interview/conversation

NEWSPAPERS AND JOURNALS

Annapolis Capital, 73, no. 43, February 20, 1959. Evening Edition.
Arklite: Arkansas Blasts Iwo, 2, no. 1 (March 15, 1945).
"Bulletin," U.S.S. *Arkansas*, September 6, 1945.
Chester County Independent (Henderson TN)
    March 27, 1930
    April 10, 1930
    April 24, 1930
McNairy County Independent Appeal (Selmer TN)
    July 1927
    August 30, 1929

Newport (Rhode Island) *Daily News*
    February 17, 1943
Princeton Alumni Weekly
    45, no. 10 (November 24, 1944)
    49, no. 28 (May 13, 1949)
The Oklahoman (Oklahoma City OK)
    January 22, 2011
The Tulia (Texas) *Herald*
    July 14, 1910
    April 9, 1920, 2, no. 15
    February 23, 1923, 14, no. 8
    May 8, 1969
    July 10, 1986

PRIVATE COLLECTIONS, PAPERS, AND UNPUBLISHED WORKS

John E. Talbott Private Collection of Papers
    Talbott Family Letters and Papers, 1943–1945
    Letter from Robert Beene to John E. Talbott, May 15, 2004
    Samuel Perkins Talbott Family Papers Collection
    Zoe E. Smith via e-mail, August 28, 2001
    Undated newspaper clipping, obituary of William Parrish Walker
    Captain Wade DeWeese Naval and Personal Papers

WEBSITES

http://www.history.navy.mil
https://testvalor.militarytimes.com.
www.tmgtips.com
http://coolblue.typepad.com/the_cool_blue_blog/2004/06/omaha_beach_and.html
http://www.maritimequest.com
www.navsource.org/archives/01/33a.htm
http://rasputin.physics.uiuc.edu/~wiringa/Ships/Period3/ UnitedStates/Battleships/Arkansas.
http://en.m.wikipedia.org/wiki/Tinian

www.waywordradio.org/tear-the-rag-off-the-bush/
www.urbandictionary.com/define.php?term=Take%20the%20rag%20off%20the%20bush/
http://www.warships1.com/US/USbb33-history.htm

Image Credits

Abbreviations
AC   Author's Collection
PD   Public domain
PR   *U.S.S.* Arkansas, *1944 Pictorial Review*
PWD   *Pacific War Diary*
WDC   Capt. Wade DeWeese Collection (author's collection)

Photo Section 1
All 14 photos (AC)

Photo Section 2
1. Luther Edward "Junior" Talbott, circa late 1942 or early 1943 (AC)
2. U.S.S. *Arkansas*, BB33, ca. 1942 (AC)
3. U.S.S. *Arkansas*, BB33, ca. 1944 (PD)
4. U.S.S. *Arkansas*, BB33, ca. 1938 (PD)
5. Captain Wade DeWeese (WDC)
6. Captain Frederick G. Richards and Rear Admiral Carleton F. Bryant (PR)
7. Captain Frederick G. Richards (PR)
8. Lt. (jg) L.L. Clardy (PWD)
9. Luther Edward "Junior" Talbott as a new graduate of the Naval Fleet Service School in Newport, Rhode Island, ca. March 1943 (AC)
10. (Inlet) Luther Edward "Junior" Talbott on board ship, ca. 1944 (AC)

11. Sailors of "F" Division (fire control) on board the U.S.S. *Arkansas*, ca. 1944. (AC)

12. "F" Division (fire control) on board the U.S.S. *Arkansas*. (PDW)

13. Luther Edward "Junior" Talbott, while a cadet at the Naval Fleet Service School in Newport, Rhode Island, ca. January 1943. (AC)

14. Luther Edward "Junior" Talbott, shortly after graduating from the Naval Fleet Service School, 1943. (AC)

15. Luther Edward "Junior" Talbott in Glasgow, Scotland, May 1944, during preparations for the invasion of France (D-Day). (AC)

16. Junior Talbott and his best friend of 65 years and Navy buddy, Philip Wilcox, 1943. (AC)

17. The masthead of the U.S.S. *Arkansas* sailors' newsletter, *The Arklite*, announcing the action of Iwo Jima. (AC)

18. Executive Officer of the U.S.S. Arkansas, P.M. Boltz, an officer Junior neither liked nor respected. (PWD)

19. The typhoon at the mouth of Buckner Bay which found Junior stuck in a tower to weather the storm and which forced the U.S.S. *Arkansas* to sail into the East China Sea to avoid significant damage. (PDW)

20. The burial at sea of Coxswain Peter Paul Konosky, an event which Junior witnessed firsthand and which left him saddened and moved until his dying day. (PWD)

21. Scenes from the U.S.S. *Arkansas* during the sail to Normandy for the D-Day invasion, June 1944. (PR)

22. The U.S.S. *Arkansas* in action at the D-Day invasion at Normandy on June 6, 1944. (PD)

23. The U.S.S. *Arkansas* delivering fire on Mount Suribachi at Iwo Jima. (PWD)

24. The U.S.S. *Arkansas* firing on Iwo Jima. (PWD)

25. Cartoon from the U.S.S. *Arkansas* sailors' newsletter, *The Arklite*, depicting their efforts to goad the Japanese out of their foxholes at Iwo Jima. (AC)

26. Some of Junior Talbott's comrades ashore at Okinawa inspecting an old native tomb. (PWD)

27. Photo taken during the battle of Okinawa demonstrating the proximity of Japanese kamikaze planes to American naval battleships. (PWD)

28. Junior Talbott remembered the German prisoners of war who were transported aboard the U.S.S. *Arkansas*. (PR)

29. An old newspaper article depicting the invasion of Okinawa. (AC)

IMAGE CREDITS

30. The U.S.S. *Arkansas* was honored on Navy Day 1945 for her role as the U.S. Navy's oldest active battleship. (United States Navy, Navy Day 1945 Brochure)

31. Faye McIntyre Talbott (AC)

32. A V-mail between Junior and Faye during their courtship. (AC)

33. A V-mail between Junior and Faye following their marriage. (AC)

34. Faye McIntyre proudly holding a photograph of her sailor. (AC)

35. Faye McIntyre and future sister-in-law, Vonnie Mae Talbott, helping Newt Talbott in his general merchandise store in 1944. (AC)

36. Newlyweds Junior and Faye Talbott, late 1944. (AC)

37. Home from the war and happy to be back forever, Junior with Faye and his parents, Newt and Varham Talbott, ca. 1946. (AC)

38. An honorable and well-earned discharge from the United States Navy. (AC)

Index

A
Abbazia di Santa Maria della Giustizia (Saint Maria of Justice), 222
Abernathy family, 15, 23
Abilene, Texas, 165
Able test (nuclear test), 272
Adams, Arch Willis, 53, 289
Adams, Estilee, 52, 289
Adams, Joseph P. "Josie," 52, 53, 289
Alaska, 292
Albany County, Wyoming, 90
Alexander family, 20
Alexander, Dave, 72, 278
Alexander, Evelyn, 278
Algeria, 153
Algiers, 131
Allen Academy, 90
Allied Armada, 171, 177, 178, 180, 181n, 183n, 189, 247
Allied convoys, 142
Allied Forces, 127, 129, 131, 171, 179, 191n, 201, 202, 203, 204, 211, 233n, 239, 242, 258, 259, 261
Allied Naval Fleet, 232, 255
Allied Naval Forces, 139, 214, 234
Allied war effort, 142
Aleutian Islands, 289
Amarillo Hotel, 102
Amarillo, Texas, 81, 82, 84
America First movement, 110, 110n
American Area Campaign Ribbon, 292
American Campaign Medal, 274
American Cancer Association, 93n
American forces, 233n
American 82nd Airborne, 181n
American 101st Airborne, 181n
American Quarter Horse Association, 85

Amerson, Icey, 55
Amerson, Mandy (Jamerson), 21n
Anderson, A.M. Sr., 90
Anderson, Mrs. A.M., 90
Andersonville Prison, 51
Annapolis, Maryland, 287
Antwerp, Belgium, 211
Anzio, Italy, 231
Arabs, 132
Arklite, 244
Arlington National Cemetery, 286
Arlington, Virginia, 286
Armistice, 244
Armstrong, C.F., Chief Specialist (USNR), 115, 115n
Asiatic-Pacific area, 243
Atlantic, Battle of the, 139
Atlantic City, New Jersey, 226
Atlantic Conference, 126
Atlantic convoys, 138
Atlantic naval campaign, 229,
Atlantic Ocean, 124, 126, 126n, 127, 136, 138, 139, 142, 155, 156, 229, 234, 265, 275
Atlantic Theatre, 223
Austin, Texas, 93n
Australia, 271
Axis navies, 126n
Axis powers/forces, 145, 190, 233n
Azores (islands), 142, 143, 144, 222

B

Bahamas, The, 235
Baie de la Seine, France, 176, 187, 193, 206
Bailey, Robert, 112
Baker test (nuclear test), 272
Baltimore, Maryland, 226
Bangor, Ireland, 136, 137, 156, 170, 176
Barber, Rudolf, 23n
Barham family, 20
Barham, Charlie, 34
Barham, Edna, 34
Barham, R.N., 30
Barksdale, Mister, 18
Barnes family, 20
Barnes, Blaine, 81, 82, 85, 85n, 93, 106

Barnes, Bruce, 32, 68
Barnes, Estelee (Bishop), 75
Barnes, Ida (Clayton), 85
Barnes, Martha Elizabeth (Plunk), 85n
Barnes, Dr. William Mark, M.D., 28, 36, 74, 74n, 75, 165
Barton, Ada (Talbott), 5, 106
Barton, Dora, 106
Barton, John, 106
Barton, Perry, 129
Barton, Thaddeus "Thad," 106
Barton, William Ivy, 70, 71
Basham, Hugh Allen, 5n, 34, 35, 35n
Bass, Robert, 42
Battery Hamburg, 204
Battleship Division Five, 209
Battleship Division Seven, 125
Bayeux-Isigny Road (France), 192
Beatties Ford Road, 160
Beauty Hill Road, 10, 10n
Bedford, Virginia, 226
Bee-Brand Insect Powders, 44
Beene, Robert, 38, 38n
Bees and Bullets, 161n
Belfast, Ireland, 137
Belgium, 172n
Berlin, Germany, 204
Berlin, Irving, 210
Bethel Springs, Tennessee, 70
Bikini Atoll, 233n, 271, 272
Bikini Atoll Lagoon, 272
Billie's Creek, 39
Billy the Kid, 96
Bishop Funeral Home, 28
Bishop & O'Neal Funeral Home, 112
Bishop & O'Neal General Merchandise, 28, 29, 74, 76
Bishop, Alsworth Guy, 38, 49, 49n, 50, 59, 112
Bishop, Dorsey "Dossie," 75
Bishop, Inetha, 75, 163, 164
Bishop, Lela (Woodward), 75
Bishop, Lorraine, 163
Bishop, Roy, 75
Blackwood, Lt. CDR Frank A., 252
Blandy, Rear Admiral W.H.P., 243
Blythe, LeGette, 161n
Bolivar, Tennessee, 70, 162

Boltz, Executive Officer Philip M., 148, 149, 150, 214, 244
Boston Courthouse (Massachusetts), 226
Boston Harbor, 223
Boston, Massachusetts, 152, 156, 173, 224, 225, 226
Boston Navy Yard, 223, 268
Bousbir Quarter, 132
Bradley, Lt. Gen. Omar N., 201n, 202
Brest, France, 126, 244
Bristol, Admiral Mark Lambert, 245
Britain, 139, 144
British Army/Armed Forces, 160, 161, 202
British Grand Fleet, 126
British Isles, 110, 132, 138, 139, 144–145, 157
British Marines, 208
British naval forces, 143
British Second Army, 202
British 6th Airborne Division, 181n
British Special Operations Executive, 172n
Brittany Peninsula, 202
Brittany ports, 219
Brock, Buford, 159
Brockman, Charles Raven, 161n
Brooklyn Navy Yard, 134, 135
Browder, Emma, 22
Brown, Guy, 290
Brown, Harrison, 67n
Brown, Ily, 32
Brown, Lillian, 67n
Brown, Mary, 290
Brown, Mary Frances (Robison), 36, 37, 290
Brown, Mr., 49
Brown, Ora Lee, 71
Brown, Orby, 46
Brown, Zannie, 290
Bryant, Capt./Rear Admiral Carleton F., 123, 124, 124n, 176, 188, 286
Buckner Bay (Okinawa), 154, 155
Buffalo, New York, 270
Bulliner-Clayton Fine Arts Building, 34n
Bullman, Bud, 112
Bullman, Elvis, 112
Bullman, George, 112
Bullman, Mrs. (Staton), 57
Bullman, Otis, 112
Bullman Store community, 112
Bureau of Naval Personnel, 122
Bush, Pres. George H.W., 288
Bushel Creek, 39, 127
Bushel Creek News, 30n
Butcher, Captain Harry C., 175
Byrd Locke Community, 19

C

Cabo Cemetery, 10n
Cabot, Arkansas, 12
Caen, France, 202
Caen-Cherbourg railway line, 193
Cairo, Illinois, 291
California, 235
Camden, Maine, 286
Camden, New Jersey, 124
Canadian armed forces, 202
Canadian First Army, 202
Canadian, Texas, 97
Canary Islands, 222
Cannes, France, 210
Cape Verde Islands, 143
Captain Wade DeWeese Memorial Honor Scholarship, 287
Carothers family, 20
Caribbean Sea, 235
Carroll place, 112
Carter, Brown, 167
Caruthersville, Missouri, 44
Casablanca, Morocco, 127, 128, 129, 130, 131, 132, 260
Casco Bay, Maine, 126, 156, 268
Catholic Church, 225
Catildas (naval officer), 152
Cattleman's Dinner and Dance, 102
Cedar Grove Cemetery, 14
Central Basin, 9
Chamerro dances, 259
Chandler place (farm), 46
Chandler, Emanuel "Manley," 82, 83, 84, 86, 290
Charlo, Private Louis, 241n
Charlotte, North Carolina, 160
Charlotte's Woman's Club, 161n

Charlottesville, Virginia, 226
Cherbourg Campaign, 203, 210, 259, 285
Cherbourg, France, ii, 126n, 187, 201, 201n, 202, 203, 204, 205, 206, 208, 209, 212, 219, 223, 229, 267, 272, 285
Cherbourg Peninsula, 175, 215
Chester County, Pennsylvania, 10
Chester County Independent, 30n
Chester County High School, 34, 78, 80, 119, 132, 222
Chester County, Tennessee, 6, 10n, 71, 81, 83, 87n
Christianburg, Virginia, 226
Church of Christ, 225
Churchill, Winston (British Prime Minister), 110, 126, 139, 143, 211
City of Miami train, 58
Civil Aeronautics Administration, 292
Civil War, 10, 160
Clanton Brothers, 96
Clardy, Lt. (jg) L.L., 264
Clark, Perry, 44
Clayton, Ada D., 37, 38n
Clayton, Cecil, 163
Clayton, Cora B., 72
Clayton, Ernest, Dry Goods Store, 28
Clayton, John P., 37, 38, 38n
Clayton, Troy, 37, 38, 38n
Clements, Turret CDR Harold, 217
Cleveland, Grover (U.S. President), 287
Coentin Peninsula, 202
Colleville, France, 192
Collier's Magazine, 196
Collins, Gen. Lawton, 204
Combat Action Ribbon, 274
Commonwealth of the Northern Marianas Islands, 237
Cone, Bill, 46
Cone, Hattie Lee (Bray) Arnold, 6, 6n, 7n
Cone, Lexie, 112
Cone, Newell, 112
Cook, Alfred, 53
Cook, Murray, 49
Corinth, Mississippi, 58

Cornwallis, Lord Charles, 160
Corpus Christi, Texas, 114n
Corsica (island), 222
Cotton Belt Railroad, 105
Cottonwood, Missouri, 43
Crerar, Gen. Henry D.G. (Canadian), 202
Crosby family, 21
Cuba, 235
Cumberland Presbyterian Church, 8

D

Daily War Diary (U.S.S. *Texas*), 174
Davidson, Annie, 78
Davis family, 20
Davis, Arl, 41
Davis, Chili, 67
Davis, Martin, 54
Davis, "Popcorn" Jimmy, 63
D-Day, ii, 148, 170, 171, 172, 172n, 173n, 174, 179, 180, 181n, 185, 190, 191, 202, 203, 208, 215, 216, 244, 259
D-Day Plus, 171
D-Day Plus One, 193, 243
D-Day Plus Seven, 199
D-Day Plus Twelve, 204
D-Day Plus Two, 193
Deaton, Ervin, 112
Decatur, Texas, 90
Dempsey, Gen. Miles, 202
Denmark, 177
Denton County, Texas, 89, 284
Devil Ship, 184, 184n, 212
DeWeese, Capt. Wade (also Cadet), 125, 265, 270, 270n, 271, 271n, 286
DeWeese, Catharine Hillman "Kitty," 287
Dewey, Thomas E. (New York Governor), 225
Deyo, Admiral Morton L., 214
Dickey, Doll, 51
Dickey, Freelin, 33, 33n, 37, 291
Dickey, G.D. (naval officer), 270
Dickey, Jack, 37, 38, 38n
Dickey, Ophelia, 51
Dinkie train, 58n
Dinwiddie family, 87n

INDEX

Dinwiddie Ranch, 88, 90, 92, 93, 97, 98, 101, 101n, 107
Dinwiddie, Rondeau Borden, 90
Dinwiddie, Elizabeth A. (Hankins), 87
Dinwiddie, Ida (Borden), 89, 104, 284
Dinwiddie, J.R. "Jim," 87
Dinwiddie, Jack D. "Doggie," 89, 90
Dinwiddie, John R., 87
Dinwiddie, John Wooten, 87
Dinwiddie, Judge William Charlie, 84n, 85, 86, 87, 88, 88n, 89, 90, 91, 92, 93, 94, 95, 96, 97, 98, 99, 101, 102, 103, 104, 105, 106, 107, 108, 109, 283, 290
Dinwiddie, Mongo Lyman, 89
Dinwiddie, Nella Vee (Anderson), 90
Dinwiddie, Otto D., 89
Dinwiddie, R.F., 90
Dinwiddie, Rondeau "Rondo," 89, 90
Dinwiddie, Sam B., 87
Dinwiddie, Willie C., 90
Divine Wind, 229, 244
Division F (U.S.S. *Arkansas*), 240
Doc Miller place, 10n
Dodd, Sally (Barry), 161n
Dollar Hill, 23
Doodlebug train, 58
Double Trestle, 57
Draper family, 41
Draper, Cora, 41
Drazdowski, T.J., 151
Droke family, 20
Droke, Elizabeth Stovall, 51
Droke, Vadie (Moore), 21n
Dry Creek, 10
Dudley, Capt. Roy, 284
Dust Bowl, 95
Dutchman, The, 90, 91
Dyer, Bailey, 93, 98, 99, 100, 101, 105, 284
Dyersburg, Tennessee, 43

E

E-boats, 178, 187, 187n
Eason family, 20
Eason farm, 24
Eason, James A., 21
East China Sea, 155

Edwards, Admiral Richard Stanislaus, 245
Eighth Fleet, 211
Eisenhower, Gen. Dwight D., i, 174, 174n, 175, 179, 211, 219
El Alamein, 127
Electric Studio (photography studio), 121
Emerald Isle, 136
England, 142, 232, 266, 267
English Channel, 173, 177, 178, 198n, 204, 206, 211, 267
English, Miss Florence, 16, 16n, 17, 33
Enville-Leapwood Road, 4, 16
Enville, Tennessee, 66
Europe, 231, 232, 266, 275
European African Ribbon, 292
European-African-Middle Eastern Area Service Record, 207
European-African-Middle Eastern Campaign Medal, 274
European Campaign, 249
European naval campaign, 206, 229
European Theatre, 208, 215, 216, 230, 262, 267, 272, 277

F

Farmer's Grain Company of Tulia, 88, 89
Farmer's Progressive Store, 28, 30
Farmers State Bank, 89
Fascism, 200
Fascists, 208
Federal Aviation Administration, 292
Federal Bureau of Investigation, 93n
Ferguson, John C., 174, 206
Fifth Amphibious Corps, 237
Findley family, 20
Findley, G.L., 20
Findley's East Side Addition, 20
Finger and Enville Road, 30, 30n
Finger Barbecue, 40, 70n, 259, 290, 291
Finger Burial Association, 28
Finger Cemetery, 57, 72n, 74, 111, 278, 281, 289, 290
Finger Church of Christ, 66, 278
Finger Depot, 25, 28, 57, 58, 225
Finger Fire Department, 36

Finger Gin Company, 29n, 71, 81, 81n, 113
Finger High School, 78, 119
Finger-Leapwood Road, 20, 25, 30n, 42
Finger Masonic Lodge, 32
Finger Methodist Church (also Finger Methodist Episcopal Church, South), 28, 32
Finger Odd Fellows Lodge, 32
Finger Post Office, 29
Finger School, 5n, 16n, 32, 33n, 34, 36, 37n, 41, 49, 49n, 74n, 78n, 80, 163, 166, 291
Finger Telephone Company, 52
Finger, Tennessee, 5, 13, 20, 22, 25, 26, 27, 28, 29, 30, 51, 54, 55, 56, 57, 58, 63, 65, 67, 68, 69, 71, 76, 78, 78n, 80, 84, 86, 89, 95, 96, 103, 108, 109, 111, 112, 114, 115, 116, 145, 146, 152, 160, 161, 165, 167, 168, 186n, 223, 224, 226, 234, 236, 259, 262, 272, 275, 276, 283, 288, 290, 291, 292
Finley Addition, 3n
First National Bank of Tulia, 88
First West Tennessee Cavalry (USA) (*also* Sixth Tennessee Cavalry, USA), 162
First World War (World War I), 10, 117, 125, 191, 191n, 222, 237, 257, 266, 270, 288
Floyd's Crossing, 39
Fon du Lac Township Cemetery (Illinois), 291
Ford, Henry, 110
Forrestal, James (U.S. Secretary of the Navy), 245
Fort Oglethorpe, Georgia, 114
Fort Smith, Arkansas, 84
Fortress Cherbourg, 203
Fortress Europe, 176
Fowler, Sarah (McIntyre), 165, 166
Fox Café, 166, 167
Fox, Mrs. (proprietor of Fox Café), 166, 167
France, 140, 156, 157, 170, 171, 172n, 202, 219, 232, 275

Free French Bureau Central de Renseignements et d'Action, 172n
Freetown, Sierra Leone, 143
French culture, 131
Frye, Conard (Deputy Sheriff), 68, 69, 70
Front Royal, Virginia, 13

G

Galbraith, Judge J.I., 50n
Gardner, Baxter, 63, 72
Gardner, Mary Harris, 72
Gardner Motors, 28
Garner, Haven, 46, 47
Garner, Vonnie Mae (Talbott) McIntyre, 9, 11, 12, 14, 15, 16, 42, 44, 159, 166, 261, 283
Garrett Tobacco Company, 18
Georges Leygues (George's Legs), 188
Georgia Robertson Christian College, 34, 78
German Air Force, 137, 139
German Armed Forces, I, 131, 177, 189, 189n, 193, 198n, 201, 202, 211, 212, 227, 258, 262, 272
German fleet, 265
German Navy, 139, 142, 229
German occupation forces, 172
German pillboxes, 183n, 229
German prisoner of war camps, 229n
German submarines (U-boats), 114n, 126n, 138, 139, 142, 143, 144, 145, 153, 191n, 229, 266
German Wolf Packs, 114n
Germany, 139
Gibraltar, 221, 245
Gilbert, Aaron, 261
Gilbert, Dewey, 53
Gilbert, Ellen (Presley), 14
Gilbert, J.E., 261
Gilbert, Junior, 261
Gilbert, Pearl, 20
Gilbert, Dr. Thomas A., 14, 15
Giles County, Tennessee, 8, 9, 10n
Glasgow, Montana, 291
Glasgow, Scotland, 157

Glidden Street Cemetery (Newcastle, Maine), 286
Good Conduct Award, 292
Goldstein, Richard, 193
Golfe de Fréjus, 217
Grandcamp les Bains, 199
Grand Canary Islands, 143
Grand Central Station (New York City), 145, 289
Grand Fleet, 188
Great Britain, 173
Great Crash of 1929, 20
Great Depression, 78, 106, 288
Green Beach, 217
Greening, H.A., 261
Greenock, Scotland, 157, 170
Griffin, Lessie, 86n
Griswell, Dan, 112n
Guam, 228, 258, 259, 269
Gulf of Frejus, Southern France, 206

H
H-hour, 181, 181n
Hamlet, iv
Hair family, 20
Hair, Cora, 17, 19
Hair, Haywood, 11
Haley, Jack, 210
Hall, Rear Admiral J.L., 200
Hand, Marvin, 75
Hansen, Sgt. Henry O., 241n
Happy, Texas, 89
Hardin family, 20
Hardin Graveyard Road, 4
Hardy, Thomas, 194, 195
Harriman, Averill (Governor of New York), 126
Harris family, 3, 20
Harris, Anna Lee, 71
Harris, Bliss, 81
Harris, Caesar, 19
Harris, Christine (Brown), 67n
Harris, Doris, 71
Harris, Ed, 16
Harris, Gretchen, 71
Harris, John R., 5, 29n, 54, 55, 57, 59, 68, 71, 71n, 72, 113

Harris, John R., General Merchandise, 29, 71, 72, 76
Harris, Julius, 16
Harris, Lela, 72, 72n
Harris, Manley L., 19, 19n
Harris, Prince, 72
Harris, Robert, 81
Harris, Thee, 55, 72, 72n
Harris, Zaida (McCaskill), 71
Hart Cemetery (Texas), 89
Hart, Texas, 89, 90
Hayman, Lt. (jg) L.W., 228
Hayre, Alma, 111
Hayre, Billy Lee, 111
Hayre, Hartle, 29, 36, 36n, 111
Hayre, Hayes, 41, 68, 69, 70, 70n, 71, 71n, 84n, 111, 112n, 114, 288, 289
Hayre, Stella (Lynch), 288
Hayti, Missouri, 43, 44, 44n, 45n
Hemingway, Ernest, 196, 197, 198n
Henderson, Tennessee, 5n, 43, 55, 55n, 58, 74, 78, 84, 224
Henderson County, Tennessee, 6n, 8, 14, 82, 87n, 115
Henry, Annie (Talbott) Peeples, 11
Henry's Place (café), 76
Herring, Benjamin Franklin, 23, 23n, 24, 25
Herring, Cassie (Matlock), 15, 22, 23, 23n
Henson, Brother Brody, 224
Henson, Brody Jr., 224
Higgins boat, 196
Hiroshima, Japan, 261
Hispaniola, 235
Historic Battleship Texas: The Last Dreadnought, 174
Hitler, Adolf, i, 125, 143, 144, 145, 173, 201, 203, 206, 208, 219, 258
H.M.S. Glasgow, 188, 191
Hodges, H.L., Produce & Commission Store, 28
Hodges, Harvey (Professor), 33
Hodges, J. Clifford, 34
Hodges, Julia, 5n
Hodges, Raymond, 5n
Hogwallow Creek, 39, 127

Holder, Annie (Davis), 51
Holder, Dolf C. "Pa," General Merchandise Store, 29, 51
Holland, 172n
Holmes, George Calvin, 112
Home Banking Company, 29, 32, 68, 69, 71, 72, 78, 113
Honolulu, Hawaii, 232
Hopewell community, 112
Honolulu, Hawaii, 228
Hoover Beach, Guam, 258, 259
Hoover, Herbert (U.S. President), 62, 62n
Hopewell Baptist Church, 66
Hopewell Cemetery, 9, 11, 14, 66
Horatio, iv
Hudson River, 125
Huerta, Victoiano, 125
Huggins Creek, 22, 25, 30, 39, 66, 70, 71, 127, 161, 222, 275
Huggins Creek Canal, 29, 50, 51n
Hun School of Princeton, 285
Hurt, Will, 41, 41n
Hutcherson, Belver N., 114, 261
Hutcherson, Johnnie H., 261
Hysmith family, 20

I

Iceland, 143
Imperial Army (Japanese), 230
Imperial Navy (Japanese), 230, 233
Indian War, 10
Ingle, Fate, 53
International Date Line, 34, 236, 237
Invasion of Southern France, ii, 207, 208, 211, 212, 217
Ireland, 136, 137, 138, 144, 145, 156
Irving Berlin Show, 210
Isigny, France, 199, 199n
Islamic culture, 131
Italy, 140, 222
Iwo Jima, 234, 237, 238, 239, 240, 243, 244, 246, 248, 268
Iwo Jima, Battle of ii, 126n, 154, 227, 232, 233, 233n, 241, 242, 249, 254, 258, 259, 261, 289

J

Jack County, Texas, 89, 284
Jack Haley Show, 210
Jack's Creek, Tennessee, 6, 8
Jackson, Tennessee, 17, 20, 69, 115n, 166, 167, 224, 278, 291
Jamaica, 235
James, Frank, 96
James, Jesse, 96
Jamestown, Alabama, 286
Jap (derisive term), 186n, 238
Japan, 237, 238, 242, 265, 269
Japanese Armed Forces, 227, 234, 241, 243, 258, 259, 262
Japanese Fleet, 153
Japanese Home Islands, 239, 264
Jaujard, Rear Admiral Robert (French Navy), 188
Jefferson County, Tennessee, 8, 10, 87, 87n
Jehovah's Witnesses, 229n
Jerry (derisive term), 183, 186, 186n, 187
Johnson, Florence, 224, 225
Johnson, George, 224, 225
Johnston, Mrs. (teacher on Guam), 259
Joint Chiefs of Staff, 248
Jones, Margaret, 16
Joyce, James, 138
Joyner, J.L., 65
Junkers JU-88 (aircraft), 185, 185n, 218
Justin, Texas, 89, 284

K

Kaiten (human torpedo), 233
Kamikaze, 229, 233, 243, 247, 248, 255, 268
Kansas City, 231
Karama Islands, 260
Karig, Commander Walter (USN), 140
Kavanagh House (Portland, Maine), 286
Kelly, R.E., MM3c (M Division), 176n
Kelly, Richard, 176, 176n
Kerama Retto (islands), 250, 251, 268
Kerby family, 20
Kerby, John Wesley, 81, 83, 84n
Key West, Florida, 125
Kilcrease, Claude, 93

INDEX

Kincaid, E.H., 122
King, Admiral Ernest Joseph, 175
Kirby (Kerby), Eulis, 81, 82, 83, 84n
Kirk family, 20
Kirk, Gordon, 53
Kirkpatrick, Eula, 66, 110
Kirkpatrick, C.H., 76
Kirkpatrick, H.H., 30
Konosky, Peter Paul (coxswain), 133
Korean War, 210, 263
Kriegsmarine, 139

L

L'Amour, Louis, 56
La Grande High School (La Grande, Oregon), 291
La Grande, Oregon, 291
Land craft infantry vessels (LCI's), 253
Landing Craft, Vehicle, Personnel (LCVP), 196, 258
Landreth family, 20
Landreth, R.J., 19
Lankenay, Commander W.E., 123
La Plaiseon, France, 193
Laramie, Wyoming, 90
Leapwood Schoolhouse, 16, 16n, 17, 19, 22, 32
Leapwood, Tennessee, 3, 4, 9, 10, 15, 16, 17, 18, 19, 21, 25, 26, 30, 63, 78, 291
Leath, Hard, 74
Leckie, Robert, 252
Les Moulins, France, 191
Lexington, Tennessee, 291
Leyte Gulf, 259, 260, 261, 262, 264
Liberator bombers, 216
Liberty Launch, 209
Lindberg, Corp. Charles W., 241n
Lindbergh, Charles, 110
Lipford, Mr. (bootlegger), 54
Lisbon, Portugal, 142
Little White House (Warm Springs, Ga.), 256
Loftin, Squire W.A., 6
Logan's Lake, 67, 68
Logan's Lake Lodge, 291
Loire River, 202

London, England, 173
Long Beach Harbor, 228
Lorraine (French battleship), 211
Lott family, 20
Loving, Jack, 23n
Lowrance, Alec, 59
Lubbock, Texas, 90
Lucilla sericata (green bottle fly), 250
Luftwaffe, 137, 139, 184, 185, 185n, 213
Lynchburg, Virginia, 226

M

MacArthur, Gen. Douglas, 214, 262, 263
Macon, Miss Nancy Louise, 124
Magruder, Capt. C.W., 122
Main Japanese Chain, 260
Malone, Marcus Dee, 66, 67, 67n
Malone, William Barney, 66
Maness, W.F., 11
Marianas (islands), 231, 237, 289
Mark V Stereo Trainer, 122
Mark 7 (fire control systems), 136
Mark 8 (fire control systems), 136
Mark 27 (fire control systems), 136
Mark 37 (fire control systems), 136
Mark 45 (fire control systems), 136
Mark 51 (fire control systems), 136
Marley, Jacob, 113
Marrs, Murphy, 88, 92, 92n, 93, 96, 98, 99, 100, 101, 102, 104, 105, 106, 107, 283, 284, 284n
Marrs, Mrs. Murphy, 92n
Mars Hill Cemetery, 17, 18, 19, 21, 24
Marshall, Gen. George, 175
Marshall Islands, 289
Marseilles, France, 211, 217, 219
Martin family, 20
Martin, Sarah Belle (Matlock), 15, 24, 25
Martin, James Nathaniel, 14
Martin, James Thomas, 14
Martin, John T., 24, 25
Martin, M.E., 24
Martin, Mary, 24
Martin, Martha Ellen, 14
Martin, Willie, 42
Martinez (sailor), 150
Maryland, 226

Mason-Dixon Line, 226
Mason, Oda, 90
Massengill family, 20
Massillon Community Hospital, 286
Massillon, Ohio, 286
Massey, Mrs. Aubrey (Orby), 68, 69
Massey, James L., 79
Massey, W.P., General Merchandise, 29, 58, 71, 76
Matlock, Ermon D., 261
Matlock, Moses M., 5
Matlock, Henry Thomas, 5, 15, 21, 22, 23, 76
Matlock, Sarah Albertine (Moore), 5, 15, 21, 21n
Maxwell House Hotel, 115
Mayo, Admiral Henry T., 265
Meadows, Lorraine, 49
Mecklenburg County, North Carolina, 160
Mediterranean Patrol, 244
Mediterranean Sea, 209, 214, 215, 221, 222, 223, 267, 275
Memphis *Press Scimitar*, 158
Memphis, Tennessee, 84, 114, 115n, 271
Messina, Italy, 222
Metropolitan Club, 64
Mexico, 125
Miami-Dade County, Florida, 225
Miami, Texas, 81, 82, 97, 102
Michels, Pfc. James R., 241n
Mid-Atlantic Range, 142
Middleton, Grady, 115, 288
Milan Army Arsenal, 167, 168
Milan-Sitka Building, 34n
Miller, Callie, 51, 52, 56
Miller, Finis E., 29, 51
Miller, Jenkins "Red," 56
Miller, Mattie, 51, 52, 56
Mitchell, J.O., 59
Mitchell, Jess O., General Merchandise Store, 29
Mitchell & Son General Merchandise, W.O., 76
Mobile Bay, 114n
Mobile & Ohio Railroad, 28, 29n, 37, 38, 55, 57
Mog-Mog, 233, 233n

Montana, 241
Montcalm (French light cruiser), 188
Montezuma, Tennessee, 288
Montgomery, Field Marshal Bernard, 127, 202
Montgomery, Professor W.E., 78, 79
Moore, George W., 15, 21n
Moore, Inez (Walker), 112, 112n
Moore, Irene, 17
Moore, James B., 21n
Moore, Jesse Alexander, 21n
Moore, John Calvin, 11, 13, 14, 21n
Moore, John Calvin "J.C." Jr., 11, 12, 13, 14, 261
Moore, John Robert, 21
Moore, John W., 21n
Moore, Katherine (Pickett), 15, 21n
Moore, Millard, 15, 21n, 112
Moore, Odie, 15, 21n
Moore, Nona "Nonie" (Talbott), 11, 13, 14, 21n
Moore, Sandra Kay, 112
Moore, W.B., 11, 12, 13, 14, 261
Moore, Washington Curtis "Curt," 15, 21, 21n
Moore, William, 21
Moore, William Nathan "Billy," 15, 21, 21n
Morocco, 126, 128, 131, 132
Morrison, Rear Admiral Samuel Eliot, 140, 188, 190, 191, 192, 200, 212, 213, 233, 286
Moseley, John C. (Sheriff), 85, 93
Mount Carmel Cemetery, 46, 56, 111, 161, 288, 290
Mount Peter, 70, 106
Mount Suribachi, 227, 238, 240, 241, 242, 243
Mulberries (artificial harbors), 203
Munroe, Rear Admiral William M., 285
Murray, Roger, 168
Murray, Thomas Jefferson "Tom" (U.S. Congressman), 168
Mussolini, Benito, 145, 208

Mc

McCann, Arthur Marion Douglas "Whig," 112n, 162, 165

McCann, Celia Weaver, 112n
McCann, Dell, 112n
McCann, Parthenia (Tacker), 162
McCann, Truman, 165
McCaskill, Alice (McIntyre), 291
McCaskill, Dennie, 60, 61
McCaskill, Logan, 60, 61, 67, 68, 69, 76, 275, 291
McCaskill, Logan, Barber Shop, 28
McCaskill, Major, 112
McCaskill, Scott, 75
McCaskill, Tom, 58
McDonald, John A. "Buddy," 224
McIntyre family, 78, 160, 163n, 290
McIntyre farm (Finger, Tennessee), 226, 292
McIntyre, Adrian, 39, 52, 52n
McIntyre, Alice (McCaskill), 28, 32, 67
McIntyre, Audrey Roberta, 165
McIntyre, Cecil (Parrish), 52, 52n
McIntyre, Earl, 42, 43, 44, 167
McIntyre, Elizabeth (Thompson), 161
McIntyre, Ella (Miller), 52, 52n
McIntyre, Ethel, 86n
McIntyre, Fannie (Carroll), 28
McIntyre, Helen, 111, 287
McIntyre, Hubert, 42, 165
McIntyre, Isaac (North Carolina), 161, 161n
McIntyre, Isaac T. (*son of* R.T.), 162
McIntyre, J.R., 11, 111, 165, 220
McIntyre, James Robert "Jim," 28
McIntyre, John Absalom, 162
McIntyre, John Sr., 160, 161
McIntyre, John Robert, 39, 42, 42n, 52n, 72, 111, 112, 112n, 162, 163, 166, 167, 223, 236, 256, 278, 287
McIntyre, Lessie, 111, 112n, 287
McIntyre, Lucille, 220
McIntyre, Maggie, 42
McIntyre, Mary Roberta "Robertie" (Coleman), 162
McIntyre, Ollie Pearl (McCann), 31, 52n, 111, 112, 162, 163, 165, 223, 257, 278, 287
McIntyre, Robert Thompson, 33n, 161, 162, 163
McIntyre, Roy, 167, 220

McIntyre, Vivian, 111, 112n, 166, 287
McIntyre, William Cogbourne, 161
McIntyre, Wilma (Sharp), 28, 32, 67
McIntyre Road, 10n
McIntyre's Farm (McIntyre's Skirmish), Battle of, 160, 161n
McLaren, Lt. CDR William F., 150, 151, 152
McKenzie, Lorraine (Brown), 67n
McManus, John C., 188
McNairy County Independent Appeal, 15, 33n
McNairy County Quarterly Court, 162
McNairy County, Tennessee, 4, 9, 11, 15, 19, 20, 21, 81, 82, 83, 106, 135, 160, 161, 278
McNairy County, Tennessee Quarterly Court, 60n
McNairy Station, Tennessee, 58, 74

N

Nagasaski, Japan, 261
Nakagusuku Bay (Okinawa), 154
Nashville, Washington Co., Illinois, 162
Nashville, Tennessee, 66, 114, 115, 115n
Nashville Basin, 9
Nashville Railway and Light Company, 66
National Quarter Horse Association, 85
National Recovery Administration, 62
National Service Life Insurance, 116
Naval Elementary Fire Control School, 136
Naval Fire Control School, 119, 121, 122
Naval Fleet Service School (Newport), 119, 135, 136
Naval Gun Factory, 245
Naval Training School (Newport), 119, 122
Naval Training Station (San Diego), 115, 121
Navy Department, 180
Navy Distinguished Service Medal, 286
Naylor, Frank, 83
Naylor, Harmon, 112
Naylor, Harrison, 58
Naylor, I.C.B. (Squire), 162
Naylor, Aunt Mary Lum, 111

Naylor, Aunt Mary Tom, 111
Naylor, Rosalind (Kerby), 83
Naylor, Thomas, 111
Nazi Party, i
New Deal, 62, 256
New Haven, Connecticut, 226
New London, Connecticut, 226
New Orleans, Louisiana, 45, 150
New Southern Hotel (Jackson, Tennessee), 224
New York City, 122, 123, 124, 125, 127, 134, 135, 136, 145, 146, 152, 156, 173, 209, 226
New York Harbor, 127, 152
New York Navy Yard, 145, 266
New York Shipbuilding Company, 124
New Zealand, 129
Newcastle, Maine, 286
Newcomb, Richard F., 241, 241n
Newport Daily News, 120
Newport, Rhode Island, 119, 120, 121, 122, 124, 245
Nicaragua, 245
Nicaraguan Campaign, 245
Nichols School (Buffalo, NY), 270
Nimitz, Admiral Chester, 232, 235
Norfolk, Virginia, 119, 124, 135, 136, 156
Normandy, France, ii, 156, 176, 180, 181, 181n, 188, 189, 190, 194, 196, 197, 201, 210, 212, 223, 229, 242, 247, 266, 272, 285
Normandy Campaign, 171, 201, 207
Normandy invasion, 126n, 154, 200, 202, 203, 208, 213, 215, 217, 258, 259, 286
North Africa, 127, 128, 132, 140, 209, 275
North African Campaign, 127, 209
North America, 138, 139
North Atlantic Ocean, 143, 152, 153, 153n
North Carolina, 160, 161n
North Texas A & M University, 90
Northern France, 173, 181n, 193, 201, 203
Nuremburg War Crimes Trials, 125

O

Oak Hill Cemetery (Huntingdon, Tennessee), 290
Okinawa, Battle of, ii, 126n, 151, 154, 227, 228, 233, 233n, 249, 250, 251, 253, 254, 255, 258, 259, 261, 264, 269, 289
Okinawa Island, 154, 242, 244, 246, 247, 248, 251, 254, 257, 260, 264, 268, 271
Oklahoma, 292
Oklahoma City, Oklahoma, 201n, 292
Old Friendship Road, 41, 84
Oldendorf, Vice-Admiral J.B., 264, 268, 269
Omaha Beach, ii, 176n, 177n, 178, 188, 189, 190, 192, 200, 201, 204, 239
Omaha Beachhead, 176
O'Neal Cemetery, 66
Operation Alacrity, 142
Operation Anvil, 211
Operation Crossroads, 272
Operation Dragoon, 211, 214
Operation Jedburgh, 172n
Operation Magic Carpet, 269, 272
Operation Overlord, 170, 172, 174, 177
Operation Torch, 131
Oran, Algeria, 209, 210, 219, 220, 223, 267
O'Rear, Capt. George McFadden, 244, 245, 246, 286
O'Rear, Virginia, 245
Oregon State College, 292
Orne River, 202
Orr, Burleen, 163
Osborne, J. Polk, 97, 98, 102, 105
Overman, Enoch, 41

P

Pacific Campaign, 249, 277
Pacific Fleet (U.S.O.), 146, 235, 237, 266
Pacific Islands, 275
Pacific Ocean, 150, 154, 155, 233, 234, 236, 242, 265

Pacific Theatre, 194n, 206, 222, 223, 224, 227, 229, 230, 233n, 234, 237, 246, 262, 268
Pacific War, 232, 242, 265, 268
Pacific War Diary, 223, 228, 258, 262, 264
Palermo, Sicily, 217, 219, 220, 221, 267
Pampa, Texas, 81, 82, 102
Panama Canal, 235, 265, 268, 275
Panama Canal Zone, 125, 235
Panhandle, Texas (town), 89
Panhandle of Texas, iii, 79, 95, 96, 103, 109
Papen, Franz von, 125
Paris, France, 202
Parrish, E.O., 58
Patterson, Allen, 54
Patterson, Cora, 106, 106n, 146
Patterson, Hobert, 81, 106, 106n, 146
Patterson, Leonard, 146, 261, 289
Patterson, Lucian, 37, 38
Patterson, Raymond, 37, 38
Patton, Gen. George C., 202
Paul's Valley, Oklahoma, 57
Pearl Harbor, Hawaii, ii, 10, 110, 110n, 146, 194n, 231, 235, 252, 257, 271, 272, 289
Peeples, Eddy C., 29, 168
Peeples, Oma, 168
Peeples, S.M., 261
Pemberton Square (Boston, Massachusetts), 226
Peoria, Illinois, 291
Petty, Arthur, 49, 50, 291
Petty, Charles Haze, 51n, 291
Petty, Pearl, 49n, 50, 51, 291
Philadelphia Navy Yard, 124, 125, 265
Philadelphia, Pennsylvania, 226
Philippine Liberation Ribbon, 274
Philippines, 194n, 259, 260, 261, 263, 269, 289
Pickett, Albert, 29
Pickwick, Tennessee, 275
Pier 92 (New York Harbor), 122, 209
Pioneer Days Festival (Tulia, Texas), 100
Pittsylvania County, Virginia, 6
Plunk Family, 23, 84
Plunk, Alfred (Alford), 71
Plunk, Mrs. Bessie (Herman), 65

Plunk, C.C., 33
Plunk, E.H., 30
Plunk, Ethel, 33
Plunk, Orby, 82, 84
Plunk, Orville, 82, 84
Plunk, W.L., 30, 41
Plymouth, England, 138, 199n
Pointe du Hoc, 192
Pope, Mark, 205n
Port-en-Bessin, 189, 190, 192, 193
Portland, Maine, 156, 226, 235, 268, 285
Portsmouth, Virginia, 135
Portugal, 142
Press Association, 237
Princeton Alumni Weekly, 285
Princeton University, 284
Professor Paz, 260
Provence Coast, 211, 213
Providence, Rhode Island, 226
PT boat (American), 187n
Puget Sound, Washington, 228
Pulaski, Tennessee, 9
Pulaski, Virginia, 226
Purdy-Lexington Road, 42
Purdy, Tennessee, 6n, 11
Pyle, Ernie, 146, 230, 232, 234, 237
Pyron family, 20

Q

Querqueville, France, 204
Quinéville, France, 199

R

R-boat, 187n
Radford, Virginia, 226
Radio San Francisco, 237
Raeder, Grand Admiral Erich, 144
Ramsay, Admiral Bertram Home, 175
Ranger battalions, 192
Rankin, Leonard, 113
Raye, Martha "The Big Mouth," 210
Redmon, Jere, 47
Revolutionary War, 10, 160
Richards, Charles Ligon, 285
Richards, Capt. Frederick Gore, 148, 149, 150, 177, 246, 270, 283, 284, 285
Richards, Frederick Gore Jr., 285

Richards, John Thorpe Lawrence, 285
Richards, Mary (Ligon), 285
Rick's Café Américain, 131
Rideout House (Annapolis, Maryland), 285
Roanoke, Virginia, 226
Roberts, Seaman David, 212, 214
Robinson, Commander D.S., 133
Robison, Lawrence "Red," 81, 113
Robison, Noah Allen, 290
Rock Island Railroad, 105, 105n
Rock of Gibraltar, 221
Rodman, Admiral Hugh, 188
Rommel, Field Marshal Erwin, 127, 201
Roosevelt, Franklin D. (U.S. President), 62, 110, 110n, 126, 143, 225, 228, 256, 257
Rose Hill Cemetery (Texas), 89
Rouse, John, 81
Royal Canadian Navy, 180
Royal Navy, 180
Rundstedt, Gen. Gerd von, 201
Russia, 143
Russom, Coy, 29n
Rutherfurd, Lucy Mercer, 256
Ryan, Cornelius, 191, 192
Ryukyu chain (islands), 248

S

S.S. *Queen Mary*, 152
Saipan, 237
San Antonio Beach, 259
San Diego, California, 115, 116, 124, 235, 271, 272
San Francisco, California, 236
San Jacinto, Texas, 205n
San Pedro Bay, California, 155, 235, 259
Santa Fe Railroad, 88
Sardinia (island), 222
Schnellboot (form of E-boat), 187n
Schrier, Lt. Harold G., 241n
Scotland, 126, 156, 157, 191n
Scotts Hill, Tennessee, 14
Scrooge, Ebenezer, 113
Sears, Roebuck & Company, 45
Seattle, Washington, 271

Second World War, ii, 10, 21, 107, 108, 117, 126, 138, 143, 147, 184n, 191, 230, 237, 247, 253, 256, 283
Seine River, 202
Selmer, Tennessee, 31, 55, 69, 71, 114, 290
Sewell family, 3, 20, 21
Sewell, Mary, 21
Sewell, Raymond Dee, 17, 17n
Sewell, W.E. "Ebb," 17, 17n, 20, 21, 23, 23n
Shakespeare's *Hamlet*, iv
Shawsville, Virginia, 226
Sheffield, Leonard, 53, 53n
Shickelgruber, 183, 183n
Shiloh National Military Park, 166
Shorty's Bus Line, 43
Shoumatoff, Madame Elizabeth, 256
Sicily, 219, 220
Silverton, Texas, 81, 82, 85
Sims, Tom, 9, 9n
Sixth Battle Squadron, 126, 188, 265
Smith, Arlie Harris, 74
Smith, Arnelia, 112n
Smith, Bud, 112
Smith, Dr. L.C. "Cube," 4
Smith, Richard, 74
Smith, Capt. Roy C., 124
Smith, Virgil, 112n
Smith, Walter, 112
Smith, Zoe E., 87n, 88n, 93n
Society of Friends (Quakers), 10
Soldier's and Sailor's Civil Relief Act of 1940, 116
Southern France, 126n, 210, 212, 213, 214, 215, 216, 217, 223, 229, 239, 259, 286
Soviet Union, 140
Spain, 143
Spanish-American War, 10, 288
Speer, Albert, 173
Sperry Gyroscope Corporation, 119
Spirit of St. Louis train, 58
Spitfire (airplane), 192, 267
Standard Oil Company, 224
Stark, Admiral Harold, 175, 285
States' Rights Party, 149n
Staton, Tom, 57

Staton, Vroner, 57
Ste.-Mère-Église, 199
Steinbeck, John, 131
Stephens, Ed, Barbershop, 28, 76
Stevens family, 20
Stewart, Tom M., 75, 75n, 76
Straits of Gibraltar, 221
Stratford, Texas, 89
Suckley, Margaret "Daisy," 256
Suriao Strait (battle), 289
Sweetlips community, 66
Swisher County Draft Board, 107
Swisher County Old Settlers' Association, 87
Swisher County, Texas, 81, 82, 84, 87, 88, 89, 90, 93, 93n, 284

T

Tacker family, 20
Tacloban, 259, 260
Taft, William Howard (U.S. President), 125, 265
Talbert, Arcana Edgar (Russell), 66
Talbert, Charlie, 5, 65n
Talbert, Willie "Will" Coleman, 5, 62, 65, 65n, 66
Talbott family, 87n
Talbott, Angie Nora (Wright), 4, 5, 8, 9, 10, 10n
Talbott, Beulah Varham (Matlock), 5, 9, 12, 15, 17
Talbott, Bryan L., 111n, 205n
Talbott, Deborah Jean, 278
Talbott, Elizabeth Ann (Walker), 6, 7
Talbott, Essie Mae (Webster) Vires, 21n
Talbott, Faye (McIntyre), 11, 12, 14, 37n, 42, 46n, 52n, 60n, 72, 72n, 94n, 111, 112n, 113n, 123n, 156, 157, 158, 159, 163, 164, 164n, 165, 166, 167, 168, 169, 205n, 220, 223, 224, 225, 235, 236, 256, 257, 271, 272, 276, 277, 278, 279, 280, 281, 283, 290, 292, 293
Talbott, Col. John, 10
Talbott, John Henry (birth name of Junior), 4
Talbott, Luther (*uncle of* Junior Talbott), 5, 9
Talbott, Mary Gilbert (Martin), 14, 15
Talbott, Michael Edward, 278
Talbott, N.P., and Sons General Merchandise, 283
Talbott, N.P., General Merchandise Store, 28, 41, 54
Talbott, N.P., Staple Groceries and Produce, 76
Talbott, Nancy Jane (Jackson), 11, 14, 15
Talbott, Newton Perry "Newt," 4, 8, 9, 9n, 11, 11n, 14, 15, 16, 18, 18n, 19, 20, 24n, 27, 28, 30, 31, 32, 40, 53, 56, 59, 60, 60n, 61, 62, 63, 68, 73, 77, 78, 81, 110, 113, 113n, 114, 157, 257, 283
Talbott, Ronald Lane, 46, 278
Talbott, Samuel Perkins "Perk," 6, 6n, 7, 7n
Talbott, Theodore (Perry), 6, 6n, 7, 8, 59, 59n, 87n
Talbott, Varham (Matlock), 22, 23, 23n, 27, 32, 42, 56, 158, 261, 283
Talbott, W.A., 6
Talbott, William Alexander "Alec," 5, 7, 8, 9
Talbott, William Perry, 14
Talbott's General Store (Finger), 18, 53, 112
Talbott's General Store (Leapwood), 17, 18
Talbott's Grocery (Finger), 290
Talleytown, 53, 55n
Tar Creek, 39, 106
Taranto, Italy, 208, 221, 222, 267
Tarawa, 289
Task Force 87, Camel Force, 214
Teague, Mrs. J.B., 33
Tedford, John, 112
Tennessee River, 68, 275
Tennessee State Militia, 10
Terminal Island, California, 272
Texas A & M University, 89
Texas & Pacific Railroad, 105n
Texas Rangers, 93n
Texas Sheriff's Association, 93n
The Wizard of Oz (film), 210

Third (3rd) Division (U.S. Army), 231
Third Naval District (U.S. Navy), 285
Third Reich, 110
Thomas, Platoon Sergeant Ernest I. Jr., 241n
Thomas, Marie (Moore), 11
Thurmond, Strom, 149n
Tidwell, Horace, 22, 24, 25, 25n
Tidwell, Miranda (Matlock), 22, 23n, 25
Tillman's Chapel CME Church, 64
Tinian, 237
Tinian, Battle of, 237
Tojo, Hideki, 145
Tokyo Rose, 184n
Toulon, France, 210, 211, 217
Townsend, Ms. Faye, 84, 85n, 93
Townsend, James Anthony, 85
Trans-Atlantic convoy(ies), 140
Trévières, France, 193
Trieste, Italy, 211
Tricolor (flag of France), 187
Truman, Harry S (U.S. President), 149n, 257, 262, 263, 275
Tsuken-Shima, Okinawa, 264
Tucker, Aline, 33
Tucker, Beulah (Harris), 72
Tucker, Dr. Nathaniel A. "Al," 29, 34, 59, 63, 70, 72, 73, 75, 112, 276, 278
Tulia High School, 89
Tulia Telephone Directory (1926), 88
Tulia, Texas, 81, 82, 83, 84, 85, 86, 90, 93, 100, 100n, 102, 106, 146, 275, 284, 290
Tunis, Tunisia, 221
Turko-Greek War, 244
Twain, Mark, 64, 125
Tweed, W.O. George, 259

U

Ulithi, 232, 233, 233n, 234, 235, 236, 237, 244, 268
Ulithi Atoll, 232
Ulithi Lagoon, 233
Union Savings Bank, 71
Union Station (Nashville, Tennessee), 115, 288
United Kingdom, 140, 266

United Service Organizations (USO), 210
United States, 140, 142, 265
United States Eighth Fleet, 209
United States First Army, 202
United States Ninth Cavalry, 87
United States VII Corps, 204
United States Supreme Court, 62
United States Third Army, 202
University of Wyoming, 90
U.S. Army, 114, 114n, 115, 115n, 149n, 174, 196, 215, 216, 268, 290
U.S. Army Air Corps (Air Forces), 90, 114, 215, 216, 288
U.S. Coast Guard, 114, 114n, 115n
U.S. Coastal Artillery Corps, 289
U.S. Fleet (Grand Fleet), 265
U.S. Marines, 196, 234, 237, 238, 240, 242, 243, 249, 254, 255, 268
U.S. Merchant Marine, 114n
U.S. Naval Academy, 123, 125, 148, 245, 270, 286, 287
U.S. Naval Academy Naval Museum, 286
U.S. Naval Intelligence, 158
U.S. Naval Reserve, 115, 274
U.S. Naval Separation Center Station, 269
U.S. Navy, 114, 114n, 115, 116, 118n, 120, 125, 133, 140, 143, 146, 147, 153, 204, 213, 215, 216, 234, 237, 242, 266, 274, 276, 285, 291, 292
U.S. Office of Strategic Services (OSS), 172n
U.S. State Department, 144
U.S.S. *Arizona*, 244
U.S.S. *Arkansas* or "Arky" (battleship), ii, iv, 117, 118, 120, 122, 123, 123n, 124, 124n, 125, 126, 126n, 127, 132, 133, 134, 136, 137, 139, 142, 143, 144, 145, 147, 149, 149n, 150, 151, 152, 153, 153n, 154, 155, 156, 157, 158, 170, 171, 173, 174, 174n, 175, 176, 176n, 177, 178, 179, 180, 181n, 183, 185n, 186n, 187, 188, 189, 190, 191, 191n, 192, 193, 193n, 194, 196, 197, 198, 198n, 199, 199n, 200,

201, 204, 205, 205n, 206, 208, 210, 211, 212, 213, 214, 215, 216, 217, 219, 220, 221, 222, 223, 224, 225, 226, 227, 228, 229, 232, 233, 234, 235, 236, 237, 238, 239, 240, 241, 242, 243, 244, 246, 247, 248, 249, 250, 251, 252, 253, 254, 255, 257, 258, 259, 260, 261, 262, 264, 265, 266, 267, 268, 269, 270, 271, 272, 276, 277, 283, 284, 285, 286, 287
U.S.S. *Ashville* (gunboat), 123
U.S.S. *Augusta*, 126, 211
U.S.S. *Boreas*, 245
U.S.S. *Bush*, 251
U.S.S. *Calhoun*, 251
U.S.S. *Charleston* (gunboat), 123
U.S.S. *Colorado*, 252, 270
U.S.S. *Converse*, 270
U.S.S. *Delaware*, 126, 265
U.S.S. *Detroit*, 270
U.S.S. *Emmons* (destroyer), 192, 251
U.S.S. *George Washington*, 126
U.S.S. *Hazelwood*, 270
U.S.S. *Hobbs Victory*, 251
U.S.S. *Hyman*, DD-732 (destroyer), 251
U.S.S. *Idaho*, 238, 252
U.S.S. *Leutze*, DD-481 (destroyer), 251
U.S.S. *Logan Victory*, 251
U.S.S. *Maryland*, 245
U.S.S. *Morris*, DD-417 (destroyer), 251
U.S.S. *Mullany*, DD-528 (destroyer), 251
U.S.S. *Nautilus*, 266
U.S.S. *Nelson*, 176
U.S.S. *Nevada*, 155, 174n, 175, 176, 179, 180, 193, 211, 212, 227, 238, 252, 267, 272
U.S.S. *Newcomb* (destroyer), 251
U.S.S. *New Mexico*, 252
U.S.S. *New York*, 238, 252
U.S.S. *Oah* (gunboat), 123
U.S.S. *Quail*, 245
U.S.S. *Quincy*, 211
U.S.S. *Pennsylvania* (battleship), 123
U.S.S. *Randolph*, 233
U.S.S. *Reid*, 270
U.S.S. *Rhode Island*, 270
U.S.S. *Rodman*, 251

U.S.S. *Rodney*, 176
U.S.S. *Saratoga* (aircraft carrier), 123
U.S.S. *Savannah*, 270
U.S.S. *Siboney*, 270
U.S.S. *Smith*, DD378, 245
U.S.S. *Stribling* (destroyer), 123
U.S.S. *Tennessee* (battleship), 146, 238, 239, 253, 289
U.S.S. *Texas* (battleship), 174, 174n, 175, 176, 180, 188, 192, 193, 197, 198, 198n, 200, 204, 205, 205n, 206, 206n, 211, 212, 227, 238, 241, 253, 267
U.S.S. *Tuscaloosa*, 175, 211, 214, 267
U.S.S. *Warspite*, 176
U.S.S. *West Virginia*, 239, 253
U.S.S. *Wyoming* (battleship), 123, 265
Ushijima, Lt. Gen. Mitsuru, 248, 254
Utah Beach (Normandy), 204

V

V-1 rockets (flying bombs), 173, 174
V-E Day (Victory in Europe), 262
V-J Day (Victory over Japan), 262
Vandiver, Alec, 62
Veracruz, Mexico, 125, 191n, 265
Vichy, France, 131
Vierville, France, 193
Vietnam War, 210, 288
Vires family, 20
Volcano Islands, 237, 243
Vought OS2U (shipboard observation plane), 249, 250

W

Wainwright, Gen. Jonathan, 263
Walker family, 6
Walker, Carroll, 76
Walker, Frank, 76, 159
Walker, *mother of* William Parrish, 7n, 59, 59n
Walker, Murray F., 112n
Walker, Lt. N.E., 119, 121
Walker, William Parrish, 7, 59, 59n
Walters, Tom (Sheriff), 85
Wamble family, 84
Wamble, Marcus A. "Mark," 84

War Between the States, 87, 161, 162
War College, 244
War Department, 158, 227
Ward family, 47
Warm Springs, Georgia, 256
Washington, D.C., 115n, 123, 226
Washington High School, 259
Weaver, Albert, Dry Goods Store, 28, 111
Weaver, Dovie (Kerby), 84n
Weaver, Lee Andrew, 71, 71n, 74, 84n, 289
Weaver's Grocery and Café, 76
Webb, Dr. Charles F., 73, 278
Webb-Williamson Hospital, 73, 278
Welles, Sumner (U.S. Undersecretary of State), 126
West Tennessee, 131, 134, 224, 275
Western Pacific, 243
Wharton family, 3, 20
Wharton, J. Matt, 19, 20
Wharton, Lizzie, 165, 166
White, Hugh (sheriff), 85, 93, 93n, 105
Wichita Falls, Texas, 146
Wilcox, Georgia Deliah (Carey), 291
Wilcox, Juanita, 292
Wilcox, Milton Earl, 291
Wilcox, Milton (*son of* Philip), 292
Wilcox, Philip Malachi, 116, 135, 201, 201n, 261, 291, 292
Wilcox, Ruth, 292
Wilkerson family, 20
Willkie Presidential Campaign, 110
Willkie, Wendell, 110
Williams, Euda, 46n
Williams, Hatton, 46, 46n
Williams, James "Chick," 78
Williams, Tom "Prof," 78
Williams, Ward, 46
Williams, Warren, 46
Wilmington, Delaware, 226
Wilson, Woodrow (U.S. President), 125, 126
Winding Ridge, 23
Winding Ridge Road, 4
Wisdom County, TN (proposed county), 6n
Wisdom, William Sargent, 6n

Wise County, Texas, 284
Wichita Falls, Texas, 289
Wolf Packs, 229
Womble, Isom P., 29
World War II (World War Two), 185n, 198n, 210, 265, 266, 277, 288, 289, 291
World War II Victory Medal, 274
Wright, Frank Lloyd, 20
Wright, G.G., 18, 18n, 19
Wright, Henry P., 8, 10, 10n
Wright, Landon, 10n
Wright, Sarah Jackson (Loyd), 8, 10n
Wright, Uncle, 18
Wytheville, Virginia, 226

Y

York River (Virginia), 125
Young, Becky, 86n
Young, Charles, 86n
Young, Clifford, 33, 33n, 37, 38n, 69, 70n, 290
Young, Ella, 111
Young, Fonzo, 111
Young, Horry, 84, 85, 86, 86n, 290
Young, James "Jim," 33n
Young, Lucy, 86n
Young, Marie, 86n
Young, Nelius, 112
Young, Nettie, 86n
Young, Rube, General Merchandise, 29
Young, Sally, 33n, 278, 290
Young, Van, 58, 75, 76
Youngster's Cruise, 125
Youngster's Cruise Album (U.S.S. *Arkansas*), 125, 287

About the Author

John E. Talbott is an attorney, lecturer, author and former educator. A graduate of both Freed-Hardeman University (B.A. History/Secondary Education) and the University of Memphis, Cecil C. Humphreys School of Law (Juris Doctor), he is the oldest grandson of the subject of this work, the late Luther Edward "Junior" Talbott. He spent approximately twenty years interviewing and discussing his grandfather's youthful experience with the man before his death in 2007. John has spent the past thirteen years researching the background behind the man's interesting and peculiar experiences.

Infused with a love of history, reading and an intense interest in interesting characters—all traits passed to him in part by his grandfather—John chose to put them to work writing this account of the man's first twenty-four years. Those twenty-four years included a great depression, itinerate labor in Missouri and the Texas Panhandle, and a world war that saw him actively engaging in five of the most important battles of

World War II: the Normandy invasion, the fall of Cherbourg, France, the invasion of Southern France, Iwo Jima and Okinawa.

The author has practiced law in Henderson, Tennessee, for more than seventeen years and has taught and lectured on the subject of history on both the high school and university levels. He is a resident of Chester County, Tennessee. The author and/or editor of six previous works of history and two works of Southern fiction, he is also the editor of the works of the late Tennessee novelist and short story writer, Jack Happel Boone.

The author has not only sought to honor the contributions of his grandfather but to also leave behind a record of his accomplishments and adventures for his own three daughters, the other descendants of Junior Talbott and those who choose to learn the story of one of this nation's greatest generation.

www.ingramcontent.com/pod-product-compliance
Lightning Source LLC
Chambersburg PA
CBHW020322170426
43200CB00006B/244